MW01415117

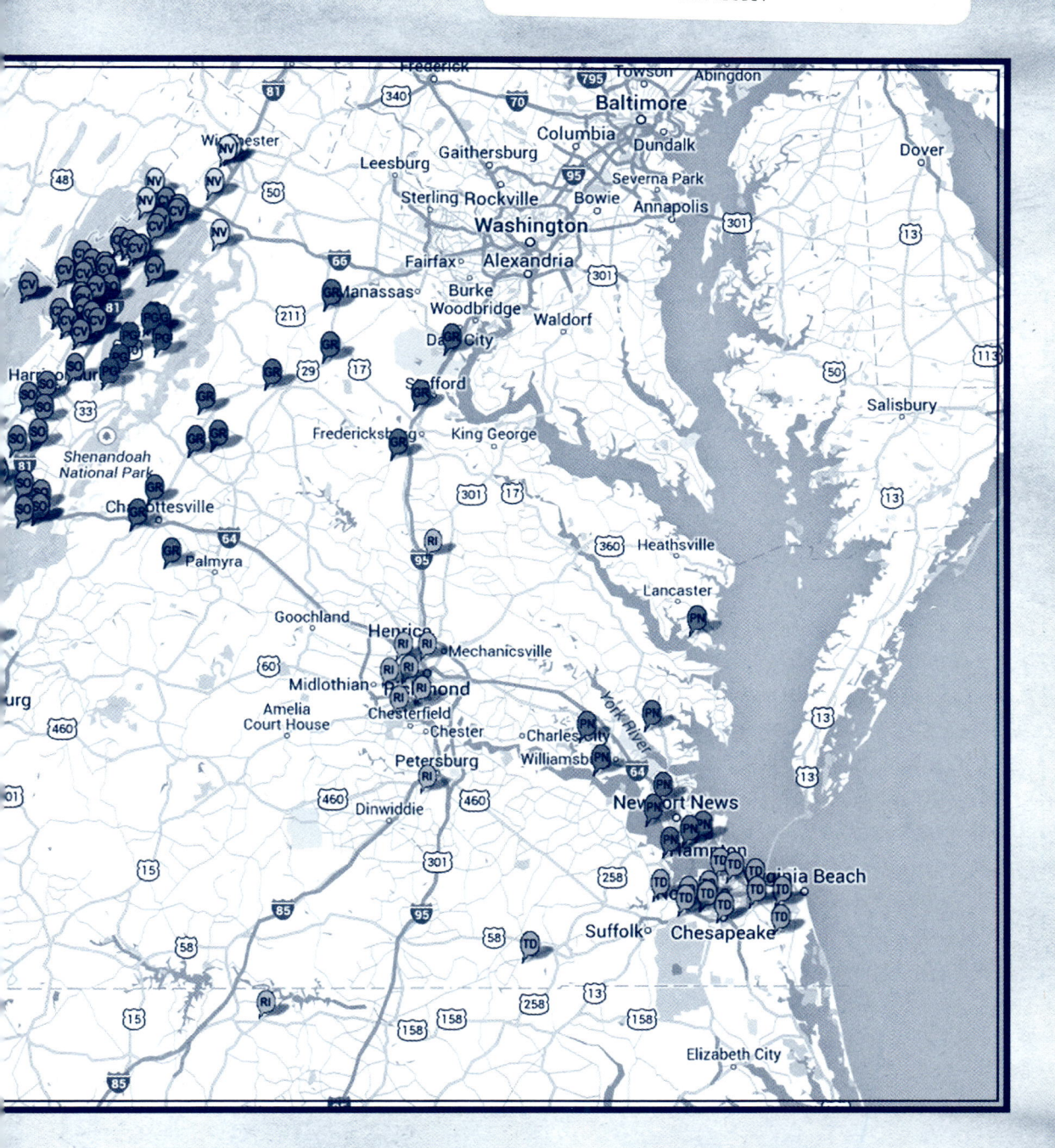

The Donning Company
Publishers

Journey Together

A History of the Virginia Synod of the
Evangelical Lutheran Church in America

1988–2012

James H. Utt

DEDICATED
in HONOR of

George A. Kegley

Editor
of the
The Virginia Lutheran
1960–

Member
of
The History Committee, 1955
for
The Lutheran Church in Virginia, 1717–1962

Contributor
to
Lutherans in Virginia, 1962–1987
and
*Journey Together
A History of the Virginia
Evangelical Lutheran Church in America
1988–2012*

In MEMORIAM

William Edward Eisenberg, D.D.
1903–2001

Author
The Lutheran Church in Virginia,
1717–1962

Paul Gerhard "Chip" Gunsten, D.Min.
1954–2012

Assistant to the Bishop, Virginia Synod
Evangelical Lutheran Church in America
1999–2012

Title page photo: Virginia Synod Assembly service of Holy Communion, St. Andrew's Roman Catholic Church, Roanoke, Virginia.

Copyright © 2015 by the Virginia Synod of the Evangelical Lutheran Church in America

All rights reserved, including the right to reproduce this work in any form whatsoever without permission in writing from the publisher, except for brief passages in connection with a review. For information, please write:

The Donning Company Publishers
184 Business Park Drive, Suite 206
Virginia Beach, VA 23462

Lex Cavanah, General Manager
Barbara Buchanan, Office Manager
Heather L. Floyd, Editor
Chad Harper Casey, Graphic Designer
Monika Ebertz, Imaging Artist
Karolyn Summers, Project Research Coordinator
Nathan Stufflebean, Marketing and Research Supervisor
Katie Gardner, Marketing Assistant

Dennis Walton, Project Director

Cataloging-in-Publication Data
Available from the Library of Congress

Printed in the United States of America at Walsworth Publishing Company

TABLE of CONTENTS

10 FOREWORD

13 PREFACE

17 PROLOGUE: AN HISTORICAL GATHERING OF LUTHERANS IN VIRGINIA

20 CHAPTER 1: VISIONING A NEW VIRGINIA SYNOD
- 20 Promises and Hopes—Anxieties and Fears
- 20 Ending the Former and Beginning the New
- 22 Electing Members of the Transition Team
- 23 The Work of the Virginia Synod/ELCA Transition Team
- 24 Constituting Convention Task Group
- 26 Constitutional and Legal Task Group
- 28 Finance Task Group
- 29 Institutions, Agencies, and Social Ministry Organizations Task Group
- 31 Headquarters Site and Staffing Task Group
- 32 Synod Functions and Activities Task Group
- 33 Nominating Task Group
- 33 Communications Task Group
- 33 Youth Ministry Task Group
- 33 Statistical Realities
- 34 Congregations Contributed and Received
- 35 Members Contributed and Received
- 35 Finances Contributed and Received
- 35 From Transition to Formation

36 CHAPTER 2: CONSTITUTING THE NEW SYNOD
The Constituting Convention
- 36 A Gathering of Virginia Lutherans
- 37 Form Follows Function
- 39 Whether Region 8 or Region 9?
- 41 Nominating and Electing New Leaders for a New Synod
- 45 Electing a New Bishop
- 51 Richard F. Bansemer—From New York to Virginia
- 52 New Bishop, New Style
- 52 A New Synod is Born

54 CHAPTER 3: IMPLEMENTING THE NEW VIRGINIA SYNOD
1988–1999
- 54 Wasting No Time
- 55 Building the Team
- 55 Keith Brown—From Engineer to Administrative Assistant
- 57 James F. Mauney—From Parish Pastor to Assistant to the Bishop
- 58 Learning the Ropes
- 60 "In the Excitement of This Hour"—The Installation of the New Bishop

- 61   A New Synod Begins
- 63   Appointing Deans of Conferences and Bishop's Representatives
- 65   Pastor John F. Byerly, Jr.—Respected Advisor
- 65   Jean Bozeman—Daughter of the Synod
- 67   From Chicago to Salem
- 67   Building Financial Resources—The Synod Trust Fund for Mission
- 71   From Many to One—The United Lutheran Appeal
- 78   From Virginia to Papua New Guinea—Beginning the Companion Synod Relationship
- 81   "The Trip of a Lifetime"
- 84   Conceived and Named—Power in the Spirit
- 89   Care of Spouses—Luncheons and Retreats
- 91   Care of the Call/Care of the Soul
- 92   Restructuring for Mission and Ministry
- 96   "That Christ May Be Seen—Strategy 2000"
- 100   A Third Full-Time Assistant and Office of the Bishop in the East
- 102   "Strategy 2000"
- 103   The Need for Church to Be a Safe Place
- 107   A Final Election and Retirement

110   CHAPTER 4: SUSTAINING THE VIRGINIA SYNOD
1999–2012 and Beyond

- 110   Electing the Next Bishop
- 114   Building the Team
- 115   Paul Gerhard Gunsten—From Parish Pastor to Assistant to the Bishop
- 117   The Installation of Bishop James F. Mauney
- 120   Ambassadors for Christ
- 121   20/20 Vision Goals
- 123   Visiting and Listening
- 125   Sustaining Ministry to Youth—A Synodical Director for Youth and Young Adult Ministries
- 128   David K. Delaney—From Parish Pastor to Director for Youth and Young Adult Ministries
- 131   Sustaining the Financial Base—The Mission Office for Planned Giving
- 132   George L. Sims—From Parish Pastor to Director of the Mission Office for Planned Giving
- 135   Lutheran Partners in Mission
- 136   Ellen I. Hinlicky—Director, Lutheran Partners in Mission
- 137   Sustaining Congregations and Leaders—Healthy Congregations and Bridgebuilders
- 142   Ambassadors Community for Theological Study (ACTS)
- 146   Forming Faith at Home—Roots & Wings
- 150   Phyllis Blair Milton—Synodical Minister for Christian Formation
- 151   Sustaining the Companion Synod Relationship—Changes and Challenges
- 156   Building Up the Ministerium
- 161   Mindy Reynolds—Diaconal Minister for Healthy Leadership and Wellness
- 163   Responses to the Issues of Human Sexuality
- 167   Response to the 2009 ELCA Social Statement, "Human Sexuality—Gift and Trust"
- 172   Moving On in Mission and Ministry

174   CHAPTER 5: EXTENDING THE MISSION OF THE VIRGINIA SYNOD
Related Institutions, Agencies, Auxiliaries, Camps, Ministries, Ecumenical Relationships, and Organizations

- 174   Roanoke College
- 175   Lutheran Theological Southern Seminary
- 176   National Lutheran Communities & Services
- 177   Chaplain Service of the Churches of Virginia
- 177   Lutheran Family Services of Virginia
- 178   Caroline Furnace Lutheran Camp and Retreat Center
- 179   Virginia Lutheran Homes

- 180 Lutheran Council of Tidewater
- 181 Hungry Mother Lutheran Retreat Center
- 181 Virginia Synodical Women
- 182 Virginia Lutheran Men in Mission
- 184 Region 9 Center for Mission
- 187 Lutheran Campus Ministry
- 190 Ecumenical Relationships

198 CHAPTER 6: CONGREGATIONS OF THE VIRGINIA SYNOD
- 198 Virginia Synod of the Evangelical Lutheran Church in America
- 198 Central Valley Conference
- 209 Germanna Conference
- 218 Highland Conference
- 225 New River Conference
- 232 Northern Valley Conference
- 236 Page Conference
- 239 Peninsula Conference
- 245 Richmond Conference
- 251 Southern Conference
- 260 Southern Valley Conference
- 271 Tidewater Conference

280 EPILOGUE: AN HISTORICAL GATHERING OF LUTHERANS IN VIRGINIA

284 APPENDICES
- 284 Appendix I: Virginia Synod/Evangelical Lutheran Church in America Statistics
- 285 Appendix II: Virginia Synod Ordinations
- 288 Appendix III: United Lutheran Appeal, First Year Report of Response By Conference
- 288 Appendix IV: United Lutheran Appeal, Response By Year
- 289 Appendix V: Power in the Spirit Programs and Leaders
- 294 Appendix VI: Ambassadors Community for Theological Study (ACTS) Courses
- 296 Appendix VII: The Ministerium Covenant, Virginia Synod/ELCA
- 296 Appendix VIII: Virginia Synod Assembly Themes
- 297 Appendix IX: Ordained Ministers in Special Situations
- 299 Appendix X: Associates in Ministry (AIM)
- 299 Appendix XI: Number of Congregations
- 300 Appendix XII: New Congregations Received
- 300 Appendix XIII: Congregations Closing or Leaving
- 301 Appendix XIV: Necrology
- 302 Appendix XV: Ambassadors Community for Theological Study (ACTS) Certificates Awarded
- 304 Appendix XVI: Synod Council Members and Officers
- 311 Appendix XVII: Ordained/Rostered Leaders Statistics
- 311 Appendix XVIII: Distribution of Congregations By Size
- 311 Appendix XIX: Worship Attendance Statistics
- 312 Appendix XX: Baptized Members By Congregation Size
- 312 Appendix XXI: Baptisms By Year
- 313 Appendix XXII: Membership Analysis

314 INDEX
- 314 Subject Index
- 316 Name Index

320 ABOUT THE AUTHOR

† FOREWORD

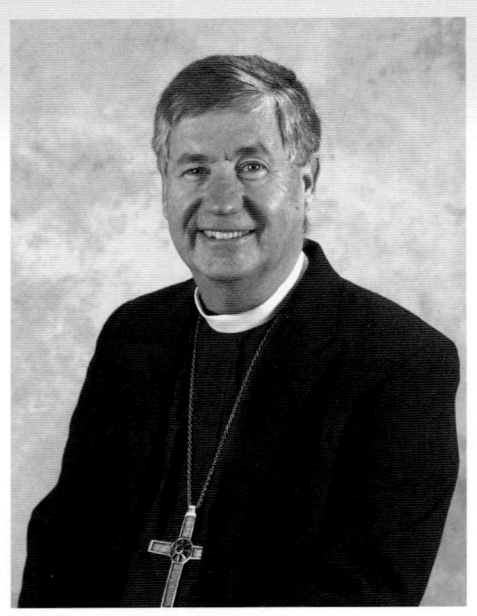

Bishop James F. Mauney

In 1987, a new Virginia Synod of the Evangelical Lutheran Church in America (ELCA) was created. Twenty-five years have passed, and the Synod Council thought it prudent to provide for the writing of a history that would include the emphases, leadership, congregations, institutions, and programs that have given glory to our Lord Jesus Christ.

I love this synod! One of its greatest characteristics is that it has emphasized relationships in Jesus Christ throughout its generations. Its sixty-plus years of summer assembly at Massanetta Springs and its forty-plus years of dynamic youth events have been visible signs of lay and clergy—and now rostered leaders—who have collaborated and worked together for the sake of the gospel. The synod's very nature is to collaborate, to form teams of lay and rostered leaders. The grandeur of our laity with their ardor for the faith is most remarkable! The intentionality of our Ministerium to build one another up with the love of the gospel has been key to our practice of ministry in this synod. I love our Ministerium and its members' desire for excellence!

So it seemed right and salutary to ask the Rev. James H. Utt to collaborate with Mr. George Kegley in gathering data, interviewing leaders, crafting a process, writing a draft, and overseeing the publication of a history of this new synod. Pastor Utt's passionate love for and decades of service to his synod and its institutions, and his giftedness in blending many details into a seamless story, made him a first-rate selection. Mr. Kegley's long career as a reporter and editor with *The Roanoke Times*, and his fifty-four-plus years of service as the editor of *The Virginia Lutheran*, made him a prime choice to collaborate with Pastor Utt. Like Lewis and Clark, they began an assignment that became a journey together, and took over three years to complete. They have produced a fine accounting of the life of our dear Virginia Synod/ELCA.

One of our many historic congregations is Grace Lutheran in Winchester, Virginia. Organized in 1759, it was the first congregation in Virginia to be recognized as a member of the Pennsylvania Ministerium. The Virginia Special Conference was formed within its building in

1793. In 1820, the first Virginia Synod in association with Maryland congregations was organized in that same sanctuary. In 1892, it was the first Lutheran congregation to support a missionary in a foreign field—the Rev. Rufus Benton Peery, missionary to Japan.

I know this because Grace's pastor from 1944 to 1967, the Rev. Dr. William Edward Eisenberg, wrote *The Lutheran Church in Virginia, 1717–1962*. This tome has been the insightful history of our synod from the founding of our first congregation, Hebron in Madison, in 1717, through the ending of the United Lutheran Church in America and the anticipation of the start of the Lutheran Church in America in 1962.

For chronicling the first twenty-five years of the Virginia Synod of the Evangelical Lutheran Church in America, we thought it fitting to return to a pastor of Grace, Winchester, the Rev. James H. Utt, and call upon him to write the history for this period, 1987 through 2012. In every way an historian like Eisenberg, Pastor Utt has written a thorough account of these twenty-five years, and has included a host of photos and appendices to amplify the message.

But more than that—for the publishing of this history, the trustees of the congregation and the Congregational Council of historic Grace, Winchester stepped forward with a gift of $15,000 from an endowed fund managed by the trustees, Heritage for the Future, in honor of their two historians and in recognition of the importance of our having an accurate history of our synod for future generations. In every one of its generations, Grace congregation has been a leading, engaging, participating, and supporting partner in the life of the Virginia Synod.

Their expressed honoring of their pastors and their strong gift of partnership are a reminder to us that the call of the gospel is to every generation and every life. It isn't that we have our grandparents' historic faith. It is that we have our grandparents' desire to be faithful to the gospel in whatever time or age. So we are called to be faithful to the gospel in these days, and in this generation. This history is a wonderful expression of what we together have been about in the name of our Lord Jesus Christ for the past years.

I want to express my appreciation to Dr. Michael C. Maxey, president of Roanoke College; Dr. Mark F. Miller, professor of history; and Rebecca Sandborg, vice president, for their helpful support and guidance through the publication process.

In addition to thanking Dr. Utt and Mr. Kegley, I want to thank the assistants to the Office of the Bishop, the Virginia Synod/Evangelical Lutheran Church in America, Bishop V.A. Moyer, Jr. and his assistants, and the officers of both synods and so many others who spent hours in the interviews which greatly aided the composing of this history. I would like to thank all of the congregations and the rostered leaders who made deadlines so that their congregations could be included within this history.

Let me also draw attention to the deep faith and leadership of former vice presidents Leroy Hamlett, Kathryn Buchanan, Mark Reed, and Charles Poston. Their love for Jesus and the Spirit within them have molded and often preserved the synod's bishops in a constancy and joy for their service. These vice presidents have chaired our synod councils with adroit wisdom, kindness, and skill. They have so often been a listening ear and wise word for the Office of the Bishop.

While the history may often focus on the visible bishop, the pages hold within them the strong undercurrent of a bishop and officers and synod council journeying together.

In every chapter you will read about the creativity of synod staff, lay leaders, pastors, rostered leaders, and deans who engendered new programs, and whose ideas, gifts, faith, and talents gave life and newness to emphases and events. In every step this synod has taken, it has been a journey together. Always a journey together, always something expressed together and done together for the glory of our Lord—this is why Pastor Utt chose the title, *Journey Together*. May it always be so in this dynamic, very gifted, and very blessed Virginia Synod.

Bishop James F. Mauney
Salem, Virginia

PREFACE

Journey Together is the story of a new collective of Lutherans in Virginia and how they envisioned, constituted, implemented, and sustained the mission and ministry of a new synod. In each chapter the emphasis of the narrative is on the people involved, important decisions made, faithful work accomplished, and the resulting dynamics of new journeys in the mission and ministry of the members, congregations, and the leaders of the new synod.

The word *synod* has its origin in two Greek words—*syn* (together), and *odos* (a going, a way). Bishop Richard F. Bansemer took note of the origin of this word so familiar to Lutherans who pride themselves on order and the work of committees, councils, and assemblies—entities most often associated with the work of a synod. As was his disinclination for meetings and things administrative, he changed the title of one of the synod's communication instruments from *Staff Letter* to *Journey Together*. Befitting his self-identity as a "spiritual pilgrim," Bansemer often described the mission and various ministries of the synod as our *journey together*. So I confess—a good Lutheran trait—that I have stolen the title of a newsletter for the title of this historical narrative.

The Rev. Dr. James H. Utt

Chapter 1 steps back in time to tell the story of the work of the Transition Team and all the efforts needed in fulfilling the vision that would shape the new synod.

Chapter 2 describes the gathering of the voting members, their work and debates on the numerous actions required, and the ballots cast to elect new leadership and form a legally constituted synod ready to begin its new mission and ministry.

Chapter 3 tells the story of the challenges and struggles of implementing the new synod through the leadership of its first bishop, his assistants, lay officers, and the Synod Council.

Chapter 4 focuses on the work of sustaining the synod guided by the leadership of a new bishop, new staff members, and lay leaders responding to the challenges of being a faithful expression of the church in a changing world.

Chapter 5 reports the work of the various institutions, agencies, organizations, and other ecclesial structures that extend the mission and ministry of the Virginia Synod through their affiliated relationships with the synod. Those most involved in these partnerships wrote the account of their work over the past twenty-five years.

Chapter 6 follows the practice of the two previous volumes of history about Lutherans in Virginia offering a brief sketch of each of the congregations of the synod with highlights of their mission and ministry and a listing of their ordained and rostered leadership.

† † †

I am indebted to so many people for their assistance in the research and writing of this historical narrative. I begin my expressions of thanks to George A. Kegley for his abundance of help and encouragement. George is the only non-ordained member of the 1955 editorial committee that assisted Dr. William Edward Eisenberg, Grace, Winchester, in his scholarly efforts over a period of eleven years in writing the widely respected tome, *The Lutheran Church in Virginia, 1717–1962*. George was also instrumental in working with Pastor George E. Handley, secretary, archivist, and assistant to Bishop V.A. Moyer, 1977–1987, in contributing to a two-volume history, *Lutherans in Virginia, Vol. 1: A 25-Year History, 1962–1987* and *Lutherans in Virginia, Vol. 2: Congregational Sketchbook*. As in those two volumes, he has taken a significant role in this history by editing the reports of the institutions, agencies, organizations, and other ecclesial structures in Chapter 5, and the historical sketches of the congregations in Chapter 6. These are the reasons for dedicating this book in his honor.

Thanks are owed to Bishop Richard F. Bansemer and Bishop James F. Mauney for their assistance and guidance in "getting it right" with some of the more tedious details during their tenures of office. I particularly appreciate the time and effort they and members of their staffs were willing to give to talk about their work and answer numerous questions. Thanks go to Keith Brown, Jean Bozeman, Chip Gunsten, Dave Delaney, Ellen Hinlicky, Mindy Reynolds, and Phyllis Milton, who helped me throughout the duration of the research and writing of the history. I want to say a special word of thanks to Jean Bozeman and Lenae Osmondson, administrative assistant for the Office of the Bishop-East, for the extra time they gave in meeting with me on occasion and the help in reading, editing, and making sure I correctly identified people and their home congregations. Jean is owed a special word of appreciation for her diligent search for photos and their captioning.

A special word of appreciation is also expressed to the officers of the synod who faithfully served in their various capacities over these past twenty-five years. They never tired of being interviewed or answering phone calls and emails: vice presidents Leroy Hamlett, Kathryn Buchanan, Mark Reed, and Charles Poston; secretaries Clif Anderson, Mark Reed, Pat Morgan, Martha Edwards, and Janet Gomez; and treasurers Kathryn Buchanan, Adolph Moller, and Skip Zubrod.

I also wish to thank the members of the administrative staff in the synod office—Sue Dugas, Debbie Worley, Billie Spencer, Becky Walls, and Kayla Fuller—for the many ways they assisted in my search for further information and for forwarding messages, emails, and various forms of printed material to me. They were very patient and supportive, offering me space and helping with the printing and copying of documents.

I want to thank the Rev. Dr. V.A. Moyer, Jr., bishop emeritus, Virginia Synod of the Lutheran Church in America, and members of the synod staff who served with him—Charles Shenberger, the Rev. George E. Handley, and the Rev. Dwayne J. Westermann—for their advice, insights, and encouragement in writing the story of the work of the Transition Team and details of the development of synod programs and emphases that moved forward from one synod to the next.

A special word of thanks is owed also to President Michael Maxey, Roanoke College, for his support and encouragement and making available professional assistance and resources of the college, especially Dr. Mark F. Miller, professor of history, and Rebecca Sandborg, vice president for information technology, and members of her staff, for their assistance in the publication process. Thanks are also due to Linda Miller, archivist, Roanoke College, and to her student assistants for providing the space for research and writing and for assistance in locating various records of the synod over the past twenty-five years.

I want to thank the staff, leadership, and members of Grace Evangelical Lutheran Church, Winchester, for their support in the early stages of my research and writing before retiring after thirty years as pastor of this historic congregation. They have demonstrated once again this congregation's love for the Virginia Synod and the importance of recording its history through their generous gift for this publication. It is a gift to all the congregations, members, pastors, and rostered leaders in this synod. The trustees of the congregation—David Behr, Jerry Kerr, and Roger Milburn—were strong in their advocacy of recommending the use of available monies in the congregation's endowment fund appropriately entitled "Heritage for the Future." I wish also to thank Mary Froehlich, archivist for Grace, for her advice and encouragement.

Finally, I wish to note the love and encouragement of Susan, my wife, and our children, Emily and Tyson, and their families, especially the love of four grandchildren who have reminded me of what is really important in life.

† † †

Three Virginia Synods have been significant in my journey of faith and call to ordained ministry. I am honored to have been baptized and confirmed at Gladesboro Lutheran Church, Hillsville, in Carroll County, a small, rural congregation of the Virginia Synod of the United Lutheran Church in America (ULCA, 1918–1962); ordained by the Virginia Synod of the Lutheran Church in America (LCA, 1962–1987) upon receiving a call to serve as pastor of Ascension, Danville (1976–1982); and retired from active parish ministry at Grace, Winchester (1983–2013), of the Virginia Synod of the Evangelical Lutheran Church in America (ELCA, 1988–).

† † †

Robert Strausz-Hupé, an American diplomat, once said, "Since we do not know whence we came and where we are going, we are likely to be mistaken when we think we know where we are."[1]

It is my hope that *Journey Together* will help this and future generations of Lutherans in Virginia understand where they have been as a synod of the ELCA and what they have accomplished throughout these past years. I hope they will be encouraged by this narrative to move into the future with the confidence God will abundantly give them for the demands and opportunities to be the church in years ahead. Finally, I trust the gift of this history will generate renewed strength in the members and congregations as they continue their *Journey Together* as an historic and evangelical witness to the gospel of Jesus Christ in today's world.

> James H. Utt, D.Min., D.D.
> Pastor Emeritus
> Grace, Winchester

---

1. Robert Strausz-Hupé, "Maxims," *Encounter*, February 1976, p. 28.

PROLOGUE
AN HISTORICAL GATHERING OF LUTHERANS IN VIRGINIA

O Holy Spirit, enter in, and in our hearts your work begin,
and make our hearts your dwelling.
Sun of the soul, O Light divine, around and in us brightly shine,
your strength in us upwelling.
In your radiance life from heaven now is given overflowing,
gift of gifts beyond all knowing.

Left to ourselves, we surely stray; oh, lead us on the narrow way,
with wisest counsel guide us;
And give us steadfastness, that we may follow you forever free,
no matter who derides us.
Gently heal those hearts now broken; give some token you are near us,
whom we trust to light and cheer us.

O mighty Rock, O Source of life, let your good Word in doubt and strife
be in us strongly burning,
That we be faithful unto death and live in love and holy faith,
from you true wisdom learning.
Lord your mercy on us shower; by your power Christ confessing,
we will cherish all your blessing.

WIE SCHON LEUCHTET
PM
Text: Michael Schirrmer, 1606–1673[1]

---

1. *Lutheran Book of Worship* (*LBW*), 459, 1979. Public Domain.

Voices of over 700 Virginia Lutherans sang out in unison this opening hymn of the Service of Celebration and Praise with Holy Communion and the Rite of Ordination on Friday evening, May 29, 1987. Historically, it was a gathering of Lutherans in Virginia from congregations with different historical backgrounds and churchwide affiliations who gathered to worship at the start of what would be a new synod. Technically, it was the second meeting of voting members, guests, and visitors attending the Constituting Convention of the Virginia Synod of the Evangelical Lutheran Church in America being held in the Bast Center of Roanoke College.

Earlier in the day they gathered to organize themselves into a constituted body of voting members representing the 165 congregations of three different Lutheran expressions present in Virginia—the Association of Evangelical Lutheran Churches (AELC), the American Lutheran Church (ALC), and the Lutheran Church in America (LCA).

Voting members came well prepared and ready to engage in forming a new synodical expression. They had already adopted an agenda and rules of procedure to guide their debates, decisions, and casting of ballots, including the first ballot earlier in the day for the first bishop of the new synod. A new constitution, bylaws, and structure had been debated, amended, and approved by overwhelming votes. There was an air of excitement and anticipation mixed with both joy and serious reflection on the tasks yet ahead. Now the time had come to do what Lutherans do best—worship.

The opening hymn announced a new thing God was doing. This new thing was visualized as three processionals composed of ordained and lay representatives of the merging expressions made their way from different locations to the center of the worship space. Each procession brought jars of water symbolic of Holy Baptism, plates of bread and cups of wine that would be used for Holy Communion, and copies of the Holy Bible for the Word proclaimed—tokens that the Holy Spirit was near to "light and cheer us." Brief statements of each expression's history and hope for the future were read, followed by an Order for Confession and Forgiveness as well as a Remembrance of Baptism. There was no mistaking the message or the purpose of this people—this new expression of evangelical Lutherans would begin and its future mission would be centered in God's Holy Word and Holy Sacraments.

Bishop V.A. Moyer, Jr., Virginia Synod/LCA, presided at the service of Holy Communion assisted by Bishop E. Harold Jansen, Eastern District/ALC. The former president of the Lutheran Church in America, the Rev. Dr. Robert J. Marshall, presiding officer of the convention, preached. The title of his sermon, "Values with Vitality," was based on John 17:15-23. Callister Dailey, a member of the Virginia Synod/LCA Executive Board, and Clarence Caldwell, treasurer, Virginia Synod/LCA, served as readers of the appointed texts for the service.

The Virginia Synod/LCA had requested the Rite of Ordination be part of the service. The candidates for ordination were Caldwell Newton Day, sponsored by Pastor Terry D. Clark; Dennis Scott Roberts, sponsored by Pastor Richard F. Bansemer; and Karl David Skole, sponsored by Mr. Gunther Skole and Pastor Dwayne J. Westermann. The newly ordained assisted in the distribution of Holy Communion. They were joined by Pastor Willetta B. Heising, AELC; Pastor Robert R.

Sala and Pastor Elmer H. Ganskopp, celebrating the fiftieth anniversary of their ordinations; along with Pastor Marshall F. Mauney, recognized for retiring from active parish ministry. Lay members assisting in the distribution of the wine represented the Transition Team. Pastor Robert J. Maier was server, assisted by Pastor John W. McCandlish. An offering of $1,188.53 was received and designated for church extension in the new Evangelical Lutheran Church in America.

Centered in Word and Sacrament for the work in this Constituting Convention, Virginia Lutherans gathered for worship on this historical occasion trusting the Holy Spirit was guiding them as they would continue in the days ahead to debate, vote, and inaugurate a new Virginia Synod of the Evangelical Lutheran Church in America.

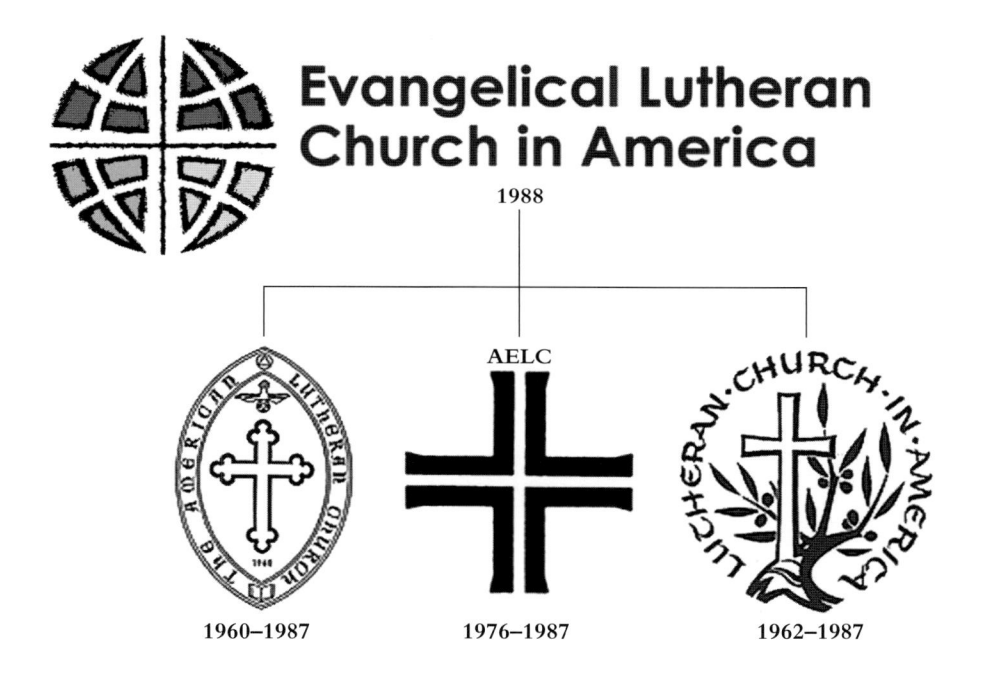

Evangelical Lutheran Church in America
1988

| 1960–1987 | AELC 1976–1987 | 1962–1987 |

CHAPTER 1

VISIONING A NEW VIRGINIA SYNOD

PROMISES AND HOPES—ANXIETIES AND FEARS

"Who's been doing all this work to start a new synod?" "What's going to happen to the old synod, just stop existing?" "How will all of these changes impact us as a congregation?" "Besides, who knows what all this talk about being an interdependent and inclusive church really means?"

These questions were asked and discussed in a "special order" time on the agenda of a church council of a Lutheran congregation in the Shenandoah Valley. The council had set aside the time to allow for discussion and questions before voting to elect their congregation's voting members to the Constituting Convention for the new Virginia Synod of the Evangelical Lutheran Church in America.

It was early spring, 1988. All types of Lutheran congregations throughout Virginia—large and small, historic and new, from different traditions and affiliated with different national expressions—were preparing for their voting members to attend pre-convention consultations, getting ready for the beginning of new and unfamiliar ways of being a church body and ending one that was comfortable, familiar.

Their questions would be answered in time. For now, such questions reflected the uneasiness often felt by people of faith when anxieties and fears of present realities meet the promise and hope of the future of God's kingdom revealed in Jesus Christ.

ENDING THE FORMER AND BEGINNING THE NEW

The concluding paragraphs of the "Report of the Bishop and Synod Staff" to the June 1986 convention of the Virginia Synod/Lutheran Church in America (LCA) give historical perspective and notice of the challenges facing the synod in the necessary work of ending the former Virginia Synod and

The Rev. Dr. Virgil A. Moyer, Jr., Bishop, 1976–1988

20 † Journey Together

transitioning to the new Virginia Synod of the Evangelical Lutheran Church in America (ELCA). Bishop V.A. Moyer, Jr. wrote,

> To properly understand that beginning we need to take a look backward. The road to this new church had its beginnings at many different points along the long road to church unity. Perhaps for our present purposes we need only to go back to the work of the Joint Committee on Church Unity that took into consideration the concerns of the American Lutheran Church and the Lutheran Church in America. Then came the concerns expressed by the Association of Evangelical Lutheran Churches, formed by the group of congregations which broke away from the Lutheran Church-Missouri Synod.
>
> Then followed adoption, by all three church conventions, of the plan that called for the appointment of the Commission for a New Lutheran Church—a group of seventy persons charged with the responsibility of planning for the new Lutheran Church. The group has made periodic reports as they made progress toward the formation of our new church. Six such reports have been issued with the final one being used as the basis for the development of the documents that will form the foundation of the congregation, synodical, and national organizations.
>
> As we look to the transition from our present synodical life and work to the new church, the most obvious change relates to the division of our present synod into three future synods. Most of our congregations will form the new "Virginia Synod," or whatever its name will be. Another group will help form a new "Metro Washington Synod," and a smaller number will help form a new "West Virginia Synod." In each case there is the addition of congregations from the American Lutheran Church and the Association of Evangelical Lutheran Churches.
>
> To assist in planning for the new synods, Transition Teams have been appointed to guide us from where we are now through the constituting convention of the new synod. They will provide specific recommendations that relate to legal matters, institutional relationships, finances, constituting conventions, nominating committees, assets, and the necessary guidelines to see that present programs related to the functions assigned to new synods are carried forward without hiatus, and a multitude of other responsibilities.
>
> We need the patience of all our people in this process of ending and beginning, but we also need your help in making sure that we do not neglect either the ending of the former or the beginning of the new. The next eighteen months promise to be busy and exciting as together we work toward a new phase in the life of God's family of which we are a vital part.[1]

It would be the work of a Transition Team for the new Virginia Synod to make certain that the ending of the former and the beginning of the new would not be neglected, but would, in fact, be done well. Bishop V.A. Moyer, Jr., because of his love for the Lord and His Church—especially the part of it called the Virginia Synod—would see to it. It would be as if the whole of his ordained career had prepared him for this work of shepherding the transition from the former to a new Virginia Synod.

---

1. Minutes, Report of the Bishop and Synod Staff, 167th Annual Convention, Virginia Synod/LCA, June 6-8, 1986, VA.

Moyer knew the church well in all of its expressions. He served congregations in Virginia as a parish pastor—Ascension, Danville, 1945–1947; Mt. Jackson Parish (Bethel, Mt. Calvary, St. James), 1947–1950; Christ, Radford, 1950–1952; St. Peter, Shenandoah, 1953–1958; and Grace, Winchester, 1968–1973. He served the synod as its first full-time assistant to the president, the Rev. J. Luther Mauney, 1959–1968. He was called by the LCA as a Regional Mission Consultant of the Division for Mission in North America, 1973–1976. He was the last president (1976–1981) and the first bishop (1981–1987) of the synod since his election in 1976. His advice and support would prove valuable to the Executive Board in its responsibilities to end the Virginia Synod/LCA and to the Virginia Synod Transition Team (VSTT) as it faced many tasks to begin the Virginia Synod/ELCA. His presence would also be important to the other synodical transition teams—the new Metropolitan Washington, DC Synod and the new West Virginia-Western Maryland Synod.

ELECTING MEMBERS OF THE TRANSITION TEAM

During its February 1986 meeting, the Executive Board of the Virginia Synod/LCA elected members of LCA congregations from across the synod to serve on three Transition Teams.[2] The following were elected from Virginia Synod congregations that would be part of the new Metropolitan Washington, DC Synod:

Pastor Duane H. Carlson	St. Mark, Springfield
Pastor Edwin L. Ehlers	Redeemer, McLean
Sam Simonovick	Bethel, Manassas
Constance Swank	Advent, Arlington

These members would be joined by a representative from the AELC, five representatives from the ALC's Eastern District, and six or seven representatives from the LCA's Maryland Synod.

The following were elected from the Virginia Synod/LCA congregations on the territory that would become part of the West Virginia Synod:

Kay Fix	St. John, Martinsburg
Pastor Philip C. Huber	Wardensville Parish, Wardensville
Pastor Richard Neal	St. Thomas, Charlestown

These members would be joined by three representatives from the ALC's Eastern District and seven to nine representatives from the LCA's Western Pennsylvania/West Virginia Synod.

The following were elected by their respective judicatories to serve as members of the Transition Team for what would become the new Virginia Synod/ELCA:

Pastor Willetta Heising	Faith, Franklin (AELC)[3]
Clifton W. Anderson	Peace, Charlottesville (ALC)

---

2. Minutes, 167th Annual Convention, Virginia Synod/LCA, June 6-8, 1986, pp. 107-108.
3. Pastor Heising was the only AELC pastor on the territory of the Virginia Synod/LCA at the time of her appointment to the Transition Team, serving the only AELC congregation in Virginia: Faith, Franklin.

Nunna See	Shepherd of the Valley, Bridgewater (ALC)
Pastor Bruce Wilder	Christ the King, Richmond (ALC)
Pastor Richard F. Bansemer	Grace, Rural Retreat (LCA)
Pastor Thomas L. Bosserman	Trinity, Newport News (LCA)
Keith Brown	St. John, Roanoke (LCA)
Pastor John F. Byerly	First English, Richmond (LCA)
Pastor Richard M. Carbaugh	Christ, Fredericksburg (LCA)
Carol Cox	Bethlehem, Lynchburg (LCA)
Humes J. Franklin, Jr.	Grace, Waynesboro (LCA)
Richard K. Gerlitz	Glade Creek, Blue Ridge (LCA)
Leroy R. Hamlett, Jr.	St. Mark, Charlottesville (LCA)
Betty Kipps	Muhlenberg, Harrisonburg (LCA)
Pastor James H. Utt	Grace, Winchester (LCA)

Staff members of the present synod or district would not serve as members of the Transition Team but rather be available as advisory members and serve on the various task groups of the Team. The Rev. K. Roy Nilsen, assistant to Bishop Harold Jensen, Eastern District/ALC, represented the ALC Eastern District staff. In addition to Moyer, representing the Virginia Synod/LCA staff were the Rev. George E. Handley, secretary and administrative assistant to the bishop; Charles E. Shenberger, assistant to the bishop; and the Rev. Dwayne J. Westermann, assistant to the bishop. There was no staff member of the AELC assigned to serve on the Team.

THE WORK OF THE VIRGINIA SYNOD/ELCA TRANSITION TEAM

The first meeting of the Virginia Synod Transition Team was held on Thursday, February 27, 1986, at Grace Evangelical Lutheran Church, Waynesboro. Richard K. Gerlitz was chosen by consensus to serve as chair; Clifton W. Anderson, secretary. Bishop Moyer presented information from the National Transition Team (NTT) listing the primary objectives of synodical Transition Teams:

1) Guide the congregations of the ALC, AELC, and LCA starting with this meeting until the constituting convention of the new synod at which time the new Synod Council will be the new governing body between assemblies.

2) Identify and accomplish those tasks necessary for transitioning to a new synod under the directives and constitutional provisions provided by the Commission for a New Lutheran Church (CNLC) and the National Transitional Team (NTT).

3) Establish meeting dates and times for the Transition Team, probably once a month, noting that some months may be devoted to task group meetings rather than to meetings of the full team.

4) Elect a chairperson and a secretary.

5) Divide the various responsibilities among task groups which will involve people outside the Transition Team.

Other responsibilities of the Transition Team would include communicating meeting dates of the Team with the CNLC and NTT and establishing means of communication with the congregations and members of the new synod to inform them of decisions concerning the formation and operations of the new synod and the rationale behind those decisions. It was agreed that a series of newsletters, *Transition News—An Occasional Newsletter from the Virginia Synod Transition Team*, would be published and mailed to all the congregations that would become part of the new synod. The newsletter would also be submitted for publication in the communication instruments of each represented church body.

Six task groups were appointed initially: Constituting Convention, Constitutional and Legal, Finance, Institutions and Agencies, Headquarters Site and Staffing, and Synod Functions and Activities. As the work of the Team progressed, other matters would need attention and three additional task groups would be appointed in 1987 and 1988 to study and recommend actions in the ministry areas of communication and youth ministry. A Nominating Task Group would also be appointed by the Team in early 1988 in time for an extensive slate of nominees to be presented to the Constituting Convention to be elected to be the new leaders and do the work of the new synod.

CONSTITUTING CONVENTION TASK GROUP

To lead the work of this task group the Transition Team selected Pastor John Byerly, First English, Richmond, as the chair, to serve along with Keith Brown, St. John, Roanoke. Charles Shenberger served as advisor to the task group.

Guidelines from the CNLC were provided to help the task group especially in determining delegate representation from congregations, items and order of business, election processes, and representative makeup of the Synod Council and other boards or committees to be elected. The task group was encouraged to note new language that would be followed indicating changes in understanding the church on the synodical level. For example, in the new church, synods were to be understood as an expression of the whole church, not just as a collective representation of the interests of local congregations within a recognized geographical boundary.[4] Therefore, congregations would be electing "voting members" to participate in an "assembly" to advance the mission and ministry of another expression of the church—the synod—rather than electing delegates to participate in a convention to conduct business for the sake of the constituent congregations.

The Transition Team encouraged the task group not to wait to make decisions relative to the time and place of the Constituting Convention. There were a number of important reasons not to delay:

---

4. For a review of the CNLC's debate about the nature and structure of the church and a description of the three tier expressions—congregations, synods, and churchwide—see Edgar Trexler's *Anatomy of a Merger: People, Dynamics, and Decisions That Shaped the ELCA*, Augsburg Fortress Press, 1991, especially Chapters 3-6.

1) Communicating reports and items for action as well as the latest recommendations and actions of the Constituting Convention of the ELCA that would be held in May just before the synod constituting conventions;

2) Appointing task groups and committees to do the work of local arrangements for the convention and the orderly conducting of its business;

3) Providing timely information to the congregation for electing voting members according to guidelines for meeting congregational representation quotas;

4) Conducting of the business of the Constituting Convention, especially outlining the timing and procedures for electing the new bishop and nominating at least two candidates for new offices, as well as a new synod council with specific numbers of nominations assuring representation from merger church bodies, as well as required gender and minority quotas.

Though the specific dates would need to be coordinated with the CNLC and NTT, it was the consensus at the first meeting of the Transition Team that the Constituting Convention Task Group find a time to convene the convention at the end of May or beginning of June 1987. It was also the consensus that the Constituting Convention should be held at Roanoke College. Moyer and synod staff members noted that both time and location would be following the custom with which most congregations were familiar. It was also noted that the presence of synod administrative support staff in the office of the synod would be helpful in preparing and printing ballots and duplicating documents containing motions and amendments needed for orderly debate and votes.

After communications with the CNLC and the NTT, the dates of May 29, 30, and 31, 1987 were set for the Constituting Convention at Roanoke College, Salem. The primary items on the agenda would be:

1) Adopting the recommended model constitution and bylaws for the new synod;

2) Finalizing the decision concerning regional alignment;

3) Approving several sets of recommendations from the Transition Team's task groups;

4) Conducting numerous elections, especially a new bishop, among the most anticipated of all actions, in addition to electing new synodical officers and a new synod council.

The Team and task group members were sensitive to the leadership of the convention, especially the importance of a strong and knowledgeable presiding officer. Rev. Dr. Robert J. Marshall, former president of the LCA and well known in Virginia, was selected by the CNLC from a

The Rev. Dr. Robert J. Marshall, President of the Lutheran Church in America, 1968–1978; Presiding Officer, Constituting Convention, May 29-31, 1987

Virginia Synod † 25

pool of names suggested by the Team. "God's People in Mission" was chosen as the theme of the convention. Bishop V.A. Moyer, Jr. accepted the invitation of the Team to serve as convention chaplain. The retired secretary of the Virginia Synod/LCA, Dr. Charles Tusing, was asked to serve as secretary of the convention. The secretary of the Virginia Synod/LCA, Pastor George Handley, offered to assist the task group in the responsibility for publishing the official roll of voting members with addresses and the congregations they represent. Secretary Handley also accepted responsibility for publishing the convention Bulletin of Reports with the assistance of the synod administrative staff. It was agreed that at least two supplements to the Bulletin of Reports would be needed to provide updates of decisions made by the CNLC, the NTT, and the ELCA Constituting Convention just before the time of the synodical constituting convention in Salem.

The task group also recommended, and the Team agreed, that pre-convention consultations should take place in the designated conferences of the new synod. These conference consultations were planned to take place during the time frame of May 10-23, 1987, with teams of members from the Team conducting the consultations.

The task group planned for an attendance of approximately 180 clergy and 320 lay voting members, following the mandated formula percentage of 40/60 for clergy/lay. From each congregation there would be a pastor and two lay voting members—a male and a female. As recommended by the CNLC, the Team agreed that in congregations with more than 400 baptized members, an additional voting member would be received for each additional 200 baptized members or portion thereof. It was also agreed that members of the Team not otherwise elected as voting members should be granted voice, not vote.

For the purpose of organizing the convention, the following committees and chairs were recommended by the task group and appointed by the Team: Official Roll, chaired by Pastor John C. Morrill, St. Paul, Roanoke; Reference and Counsel, chaired by Pastor Kenneth Crumpton, associate director, Church Extension/Division for Mission in North America; Minutes, chaired by Robert Shaver, Ascension, Danville; and Conduct of Elections, chaired by Kate Miller, St. Mark, Charlottesville. Members of the committees would be recruited by the Team giving attention to representation from congregations of the ALC and AELC. It was the consensus of the Team that no "Youth Convo" be held during the convention.

To resolve questions or issues that might arise during the convention, it was recommended by the CNLC that the Team serve as the governing body of the convention. It was also agreed that the Team and task groups would cease to function at the adjournment of the convention at which time the newly adopted synod constitution and bylaws would take effect and the newly elected bishop and Synod Council would assume leadership and address matters to come before the new synod before January 1, 1988, the new synod's official beginning date.

CONSTITUTIONAL AND LEGAL TASK GROUP

To lead the work of this task group the Transition Team appointed as chair Leroy R. Hamlett, Jr., St. Mark, Charlottesville, a well-known leader in the synod and a respected attorney. Pastor

Richard Carbaugh, Christ, Fredericksburg, was appointed to serve with him. It was agreed that Moyer and Tusing would serve in advisory capacities to assist the task group.

The primary task before this group would be to review the recommended model constitution and bylaws for the new synods of the ELCA. These governing documents were developed with vigorous debate during the course of the work of the CNLC and placed before the convention of the merging bodies and their synods, districts, and congregations. Their adoption at the Constituting Convention of the new Virginia Synod would be among the most significant actions necessary for authorizing the legal steps required for incorporating the new synod on the territory of the Commonwealth of Virginia. Because of legal requirements and as a demonstration of unity among synods within the ELCA, model constitutions for synods were to be adopted with the caveat that no amendments would be considered until the synods' first assemblies.

Congregations would be given a four-year window of opportunity to adopt the model constitution for congregations of the ELCA. Each voting member would be provided copies of the recommended constitution and bylaws of the Virginia Synod of the Evangelical Lutheran Church in America in the Bulletin of Reports.

The task group also assisted the Team in developing the necessary Rules of Procedure, noting the following explanation in the opening paragraph of its report to the convention: "This convention is a constituting and organizing convention. There are no rules of order with authority at this time. The first order of business should then be to adopt the necessary and desirable procedures, rules, and authority."[5]

Thirteen rules of procedure were adopted addressing the following: establishment of a quorum; approval of an agenda as the official program with no departure except by unanimous consent or a two-thirds vote; announcing details of each ballot in every election; directing of typewritten resolutions and reports in triplicate to the secretary; defining the role of the Committee of Reference and Counsel; procedures for reviewing and approving any special appeal or amendment to the proposed budget; limitations on speeches (amount of time on debating motions and the number of times allowed to speak in favor or opposition, including the number of times allowed to speak if others who have not spoken desire to speak); review of most frequent motions (debatable and non-debatable); authority of the chair to exercise flexibility of agenda, especially to receive the report of ballots and to proceed with additional ballots as necessary; governing of parliamentary law by Robert's Rules of Order except as otherwise provided in the constitution or bylaws of the Evangelical Lutheran Church in America; and the sequence of elections and election procedures as set forth to guide the convention in the host of ballots to be cast for new leaders.

The task group was also asked to assist the Institutions, Agencies, and Social Ministry Organizations Task Group in reviewing legal matters concerning the new synod's relationship to the institutions, agencies, social ministry organizations, and various ecumenical groups that would be affiliated with the new synod.

---

5. Minutes, Report of the Transition Team, Constituting Convention of the Virginia Synod/ELCA, May 29-31, 1988, p. 56.

FINANCE TASK GROUP

To lead the work of this task group the Transition Team appointed as chair Mr. Keith Brown, St. John, Roanoke, to serve with Team member Leroy Hamlett, Jr. It was agreed that the Rev. George Handley, secretary of the synod/administrative assistant to the bishop, would serve in an advisory capacity from synod staff. In addition, the Team agreed that it would also be helpful to have Paul Kipps, Muhlenberg, Harrisonburg, and James A. Lambie, College, Salem, former members and leaders of the Finance and Budget Managing Group, Virginia Synod/LCA.

By the time of the convention, the Finance Task Group had become the Finance and Budget Task Group. The task group had important work to do to recommend a budget and give guidance to help the new leadership of a new synod manage anticipated fewer funds for a first-year thirteen-month budget. There would be necessary transitional costs along with continued administrative costs even though there would be one less synod staff member and one less administrative office staff member. Support of institutions, agencies, and camps would be expected to continue and congregations and pastors would anticipate continued support of popular synodical programs and services. There was also the expectation that synods would be sending a higher percentage of benevolent funds for support of the churchwide expression and support of the new Regional Centers for Mission.

The report of the task group to the convention provides the best summary of its work in attempting to address the financial realities of a new synod:

A three-level Budget of Disbursement has been developed to support the proposed program of the synod for mission and ministry and sets certain priorities. The budget reflects and supports the organization and staffing of the synod as proposed by the various transition team task groups. It further reflects funding requests from institutions and agencies in support of Roanoke College, the Lutheran Theological Southern Seminary, outdoor ministries and campus ministry. Projected receipts are based on 1986 receipts from congregations comprising the new synod.[6]

Four recommendations were placed before the convention for adopting a proposed budget and asking the convention to give authority to the Synod Council to exercise careful stewardship in the new synod's first year of operation:

    a. *That the Virginia Synod of the Evangelical Lutheran Church in America adopt a 1988 (13-month fiscal year) budget of $1,725,000, and*

    b. *That the Synod Council be authorized to establish an initial expenditure authorization consistent with 1988 anticipated income, and*

    c. *That the Synod Council be authorized to review and adjust (increase or decrease) the approved 1988 budget in the light of actual 1988 experience, and*

    d. *That the synod requests the church council for an exception to the 55% minimum distribution of unrestricted congregational benevolence from the synod to the ELCA.*[7]

---

6. Ibid., p. 107.
7. Ibid.

The recommended budget presented the familiar "three-level" budget of disbursements using 1987 budgeting experience of essential, anticipated growth, and additional urgent needs as definitions of the three levels.

Recommended budgeted remittance to the churchwide organization in the three-level categories were $725,000 essential funds in Level 1, an additional $45,000 ($770,000) of anticipated growth in Level 2, and $120,000 ($890,000) of additional urgent needs in Level 3. Budgeted support for Virginia Synod causes was $740,000, $770,000, and $850,000 respectively. The total anticipated support needed for ELCA and the Virginia Synod was Level 1, $1,450,000; Level 2, $1,525,000; and Level 3, $1,725,000.[8]

The task group urged adoption of the recommendations and that the convention authorize financial consultations with congregations in the fall of 1987. The task group also recommended that the proportionate share of regular benevolence in 1988 be based on two factors: 65 percent on the confirmed, communing members in each congregation, and 35 percent on the current operating expenses of each congregation.[9]

INSTITUTIONS, AGENCIES, AND SOCIAL MINISTRY ORGANIZATIONS TASK GROUP

To lead the work of this task group the Transition Team appointed as chair Pastor James H. Utt, Grace, Winchester, to serve with Team members Humes Franklin, Jr., Grace, Waynesboro, and Nunna See, Shepherd of the Valley, Bridgewater. It was agreed that Bishop Moyer, Virginia Synod/LCA, and Dr. K. Roy Nilsen, assistant to the bishop, Eastern District/ELCA, would serve in advisory capacities. It was also agreed by consensus that Pastor Fred Donahoe, member of the Board of Chaplain Service of the Churches of Virginia; John Edwards, member of the Board of Virginia Synod Lutheran Homes, Inc.; and Robert Hanson would serve on this task group. The Rev. Wayne Williams, director, Lutheran Outdoor Ministries, also assisted the task group.

The primary tasks before this group would be directed by the guidelines and mandates from legal counsel of the CNLC and the National Transition Team:

1. Identify all the institutions, agencies, and social ministry organizations with which the Virginia Synod/LCA was affiliated.

2. Communicate transitional concerns with the directors of these institutions, agencies, and social ministry organizations.

3. Receive and review requests for affiliation with the Virginia Synod/ELCA from the various institutions, agencies, and social ministry organizations.

4. Recommend actions on the request for affiliation from the institutions, agencies, and social ministry organizations.[10]

---

8. Ibid., p. 108.
9. Ibid., p. 109.
10. Ibid.

For the new synod as well as the institutions, agencies, and social ministry organizations seeking to be affiliated with the synod, important issues such as ownership of property in the new church; concern for "ascending liability" (protection of church assets at higher corporate levels from liability suits); formulas for apportioned financial support from related synods; appointment, election, or confirmation of members of boards by the Synod Council; and governing documents defining relationship with the new church structures were discussed. In addition, accountability and relationship to synodical and national church structures would all need to be reviewed, revised according to new governing documents, and approved by the synod and the governing boards of each related institution, agency, and social ministry organization.

During the beginning stages of the task group's work, the CNLC and NTT made the decision that church-related colleges and seminaries would have their own "transition teams" given their unique historical relationships to one or more of the new supporting synods or church entities. Also, each is incorporated with their own constituted governing boards, fiduciary powers and responsibilities, and governing documents necessary for meeting requirements of accreditation as an educational institution. For some of the same reasons, the NTT also decided that campus ministries would not be the responsibilities of synodical transition teams.

The focus of the work of the task group would center on the following:

Ministry Program Agencies: Caroline Furnace Lutheran Camp, Fort Valley; Hungry Mother Lutheran Camp, Marion;

Social Ministry Organizations: Lutheran Family Services of Virginia, Salem; Virginia Synod Lutheran Homes, Roanoke; National Lutheran Home for the Aged, Rockville, Maryland; Lutheran Council of Tidewater, Norfolk; Lutheran Social Services of the National Capital Area, Washington, DC; Zion Place/Luther Manor, Virginia Beach; Fellowship Square Foundation, Washington, DC;

Virginia Ecumenical Groups: Virginia Council of Churches; Chaplain Service of the Churches of Virginia; Virginia Center for Public Policy, Richmond.

Given the realignment of synodical boundaries, the new synod would cease to have an ongoing relationship with Lutheran Social Services of the National Capital Area and Lutherock Outdoor Ministry in North Carolina.

The task group placed nine recommendations before the Constituting Convention recommending various levels of affiliation and terms of board representation. Caroline Furnace Lutheran Camp and Hungry Mother Retreat Center were approved to seek their own incorporations. The convention approved the participation of the Metropolitan Washington, DC and West Virginia Synods in both of these new corporations on the territory of the synod. The task group also recommended that the new Synod Council prepare, file, and execute such legal documents as necessary to carry out the actions of the convention. Recommendations were also made that the Virginia Synod/ELCA would provide financial support to the International Seaman's House and the Commission on Religion in Appalachia.

HEADQUARTERS SITE AND STAFFING TASK GROUP

To lead the work of this task group the Transition Team appointed as chair the Rev. Tom Bosserman, Trinity, Newport News, to serve with team members the Rev. Bruce Wilder, Christ the King, Richmond; the Rev. Richard Bansemer, Rural Retreat Parish, Rural Retreat; and Betty Kipps, Muhlenberg, Harrisonburg. The primary tasks before this group would be to study and make recommendations for the location of the Office of the Bishop of the new synod and to study and recommend staffing for the new synod.

In the recommendation of a location for the synodical offices the following factors were weighed: 1) accessibility, including access of synod staff to congregations and vice versa, access of synod staff to air transportation, access of regional staff to synod headquarters; 2) adequacy for staff and program needs; 3) costs; and 4) linkage afforded to institutions, agencies, and the headquarters of other denominations. On the basis of these factors, four geographical areas were studied in some detail: Richmond, Charlottesville, Staunton/Waynesboro, and Roanoke/Salem. Of these four possibilities, a headquarters site, Salem on the campus of Roanoke College, best met our criteria and is, therefore, recommended.[11]

An early decision of the Transition Team affirmed that the office of the new Virginia Synod/ELCA would remain on the campus at Roanoke College, Salem.

---

11. Ibid., p. 97.

The task group acknowledged that the Roanoke College campus in Salem was not the most geographically central to the congregations of the synod. It recommended that the various "working arms" of the new synod strive to meet as often as possible at more geographically centered locations, giving consideration to Staunton, Waynesboro, and Charlottesville sites along Interstate 64 East. The task group also suggested that the new bishop and staff give consideration to planning blocks of time and have an office in residence in various areas of the synod.

The task group's attention to staffing considerations began with the mandated synod staff positions of bishop, vice president, secretary, and treasurer with clarification of the specific responsibilities each office would assume. It was also recommended by the CNLC that assistants to the bishop's office be limited to not more than two.

Our idealizing of the bishop's office was then married to the emerging function and structure of the new synod, the CNLC recommendations and the emerging budget for the new synod. The result of this process for the office of the bishop was the recommendation of several modifications to the CNLC's description of the bishop's responsibilities, primarily in order to emphasize the spiritual and pastoral functions of the office and to free the bishop from some of the managerial burdens of the office by encouraging the bishop to delegate board and committee responsibilities as much as possible.

The number of assistants to the bishop and their responsibilities were discussed at great length. In the end, the proposals of the Function and Structure Task Group, the wisdom of beginning "lean" with staffing, and the realities of budget projections led to the recommendation of two assistants, one having primary administrative responsibility, the other having primary programmatic and communications responsibility.[12]

A total of four recommendations were forwarded to the Constituting Convention calling for approval of two executive assistants to the bishop; encouragement of the bishop to exercise "power of delegating responsibilities," especially in administrative duties; and employment supervision of the support staff necessary to facilitate the operations of the synodical office. It was also recommended by the task group that attention be given to the policy of inclusiveness in the fulfilling of these staff positions.

SYNOD FUNCTIONS AND ACTIVITIES TASK GROUP

To lead the work of this task group the Transition Team appointed the Rev. Richard Bansemer as chair to serve with team members the Rev. Tom Bosserman, the Rev. Willetta Heising, the Rev. John Byerly, the Rev. Bruce Wilder, Betty Kipps, and Carol Cox. It was agreed that the Rev. Dwayne Westermann, assistant to Bishop Moyer, would serve in an advisory capacity. It was the consensus of the Transition Team that the task group be creative and not be obligated to follow past organizational plans and structures in providing a narrative design for the new synod. While the model constitution and bylaws would mandate certain necessary structures and functions for new synods, what could be new about the synod were

---

12. Ibid.

its functions and new structures which synod leadership could describe and authorize as their form and functions through standing resolutions.

The primary responsibility of this task group would be to write a draft of the synod's functions and structures. Four drafts would be written and submitted to the Team for discussion. The fourth and final draft would be written in time for the Team's debate, action, and recommendation to the Constituting Convention. Details of the narrative design are examined in the next chapter.

NOMINATING TASK GROUP

Another important task placed before the Transition Team was the appointment of a Nominating Committee. This task group would be responsible for nominating the correct number of candidates for certain synodical leadership positions and to insure compliance with specific mandates for quotas and minority representations among the nominees for leadership positions. The work of the task group is reported in the section on elections in next chapter.

COMMUNICATIONS TASK GROUP

No written record of meetings of this task group was found recorded in the minutes or reports of the Transition Team. However, a report and recommendation was approved by the Team and recommended to the Constituting Convention. Details of the recommendation and action of the Constituting Convention are provided in the next chapter.

YOUTH MINISTRY TASK GROUP

No written record of meetings of this task group or recommended actions were provided by the Transition Team to the Constituting Convention. Apparently there was little to no initial enthusiasm for the CNLC proposal of a National Youth Organization. There was enthusiasm for continuing the current popular youth ministry events in the synod. Attention to the new synod's participation in the proposed National Youth Organization and how the current synod model would fit with the proposed national model are examined later.

STATISTICAL REALITIES

Among the last of his reports to the Virginia Synod/LCA, Bishop Moyer wrote,

In these shifts we need to recognize that there will be both pluses and minuses. The size of each of these synods will be smaller than our present synod. To state the obvious, it will mean fewer resources to work with than we presently have, but it will also mean that more individual attention can be given to pastoral and congregational needs.[13]

---

13. Minutes, Report of the Bishop and Synod Staff, 167th Annual Convention, Virginia Synod/LCA, June 6-8, 1986, p. 41.

Moyer was diplomatic in his assessment of the impact that the formation of three new synods would have upon the new Virginia Synod. There would be pluses for the new synods as new bishops and synodical programs would be more attentive to the needs of their pastors and congregations. There would be three new bishops elected to serve those pastors and congregation. New elected and appointed lay leaders would be available to serve pastors and congregations to be more fully engaged in its particular context for mission and ministry.

However, Moyer also noted there would be minuses. No doubt he was thinking of the impact these "contributions" to the two new synods would have upon the new Virginia Synod. In an interview with Moyer in 2012, he noted that the minuses for the new Virginia Synod were more than a matter of the loss of congregations, members, pastors, and finances. For him the more significant minus would be the loss of gifted leaders, ordained and lay, in addition to the losses of significant membership and financial resources. He expressed his concern that smaller synods might receive more pastoral attention of a bishop and staff, but feared that more financial resources from fewer congregations would be used to support the operations of the new synods, Regional Centers for Mission, and a stronger centralized national expression. He was reluctant in his interview to do more than express these concerns that he held then for the new synod that the Virginia Synod/LCA helped to create.

Facing their multiple responsibilities for planning a strong and confident start to a new synod, the Transition Team needed to know the realities of the "numbers of the new synod"—congregations, membership, and anticipated financial support. The statistics would be based on the 1986 statistical reports to the synod/district and churchwide expressions.

CONGREGATIONS CONTRIBUTED AND RECEIVED

To the new Metropolitan Washington, DC Synod/ELCA, the Virginia Synod/LCA would be contributing eighteen congregations. These would be those congregations in the Northern Virginia Area located in the counties of Virginia bordering the Potomac River west and south of the District of Columbia. This number represented just over 10 percent of the 177 congregations of the Virginia Synod/LCA.

To the new West Virginia-Western Maryland Synod/ELCA, the Virginia Synod/LCA would be contributing nine congregations all located in the border counties of West Virginia. This number represented just over 5 percent of the congregations of the Virginia Synod/LCA. There was one exception allowed for a congregation in West Virginia wishing to be in the new Virginia Synod. Immanuel, Bluefield, in Mercer County, West Virginia, petitioned by congregational vote to remain in the new Virginia Synod. The congregation's action was allowed by the CNLC and accepted by the Transition Team.

Seven congregations were received from the Eastern District of the American Lutheran Church: Martin Luther, Bergton; Peace, a new mission start in Charlottesville; Grace, Chesapeake; Hope, Hampton; Shepherd of the Valley, Harrisonburg; Christ the King, Richmond; and Prince of Peace, Richmond.[14]

---

14. Prince of Peace voted to disband and had their last worship service on Sunday, April 12, 1987. Their membership totaled 180 baptized members, 159 confirmed.

The Virginia Synod/LCA had a total of 177 congregations in 1986. Counting total numbers of congregations contributed to the two new synods (twenty-seven) and then adding the seven received from the ALC and the one congregation from the AELC there would be a total of 158 congregations in the new Virginia Synod.

MEMBERS CONTRIBUTED AND RECEIVED

Members contributed to the new Metropolitan Washington, DC Synod totaled 11,360. This represented 20.4 percent of the total of 55,685 baptized membership of the synod. Members contributed to the new West Virginia-Western Maryland Synod totaled 2,746. This represented 4.9 percent of the total baptized membership of the synod. A total of 14,106 baptized members were contributed to the two new synods, over 25.3 percent of the total baptized membership of the Virginia Synod/LCA.

FINANCES CONTRIBUTED AND RECEIVED

Total apportioned benevolent offerings received from the congregations of the Virginia Synod/LCA going into the Metropolitan Washington, DC Synod/ELCA based on 1986 receipts totaled $401,834 or 21.6 percent of total apportioned benevolent offerings of $1,855,514 received from the 177 congregations of the Virginia Synod/LCA. Apportioned benevolent offerings received from the congregations going into the West Virginia-Western Maryland Synod based on 1986 receipts totaled $67,828 or 3.6 percent of total apportioned benevolent offerings. A total of $469,662 apportioned benevolent offerings were given representing 25.2 percent of total apportioned benevolent offerings to the Virginia Synod/LCA in 1986.

† † †

The statistical realities indicated that the new Virginia Synod would be smaller in all the numbers—congregations, membership, financial resources, and the pool of leaders for the new synod. For many leaders and members of the former synod, it would prove difficult to see the pluses of a new church body as the work of transition would change to the realities of forming the work and ministry of the new Virginia Synod/ELCA. However, hope and promise for a new expression of Lutheran congregations in Virginia proved more powerful than any fears or anxieties confronting the Transition Team.

FROM TRANSITION TO FORMATION

The Transitional Team did its job. A new Virginia Synod was envisioned for the future. Now it would be the work of the voting members attending the Constituting Convention to receive their recommendations and take the actions necessary to form a new Virginia Synod of the Evangelical Lutheran Church in America.

CHAPTER 2

CONSTITUTING THE NEW SYNOD

The Constituting Convention

A GATHERING OF VIRGINIA LUTHERANS

The work of the Transition Team culminated in the actions of the Constituting Convention of the Virginia Synod of the Evangelical Lutheran Church in America held May 29-31, 1987, at Roanoke College, Salem. Of the 580 persons registered to attend the convention, 316 were lay voting members, 140 were ordained pastors in congregations or in a special call, twenty were ordained rostered leaders on leave from call or retired, fourteen were official guests, and ninety were visitors. The debates, decisions, and votes of these lay and ordained voting members to this inaugural convention would be the genesis of forming a new Lutheran church body in the Commonwealth of Virginia.

This unprecedented gathering of voting members from three different expressions of Virginia Lutherans would be busy. There would be debates and votes taken on twenty-six recommendations from the Transition Team and its task groups. A new constitution, along with bylaws and standing resolutions, would be debated and motions made to amend these governing documents intended to assure conformity to new governing realities such as lay leadership roles with male/female and minority representations mandated in leadership structures. Relationships with institutions, agencies, and social ministry organizations would be redefined, including the adoption of new corporate relationships of the synod to governing boards and ownership of property of some agencies in order to address the concern of "ascending liability" as required by the Commission for a New Lutheran Church (CNLC) and the National Transition Team (NTT).

A "thirteen-month" budget—January 1988 through January 1989—for the first fiscal year would be recommended, debated, and adopted. Because of the loss of significant financial resources from the congregations in Virginia becoming part of the new Metropolitan Washington, DC Synod, it was recommended that the new Synod Council be given additional flexibility to adjust as necessary the operational budget of the new synod. The newly elected Synod Council requested of the ELCA Church Council an exception to the 55 percent minimum distribution of unrestricted congregational benevolence from the synod to the ELCA.

Recommended changes to geographical designations within the synod would be debated and amendments offered for organizing congregations for cooperative ministry and fostering collegial support among pastors. Areas would become conferences. Each conference would be served by a dean appointed by the bishop. Deans would take on more responsibilities than in the former areas, serving as the "eyes and ears" of the bishop. Deans would be more involved in the installation of new pastors, calling meetings of the pastors and conference councils composed of pastors and lay representatives from the congregations of each conference. Conference councils were expected to meet and address local concerns and explore cooperative ministry opportunities between the conference congregations. Concerns were expressed and actions were taken to assure that the new synod would be attentive to the synod's outdoor ministry programs. Action would also be taken to assure the new synod's continuing a tradition of strong financial support of campus ministry at the colleges and universities in Virginia which had significant Lutheran student presence from many synods throughout the church.

FORM FOLLOWS FUNCTION

The report of the Synod Functions and Activities Task Group as recorded in the minutes of the convention totaled thirty-four pages of the Transition Team's fifty-four-page report to the convention. Within the report were the texts of the mandated model constitution, bylaws, and standing resolution for synods which prescribed the proposed structures of synods as well as their functions. The report provided the following outline of the mandated structure:

As prescribed by the model constitution for the ELCA synods, the proposed structure of the synod shall include:

The Synod Assembly
The Synod Council
Four Elected Officers
    – Bishop
    – Vice President
    – Secretary
    – Treasurer
In addition, the programmatic structure of this synod shall include:
Synod Council Standing Committees
Executive Committee
Consultation Committee
Committee on Discipline
Commissions
Congregational Life
Ministry
Outreach
Conferences

Conference Deans
Conference Pastors' Groups
Congregational Partnerships
Conference Partnerships

Each of the above officers and structures has specific functions (responsibilities) which include, but are not necessarily limited to those listed below. The organizing principle which relates functions to structures is that functions precede and inform structure; structures do not dictate functions. Structures are created only in response to recognized needs. As needs change, structures change in order to maintain the highest level of responsiveness. Regular needs assessment is essential with consequent reevaluation and, if necessary, reorganization of those structures which are not constitutionally mandated. Therefore, a minimum amount of constitutionally mandated structure is urged, allowing maximum flexibility for change as needed.[1]

Also included within the text of the task group's report were recommendations for additional structures and their responsibilities beyond those mandated in the constitution and bylaws. For example, to the Synod Council the task group added two additional committees: a Finance and Budget Committee to assist the council in all matters related to finances, including preparation and general supervision of the annual budget, and a Mutual Ministry Committee to provide guidance and counsel to the bishop and the assistants to the bishop.

Responsibilities were added to the Office of the Bishop: attention to strategic planning, development of synod support for churchwide ministry, fostering of partnerships of conferences and congregations, providing for the oversight of bookkeeping, keeping records on the life and work of the synod, maintaining the archives of the synod, cooperating with other synods in supporting the work of the Regional Center for Mission, providing staff assistance in planning and implementing programs of the synod's committees and task groups, interpreting the work of the church to congregations and the public, serving as contact for *The Lutheran* magazine, encouraging congregations to subscribe to the church's periodicals and be responsible for editing the synodical insert to *The Lutheran*, developing video programming, and providing for communications between congregations, conferences, as well as between the synod and Regional Centers for Mission, churchwide structures, and the public.

A total of thirty-seven additional functions and responsibilities in the narrative design of the new synod's structure were added to the three commissions, eleven conferences and deans, the council of deans, pastors' groups, congregational partnerships, and conference partnerships. Given the breadth and depth of the task group's report and the expected volume of amendments, the agenda of the convention allowed consideration of the report early in the first meeting. To explain the design narrative a skit was presented depicting a conversation between "Founding Fathers" Benjamin Franklin and James Madison on the importance of the constitution, function, form, and order of a governing body. The skit must have been helpful. Only three amendments were offered. The first would allow for the election of deans by conferences with a term limit of two

---

1. Minutes, Report of the Transition Team, Constituting Convention of the Virginia Synod/ELCA, B. Narrative Design: Synodical Functions and Structures, pp. 62-63.

years. The amendment was defeated. The second called for conferences to also become involved in "fostering interdependent relationships among congregations, institutions, and synodical and churchwide units for mission purposes." This amendment was adopted. The third amendment called for conferences to operate somewhat like a mini-synod with annual or semi-annual conventions in alternate churches of the conference, with each conference electing officers, managing a treasury, and disbursing funds as conference councils decided consistent with the objectives of the conference and approval of the Executive Committee of the synod. A motion was made to refer this proposed amendment to the Synod Council for action and report to the next Synod Assembly.[2]

Five editing revisions were offered for the purpose of finalizing language in the constitution and bylaws in light of the task group's narrative for functions and activities of the structures of the synod.[3] The recognition of the need for these revisions was approved. Following these actions, the Constitution of the Virginia Synod/ELCA was adopted by standing vote of the convention.[4]

Two amendments were offered to the bylaws. The first added a new paragraph 3, Section III, Officers, "As the synod's pastor, the bishop shall therefore provide spiritual leadership for the people of this synod." To Section VIII, Conferences, a new item 2a, "Foster interdependent relationships among congregations, institutions, and synodical and churchwide units for mission purposes." These amendments were adopted. Noting the needed editorial changes in the numbering of items in the bylaws, the motion to adopt the bylaws of the new constitution was approved.

One final "function and activity" item needed action by the convention to complete the task group's extensive report. It was a proposed "Standing Resolution" for synods to implement the constitutional mandate S6.04.A87.

It is the goal of this synod that 10% of the membership of synod assemblies, councils, committees, boards and/or other organizational units be persons of color and/or persons whose primary language is other than English. By the time of this synod's second assembly, a plan shall be established to attain this goal within 10 years.[5]

The Standing Resolution was adopted. With these actions, the reports of the Functions and Activities Task Group and the work of the Constitutional and Legal Task Group were concluded.

WHETHER REGION 8 OR REGION 9?

One item of business that stirred emotion and debate among the voting members concerned the unresolved question of the new synod's regional alignment: Should the synod align with Region 8 to the north or Region 9 to the south? The report of the chair of the Transition Team in the Bulletin of Reports laid out the situation and the resulting recommended process of debate and resolution of the matter as proposed by the Team.

The Commission for a New Lutheran Church (CNLC) originally placed the Virginia Synod in the Southeastern Region, Region IX. Region IX contains the Virginia Synod, North Carolina Synod,

---

2. Ibid., pp. 28-29.
3. Ibid., p. 29.
4. Ibid., p. 32.
5. Ibid., p. 33.

South Carolina Synod, Southeastern Synod (Tennessee, Mississippi, Alabama, Georgia), Florida Synod, and the Caribbean Synod. The Virginia Synod/LCA, at its 1986 Convention, voted on the following resolution:

"Resolved that the Virginia Synod of the Lutheran Church in America convey to the CNLC that it is the sense of the Virginia Synod in Convention that the newly formed Virginia Synod be assigned to the Mid-Atlantic Region." The vote was: Yes-150; No-106; Abstained-41. The Mid-Atlantic Region, Region VIII, is composed of the West Virginia Synod, five synods in Western Pennsylvania, the Metro-Washington DC Synod, and the Synod composed of Maryland and Delaware.

The CNLC considered this resolution in its final meeting. Their conclusion is given in their "Report and Recommendations," dated August 29, 1986, Page XIX. This states, "That the Regional alignment of the Virginia Synod be referred to the Constituting Convention of the Virginia Synod for decision."

The Transition Team is not aware of any decisions or other expressions from the ALC or AELC congregations in the Virginia Synod relative to regional alignment.

The regional alignment issue was thoroughly discussed at the March 12, 1987 meeting of the Virginia Synod Transition Team. At the end of this discussion period, the following motion was made, seconded, debated, and passed:

"Moved, after considerable discussion of staffing, financing, seminary considerations, Virginia Synod additions to regional strength, mission fields, distances, educational ministry, youth ministry, the relative effect of Virginia Synod benevolence dollars, seminary students from the Synod, seminary affiliation of the Virginia Synod clergy roster, and outdoor ministry, that we believe the primary basis on which to make the regional alignment decision should be where we can most effectively minister to the whole church and we recommend that the Virginia Synod relate to Region IX."

Recommendation #4 – Special Rule, Alignment Vote

The following special rules apply to the selection/election of the regional alignment of the Virginia Synod in the ELCA:

1) Convention vote will be by secret ballot.

2) Majority vote will decide the issue.

3) The ballot will read: I vote in favor of

_____ Region VIII (Mid-Atlantic)   _____ Region IX (Southeastern)

4) All speeches during discussion shall be limited to three minutes.

5) Total presentation and debate time will be limited to one hour.[6]

A motion proposing no written material to be placed before the members of the convention was offered and adopted at the time of taking up the original recommendation. Marshall reminded everyone of the rules of debate and opened the floor for discussion. Eight members spoke in favor of Region 9; nine spoke in favor of Region 8.

---

6. Ibid., p. 60.

Following the debate, the secret ballot vote was taken. After the votes had been collected, Moyer expressed appreciation to the presiding officer, former LCA President Robert J. Marshall, for his handling of this item of business. The results were given by Kate Miller, chair of the Committee on the Conduct of Elections, later in the same session:

448 Ballots Cast	230 Region IX
448 Valid Ballots	217 Region VIII
0 Invalid Ballots	1 Abstention

NOMINATING AND ELECTING NEW LEADERS FOR A NEW SYNOD

While the issue of regional alignment may have stirred emotions among the voting members, the most anticipated casting of ballots would be for the electing of leadership for the new synod, especially its first bishop.

Securing sixty names for the nominations of persons to be elected for various leadership positions proved to be a complicated and time-consuming process for the Nominating Committee of the Transition Team. The committee was chaired by Pastor Bruce Wilder, Christ the King, Richmond, along with twelve members representing congregations from the merging church bodies in different areas of the synod, with five pastors, seven lay members, and two advisory members from the staff of the Virginia Synod/LCA.

Wilder noted the following information on the work of the committee in his report to the Constituting Convention:

The committee first met on Tuesday, February 24, [1988] at Grace, Waynesboro. Over 200 names had been submitted to the chair prior to this initial meeting. Committee members also brought a goodly number of prospective nominations. Clearly, the task of securing 37 nominations for the various offices and committees of the new synod was not hampered by a lack of suggestions.[7]

The committee gave lengthy consideration for including representation of ALC and AELC on the new Synod Council as well as in other organizational structures of the new synod. The report of the chair describes best the lengths to which the committee struggled with its task:

The first elected council of the new synod meets immediately after the assembly adjourned.

As the committee considered ways to insure denominational inclusiveness in the new council, the following recommendations were made to the transition team, and presented at its March 12 meeting:

---

7. Ibid., p. 30.

1. That two "slots" on synod council be filed by ALC persons.
2. That committee nominees NOT elected to office be automatically included in the slate of council.

These recommendations were discussed at great length by the team. The team also desired to include an AELC "slot" on the synod council. The chair of the nominating committee was directed to secure nominations for one ALC and one AELC "slot." Non-elected nominees will be carried over to the next ballot. In addition, the team instructed the committee chair to secure nominations so as to ensure six council members will be female and male, regardless of lay/clergy state.

After hours of phone calling, letter writing and explaining proposed by-laws, the following persons have accepted the nominations of the nominating committee for election at our constituting convention in May.[8]

Position/Nominees	Male/Female (M/F)	Clergy/Lay (C/L)	Minority/Language Other Than English	Denomination (AELC/ALC/LCA)
For Vice President				
Leroy R. Hamlett, Jr.	M	L		LCA
Betty Kipps	F	L		LCA
For Secretary				
Clifton W. Anderson	M	L		ALC
Anabel Profitt	F	L		LCA
For Treasurer				
Robert C. Bleienfernish	M	L		ALC
Keith Brown	M	L		LCA
For Youth Member of Synod Council				
Kendra Brown	F	L		LCA
Bill Kipps	M	L		LCA
For Synod Council (AELC)				
Willetta Brand Heising	F	C		AELC
Robert L. Koenig	M	L		AELC
For Synod Council (ALC)				
Cecil D. Bradfield	M	C		ALC
Else Nohr Meintzer	F	L	★	ALC
For Synod Council (Clergy)				
James H. Bangle	M			LCA
Richard M. Carbaugh	M			LCA

---

8. Ibid.

Lucille Scheels Dorband	F			LCA
William H. King	M			LCA
Mark Wm. Radecke	M			LCA
Marshall F. Mauney	M			LCA
Bruce K. Modahl	M			LCA
Thomas A. Prinz	M			LCA
T. Joseph Shumate	M			LCA
Susan Lee Springer	F			LCA
For Synod Council (Lay/Female)				
Callister Dailey			★	LCA
Maxine Dellinger				LCA
Loutisha James			★	LCA
Sue Stirewalt Lane				LCA
Helen B. Neese				LCA
Sue Brown Pickett				LCA
Mary R. Powe				LCA
For Synod Council (Lay/Male)				
Robert Benne				LCA
Humes J. Franklin, Jr.				LCA
Fred Fluckinger				LCA
Richard K. Geriitz				LCA
George A. Kegley				LCA
Wayne R. McAfee				LCA
Regional Center for Mission (Clergy)				
Ronald K. Chelton	M			ALC
William H. Hail II	M			LCA
J. Christopher Price	M			LCA
Regional Center for Mission (Lay/Female)				
Martha A. Edwards				LCA
Katherine J. Reier				LCA
Regional Center for Mission (Lay/Male)				
C. William Hill				LCA
William R. Matthews				LCA
The following nominations are one for each position:				
For Consultation Committee				
Kenneth R. Carbaugh	M	C		LCA
Philip Fauber	M	L		LCA
Richard V. Frisby	M	L	★	LCA

Frances S. Hammond	F	L	LCA
Robert H. Jones	M	C	LCA
Roger S. Kluttz	M	C	LCA
Glenn L. London, Jr.	M	C	LCA
Henry E. Mallue, Jr.	M	L	LCA
Ruth Poole	F	L	LCA
Diane Shearer	F	L	ALC
Robert R. Ward	M	C	LCA
Tommie Whitman	F	L	LCA
For Committee on Discipline (Lay)			
Richard W. Hogan	M		LCA
Constance M. Koiner	F		LCA
Robert K. Woltz	M		LCA
For Committee on Discipline (Clergy)			
William E. Kinser	M		LCA
J. Luther Mauney, Jr.	M		LCA
John D. Yeich	M		LCA

The following nominations were made from the floor: For Secretary: The Rev. John M. Koehnlein; ... For Vice President: Mr. Humes J. Franklin, Jr. ... For Synod Council: The Rev. C.J. Martin, Rodney L. Racey, James Weisenborn, Kate Miller and James A. Hepner. ... For Committee on Discipline: J. Allen Kagey. ... For Regional Center for Mission: The Rev. James E. Baseler.[9]

The casting of ballots for each position of the new synod's lay leadership would take time and patience. Marshall provided attentive leadership to all the details of each election, making sure that nominations from the floor and voting procedures were followed. Biographical information was provided for voting members in a timely manner before each ballot. The members of the committee and synod office administrative staff gave considerable time and effort in preparing printed biographical information on nominees and distributing, collecting, counting, recounting, and announcing the results of each ballot. Their work was commended by Marshall and appreciation shown by the voting members with resounding applause.

The following were the results of the elections:

Officers of the Synod: Leroy R. Hamlett, Jr., St. Mark, Charlottesville, was elected vice president of the Virginia Synod/ELCA on the second ballot. Clifton Anderson, Peace, Charlottesville, was elected secretary on the second ballot. Keith Brown was elected treasurer on the first ballot.

---

9. Ibid., pp. 31-32.

Synod Council: Youth Member: Kendra Brown (LCA); AELC Member: Pastor Willetta Heising; ALC Member: Pastor Cecil Bradfield; LCA Clergy Members: Pastor Marshall Mauney, Pastor Susan Springer, Pastor James Bangle, and Pastor Mark Radecke; LCA Lay Female Members: Sue S. Lane, Frances Hammond, Anne Ashby, and Betty Kipps; LCA Lay Male Members: Robert Benne, Richard Gerlitz, and George Kegley.

Regional Center for Mission Representatives: C. William Hill, Jr., Pastor Chris Price, and Katherine J. Reier.

Consultation Committee: Pastor Kenneth R. Carbaugh, Philip K. Fauber, Richard V. Frisby, Frances S. Hammond, Pastor Robert H. Jones, Pastor Roger S. Kluttz, Pastor Glenn L. London, Henry E. Mallue, Ruth B. Poole, Diane Shearer, Pastor Robert R. Ward, and Esther "Tommie" Whitman.

ELECTING A NEW BISHOP

Most dramatic of all the elections would be the ballots for the new bishop. During the first meeting of the convention, Marshall moved quickly through the necessary procedural items of organizing the convention—adopting the program with an agenda and appointing the necessary convention committees, recognizing guests, establishing a quorum, and reviewing and adopting rules of procedure. Within two hours of the start of the convention on Friday afternoon, Marshall called upon Kate Miller, chair of the Conduct of Elections Committee, to review the rules as set forth by the CNLC and NTT communicated through the Transition Team's report, Recommendation #3, Sequence of Elections and Election Procedures:

1) Sequence of elections:
   a) Bishop, by ecclesiastical ballot
   b) Secretary, Vice President and Treasurer
   c) 3 Synod Council Members: 1 AELC, 1 ALC, 1 Youth Member
   d) Remaining 10 Synod Council Members
   e) Consultation Committee, Committee on Discipline, and Representatives to the Regional Center for Mission.

2) The bishop of the Virginia Synod shall be elected under the following procedures:
   a) That the first ballot be a nominating ballot, and that a unanimous vote be required for election.
   b) That the second ballot be limited to those persons nominated on the first ballot, and that at least a 75% vote of those voting be required for election.
   c) That following the second ballot, biographical data of the seven persons (plus ties) receiving the highest number of votes and all persons who received 7% or more of the total vote be secured and distributed to the members of the constituting convention.
   d) That the third ballot be limited to the seven persons (plus ties) receiving the highest number of votes on the second ballot and all persons who have received 7% or more of votes cast, and that at least a two-thirds vote of those voting be required for election.
   e) That the three persons receiving the highest number of votes on the third ballot be asked to address the assembly, and that speeches be limited to three minutes.

f) That the fourth ballot be limited to the three persons (plus ties) receiving the highest number of votes on the third ballot and all persons who have received 8% or more of the votes cast, and that at least a 60% vote of those voting be required for election.

g) That the subsequent ballots be limited to the two persons (plus ties) receiving the highest number of votes on the fourth ballot and all persons who have received 9% or more of the votes cast, and that a majority of those voting be required for elections.[10]

Marshall called upon the chaplain of the convention, Bishop Moyer, to pray before the casting of the first ballot for bishop. The first ballot was cast before the recess of the first meeting.

The Report of the Committee for the Conduct of Elections was the first item of business called by Marshall following Morning Worship which opened the Third Meeting of the Convention on Saturday, May 30. Miller shared the following details of the report of the first ballot for bishop:

425 ballots cast

425 votes needed for election (100%)

421 valid ballots

4 invalid ballots

The first ballot nominated sixty names for bishop. Their names and the number of votes for each were printed and distributed to members of the assembly as follows:

Name	Votes	Name	Votes
George Handley	135	Chris Price	2
John Byerly	75	Carroll Wessinger	2
Richard Bansemer	44	William Batterman	1
Dwayne Westermann	15	Richard Bland	1
W. Richard Fritz, Jr.	12	Greg Briehl	1
Robert Marshall	12	Kenneth Carbaugh	1
Tom Bosserman	9	Richard Carbaugh	1
Marshall Mauney	9	Eugene Copenhaver	1
Joseph Shumate	7	Kenneth Crumpton	1
William Kinser	6	W. David Fritz	1
Al Kuhn	6	Mark Graham	1
Jim Utt	6	Jesse Hangen	1
Harold Jensen	5	Ed Harper	1
M.L. Minnick, Jr.	5	Richard Harris	1
Virgil Moyer, Jr.	5	Willetta Heising	1
Elmer Bosserman	4	John Herman	1
Lucille Dorband	4	Paul Himmelman	1
James Crumley	3	Robert Hock	1
Jacob L. Mayer	3	Robert Holley	1

---

10. Minutes, Report and Recommendations of the Virginia Synod Transition Team, Constituting Convention of the Virginia Synod/ELCA, 1987, Appendices: "Sequence of Elections and Procedures," p. 58.

Peter Olsen	3	Robert Hughes	1
Thomas Prinz	3	Glenn London	1
James Bangle	2	Jack Martin	1
Conrad Christianson	2	Luther Mauney	1
William Hall II	2	John Morrill	1
Robert Humphrey	2	Jack Nussen	1
John Keister	2	Douglas Stowe	1
John Largen	2	Charles Tusing	1
Mike Lippard	2	Richard Umberger	1
Jim Mauney	2	Bob Ward	1
Steve Moose	2	Bruce Wilder	1

Following the report, Marshall noted that the second ballot must be limited to those names on the first ballot and 75 percent of votes cast would be necessary for election. The second ballot was cast following a prayer by the convention chaplain.

At the end of the third meeting of the convention, Marshall called upon Miller to share the details of the second ballot for bishop.

448 ballots cast

336 votes needed for election (75%)

447 valid ballots

1 invalid ballot

Twenty-one names received votes. The results were as follows:

George Handley	184	Bruce Wilder	3
John Byerly	115	M.L. Minnick, Jr.	2
Richard Bansemer	72	Conrad Christianson	1
Dwayne Westermann	17	James Crumley	1
W. Richard Fritz, Jr.	10	Richard Harris	1
Robert Marshall	9	Harold Jansen	1
Tom Bosserman	9	John Keister	1
Bill Kinser	6	Jacob Mayer	1
Al Kuhn	5	Steve Moose	1
Marshall Mauney	4	Virgil Moyer	1
Joseph Shumate	3		

Marshall called for distribution of biographical information for the seven persons having received the highest number of votes who were eligible for election—Handley, Byerly, Bansemer, Westermann, Fritz, Marshall, and Bosserman. The third ballot was cast just before lunch.

The report of the results of the third ballot for bishop was among the first items at the beginning of the fourth meeting of the convention on Saturday afternoon. Marshall called upon Miller to share the details of the report of the third ballot for bishop.

447 ballots cast
298 needed for election (66.6%)
447 valid ballots

George Handley	187	Richard Fritz	7
John Byerly	139	Tom Bosserman	4
Richard Bansemer	80	Dwayne Westermann	4
Robert Marshall	26		

Marshall invited Handley, Byerly, and Bansemer to address the convention, speaking for no more than three minutes each. Following their comments, Chaplain Moyer made remarks on the role of the bishop and then led the convention in prayer before the fourth ballot for bishop was cast. The results of the fourth ballot were reported following a recess called by Marshall.

442 ballots cast
442 valid ballots
265 needed for election (60%)

George Handley	161
Richard Bansemer	141
John Byerly	140

Having received 8 percent or more on the fourth ballot, Byerly continued onto the fifth ballot. The fifth ballot for bishop was cast and the report given within minutes of closing of the ballot.

443 ballots cast
443 valid ballots
222 needed for election (simple majority)

George Handley	168
Richard Bansemer	150
John Byerly	125

No one having received the required number of votes, a sixth ballot for bishop was cast following a prayer by Chaplain Moyer. During the counting of the votes, the assembly participated in a time of hymn singing. Dr. Marshall asked the convention to amend the agenda by unanimous consent and move the recognitions of the fiftieth anniversary of ordinations and retirement in order to receive the report of the sixth ballot, thus allowing time for the casting of a seventh ballot if needed before the scheduled 5:00 p.m. recess. Miller gave the following report of the sixth ballot:

447 ballots cast
447 valid ballots
224 needed for election (simple majority)

George Handley	187
Richard Bansemer	182
John Byerly	78

The three pastors would go to a seventh ballot that was cast before the convention recessed for dinner.

The fifth meeting of the convention convened at 7:00 p.m. After calling the delegates to order, Marshall called for a report of the seventh ballot for bishop. Miller gave the following results:

443 ballots cast
443 valid ballots
222 needed for election (simple majority)
Richard Bansemer   215
George Handley   195
John Byerly   33

Byerly did not receive the necessary percentage of votes to continue onto the eighth ballot. Moyer was called upon again to offer a prayer and the eighth ballot was cast. Other elections were conducted and ordination anniversaries and retirements were celebrated, but the attention of the convention was focused on what would be the results of the eighth ballot for bishop.

As she had done seven times before, Kate Miller, chair of the Conduct of Elections, reported on the eighth ballot for bishop as follows:

421 ballots cast
419 valid ballots
2 invalid ballots
211 votes needed for election
Richard Bansemer   225
George Handley   194

Having received the required number of votes cast, Marshall declared the Rev. Richard F. Bansemer elected as bishop of the Virginia Synod/ELCA. A relieved assembly offered acclamation with standing applause as Bishop-elect Bansemer and his wife, Mary Ann, were presented to the convention.

Bansemer addressed the assembly noting his surprise and expressing his appreciation for the confidence in his leadership that had now been shown to him by his election. The Rev. George E. Handley and the Rev. John F. Byerly, Jr. came forward to offer their support to the bishop-elect. Bansemer concluded his remarks by asking those gathered to pray for him and the new synod. He closed his remarks with a prayer for guidance and hope for the new synod.

The convention recessed for the evening with the options of attending a musical presentation in Antrim Chapel or a dramatic presentation in Olin Hall Theatre. Given the events of this historic day in the formation of the new Virginia Synod, it would be safe to say that with all the hymn singing, prayers, and ballots necessary for electing the new synod's first bishop, most voting members had shared in enough music and drama for one day.

Reflecting upon his election as bishop years later, Bansemer acknowledged that he was the least known of the final three candidates. Handley and Byerly had served congregations and the synod at various levels of responsibility and leadership for a number of years, and

The Rev. George Handley

both were known for their leadership and work on the churchwide level.

George Elliott Handley, Jr., was born on April 12, 1930, in Newburgh, New York. He graduated from Wagner College, Staten Island, in 1952 and from Philadelphia Seminary in 1956. He was ordained in 1956 by the New York/New England Synod/ULCA, and had served as pastor in congregations of that synod until he was called as pastor of Grace, Waynesboro in 1964. In 1974, he was called to serve as assistant to President J. Luther Mauney, Virginia Synod, 1974–1976. In 1976, he was called as administrative assistant to President/Bishop V.A. Moyer, Jr. as well as elected secretary of the synod by the Executive Board upon the nomination and recommendation of Moyer. As secretary of the synod, 1976–1987, Handley served as clerk of the Executive Board, archivist of the synod, statistician, necrologist, and secretary of the corporation. As administrative assistant he made arrangements for congregational pulpit supply, provided staff support, and attended meetings with the Council for Missions and its numerous managing task groups and other task groups throughout his tenure. Having served the synod faithfully with these responsibilities, Handley was well known throughout the congregations of the synod. Handley was also known for having authored *Lutherans in Virginia,* a two-volume set: *A 25-Year History, 1962–1987* and *Congregational Sketchbook.*

Of the three, John Franklin Byerly, Jr. was the only native Virginian. Byerly was born at Mt. Clinton, Rockingham County, on July 7, 1926. A graduate of Roanoke College (1950) and Philadelphia Seminary (1953), Byerly was ordained in 1953 and served all of his years of active ordained parish ministry in three Virginia congregations: St. Mark, Charlottesville, 1953–1960; St. Stephen, Williamsburg, 1960–1973; and First English, Richmond, from 1973 until his retirement in 1988. Byerly's leadership and skill as pastor and preacher were well known throughout the synod. He served on the Executive Board of the Virginia Synod/LCA, in 1969–1978 and 1981–1982. He was also recognized as a leader

The Rev. John Byerly

on the national level, having served on the LCA Commission on the Congregation, 1964–1966, and the LCA Bishop's Task Force on the Ministry of the Laity, 1984–1987.

RICHARD F. BANSEMER—FROM NEW YORK TO VIRGINIA

Richard Francis Bansemer was born into an active Lutheran family on May 26, 1940, in Oswego, New York. Bansemer was baptized at home on November 8, 1940, because of serious medical procedures that required an extended hospitalization and a number of blood transfusions.

The family moved in 1950 to Cantonment, Florida, north of Pensacola. The nearest Lutheran congregation was Missouri Synod, where he well remembers two years of catechetical classes taught twice a week by the pastor. In was during this time that he also remembers being "in love with the Lord." He especially remembers his father giving him a scooter in his teen years which he rode to various churches within miles of his home to attend their midweek "preaching services." Recalling those times in a 2013 interview, Bansemer stated, "I went to these churches just to listen to the sermons."

It was in these years that he felt a strong sense of the call to preach the gospel. During this time of his youth, his family became involved with a mission congregation, St. Paul, Pensacola, started by the Florida Synod/ULCA. He developed a relationship with the mission pastor, the Rev. Adolph Kleindt, who encouraged him to consider a Lutheran college. He found a write-up about Newberry College, Newberry, South Carolina, in the back of a dictionary noting that it was a Lutheran College. Bansemer remembers saying to himself, "That was good enough for me."

Bishop Richard Bansemer

Bansemer graduated from Newberry in May 1962 and married Barbara Anne Gallmeir from Coral Gables, Florida, who also graduated from Newberry that year. Together they moved to Columbia, where she taught in an elementary school and Bansemer attended classes at Lutheran Theological Southern Seminary. His introduction to Virginia came during his internship year serving three small congregations—Corinth, Kimberlin, and Pleasant Hill—in southwest Virginia. He was supervised by Pastor Albert Shumate, who was serving the Rural Retreat Parish—Grace and St. Paul—at that time. The Bansemers celebrated the birth of their son, John David, during his internship.

Bansemer graduated from seminary in May 1966 and accepted a call as associate pastor at University Lutheran Church, Gainesville, Florida. He was ordained by the Florida Synod on

May 23, 1966, in West Palm Beach, Florida. He returned to Virginia in 1968 upon accepting a call to become pastor of St. John, Roanoke. His return to Virginia began with the unexpected death of his wife, Barbara, who died in the hospital with a rare form of pneumonia within days of their arriving and unpacking their belongings for their new home in Roanoke. Bansemer was supported by family, friends, and a new congregation just getting to know him. He continued to serve St. John while rearing his young son, John David.

During these years, he met Mary Ann Troutman. They were married in 1971. A son, Aaron Richard, was born to them before he accepted a call from the Board of American Missions of the LCA to develop a mission congregation in Dillon, Colorado, in 1973. Bansemer jokes to this day that he developed and served the highest calling in the LCA when Lord of the Mountain Lutheran Church was organized and its new sanctuary dedicated at an altitude just under 9,000 feet in the Colorado Rocky Mountains west of Denver. Another son, Andrew Christopher, was born while the Bansemers lived in Dillon. He returned to Virginia in 1978 to serve in a parish familiar to him from his internship days—Rural Retreat Parish.

NEW BISHOP, NEW STYLE

Through his life experiences and years of serving as a parish pastor, Bansemer brought a heart of compassion and a set of skills of a pastor known for his preaching, pastoral care of members, and uplifting the life and unity of the community of faith in the congregations he served. These skills would serve him well in his years as bishop of a new Virginia Synod. At the time of his election he had made it known he would not make attending meetings a top priority for use of his time, nor would he give most of his energy to administrative matters. All of his skills would be needed to form this new synod while attending to the emphases of caring for congregations and pastors. It would be a synod with fewer resources to meet the growing needs of congregations and pastors in an emerging culture less supportive and at times even hostile to a progressive, inclusive vision of the church. At the age of forty-seven, Bansemer was ready for the challenge.

A NEW SYNOD IS BORN

The Constituting Convention had given birth to a new synod. The Virginia Synod of the Evangelical Lutheran Church in America would have new leadership committed to being intentional in its efforts to include more lay people and persons of color or whose primary language was other than English in roles of leadership. It would be a synod with new structures committed to the mission of proclaiming Jesus Christ as Lord and Savior to all the world. It would be a synod with fewer congregations and financial resources. The work would be demanding and take its toll. From the beginning, Bansemer knew he would need help in implementing all the decisions that had been made by an historic Constituting Convention. The years ahead would prove challenging for the new synod—its first bishop, synod staff, newly elected leaders, the congregations, their members, and their pastors.

Ruby and Richard Ballard, First, Portsmouth, on June 7, 2008, presenting a plaque in observance of the church's founding. The plaque, a gift from the Ballards and their family, lists the thirty-nine charter members of the church.

Friends enjoying a light moment between sessions: Gene Gomez, Apostles, Gloucester; Diana Shane, Resurrection, Fredericksburg; Martha Carroll and Janet Gomez, Apostles, Gloucester; Jim Stensvaag, St. Paul, Hampton; and Elizabeth Smythe, Ebenezer, Marion.

Pastor Bill Stewart administers Holy Communion during a Power in the Spirit worship service.

Daily worship led by Pastor Steve Beyer, Navy chaplain, and the Rev. CeCee Mills, pastor of Rejoice, Chesapeake.

CHAPTER 3

IMPLEMENTING THE NEW VIRGINIA SYNOD

1988–1999

WASTING NO TIME

The work of implementing a new Virginia Synod would not wait until its official beginning date, January 1, 1988. The synod-to-be had a newly elected Synod Council ready to implement actions authorized by the Constituting Convention. A young and energetic bishop was eager to start his work.

As part of its first meeting, members of the new Synod Council and the bishop-elect met jointly with the Executive Board of the Virginia Synod/LCA on June 29-30, 1987, to finalize transitional details. The new leadership requested the board to consider authorizing an earlier "start-up" time for the bishop and staff of the new synod. The board, however, reaffirmed the National Transition Team's recommendation that new bishops begin their duties on November 1 and new synod staff members—assistants to the bishop and synod office staff—begin on January 1, 1988, the date set by assembly actions and legal documents of incorporation. The council would meet once more before the start of the new synod, October 19-20, 1987, just after the installation of the new bishop. However, Bansemer did not wait to be installed or to start on November 1, 1987. There were too many personal matters to attend to and decisions to be made in the months to come in order to implement well the beginning of the new synod.

Bansemer wasted no time in making plans for his move to Salem and the Synod Office on the campus of Roanoke College. Celebrations of his nine years as pastor of Rural Retreat Parish were held soon after the Constituting Convention to give thanks for his leadership. The celebrations also provided occasions for members of the parish to join in the joy and pride of his being elected bishop of the new synod. Reflecting on that time of transition for him and the parish, Bansemer noted with appreciation how "the members and leadership of the parish were supportive and freed me up so I could turn my focus early on to my new call." By the end of August a new home would be found on a secluded knoll in the countryside outside of Salem, just a few miles from his new office.

BUILDING THE TEAM

Before their move to their new home, Bansemer had given much thought to what he knew would be among the most important of his initial decisions: Whom would he ask to serve with him as assistants to the Office of the Bishop? He knew his strengths were not in attending to the details necessary for managing the synod office with a staff or overseeing the synod's annual budget and extended financial complexities associated with the various accounts and funds of the synod. Bansemer would need a strong administrative assistant with a skill set for attention to details and financial management—a lay person, someone well known and trusted throughout the synod. That someone would be Keith Brown. Bansemer asked him to be his administrative assistant before the end of July.

Bansemer also knew he would need an ordained assistant to take initiative and give energetic leadership to the ministry programs of the synod intended to support congregations and pastors in their congregational setting. He was particularly concerned not to lose any momentum in the growing popularity of the synod's youth events, especially Lost and Found for junior high and Winter Celebration for senior high youth. Without a third assistant and anticipating that congregations and pastors would continue to have high expectations of strong support from synod staff, Bansemer was cognizant that many demands would be placed on both himself and his new "program assistant." He needed a young, gifted, and well-known pastor familiar with synod's programs, known among pastors, lay leaders, and youth. Bansemer wanted someone he knew personally and could trust. He needed an assistant who would "represent the bishop in congregational, synodical, regional or churchwide responsibilities and ceremonies as assigned" and "fulfill administrative responsibilities of the bishop's office in the absence of the bishop."[1] That someone would be Pastor James F. Mauney. Bansemer asked him to be his program assistant before the end of July.

KEITH BROWN—FROM ENGINEER TO ADMINISTRATIVE ASSISTANT

Bansemer had come to know Brown while serving with him on various synodical boards and committees in the Virginia Synod/LCA. In an interview, Bansemer noted,

I was always impressed with Keith's commitment to the church, his dedication to the work of the synod, and his command of details, especially financial details. He was always prepared with the facts and figures. He had answers to specific questions about finances. I remember feeling confident about Keith's ability to attend to administrative matters. He was just who I was looking for to help get things started on the right foot.

Keith Brown

---

1. Position Description: Assistant to the Synod Bishop, Virginia Synod/ELCA, 1987, Appendices: "Sequence of Elections and Procedures," p. 58.

Brown's financial management skills and his strong work ethic for the Church were known by many throughout the synod. His reputation as a gifted lay leader had been affirmed at the Constituting Convention of the new synod with his election on the first ballot as the synod's first treasurer. Brown was excited for the future of the new synod. In an interview, Brown shared,

I felt called to this position since I felt that with my strong points of ability to organize and give attention to details, I would be able to help Bishop Bansemer as he led the synod. I was ready to serve the church wherever I would be asked to serve.

Brown knew there would be significant financial challenges due to the loss of strong benevolent support from the congregations in Northern Virginia that created the new Metropolitan Washington, DC Synod/ELCA. Close attention to financial realities, budget management, and tough fiduciary decisions would be needed at the beginning of the synod. Bansemer placed his trust in Brown to be the one who would know the facts and figures and have the skills to manage the day-to-day operations of the synod's administrative functions. Brown was open to the challenge and accepted the bishop's offer to join his team within days of the asking.

Becoming the administrative assistant to Bansemer would necessitate the election of a new treasurer at the first assembly of the synod scheduled for May 13-15, 1988, at Roanoke College. It should be noted that for the first five months of the new synod, Brown served in both capacities until Kathryn Buchanan was elected on the first ballot to be the new treasurer.

At the time he was asked to be the new synod's administrative assistant Brown was employed by General Electric of Salem as an electrical engineer. A 1958 graduate of Michigan State University with a B.S. in electrical engineering, his career with General Electric spanned twenty-nine years beginning in Syracuse, New York, and continuing with promotions in the corporation to Philadelphia, Pennsylvania. This was followed by a tour of military duty as an ordnance officer stationed in Korea and then an ordnance instructor in Albuquerque, New Mexico. He returned to Syracuse with his wife, Genie. From Syracuse they moved to Daytona Beach, Florida, back to Pennsylvania, and then to the GE plant in Salem. While with GE in Florida, Brown earned a Master of Business Administration degree from Stetson University, Stanford, Florida.

Brown recalls that he and his wife, Genie, along with their two daughters, Sabra and Janette, became very involved in the first Lutheran church they joined, an LCA congregation in Daytona Beach. They continued their active involvement in church when they moved to Erie, Pennsylvania, and joined another LCA congregation, St. John. Brown notes that it wasn't until the family moved to Virginia in 1972 and became active at St. John, Roanoke that he was first asked to serve on the synodical level. He was elected to the synod's Executive Board at the 1978 convention and served on the synod's finance committee. In 1982, he was elected as a lay delegate to the LCA convention in Seattle, Washington.

As with Bansemer, Brown did not wait to begin his work until the starting date of the new synod. While finalizing his career as an engineer in the fall of 1987, he turned his attention to the administrative and financial management tasks that lay ahead for the new synod. Brown brought the heart of a servant for Christ's church along with the skills and dedication to do his job to get the new synod off to a good start. He began his work as administrative assistant to the Office of the Bishop on January 1, 1988. He came to the position already prepared to do the job.

JAMES F. MAUNEY—FROM PARISH PASTOR TO ASSISTANT TO THE BISHOP

Bansemer wrote a letter dated July 29, 1987 offering the position of "Program Assistant" to Pastor James F. "Jim" Mauney, Christ Lutheran, Richmond. In the letter, Bansemer notes with candor his

daily struggle with the major decision of whom to interview and invite to consider the position of Program Assistant to the Bishop. By this letter, I am asking you to give this post serious consideration and to meet with me so that we might share ideas and concepts of what the position might become.[2]

Bansemer and Mauney were acquainted as colleagues, having known one another through synodical involvements since Mauney returned to Virginia in 1981 to accept the call to Christ, Richmond. Ordained by the Virginia Synod/LCA in 1978, Mauney's first call was as assistant pastor at Christ Lutheran in San Diego, California, where he had been an intern two years earlier. In the July letter, Bansemer expresses the hope that

this prospect brightens your day and fills you with some excitement. Your work with the youth and your initiatives in the men's group meeting at Massanetta have been noticed. I'd like to see just how creative you are, or might become.

The Rev. James F. Mauney, Assistant to the Bishop, 1988–1999

It would be a couple of weeks before Bansemer and Mauney would have that meeting. Afterwards, Mauney was reluctant to give Bansemer a positive response. "I was so very happy being pastor at Christ. I loved preaching, teaching and visiting the members and watching the congregation grow. I did not want to leave. I was in a good place."

Mauney's initial response was "no" to Bansemer's telephone call following their first meeting. Asking him to give it some time, more thought and prayer, Bansemer called again after three days to once again hear "no." Bansemer responded he would be in Richmond in a few days and invited Mauney to have lunch and talk.

Throughout all of these conversations, Mauney had turned to his wife, Lynda, to help discern whether or not he should accept the new bishop's offer. As Mauney noted in an interview,

The conversations with my wife and our prayers together, combined with Richard's persistence, finally turned my negative reluctance to an affirmative acceptance of this new call to serve as pastor in a different expression of Christ's church.

---

2. Letter, the Rev. James F. Mauney from Richard Bansemer, Bishop, Virginia Synod/ELCA, 1987.

Mauney brought with him the heart of a maturing pastor, youthful energy, and the skills for working with youth and adults—gifts that Bansemer had noticed years earlier at a Massanetta Summer Assembly. Mauney also brought a heart for being a servant partner with other leaders in the synod—lay and ordained. Possessing an abundant amount of energy for serving God's people and confident in the purpose of his call to serve with Bansemer and Brown, Mauney began his work as program assistant to the bishop on February 1, 1988.

LEARNING THE ROPES

By the end of July 1987, sixty-six bishops had been elected to lead the new church and its synodical expressions. Herbert W. Chilstrom was elected the first bishop of the new ELCA at its Constituting Convention held April 30-May 3 in Columbus, Ohio. Elected on the ninth ballot, he came to the position with eleven years of experience, having served as bishop of the Minnesota Synod, the largest synod in the LCA, which also included an area that had the largest number of ALC members. Of the sixty-five synod bishops elected that spring and early summer, only twenty-six had previously served as a bishop. Thirty-nine new bishops—60 percent of the new church's bishops—were elected at those synod assemblies.[3] The late summer and fall of 1987—appropriately the season of Pentecost—would be a busy time for Bansemer and the other newly elected bishops. The Holy Spirit had moved to create a new, unprecedented expression of Lutheran unity in North America. It was a new church with new leaders!

Few bishops knew each other. Synod boundaries were new with most composed of new constituent congregations from former ALC, LCA, and AELC expressions. New constitutions, bylaws, and continuing resolutions, along with other new operational principles and structures—quotas and Regional Centers for Mission, just to name two—needed to be learned and implemented in order to make functional a new church that understood itself to be composed of three interdependent expressions—congregation, synod, and churchwide. There were a lot of "ropes" for the new bishops of a new church to learn.

Bansemer's instincts were right in getting an early start on major decisions, particularly moving ahead with staffing choices. In early August he would attend the first meeting of the new bishops in Chicago, followed by three more meetings—twice in November, the 9th-10th in Charlotte, North Carolina, and the 24th in Chicago—and once more on December 14th-16th again in Chicago before the official start of the new church. He and the other bishops would travel once again to Chicago on October 10th for Chilstrom's installation, there to join with over 3,000 ordained and lay members of the ELCA with numerous national and international church leaders and guests gathered in the pavilion of the University of Illinois-Chicago campus. Just over a week later, Bansemer would be installed by Chilstrom on Sunday, October 18, Chilstrom's fifty-sixth birthday.

---

3. Edgar Trexler, *High Expectations: Understanding the ELCA's Early Years, 1988–2002*, Augsburg Fortress Press, 2003, p. 6.

Bansemer traveled to Atlanta in September for the first meeting of the Coordinating Council for the Region 9 Center for Mission. He would make trips to Columbia, South Carolina, to join with other bishops in welcoming and meeting with Cardinal Willebrands on the campus of Lutheran Theological Southern Seminary and also attend a Board of Trustees meeting in October.

In addition to all these trips and meetings, Bansemer traveled to Richmond on at least three occasions to attend meetings, conferences, and assemblies of partner ecumenical groups and their leaders, especially the Virginia Council of Churches. He attended the Lutheran, Anglican, and Roman Catholic (LARC) ecumenical gathering in Fredericksburg in November.

Throughout these months, Bansemer met with several congregations and pastors in the synod. He scheduled gatherings of congregational leaders and pastors from all eleven conferences, some conferences joining together to host an evening of "getting to know our new bishop." Before and after each conference meeting, he remembers having one-on-one meetings with individual pastors and lay leaders. Recalling this time of traveling the synod and getting to know the lay leaders and pastors, Bansemer noted,

Already I had pastors seeking support and advice with troubles they were having at home or in congregations, and others expressing a desire to seek another call or feeling ineffective and seeking help. I realized that I was getting a "foretaste" of what was to come.

Bishop V.A. Moyer, Jr. traveled with Bansemer to some of these conference gatherings. He was appreciative for Moyer's introduction of him to those that gathered. Bansemer was concerned that he was not that well known in many conferences of the synod, especially in the east. Traveling together also gave Moyer and Bansemer time to discuss issues facing the synod, the importance of the conferences and the deans, and other concerns of transition and operations of the bishop's office. Bansemer noted,

Moyer's advice and counsel were very helpful. He did not hold back in letting me know what I was going to face in terms of congregational conflicts and unhappy pastors. I appreciated every moment he could give me. He was very helpful especially in explaining the call process, the importance of mobility and how to handle requests from pastors outside the synod seeking a call within the synod.

He shared in a 2012 interview,

I particularly remember the times we met at the synod office and he also showed me how files were kept and explained the assets of the synod, the various funds and money accounts, those designated and undesignated. He was great helping me to be ready come January 1st.

"IN THE EXCITEMENT OF THIS HOUR"—THE INSTALLATION OF THE NEW BISHOP

The installation of the Rev. Richard F. Bansemer as bishop of the Virginia Synod/ELCA was held at 5:00 p.m. on Sunday, October 18, 1987, at Trinity Episcopal Church, Staunton, Virginia. Newly elected and recently installed bishop[4] of the ELCA Herbert W. Chilstrom was present and served as the presiding minister and preacher for the historic occasion. Bishop V.A. Moyer, Jr., Virginia Synod/LCA, assisted at the prayers and served as a communion assistant along with the officers of the new synod and members of the Synod Council. The late afternoon time and central location of the installation allowed for an estimated gathering of over 400 pastors and members of congregations from all across the territory of the synod and numerous ecumenical guests.

Sharon Porter Shull served as organist for the service. An adult choir composed of members from area congregations offered special anthems under the direction of Lavelva Stevens. A children's choir from the congregations of Lutheran Mountain Ministries in the Highland Conference of the synod offered special music under the direction of Ellen Schaack. A brass quartet provided accompaniment to organ prelude selections and the singing of festive hymns. Scripture lessons were read by the brothers of the new bishop, Ronald W. Bansemer, Isaiah 42:5-9, and David C. Bansemer, Romans, 12:4-8. Callister Dailey, member of the new Synod Council, read the gospel, John 10:7-18.

The Rev. Richard Bansemer was installed by ELCA Presiding Bishop Herbert Chilstrom as the Virginia Synod's first bishop, October 18, 1987.

Bishop Bansemer wearing the stole of material called "servant's cloth."

---

4. The title "Presiding Bishop" for the church's chief officer did not come into use until 1995.

The offering received at the service was designated for the World Hunger Appeal. Bansemer wore a special stole representing the ELCA's mission to Peru that had it roots in Virginia through the work of Pastor David Tholstrup, a missionary from the Virginia Synod serving at that time in Peru. Tholstrup explained that the material in the stole was known as "servant's cloth," woven and used by the poor. A reception was held in the Parish House of Trinity Church following the service hosted by area congregations.

Two petitions in the prayers captured the emotions and the historical significance of Bansemer's installation service:

Heavenly Father, in the excitement of this hour, we pause for a moment to remember our past. You have been good to us, and we thank you. We are grateful for Bishops Moyer, Jansen, and Hersfeld, and for their assistants who served you by serving us as your body, the Church. Hear our quiet thank you's for Virgil, Harold and Will, for K. Roy Nilsen, for George Handley, for Charlie Shenberger, and for Dwayne Westermann, along with the many others on this territory who did more, and loved more than duty called for.

Heavenly Father, this moment is a holy moment. Let us hold it close, and never forget the joy of this new beginning. We ask that Richard be granted a wisdom beyond his own, a wisdom that only you can provide, so that together as your people, we may be faithful, joyful, and constantly in love with you and one another.[5]

A NEW SYNOD BEGINS

In their plans for the first Synod Assembly, Bansemer and the Synod Council chose the theme "We, the Family of God." The theme was developed with the assistance of Lutheran Family Services of Virginia (LSF/VA) in recognition that 1988 marked the one-hundredth anniversary of the ministry to children and families accomplished in the name of the church through the previous expression of its ministry, Lutheran Children's Home of the South. The first assembly of the new synod would provide a venue for this new expression of social ministry related to the synod that would provide a broader range of services in a culture impacting family structures. In addition to the meeting time required for action on items of business—adoption of a budget, elections and appointments, reports and recommendations coming from the council, along with motions from the floor and resolutions brought to the assembly by the Committee on Reference and Counsel—other assembly time would include workshops for voting members and visitors to the assembly to explore and discuss the changing expressions of family life in today's society.

No doubt the council looked with excitement on the first assembly and wanted to encourage a sense of family among this new gathering of voting members, lay and pastors, from the synod's 160 congregations. It would be the first gathering of this "new family" or at least a different family.

Lay voting members (292) would almost double the number of clergy members (153) as compared to the lay delegates (210) and clergy delegates (181) attending the last convention

---

5. Service Booklet, "The Installation of the Reverend Richard F. Bansemer as Bishop of the Virginia Synod, Evangelical Lutheran Church in America, Trinity Episcopal Church, Staunton, Virginia," Oct. 18, 1987.

of the Virginia Synod/LCA.[6] Fifty percent of the lay voting members would be women and every effort was made by the Synod Council to have 10 percent of the voting members be persons of color or whose primary language was other than English.

In his first written report to annual assembly of the synod, Bansemer chose to focus his first report on a specific theme.

I can think of no more appropriate theme than, "We, the Family of God," to inaugurate our life together as The Virginia Synod, ELCA. Alone, we are something less than the church, the BODY of Christ. Although we are individually members of the Body, it is still the Body, the Family of God, that is the church.[7]

The first staff of the new synod. Front row (left to right): Linda Wells, Rosemary Thompson, Keith Brown, Sue Clark, and Sharon Williams; back row: Bishop Bansemer and Jim Mauney.

At the beginning of the life of this new synod, Bansemer would skillfully use the analogy of family to show that his would be a different style of leadership that would call upon others to fulfill roles and expectations of the Office of the Bishop so that he might focus more of his time on the pastoral care of congregations and pastors. He would most clearly demonstrate this new style in his partnership with the deans of the eleven conferences and in his appointments of "Bishop's Representatives" to serve in his stead on the numerous boards of the various institutions, agencies, and social ministry organizations related to the synod.

Two paragraphs from his first written report set forth his concerns for the use of his time, the effective delivery and reception of ministry from one another, and his intent to be a pastoral care bishop.

As the Lutheran family of God in this synod, we are trying to organize ourselves in ways to deliver and receive ministry to and from one another. As the new deans receive endorsement by the conferences they represent, the hope is that each one of these persons will receive respect from those they represent, and be accepted for celebrations, installations, and vacancy counseling when I cannot be there myself. Having completed eleven air trips, and driven 2,500 miles monthly since assuming office, there is a need for this family to accept the presence of someone other than the bishop for many functions.

---

6. Minutes, Report of the Committee on Official Roll, 167th Annual Convention of the Virginia Synod/LCA, June 6-8, 1986, p. 189.
7. Minutes, Report of the Bishop, 167th Annual Convention of the Virginia Synod/LCA, June 6-8, 1986, pp. 34-35.

Because of my commitment to the family of God in this synod, I have limited my involvement in institutional work to Lutheran Theological Southern Seminary and Roanoke College. Other institutions are served by personal representatives, and I am grateful for their able assistance.[8]

APPOINTING DEANS OF CONFERENCES AND BISHOP'S REPRESENTATIVES

Section IX of the new constitution for the synod provides the authority for the bishop's appointment of deans, a listing of responsibilities for assisting the bishop and representing the synod at congregational events, and the establishment of a Council of Deans which will be

responsible for providing advice and counsel to the bishop concerning the work of the bishop generally and specifically regarding the bishop's work in each conference. The Council of Deans shall advise the bishop of issues and concerns which arise at the parish level. The deans shall also work to interpret the work of the bishop to the parishes in their respective conferences.[9]

Throughout his tenure, Bishop Bansemer sought to appoint deans well known and respected among their fellow pastors and by members of the congregations of the conference in which each dean served. He was consistent in his reports to the Synod Council and in his annual reports to the Synod Assembly noting his appreciation for his partnership with the deans in the work of the synod, especially at times of transition in pastoral leadership, celebrations such as anniversaries in the life of congregations, and assistance with congregations in conflict.

The Council of Deans has been diligent in its work, providing guidance and assistance to the synod in many ways. Most installations are now conducted by Deans, and each serves as an important liaison between synod and conference. The brain storming of this gifted group of leaders will directly affect our Consultation program this fall.[10]

In an interview following his years as bishop, Bansemer noted, "I don't know what I would have done without the Deans' help, especially with the installation of new pastors coming to the synod."

The following is a listing of the synod's conferences and their deans and year of appointment by Bansemer throughout his tenure as bishop of the synod:

Highlands: 1988, Pastor James H. Bangle, Ebenezer, Marion; 1995, Pastor Roger S. Kluttz, Retired; 1998, Pastor Steven P. Ridenhour, Holy Trinity, Wytheville

New River: 1988, Pastor Michael A. Lippard, Our Savior, Christiansburg; 1989, Pastor Jacob L. Mayer, St. Michael, Blacksburg; 1998, Pastor John W. McCandlish, Christ, Radford

Southern: 1988, Pastor Robert Maier, Glade Creek, Blue Ridge; 1998, Pastor Mark A. Graham, St. John, Roanoke

Tidewater: 1988, Pastor Sidney K. Nelson, St. Timothy, Norfolk; 1994, Pastor Frederick P. Guy, Messiah, Virginia Beach; 1997, Pastor James G. Cobb, First, Norfolk; 1999, Pastor William W. Boldin, Grace, Chesapeake

---

8. Ibid.
9. Bylaws of the Virginia Synod/ELCA, Section IX, Deans.
10. Minutes, Report of the Bishop, 2nd Annual Synod Assembly, 1989, Virginia Synod/ELCA, p. 45.

Peninsula: 1988, Pastor Thomas L. Bosserman, Trinity, Newport News; 1996, H. Alvin Kuhn, Retired

Richmond: 1988, Pastor Lance K. Braun, Campus Pastor, Richmond; 1989, Pastor J. Christopher Price, Epiphany, Richmond; 1996, Pastor John W. Bengston, St. Luke, Richmond; 1997, Pastor John F. Byerly, Jr., Retired

Germanna: 1988, Pastor Robert R. Ward, Rapidan Parish, Orange; 1991, Pastor James E. Baseler, Hebron, Madison; 1995, Pastor William T. Stewart II, Peace, Charlottesville

Southern Valley: 1988, Pastor Glenn London, Grace, Waynesboro; 1989, Pastor John L. Derrick, Muhlenberg, Harrisonburg; 1992, Pastor Tracie L. Bartholomew, Good Shepherd, Lexington; 1994, Pastor Sharon Israel, Rockingham Parish; 1997, Pastor Arthur J. Henne, Retired

Page: 1988, Pastor JoAnn K. Bunn, St. Luke, Stanley; 1989, Pastor Kenneth Bowman, Stony Man Parish, Luray; 1994, Pastor R. Nicholas Eichelberger, St. Mark, Luray

Central Valley: 1988, Pastor John M. Koehnlein, Orkney Springs Parish, Orkney Springs; 1991, Pastor George L. Sims, Reformation, New Market

Northern Valley: 1988, Pastor James H. Utt, Grace, Winchester

Implementing the new synod presented Bansemer and the Synod Council with two realities needing immediate attention. The first was the need for more staff to attend to the demands for support for pastors and congregations placed on the Office of the Bishop. The second was the reality of reduced financial support for increased expenses given the loss of the congregations in Northern Virginia that were now part of the Metropolitan Washington, DC Synod. Thoughtful leadership by both the bishop and council proved helpful and timely in addressing both needs.

The mobility of pastors, particularly those outside of the synod wishing to be considered for a call to a congregation within the Virginia Synod, dramatically increased in the first three years. Statistics from the Reports of the Secretary to the 1988, 1989, and 1990 assemblies (January 1, 1988–August 1, 1990) reveal the following numbers: Accessions, twenty-four by ordination, twenty-three by transfer; Dismissals, eighteen to other synods; Resignations (retirements, changes in calls within the synod, and "on leave from call"), fifty-nine; and Acceptances of calls within and to Virginia Synod congregations, sixty-eight.

One has only to think about the demand of time these numbers placed upon the new bishop and staff—the number of congregational council and call committee meetings that would need to be attended; the number of mobility papers and congregational profiles that would need to be read and evaluated; the amount of correspondence; the number of meetings with pastors and candidates in and beyond the synod; and the number of services of ordination.

The opening paragraphs of the 1989 Report of the Bishop to the Assembly of the synod gathered at the College of William and Mary, Williamsburg, May 26-28, set forth Bansemer's concerns and rationale of the actions of the Synod Council. He had already addressed the need for additional staff in implementing the new synod—and facing the realities of limited financial resources.

Our journey together has had a year of significant base-building and transition. Our base-building includes personnel additions. Because of financial constraints, we had to find innovative ways to provide the

amount of leadership necessary to meet the expectations of our membership, and to accomplish new goals. By the time our synod meets in Assembly, we hope to have added two new part-time positions, with minimal financial obligations from the synod. Dr. John Byerly has come on board as a 52-day-a-year assistant to the bishop in vacancy counseling, the most time-consuming task of the bishop's office. Working under the principle that "two heads are better than one," Dr. Byerly's skills, intuition and knowledge of ministry will greatly assist in matching pastor to parish in consultation with the bishop.

The second position, provided by a leap of faith and a desire to more directly serve our synod, has been established by a courageous Lutheran Family Services Board. As of this writing, the search committee was nearing completion of its task. We hope that this new assistant, both to LFS and the bishop (funded entirely by LFS) will be on location during the summer of 1989. An average of two days weekly is directly available to the bishop's office, and the remainder of the work week will create new ministries to pastors and parishes through the outreach of LFS.[11]

PASTOR JOHN F. BYERLY, JR.—RESPECTED ADVISOR

Pastor John Byerly was a wise choice by the bishop to assist him in vacancy and mobility counseling. He was well known to the synod, trusted among pastors, and respected by congregations. Byerly would work directly with the bishop, assisting him as a "Vacancy Counselor." Primary responsibilities of this staff position would include receiving and acknowledging mobility papers for placement in the synod, conducting interviews of candidates, evaluating needs of candidates and congregations, assisting in the appointment of vice-pastors, assisting with recommendations, and upon request, representing the bishop at meetings with congregational councils, call committees, and congregational meetings voting to call pastors.[12] The position would be funded from non-budgeted income sources.

JEAN BOZEMAN—DAUGHTER OF THE SYNOD

Like Byerly, the second part-time assistant had also grown up Lutheran in Virginia. This new assistant also had a distinguished career of "church work" beginning in 1961 at the age of twenty-three. Though most of her professional career was in congregations and agencies of other synods and the churchwide expression, as the Commission on Youth Ministry in Philadephia and the Lutheran School of Theology at Chicago, Jean Bozeman was well known among many members and pastors of the congregations in the Virginia Synod/LCA.

As in other synods, her presence and skills as leader of synod workshops in education and youth ministry held in Virginia were well known and appreciated. She was a preacher and teacher at Massanetta Summer Assembly. In

The Rev. Dr. Jean Bozeman

---

11. Ibid., p. 44.
12. Minutes, Report of Synod Council, 2nd Annual Synod Assembly, 1989, Virginia Synod/ELCA, pp. 97-98.

1983, she was the "preacher for the week" with the distinction of being the first and only woman to preach at the only ordination service conducted at a summer assembly—the ordination of John Blair Fields, July 17, 1983. That was about to change with the selection of Bozeman to be the first director of the newly created Office of Parish Services of Lutheran Family Services of Virginia and her call by the Synod Council to be the new part-time assistant to the bishop.

Bozeman was baptized (December 4, 1938), confirmed (June 1, 1952), and ordained (November 14, 1976) all in her home congregation, First Lutheran Church, Norfolk. As she grew in faith, Bozeman became very involved in Luther League, spending much of her free time at church and becoming involved in the leadership of the youth group. After high school, she attended Madison College, Harrisonburg, for two years prior to teaching third grade in Norfolk County Schools. In addition to her public school teaching, she became president of the Senior Luther League, taught Sunday School, and directed Vacation Bible School.

The pastor of her childhood, youth, and young adult days at First, Pastor Luther Warren Strickler, encouraged her career in education and responded positively to her dream of someday having a "church career" in a time when ordination was not an option for a woman. With his encouragement and with some financial assistance from the Virginia Synod/United Lutheran Church in America (ULCA), she received a scholarship in the form of a "promissory note" on which she remembers the word "man" had been marked through and the word "woman" handwritten in its place. According to Bozeman, she was the first woman to receive such financial assistance from the synod, and along with other scholarships, this afforded her the opportunity to continue her college education at Lenoir Rhyne in 1959 and graduate in 1961 with a Bachelor of Arts in Religious Education.

Her career serving the church began with an appointment from the Board of American Missions of the ULCA and later the LCA as a "parish worker" serving congregations in Virginia, Florida, Missouri, and Kansas from 1961 through 1964. In September 1964, she became the director of Christian Education and Youth Ministry at St. Paul's Lutheran Church, York, Pennsylvania. In 1968, she became a member of the LCA churchwide staff as an administrative assistant and, later, associate director of the Commission on Youth Ministry (CYM) in the unit's headquarters at 2900 Queen Lane, Philadelphia, Pennsylvania. During this time she and the Rev. Robert Bacher, CYM associate director, initiated the LCA Youth Staffer Program. She conducted numerous Christian Education and Youth Ministry workshops throughout synods and congregations in the LCA. Her work caught the attention of the leadership of the Lutheran School of Theology at Chicago (LSTC), which wanted to expand its course offerings in Christian Education. She became a faculty member at LSTC in 1971, was appointed dean of students in 1975, and was granted tenure in 1980.

Bozeman earned a master's degree in education from Temple University while serving on the staff of the LCA in Philadelphia. In Chicago, she earned a Master of Arts in Religious Studies from the University of Chicago Divinity School. She was approved as a candidate for ordination by the Northern Illinois Synod/LCA and received a call to ordained ministry as a member of the LSTC faculty.

Three historical notes should be mentioned. She was the first daughter of a Virginia Synod congregation ordained by the Virginia Synod/LCA. She was the first candidate and the first woman ordained by the new president[13] of the Virginia Synod/LCA, the Rev. Dr. V.A. Moyer, Jr., elected in June 1976. Her ordination was the last one in which Dr. Charles G. Tusing, distinguished former secretary of the Virginia Synod/ULCA and LCA, participated.

FROM CHICAGO TO SALEM

Bozeman brought with her an impressive resumé as a church professional skilled as an educator and knowledgeable of new directions in faith formation for children, youth, and adults, and the importance of family in children's faith formation. She was also highly experienced in working with congregations and familiar with synodical structures and churchwide resources available to congregations and their leaders. Her years of conducting workshops at all levels of the church would be helpful in planning, communicating, implementing, and evaluating programs for both the synod and the Lutheran Family Services of Virginia (LFS/VA). These were exactly the "skill sets" both Ron Herring, LFS executive director, and Bansemer were seeking.

For LFS/VA, the calling of Bozeman would mark a significant development in the social ministry organization's entering its "Second Century of Caring" for children and families, hopefully serving and more effectively connecting one of the historical social ministry organizations of the new synod to its constituent congregations. For the new synod, her calling would bring a new partner to the Office of the Bishop able to offer more attention to congregations, pastors, and associates in ministry.

† † †

Bozeman and Byerly were installed to their new positions on the synod staff during the Assembly Service of Holy Communion with Ordination and Installation on Friday, May 26, 1989, held at Williamsburg United Methodist Church with the Rev. Herbert W. Chilstrom, bishop, Evangelical Lutheran Church in America, presiding, and Bishop Richard Bansemer, preaching. Bozeman would be installed once again at College Lutheran Church, Salem, Virginia, with staff members from LFS/VA and the synod office present.

BUILDING FINANCIAL RESOURCES—THE SYNOD TRUST FUND FOR MISSION

In the final paragraph of his report to the 1989 assembly in Williamsburg, Bansemer noted,

Finally, our base-building is evident in the establishment of the Trust Fund for Mission. Approval of documents and election of Trustees at this assembly will begin a new opportunity for all of us to make sure that our God-given gifts continue to work for generations to come. I heartily endorse this Trust Fund for Mission for consideration of a portion of your estate planning.[14]

---

13. The title "Bishop" for chief executives of synods of the LCA was approved for use in 1978.
14. Minutes, Report of the Bishop, 2nd Annual Synod Assembly, 1989, Virginia Synod/ELCA, p. 45.

The Trust Fund for Mission had its origins in the early actions of the Synod Council in 1988. A "Committee to Study Synod Endowment Fund" was appointed by the council "to study the possibility of establishing an endowment fund to support various types of synodical ministries." The committee was chaired by Dr. Marshall F. Mauney. Members of the committee were Pastor Robert R. Sala, Pastor William E. Kinser, and Connie Koiner. The committee met on several occasions and surveyed what other synods were doing in developing this type of endowment fund to expand financial support of synodical programs beyond general giving by congregations.

The committee presented a written case statement in the form of an extensive written report to the 1988 assembly. The case statement presented the rationale:

The need for the church in all of its expressions to have additional resources to carry forward its mission is a constant fact of its life. Even though the stewardship record of our synod is excellent, our opportunities for ministry always outstrip our resources with which to support them. At the same time there are potential resources which could be available to the synod through effective cultivation and enlistment. The cultivation of "perpetual stewardship" through bequests, annuities, and deferred giving might well provide resources we do not now have for ministries and service we are not able to provide. The corpus of this endowment fund will be held and invested to provide an annual income to support projects now normally covered by the annual budget of the synod.[15]

The committee offered compelling reasons why they believed there would be strong support for the establishment of such a trust fund: Members of the synod believe in the work the church is doing through its synodical activities and have concern for the long-term viability of these ministries as well as a growing desire among many members to use their assets for long-term, well-managed use to support current ministries and ministries that as yet are not being funded through general giving. The committee also noted that planned giving and "stewardship expressed beyond death" were not presently being promoted at a time when a growing number of older people are drawn to deferred giving and who are among the most generous givers in terms of percentage of income.[16]

The case statement also included types of projects and programs that would be supported, such as expansion of the synod's camp facilities; scholarships for persons to attend camp programs; grants to underwrite youth events; funds to assist small congregations to provide salaries, internship sites, or help meet minimum levels of salaries and benefits; grants to assist newly organized congregations; the opportunity of responding to special financial needs of institutions of the synod; and providing stewardship programs.

The administration of the fund would initially be the responsibility of the Synod Council through the formation of a special committee to promote the fund, publicize giving opportunities, suggest projects to consider to promote giving to the endowment, recommend where funds would be invested, manage the funds, and oversee the reporting of the progress and use of the

---

15. Minutes, 1st Annual Synod Assembly, Virginia Synod/ELCA, 1988, pp. 46-67.
16. Ibid.

funds generated. The special committee and Synod Council would report annually to the synod in assembly. The case statement made a special point of noting that no congregational campaign would be used to solicit gifts for the fund and that the fund would not be seen as replacing the support of the legitimate items in the synodical budget and special appeals approved by synod assembly or church assembly of the ELCA.[17]

Following discussion on the assembly floor and approval of an amendment, the following resolution was adopted by the assembly:

That the Virginia Synod Assembly of the Evangelical Lutheran Church in America hereby authorize the endowment of the Virginia Synod Trust Fund for Mission and that the Synod Council be authorized to implement and oversee this program. The Council shall report the Trust Fund status to the Assembly in 1989 and annually thereafter.[18]

The committee established by the Synod Council to implement and oversee the Virginia Synod Trust Fund for Mission drafted a "Trust Agreement" to govern the operation of the fund. The council approved the agreement and recommended its adoption to the 1989 assembly held in Williamsburg. The agreement set forth in legal terminology the following governing provisions of the fund: Powers and Duties of Trustees; Powers Reserved to the Grantor (The Virginia Synod); Trustees; Charitable Purposes; Non-Investment; and Dissolution.[19]

Upon recommendation of the Synod Council and in order to fulfill terms of the Trust Agreement, especially in exercising the necessary fiduciary responsibilities set forth in the agreement, the following were elected at the assembly as the first trustees of the Trust Fund for Mission: Dr. Norman F. Fintel, Mr. Warren Kindt, and Dr. Martin Sipos. Others who have served as trustees of the fund over the past twenty-five years are Frances Hammond, Richard Wertz, Leroy Hamlett, Shelly Kelley, John Jung, James Wilson, Kathryn Buchanan, Martha Edwards, and Mark Reed.

Given the positive actions of the assembly to establish the Trust Fund for Mission, the Synod Council asked that the Committee to Study Synod Endowment become the Endowment Fund Committee, which would assume the responsibilities of promoting the fund among the members, congregations, and friends of the synod. At the January 1990 meeting of the Synod Council, the committee recommended and council approved

that congregations be advised that the offering at the Ordination Service during the 1990 Synod Assembly will be designated for the Trust Fund for Mission, and that congregations be encouraged to send through their delegates a special gift to launch this fund. Furthermore, we recommend that congregational gifts of record made at this service be reported in a subsequent issue of the Virginia Lutheran.[20]

---

17. Ibid.
18. Ibid.
19. Minutes, Report of the Synod Council, Virginia Trust Fund for Mission, 2nd Annual Synod Assembly, Virginia Synod/ELCA, 1989, pp. 98-100.
20. Minutes, Report of the Endowment Committee, 3rd Annual Synod Assembly, Virginia Synod/ELCA, 1990, p. 98.

The Synod Council agreed that a mailing be sent to all the congregations of the synod notifying them of this action. The letter was sent in March. In addition, the council proposed that a "tithing demonstration" be connected with this request for a special offering because of the emphasis that would be placed on MISSION90 and its goal that the ELCA become a church of "tithers by the millions." Two special offerings, one for the Virginia Synod Trust Fund for Mission and one for the ELCA's World Hunger Appeal, were established and it was proposed that

each delegate be asked to make as his/her offering at each of the services a tithe of one day's salary equivalent. This will give each of us an experience of tithing a day's salary ... and it will give to us as a synod a demonstration of what our potential is when we take tithing seriously. Thus we will have two valuable learning experiences and will give responsible support to two critical synod causes.[21]

Also among the first-year efforts of the Endowment Fund Committee would be the development of a color brochure and its distribution

to a list of potential donors (fully paid by special gifts). Procedures for responding to inquiries and following up on them have been developed. Plans for more aggressively promoting and developing the fund are under consideration.[22]

At the May 1991 meeting of the Synod Council, the committee proposed a resolution for the council to adopt and place before the Synod Assembly to be held following the meeting at Roanoke College. The resolution set forth goals for the Fund and lifted up deferred giving as a means of extending the Mission of the Church.

The Synod Council resolves that

All congregations of the Virginia Synod conduct an awareness program to inform its members about deferred giving as a means of extending the Mission of the Church; and

Each congregation report its progress in deferred giving for the Virginia Synod Trust Fund for Mission through wills, life insurance, or similar documents by year-end in the annual congregational report; and

The Virginia Synod accept as its goal the sum of $5,000,0000 in deferred giving by year-end 1995, and a goal of $10,000,000 by year-end 2000; and

That these funds be used by the Virginia Trust Fund for Mission for the purposes set out in the trust agreement.

A year following adoption of the resolution, the trustees reported cash on hand—checking account and money market accounts of $13,377.77 ($5,979 of that amount had been received as a special "designated offering" at the 1990 assembly)—and deferred gifts of record totaling $61,000.[23] A "Fund Status" report as of January 31, 1996, from the trustees (end of the fiscal year February 1995–January 1996) notes the following details: Unrestricted Cash, $44,168.61; Restricted Cash Account-Youth Programs, $56,745.70 (to be invested); Restricted Equities-Youth Programs, $41,743.13; Insurance Policies (deferred giving), $164,200; and Accumulated Interest, $5,808.88.[24] At the end of the 2000 fiscal year the following details were reported: Checking

---

21. Ibid.
22. Ibid., p. 123.
23. Minutes, 5th Annual Synod Assembly, Virginia Synod/ELCA, 1992, p. 114.
24. Minutes, 9th Annual Synod Assembly, Virginia Synod/ELCA, 1996, p. 125.

Account Balance, $4,908.92; Account Balances-Youth (Restricted), $154,029.33; Mission (Restricted), $490,188.44; Unrestricted, $89,248.51; Income From Interest and Dividends-Youth (Restricted), $3,015.98; Missions (Restricted), $9,050.85; Unrestricted, $4,316.75; Deferred Gifts-Insurance Policies, $158,500; and Charitable Remainder Trusts, $240,000.00.[25]

FROM MANY TO ONE—THE UNITED LUTHERAN APPEAL

Requests for special financial appeals to congregations from related institutions, agencies, and social ministry organizations came before the Synod Council early on in the life of the new synod. Fearing a "disconnect" from congregations because of redefined relationships to synods in the new church, they were anxious to stay connected and maintain important financial support from constituent congregations. All of these requests came at a time when synodical and churchwide leadership was already struggling to meet basic operational demands with the benevolent dollars available from congregations.

The United Lutheran Appeal check is presented to the assembly in 2005.

The Synod Council reported to the second Synod Assembly meeting in 1989 in Williamsburg that it had approved the designation of a Caribbean Synod Sunday, the exact date to be determined by the bishop of the synod.[26] At its January 1990 meeting, the Synod Council reported its actions of approving the requests of several agencies and institutions to establish additional designated Sundays that would provide opportunities for them to distribute to congregations Sunday bulletin or newsletter inserts about their ministry to congregations, including an offering envelope for those who wish to make a gift.

February 11, 1990 as Virginia Synod Homes Sunday. In subsequent years, the second Sunday in February will carry this designation.

May 6, 1990 as Lutheran Family Services Sunday. In subsequent years, the first Sunday in May shall carry the designation.

April 1, 1990 as Roanoke College Sunday.[27]

At its meeting in March, the Synod Council was asked by Lutheran Family Services of Virginia (LFS/VA) to recommend to the May 1990 Synod Assembly a "capital fund for endowment" campaign within the synod. The council approved the request in the form of a resolution:

---

25. Minutes, 14th Annual Synod Assembly, Virginia Synod/ELCA, 2001, p. 127.
26. Minutes, 2nd Annual Synod Assembly, Virginia Synod/ELCA, 1989, p. 101.
27. Op. cit., p. 107.

Resolution #8

In response to the request of Lutheran Family Services of Virginia, the Synod Council hereby recommends to the Virginia Synod Assembly that a capital campaign for endowment purposes be authorized for the benefit of Lutheran Family Services of Virginia. The campaign is to be conducted in phases as follows:

Preparatory Phase: June–December, 1990; Intensive Phase: January–December, 1991; Commitment Payment Phase: January, 1992–December, 1993.[28]

When the resolution was brought to the floor for action by the assembly, a pastor asked for a member of the council to explain why the recommendation was being made at this time. Leroy Hamlett, vice president of the synod, responded on behalf of the council and gave the opportunity for the representative of LFS/VA and organizers of the campaign to speak to the timing and purpose. The responses must have offered a satisfactory answer to the question. The resolution was adopted without further questions or debate.

Another request came from the Lutheran Theological Southern Seminary Board of Visitors seeking the synod's approval of a campaign among congregations corresponding to the seminary's 160th anniversary. The Synod Council also recommended approval of this request to the 1990 Synod Assembly held at Roanoke College.

Objectives of the campaign are 1) to identify highly gifted prospective candidates for the public ministry; 2) to gain understanding and support from the leadership of congregations for Southern Seminary and for the paired relationship with Trinity Seminary; and 3) to gain the full participation of congregations for a Seminary Sunday observance.

Following the 1990 assembly, the Synod Council committed itself to clarifying the synod's policy governing such requests for designated Sundays and appeals to congregations. At its March 1991 meeting, the council approved two "standing resolutions" dealing with these matters to be forwarded to the next assembly. The resolutions were shared with the Council of Deans, who discussed the concerns of the appeals and dedicated Sundays with Bishop Bansemer. A background paper was written by the deans expressing several concerns and containing recommendations for consideration by the Synod Council. The paper was shared with the bishop and the Synod Council, who in turn decided to withdraw the standing resolution titled "Special Financial Appeals" and pursue the following course of action:

a. Appointment of a Task Force on Special Financial Appeals for a one-year study of special financial appeals in the congregations of the synod.

b. The Task Force to complete its work and report to the Synod Council on or before March 1, 1992.

c. The Synod Council to recommend an approach to Special Financial Appeals to the 1992 Assembly.

d. The study to include, but not be limited to, the three-year combined approach suggested by the Council of Deans Committee Report dated May 20, 1991 and the one-year approach suggested by the Synod Council.

e. The Task Force should include at least two representatives from each of, the Council of Deans, the Synod Council, and related agencies and institutions in the synod.[29]

---

28. Op. cit., p. 109.
29. Minutes, 4th Annual Synod Assembly, Virginia Synod/ELCA, 1991, pp. 66-67.

Voting members and synod staff at the 1991 Churchwide Assembly, Orlando, Florida. Front row (left to right): George Kegley, Sergio Mendes, Bishop Bansemer, Josiah Tlou, and the Rev. James Utt; middle row: the Rev. Susan Springer, Kate Miller, the Rev. Jean Bozeman, Frances Hammond, and Anne Ashby; back row: the Rev. James Mauney, the Rev. Mark Radecke, and Keith Brown.

The resolution came to be titled, "Sunday Dedication for Uplifting a Special Mission or Ministry" and was recommended for adoption at the 1991 Synod Assembly. Guidelines for scheduling dedicated Sundays for the different institutions, agencies, and social ministry organizations in the synod were delineated and Sundays assigned.

(1) The dedication of Sundays for the uplifting of a special mission or ministry shall be limited to ten.
(2) Two consecutive Sundays shall not be dedicated.
(3) No more than two Sundays shall be dedicated in any one calendar month.
(4) For purposes of this section a 'dedicated Sunday' is one set aside in the congregations of the synod for the raising up of a special mission or ministry. A special offering may be received.
(5) The following Sundays have been previously dedicated:
Second Sunday in February—Virginia Lutheran Homes
Third Sunday in March—Outdoor Ministries
Fourth Sunday in April—Roanoke College
First Sunday in May—Lutheran Family Services
Second Sunday in November—National Lutheran Home[30]

---

30. Ibid., p. 82.

This proposed resolution from the Synod Council generated extensive discussion and numerous questions from the voting members attending the assembly. Two amendments were offered: first, that no more than one Sunday shall be dedicated in any one calendar month; second, that two consecutive dedicated Sundays shall not be advisable. Considerable discussion ensued following each amendment. The first was adopted. Before a vote was called on the second amendment, a motion was made to refer the now amended standing resolution to the Task Force on Special Financial Appeals. The motion to refer was adopted.[31]

The task force appointed by the Synod Council was chaired by the secretary of the synod, Clif Anderson, and included the following members and representation: Pastor Floyd Addison, Jr., Virginia Synod Lutheran Homes; Pastor Renee Ahern, Trinity Lutheran Seminary; Anne Ashby, Synod Council; Bishop Richard F. Bansemer; Kathryn Buchanan, Roanoke College; Ron Herring, Lutheran Family Services; Warren Kindt, Caroline Furnace Lutheran Camp; Pastor Chris Price, Council of Deans; Pastor Harold Uhl, Virginia Synod Lutheran Homes; James West, Lutheran Theological Southern Seminary; and Pastor James Utt, National Lutheran Home and Council of Deans.

The task force had two meetings and at least one sub-committee meeting. Advice and counsel was sought from others in the fields of research, planning, and fundraising. Dr. Daniel L. Larsen, executive director, Institute of Research and Planning, Roanoke College, and the Rev. Harvey A. Stegemoeller, executive director, ELCA Foundation, Chicago, Illinois, consulted with the task force. Materials were received and consideration given to models of appeals being conducted in other synods of the ELCA, especially the Southeastern Pennsylvania Synod, which was conducting an annual "Lutheran Charities Appeal." The task group understood this model to be a congregation-based appeal, conducted on one Sunday of the year, with an appeal for a gift to be given which could be designated to one or more or equally divided among all of the participating institutions and agencies. The task force reviewed options and after much discussion proposed a continuing resolution titled, "Synod-Wide Fund Appeals," to the Synod Council at its March 1992 meeting. The resolution approved by the Synod Council to go before the May 15-17, 1992 assembly was an extensive set of principles and guidelines recommended to govern any and all fundraising appeals on the territory of the synod.[32]

The following is a summary of the key recommendations: No congregation-based synod-wide capital fund appeals would be allowed within the synod by any of its related institutions or agencies; an annual appeal on a Sunday determined by the Synod Council would be conducted for the purposes of raising funds for all participating agencies and institutions officially related to the synod and for other synod causes as determined by the council; all gifts to the appeal would be viewed as distinct from the proportionate benevolence offerings of congregations; participating

---

31. Ibid., p. 136.
32. Minutes, 5th Annual Synod Assembly, Virginia Synod/ELCA, 1992, pp. 110-114.

agencies and institutions would be responsible for promoting and providing the materials for the uplifting of their mission and ministry; costs of the appeal would be the responsibility of the participating agencies and institutions; the synod would be responsible for the gathering, recordkeeping, and distribution of the funds; person-to-person solicitations would be allowed by the participating institutions and agencies if a donor "self-identified" as having a specific interest for a particular cause of one of the participants.

Guidelines for identification and contact would be provided by the Synod Council. The appeal would be administered by a "Special Appeals Council" consisting of not more than twelve representatives of the participating agencies and institutions, all of whom would be elected by the Synod Council and serve limited terms. The Special Appeals Council would have one representative from the Synod Council and the Council of Deans and report at least annually to the Synod Council. Dedicated Sundays would be understood to be "a Sunday set aside for raising up a special mission or ministry of an institution or agency within a dedicated month and is officially related to the synod or for another synod cause." Envelopes would not be distributed on these dedicated Sundays and no two dedicated Sundays would occur in a given month or consecutively. Congregations could deviate from the authorized calendar as necessary to fit the local calendar. The following months and Sundays were recommended for dedication:

February	Second Sunday	Virginia Lutheran Homes
March	Third Sunday	LTSS and Trinity Seminaries
April	Third Sunday	Outdoor Ministries
May	First Sunday	Lutheran Family Service
September	Third Sunday	Roanoke College
November	Second Sunday	National Lutheran Home[33]

The resolution was presented to the assembly. No record is given in the minutes of any discussion or questions asked by voting members. The resolution was adopted.[34]

At a special meeting of the Synod Council immediately following the assembly, the council directed Clif Anderson, secretary, to convene an organizational meeting of the agencies and institutions affiliated with the synod. After consultations with those agencies and institutions to be represented, Anderson recommended to the council at its January 1993 meeting the appointment of the following representatives to the Special Appeals Council:

Rev. Floyd Addison, Jr.—Virginian Lutheran Homes, Inc.
Rev. Renee Ahern—Trinity Lutheran Seminary
Kathryn K. Buchanan—Roanoke College
Rev. Gary Danielsen—Lutheran Council of Tidewater
Ronald L. Herring—Lutheran Family Services of Virginia

---

33. Ibid., pp. 110-113.
34. Ibid., p. 114.

Rev. Kenneth A. Nilsen—Caroline Furnace Lutheran Camp and Retreat Center
Rev. George F. Ricketts—Chaplain Service of the Churches of Virginia
Rev. Edward R. Schaack—Hungry Mother Lutheran Retreat Center
Rev. Harold J. Uhl—Chair
Rev. James H. Utt—National Lutheran Home for the Aged
Rev. James N. West—Lutheran Theological Southern Seminary[35]

At the same meeting, the Synod Council authorized

the appeal to be fully implemented in 1994 and annually thereafter and that this timing of the implementation be communicated to the pastors and congregations of the synod through Journey Together, the synod newsletter.

"No more Synod-wide capital funds appeals! No more coming all through the year to congregations for funds!" These were the headlines of the opening paragraphs of the first Special Appeals Council report written by its chair, Pastor Harold J. Uhl, to the Synod Assembly, held May 14-18, 1993, at Roanoke College.[36]

The Special Appeals Council met four times in preparation for the launch of the appeal. It would be called the United Lutheran Appeal—Faith in Action. The costs of the appeal were to be borne initially by the agencies and institutions with an agreement that eventually the costs would be covered by a percentage of the contributions. It was agreed that the synod would be the administrator of the appeal and distribute the funds as well as provide the names and addresses of those who indicated a special interest in given agencies and institutions. The Special Appeals Council also emphasized the importance of communicating with the congregations to encourage strong support. The council also requested that the 1992 continuing resolution authorizing the appeal be altered to note that this would be the only "synod-wide or general" appeal to congregations for agencies and institutions officially related to the synod, and that membership on the council not be limited to three-year turnover terms of individuals from agencies or institutions, but that each agency or institution identify their own representatives.[37]

The report of the Special Appeals Council to the 1994 Synod Assembly noted that the council had been busy preparing to initiate the first appeal. Administrative details were finalized. Promotional materials were developed and printed emphasizing "the extensions of the Lord's work" by the missions and ministries of the ten agencies and institutions related to the Virginia Synod. "Their deeds require our charitable financial support." Response envelopes were designed for distribution to all the congregations with the hopes that the "success of the appeal will reduce suffering, provide hope, restore dignity, and aid in the understanding and acceptance of the Word of God." The funding for these preparations was provided by the participating agencies and institutions. This report stated,

Beginning in the late summer of 1994, Pastors and Church Councils will receive materials and information on the appeal. As a Synod Assembly-directed program, it will be expected that every congregation

---

35. Minutes, 6th Annual Synod Assembly, Virginia Synod/ELCA, 1993, p. 76.
36. Ibid., p. 126.
37. Ibid., p. 127.

participate in the manner in which it decides. The suggested time line for the Appeal will be February of each year, culminating on the Sunday before Lent.

Members will be asked to support the Appeal as a whole, generously, but will be able to indicate interest and designate gifts to certain ministries. All monies and information will be handled by the Synod Office. Because of special concerns for our seminaries, one-third of all undesignated gifts will go to the Seminaries.[38]

The first United Lutheran Appeal was conducted in congregations throughout the synod on Transfiguration Sunday, February 26, 1995. The report of United Lutheran Appeal Council (formerly the Special Appeals Council) to the 1995 assembly indicated that a few congregations participated at other times. The council gave a full listing of each congregation participating and the amount given by each and the total for each conference of the synod. A summary of the detailed report was printed in the "Bulletin of Reports for the Assembly" and the printed minutes of the 1995 assembly.

The number of congregations participating was considered significant by the appeal council, noting in its report written in early March that receipts "show a widespread and generous response." Of the $72,655.60 total gifts received, $48,287.10 were undesignated, and $24,368.50 were designated. The total number of members in the congregations in the synod that made a gift was 1,235.

The United Lutheran Appeal Council worked to improve the planning, communicating, implementing, and evaluating of each appeal, especially in the early years.

The 1997 United Lutheran Appeal total exceeded that of each of the preceding years. Receipts were 28% higher than in 1996 and 7% higher than in 1995. The number of congregations participating in the Appeal continues to increase. In 1997, 132 of 163 congregations or 81% participated by making remittances to the Appeal. In 1996 we had 67.5% participation and in 1995 the percentage was 74.8%. Five congregations participated for the first time in 1997, however, there are 16 congregations which have not participated in any of the Appeals.[39]

The council, its chair, and a coordinator—a position added in 2000 which worked closely with the chair and Synod Council—developed more precise understandings and guidelines for the significant support and leadership given by the representatives of the agencies and institutions. Because of the growing number of congregations participating, more attention was also needed to manage the increasing demands and costs of the appeal. All of the partners in the appeal—the appeal council and the representatives of the institutions, agencies, and social ministry organizations, along with the Synod Council, bishop and staff, as well as the pastors and congregations—made the United Lutheran Appeal a significant means of providing additional funding on an annual basis to these important ministries of the church.

Throughout the years, the United Lutheran Appeal has been well served by gifted coordinators and committed representatives from the ten church-related participants affiliated

---

38. Minutes, 7th Annual Synod Assembly, Virginia Synod/ELCA, 1994, pp. 117-118.
39. Minutes, 10th Annual Synod Assembly, Virginia Synod/ELCA, 1997, pp. 100-101.

with the synod. They extend the work of the synod in the name of Jesus Christ into all areas of human need. The United Lutheran Appeal has developed a stronger sense of relatedness to the synod and its congregations. Thus it has been a united appeal of Lutherans in Virginia who understand better the broader reach of the church to a broken world, generating new alliances of service to far more citizens of our commonwealth than any one congregation or synod could do on its own. Greater financial support and stronger awareness of the ministries of our institutions, agencies, and social ministry organizations have connected the congregations to these ministries.

FROM VIRGINIA TO PAPUA NEW GUINEA—BEGINNING THE COMPANION SYNOD RELATIONSHIP

The development of the Companion Synod Program was part of MISSION90 and its emphasis on the mission of the baptized people of God "to see, grow, and serve." Its intent was to connect Lutheran church structures and congregations all around the world with ELCA synods and their congregations. Visits were encouraged between synods and their global companion to establish personal relationships allowing for the development of concrete expressions of mutual fellowship and support. The program's implementation would become a major component of the ELCA's Division for Global Mission.[40] In the young Virginia Synod, its implementation would be the responsibility of the Global Missions Task Group of the Commission for Outreach. It would not be an easy task.

The following members of the task group were appointed in 1989: the Rev. Robert Ward, chair; the Rev. Frank Honeycutt, Abingdon; the Rev. Robert Jones, Front Royal; the Rev. G. Wayne Sipe, Woodstock; Betty Gerlitz, Waynesboro; Lois Kindt, Roanoke; and Sylvia Moore, New Market. Others appointed in 1990 and 1991 included the Rev. Harold Harter, Newport News; Sue Lane, New Market; Jane McAllister, Stephenson; Judy Ann Fray, Madison; Susie Mahanes, Richmond; the Rev. Steve Ridenhour, Pulaski; and the Rev. Ted Schulz, Gloucester. The task group became the Global Missions Committee (GMC) in 1991.

Synods were given the option of selecting their companion relationship from numerous global candidates to be considered. Which one to choose would prove to be a bit of a challenge for the committee. The predecessor bodies of the synod had developed long and historic relationships with leadership structures, congregations, and educational institutions in Japan and India. Congregations in the new synod were already taking global ministry initiatives and actively supporting mission efforts in congregations in Peru and Africa, especially in Tanzania and Malawi.

---

40. Edgar Trexler, *High Expectations: Understanding the ELCA's Early Years, 1988–2002*, Augsburg Fortress Press, 2003, pp. 174-176.

The Rev. Paul and Carrie Schulz were ALC missionaries in Papua New Guinea from 1947 to 1970. Their son, the Rev. Ted Schulz, pastor of Shepherd of the Valley, Dayton, was born and raised in Papua New Guinea. Pastor Ted Schulz traveled with the Virginia Synod delegation to Papua New Guinea in 1995 and 2002 because of his fluency in the "pidgin" language and familiarity with the people, places, and culture.

These historical connections and current mission efforts of congregations pressed the committee's considerations, but the committee was aware this was a new synod and an opportunity for a new history to be made. It is the longtime "Lutheran world missions voice" in Virginia, Sue Lane, who is remembered by some of the members of the committee for advocating the choice of the synod's global companion to come from Papua New Guinea. It was helpful to have a member of the committee, the Rev. Ted Schulz, Shepherd of the Valley, who was born to missionary parents, the Rev. Paul Schulz and wife, Carrie, and lived in Papua New Guinea from 1953 to 1960, to support Lane's suggestion. In addition, some relationships were already being established with leaders, pastors, and members of the Islands District of the Evangelical Lutheran Church in Papua New Guinea (ELC-PNG). The Rev. Matthew Wamuna from Papua New Guinea was officially welcomed to the Virginia Synod at the 1989 Synod Assembly in Williamsburg. He was serving as Pastor-in-Residence at First Lutheran, Norfolk. The Rev. Gerriec Sungga, bishop of the Islands District of the ELC-PNG, visited congregations in Orange, Madison, Williamsburg, and in the Peninsula and Tidewater conferences during a visit to Virginia in November 1991. Judy St. Pierre, Trinity, Newport News, participated in an ELCA program, "Woman to Woman," and traveled to Papua New Guinea in June 1992. She brought greetings from the Lutheran Women of the ELC-PNG to the convention of the Virginia Synodical Women's Organization meeting at Roanoke College, Salem, July 31-August 2, 1992.

While the 1990 report of the Global Missions Task Group notes a "linkage under this program" with the Islands District of the Evangelical Lutheran Church/Papua New Guinea, the "companion synod" relationship was not officially announced until the report of the GMC to the 1992 Synod Assembly.[41]

The current focus of the Global Missions Committee is the implementation of the ELCA Companion Synod Program. Through this program the Virginia Synod, ELCA and the New Guinea Islands District, Evangelical Lutheran Church/Papua New Guinea have been paired to support one another in mission and ministry. As this new program slowly develops, we ask that members of the Virginia Synod pray for our sisters and brothers in Christ

---

41. Minutes, 3rd Annual Synod Assembly, Virginia Synod/ELCA, 1990, p. 142.

in the Islands District and for their Bishop, the Rev. Gerriec Sungga. The Global Missions Committee is working on a brochure to explain the Companion Synod Program and introduce the companions to each other. We are currently waiting for information from Bishop Sungga for the brochure. It is also our hope to be able to send a small delegation from Virginia to the Islands District that we might begin this program on the firm foundation of one-to-one contact with our partners in New Guinea. The Committee will also be developing various information items and media displays to help congregations learn about the New Guinea Islands District and the Companion Synod Program.[42]

The Companion Synod relationship with our sisters and brothers in Christ in the Islands District developed very slowly. In fact, it almost did not develop at all. Throughout 1992 and 1993, the GMC, now chaired by Pastor Steve Ridenhour, Trinity, Pulaski, moved forward with plans to educate congregations about the synod's partnership with the Islands District. The Rev. Paul Schulz and Judy St. Pierre agreed to be available to congregations as resource persons and speakers. The Schulzes, parents and son, spoke to several congregations. St. Pierre led a workshop at Power in the Spirit in the summer of 1992. Plans were made to print a brochure to interpret the Companion Synod Program, educate members about the mission and ministries of the Islands District congregations, and develop packets of educational materials to be distributed to each congregation at the 1993 assembly.

The requests for information and assistance from ELC-PNG leadership in developing the needed promotional materials went unanswered. Throughout 1994, the committee continued to struggle with the lack of communication with leaders in the Islands District even to the point of discussing the option of changing the relationship or at least consider a partnership with another PNG District. In April, members attended a conference held in Richmond and sponsored by the ELCA's Division for Global Mission. Representatives from four other synods with Companion Synod relationships with other districts in Papua New Guinea attended. The Virginia Synod had not been alone in its frustrations over the lack of communication. The conference helped the committee understand the problems related to communication and stressed the necessity for a trip by the bishop and representatives of the synod in order to overcome problems of communication.

Our progress in the promotion of the companion synod program has been stalled by the lack of communication from the leaders of the Islands District and the leaders of the ELC/PNG. This has kept our committee from moving ahead with further plans for promoting our Companion Synod Program. We are continuing to work on this problem through the assistance of the Division for Global Mission of the ELCA.

The ELCA Division for Global Mission has recommended that our synod send a delegation to visit PNG. Our committee made recommendations to the Synod Council, that funding be set aside to send the Bishop and a delegation from the Virginia Synod to PNG by 1996. We have been informed by the Synod Council that funding for such a trip will not be available from the Synod budget due to a lack of funds. The Synod Council did advise us to explore other funding resources for this trip.[43]

In June 1994, Bishop Bansemer and the committee met to reaffirm and renew the synod's commitment to continue the Companion Synod relationship with the Islands District. Contact

---

42. Minutes, 5th Annual Synod Assembly, Virginia Synod/ELCA, 1992, pp. 72-73.
43. Minutes, 7th Annual Synod Assembly, Virginia Synod/ELCA, 1994, pp. 107-108.

was made with the new bishop of the Islands District, the Rev. Furu Tierape. Correspondence from him indicated his desire to continue the relationship. He welcomed the idea of Bishop Bansemer and a delegation from the synod making a trip to ELC-PNG as soon as details could be arranged.

Bansemer submitted plans for a mission trip to the committee in September 1994. He was confident funds for the trip would come from resources and gifts available to the synod beyond the regular giving to the budget. Grants were secured from the Porter-Hess Fund and from the Division for Global Mission/ELCA. He also recommended that a delegation from the synod include his wife, Mary Ann; Pastor Steve Ridenhour, chair of the committee; Pastor Ted Schulz, fluent in the "pidgin" language; and at least one other member of the committee. The committee approved a request from the Virginia Synodical Women's Organization (VSWO) of the Women of the ELCA to send two representatives as members of the delegation—Judy Ann Fray, president, and Diane Giessler, board member. Through the support and guidance of the Division for Global Mission and the renewed commitment for better communications from district and national ELC-PNG leadership, the synod's first mission trip was scheduled for February 1-14, 1995.

"THE TRIP OF A LIFETIME"

The opening paragraphs of the Report of the Bishop summarize well the experience of the synod's first delegation to travel to the Islands District of the Evangelical Lutheran Church in Papua New Guinea.

"The trip of a lifetime" is no overstatement regarding our delegation's visit to Papua New Guinea, just north of Australia. Sing-sings, worship, joys, sorrows, and tropical scenery are surpassed only by the memory of brothers and sisters on the other side of the world in love with the same Christ we worship.

Very few people travel to this part of the globe, for the tourist industry has not yet found it feasible to be there. Those who travel as tourists could never have the experience that was our privilege to have as Lutheran Christians who went to be with other Lutheran Christians. It was not the places we saw (the buildings were very modest), nor the historical sights, which were few. It was the people, solely the people, who won our hearts as they shared their faith.

Our goal is to be in as many places as invitations are extended to share the experience and encourage both congregations and synod to strengthen relationships with our companions on the other side of the earth. To that end, the Global Missions Committee will coordinate relationships, so that congregations from Virginia may be appropriately paired with congregations in PNG.[44]

The Global Missions Committee made its written report of the trip to the 1996 Synod Assembly. In the report, the committee noted the goals of the mission trip, highlights of each day's journeys to the headquarters of the ELC-PNG, Martin Luther Seminary in Lae, and to

---

44. Minutes, 8th Annual Synod Assembly, Virginia Synod/ELCA, 1995, p. 10.

congregations, pastors, and ELCA world missions staff in Lae, Kimbe, Bialle, Rabaul, and Kavieng. In Kimbe, approximately 2,000 people attended a gathering of welcome. At this gathering the delegation presented a quilted banner incorporating the logo of the synod and a fabric painting of each of the eleven conferences. After this event, the delegation was greeted by over 2,000 more as they journeyed to three other parishes near Kimbe. One thousand or more gathered for an evening worship service in the village of Bialle. In Rabaul, the delegation was given a tour of the city which had been devastated by the September 19, 1994 eruption of the nearby volcano. Hundreds gathered in a refugee center in Kokopo for an evening of worship services. Numerous meetings were held with village leaders, pastors, ELCA missionaries Kevin Jacobson and Rhoda Carlstadt, and with Island District officers. The delegation also had a visit with the vice-prime minister of Papua New Guinea. Travel from village to village was primarily by boat.

In each of the parishes, special worship services and programs were held in our honor. Members of the delegation were showered with gifts. Each parish reenacted the story of the coming of the first missionaries. The festivities included traditional dancing (sing-sing), dramas, and a moo moo, food cooked in a pit with heated rocks. Generally members of the delegation were asked to address the congregation or to preach.

The Lutherans of the Island District PNG were truly honored that we came to visit. In every village we were warmly welcomed. Our companions are people who exhibit a deep faith in Jesus Christ. They are truly alive and on fire with the Spirit of God.[45]

The 1996 report concludes with appreciation expressed for the support of the synod. It notes that upon return to the synod, members of the delegation made presentations about our companion synod relationship in congregations and presented programs in various synodical settings, including displays for the Synod Assembly and classes offered at Power in the Spirit.

We asked that our gifts be used by the District Council of the Islands District. We trust that you know your most urgent needs much better than we do ... we are deeply concerned for the people of Rabaul as they rebuild their lives and congregations after the volcano's destruction.[46]

Plans of the Global Missions Committee made in 1996 came to fruition in 1997, highlighting the synod's closer connections with the Islands District/ELC-PNG. With the help of the new chair of the committee, Pastor Ted Schulz, Shepherd of the Valley, Bridgewater, plans were finalized for Pastor Paul Senff and wife, Marie, to arrive in March 1997 as "Missionaries in Residence." The Senffs would be in Virginia for at least three months making presentations to congregations and at the Synod Assembly. They had served for thirty-two years in Papua New Guinea. Also in 1997, plans began to take shape for a student from the Islands District to begin undergraduate courses at Roanoke College in either 1997 or 1998. Dean of Admissions Michael Maxey was valuable in assisting the committee to achieve this goal with the arrival of Mary Tankulu in time for the 1998 fall semester. Recommended by the ELC-PNG, Tankulu came as a high school graduate with successful further studies at the University of Papua New Guinea

---

45. Minutes, 9th Annual Synod Assembly, Virginia Synod/ELCA, 1996, p. 115.
46. Ibid.

in Port Moresby. Roanoke College covered fees and tuition totaling $15,800 with gifts through the Virginia Synod covering her traveling and living expenses. Coordinating with the committee, Tankulu agreed to be available on occasion to visit congregations, join in synod youth and young adult events, and make presentations about her life and church in her native country. A goal was set in 1997 by the committee to finalize plans for an exchange of visiting delegations, with the hope that delegations from each would be able to visit the other beginning sometime in 1999. At the end of 1997, word was received from ELC-PNG leadership that the nation was suffering from an unprecedented drought with over 300,000 people facing starvation. In response, the ELCA sent $40,000 and the Virginia Synod sent $11,355.32 by March 1998.

By 1999, it was clear that the new ELCA Division for Global Mission program, Companion Synod, had firmly been implemented and well established in the Virginia Synod/ELCA. New chair of the committee Pastor Paul Pingel, Zion/St. Mark, Floyd-Willis, noted the following in his report to the Synod Assembly:

Our communications with PNG were greatly increased with the election of a new President of the Islands District, Roewec Roenuc. Members of the 1995 delegation are familiar with "Pastor Roy" as they called him ... Pastor Roy has been much more available to the Global Mission Committee ... enhanced by the purchase of a fax machine for the Islands District by our committee as part of a $500 communications grant sent to PNG.

As a result of more frequent communication and being able to discuss goals and plans at length with our brothers and sisters in PNG:

- The hoped-for visit from a delegation from Papua New Guinea will occur in 1999.
- Our synod's Youth to Youth project for 1999 will be a project to build school spaces at the Martin Luther Seminary in Lae, where many New Guinea Islands District pastors and families go for seminary training.
- We are able to make sure Mary Tankulu, a PNG student attending Roanoke College, would be able to come on time, and better prepared to begin school in the United States.[47]

In addition to others already named, the following also served on the Global Missions Committee: Judy Wagner St. Pierre, Newport News; Bob and Nancy Walkins, Luray; Bill May, Church Road; Crystal Bunting, Portsmouth; Geneva Fritts, Macon, North Carolina; Till Blackwelder, Chesapeake; Stephanie Strandberg, Newport News; Sophie Wilson, Richmond; Pastor Harold Burnette, Edinburg; and Pastor Gerald Weeks, Hampton.

In his final Report of the Bishop to the Assembly in 1999, Bansemer noted what he considered to be the twelve most significant positive changes implemented in the life of the new synod during his tenure as bishop. The establishment of a Companion Synod in the Islands District of Papua New Guinea was first on his list.[48] A word of thanks is due to many in the new synod who worked hard and traveled great distances to implement this new global mission emphasis in the synods of the ELCA.

---

47. Minutes, 12th Annual Synod Assembly, Virginia Synod/ELCA, 1999, p. 109.
48. Ibid., p. 10.

Changes and challenges to this special relationship would come in the years ahead. As with its beginnings, trust and cooperation would be dependent on the commitment of both companions to open and honest communication. If so, this new synod-based global mission relationship would move to deeper levels of walking together as equal companions in service to God's mission in Christ in the Islands District of the Evangelical Lutheran Church in Papua New Guinea and in the Virginia Synod of the Evangelical Lutheran Church in America. Evidence of that trust and commitment would come. The story of those journeys is told in the chapter to follow.

CONCEIVED AND NAMED—POWER IN THE SPIRIT

"New events still to be conceived and named may be guided by the Massanetta experience."[49] With this quote from the Synod Staff Letter, the Rev. George E. Handley concluded his review of "The Lutheran Summer Assembly at Massanetta" in his twenty-five-year history of the Virginia Synod/LCA, 1962–1987. The popular summer gathering of Lutherans had been held for fifty-five years at the Presbyterian Conference Center, Massanetta Springs, just off Route 33 east of Harrisonburg. By the 1980s, its popularity among Lutherans in Virginia began to wane as other family options such as summer church camps, longer vacation times, and family camping adventures became popular. Costs increased and attendance decreased. From 1976 to 1984, the total cost of the assembly jumped from $37.50 per person to $137.00. Attendance dropped from 940 participants in 1976 to 486 in 1983.[50] In its last year, 1984, only 245 attended.

The synod's Executive Board voted to discontinue the assembly when only 142 people responded to a survey requiring an attendance by 260 people. A synod subsidy of $5,500 would have been required even if 260 had planned to attend.[51]

Handley's words written in 1984 would prove to be prophetic for the new synod as it sought to conceive a new summer fellowship event yet to be named.

The new event was first conceived as a summertime convocation by the Worship Managing Group of the Virginia Synod/LCA as noted in its report to the synod's convention in June 1986 at Roanoke College.

In the fall of 1985 a joint meeting of the Worship Managing Group and the Evangelism Managing Group was held at Massanetta Springs. This overnight conference highlighted the importance of the climate for growth in a congregation of which worship as well as witness play an important part. Out of this meeting a planning committee was formed representing both Evangelism and Worship committees. On July 24th-July 26th, a convocation will be held at Roanoke College. This convocation will feature top persons in the field of worship and evangelism. This convocation is aimed at Pastors, Musicians, choirs, worship and evangelism committee members from our synodical congregations. We are excited about this joint effort and hope it will

---

49. George E. Handley, *Lutherans in Virginia: A 25-Year History, 1962–1987*, Vol. 1, Virginia Synod/LCA, Chapter 7: Summer, Camping and More, The Lutheran Summer Assembly at Massanetta, p. 68.
50. Minutes, 1986, 166th Annual Convention, Virginia Synod/LCA, 1985, p. 131.
51. Op.cit., p. 67.

84 † Journey Together

be the forerunner of other joint projects among the various managing groups and task groups as the need and occasion arise.[52]

Even with a year's hiatus, the first of these summer events generated a positive response among pastors and congregational lay leaders. The first of these convocations was planned and implemented by the Worship and Evangelism Managing Group and held in 1986. The three-day event—Thursday, Friday, and Saturday—featured the Rev. Jerry Schmalenberger, Gordon Beaver, and the Rev. James Connelly, popular Lutheran leaders in the disciplines of evangelism, church music, homiletics, and worship leadership. The success of the first with its positive evaluations from the 145 participants attending the event held July 30-August 1 at Roanoke College would assure plans for a second convocation in the summer of 1987 that began taking the name "Power in the Spirit." The Rev. Bob Maier, Glade Creek, Blue Ridge; Dr. Robert Benne, professor, Roanoke College; and Sue Clark, administrative staff, Virginia Synod/ELCA worked with others from the Worship and Evangelism committees during the time of the transition between synodical expressions. They met with Handley to get advice and make plans for continuing a summer program that might serve as a forerunner to a new summer program in the new synod. They succeeded in their efforts and the new synod would be the beneficiary of their and others' efforts to offer a meaningful learning and fellowship event during the summer for the Virginia Synod/ELCA.

In the Worship and Evangelism committees' joint report written for the "Record of Reports—1986," the first record of a name—"Power in the Spirit"—was given to the new mid-summer convocation held at Roanoke College before the beginning of the new synod. Perhaps the name of the new event came from the power of remembering the spirit of the past summer assemblies of Virginia Lutherans gathering at Massanetta Springs, or maybe it was the awareness that there would soon be a new synod with the potential of its own summer event— whatever the motivation, the new summertime event for congregational leaders would become known as "Power in the Spirit."[53] During this time of transition and for years to follow, Maier served as coordinator of the Power in the Spirit planning group. Bozeman recalls,

Bob Maier was great to work with and there was nothing he was not willing to do. He shared with me that he served as the first coordinator beginning in 1986 through 1998, excluding 1988, for a total of 12 years.

No Power in the Spirit conference was held in 1988 as the implementation of a new synod required total attention. New staff leadership and a new Synod Council were committed to taking their time getting started by taking a "fresh look" at every aspect of the synod's responsibilities and programs. As noted by the new synod's vice president, Leroy Hamlett, St. Mark, Charlottesville, in his first report to the Synod Assembly,

---

52. Minutes, 1987, 167th Annual Convention, Virginia Synod/LCA, 1986, p. 113.
53. Record of Reports, Virginia Synod/LCA, 1986, p. 109.

With three different traditions in our history, it would have been easy for the "we always did it this way" syndrome to be prevalent. Instead the Council has viewed each situation as an opportunity to take a fresh look. While a certain amount of "nuts and bolts" is, by necessity, to be done in the first year, a substantial amount of time has been given to brainstorming: What is the mission of the Virginia Synod and how do we accomplish this mission?[54]

In his 1989 Report of the Bishop to the Assembly, Bansemer notes his appreciation for the work of Pastor Jim Mauney, program assistant, especially in his efforts to "reinstitute Power in the Spirit ... a summer program for congregational leaders." An additional report of the Commission for Outreach and the Commission for Congregational Life noted plans for developing the Power in the Spirit conference scheduled for July 20-22, 1989 at Roanoke College, calling it a "visible and popular means of sharing program and people resources for congregations, pastors, and lay leaders throughout the new synod."[55]

It should also be noted that a resolution entitled "Synodical Summer Assembly" was placed before the 1989 voting members asking the Synod Council to report to the 1990 assembly the council's reflection and advice on the matter of considering "some event on the territory or close proximity (such as Power in the Spirit) which might provide opportunities for all ages."[56] The resolution was adopted.

The Synod Council asked the Commission for Congregational Life to review and advise the council's response to the resolution.

The Commission for Congregational Life brought the renewed interest in a family-oriented synod-wide event to the attention of the "Power in the Spirit" planning group. That group concluded, and the commission concurred, that "Power in the Spirit" was needed and well used as an inspirational event designed to better equip congregational leaders for ministry in the parish. It was agreed that an attempt to merge this goal with the aims of those who desire a family-oriented event would not be feasible.

At this time, therefore, it is the conclusion of the Synod Council that the same basic obstacles which prevented continuation of Massanetta Summer Assembly continue to exist, and that no formal plan for a new synodical event be initiated at this time.[57]

Implementing Power in the Spirit for congregational leaders—lay and ordained—continued to be focused in the Commission for Congregational Life of the new synod. With synod support that came especially from staff, along with "seed money" from the Synod Council, and a good working relationship with Roanoke College as the choice of a permanent location, a Power in the Spirit Planning Group evolved over time. Some members of the planning teams have included Pastor Robert Maier, Glade Creek, Blue Ridge; Pastor Hank Boschen, ELCA regional missions director; Pastor Robert Maier, Pastor Terri Sternberg, Trinity, Pulaski; Pastor Harvey Atkinson, Walker Mountain Parish, Crockett; Cary Mangus, St. John, Roanoke; Debbie Mintiens, Emanuel, Woodstock; Gene and Janet Gomez, Living Water, Kilmarnock;

---

54. Minutes, 1st Annual Synod Assembly, Virginia Synod/ELCA, 1988, p. 36.
55. Ibid., pp. 45, 113, and 136.
56. Ibid., p. 131.
57. Minutes, 3rd Annual Synod Assembly, Virginia Synod/ELCA, 1990, p. 110.

Heather Repass, Holy Trinity, Wytheville; Stephanie Garst, Church Relations, Roanoke College; and Anna Merz, St. James, Chilhowie. This group, along with other leaders over the years, developed a set of "blueprints" for building the annual event, accepting the responsibility of planning and implementing what has become the popular annual summer leadership convocation of the synod.

Leadership and support has come from outside the synod as well. The Rev. Ray Blansett and Vickie DeVilbiss, Celebration Art, Annapolis, Maryland, coming from our sister synod, Metropolitan Washington, DC, have given their time, creativity, and resources to strengthen worship experiences and support congregational ideas through workshops with a sense of joy and life in all the years they have been a part of Power in the Spirit.

Power in the Spirit coordinators the Rev. Jean Bozeman, 1990–2005, and Elizabeth Smythe, 2006 –.

Bozeman served as synod staff liaison from 1990 through 2005. As her responsibilities shifted in the synod toward leadership in the Office of the Bishop-East, Elizabeth Smythe, Ebenezer, Marion, was invited to assume the leadership role of the planning group. Smythe was handed the reins of Power in the Spirit in 2006. In an interview in 2013, Bozeman noted,

Elizabeth was a natural for this position with her background as a public school teacher and her already polished skills in congregational service. She was among the first of the ACTS students who commented about how much ACTS had changed her life. Assuming this leadership role for Power in the Spirit she would find out just how much her life had changed.

According to Smythe, the planning team normally met three times a year— September, January, and sometime in April or May. In an interview, Smythe reported about the work of the planning group:

We all would get so excited about the major decisions we made, like the theme for that year, and also the names of the key leaders we wanted to ask— keynoter and bible study leader. We had great support.

Power in the Spirit has become an important source of support for congregational leaders in the synod. The mid-summer schedule has worked well. Roanoke

Roanoke College leaders for Power in the Spirit: Kathryn Buchanan, Church Relations, and Robert Benne, Center for Religion and Society.

Virginia Synod † 87

Dr. Susan McArver, professor from Lutheran Theological Southern Seminary and Power in the Spirit presenter of "Nurturing Faith in Home, Church and School," baptismal themes.

College has been a partner in the sponsorship of the program, especially with Kathryn Buchanan, director, Office of Church Relations, serving on the planning committee along with Dr. Robert Benne. The hospitality shown by all levels of the staff at the college in providing whatever facilities are needed, technical support, staff support, and the great meals prepared by the dining personnel have helped to make Power in the Spirit a special summertime event in the life of the synod. Members from across the synod who attend experience a unique opportunity for fellowship, creating new and sustaining relationships among the many lay leaders and pastors of the synod.

Power in the Spirit has also provided some of the most popular theologians, pastors, teachers, musicians, and experts in their respective fields coming to Virginia to help make us a stronger synod. One might say about its development and years of success that trusting in the "Power in the Spirit," once conceived and named for a new summer fellowship in the synod, has proven to be instrumental in the implementing and sustaining of a new synod.

In a report, Bozeman shared,

While invited speakers and musicians are important to the fabric of Power in the Spirit, the heart of this event has been the numerous people—lay and rostered—who have sat through numerous planning meetings, planned worship services, led workshops, designed, hauled, and set up stage designs, stuffed packets, staffed registration tables, prepared displays, provided transportation for presenters, and on and on to so many tasks necessary for such an event.

Each year as participants begin to arrive, voices ring out hellos and raise in praise through worship, and friends—old and new—embrace Bible study, gain new theological insights, and grow in their relationship to Christ and his church. The mission of a small synod doing big things is affirmed as each participant experiences a new level of Power in the Spirit and takes to their home congregation a renewed enthusiasm for the church.

CARE OF SPOUSES—LUNCHEONS AND RETREATS

A more intentional approach by the synod for the care of the clergy spouses (and later all rostered leader spouses) has its origin in one of the many gifts that Pastor Jean Bozeman brought when called by Lutheran Family Services of Virginia (LSF/VA) and the Virginia Synod/ELCA to serve families, pastors, and congregations. Reflecting on her interview with the Search Committee, Bozeman shared the following:

When I interviewed for this position, they invited me to talk a bit about some things I could especially bring to this position. Well, of course we talked about my education background, churchwide experiences and contacts, the areas of leadership support having been in the seminary community setting for eighteen years. I also told them about retreats that I had led for clergy spouses in some other synods. These were very special times of building community and helping them to see their roles not just as the pastor's wife (few men at that time), but also as a child of God who comes to a congregation serving and responding to God's call in their own unique way. I told the call committee that was an area in which I would have great interest.

Within six months of being on staff at LSF/VA and the synod, Bozeman developed a survey to communicate with the spouses of clergy in order to receive some input on whether they would be interested in working together to develop more intentional ways of support for clergy spouses. Bozeman was surprised at the response.

Even where people are deeply invested, there is little interest in surveys and the return is usually about 15%. Well, we had a huge response. There was a lot of negativity and suspicion expressed. But, there was also a good amount of openness and ready to go.

Working with the Leadership Support Committee, Bozeman developed plans for the first retreat and set the date and place—November 15-17, 1991, at the Eagle Eyrie Conference Center, Lynchburg. The theme centered on Ecclesiastes 3:1, "For Everything There Is a Season." Funds to underwrite the retreat and assist in covering costs, if needed, were approved by the Synod Council. This helped to keep the cost to $58.00 per participant. Sixteen spouses registered and participated in the first Virginia Synod Clergy Spouse Retreat. Reflecting on that first retreat, Bozeman shared,

They generally did not know each other, which was a surprise to me. By the end of the retreat there was no question about "if" there would be another retreat, but only "when." I could not believe the changes in those women in just one weekend. They were no longer alone in the synod. They knew there was a broader base of support as they now had a new network of folks who understood their issues. They learned a lot. It was a great beginning.

The second spouse retreat, November 13-15, 1992, Massanetta Springs, had grown from sixteen to twenty-six participants.

In addition to the retreats, clergy spouse luncheons were initiated during the time of the annual synod assemblies in the new synod. The luncheons were open to any and all spouses of clergy and associates in ministry attending the assembly. In addition to expanding contacts and an opportunity for expressing support for spouses, the luncheons afforded the opportunity for spouses who had attended retreats to have a "reunion experience" and to encourage the participation of other spouses to attend. In her reflections on the luncheons and retreats, Bozeman noted,

The luncheons and the retreats are not for everyone. We will never get some folks to retreat, but for a number over the years they "fit the bill." I do believe that, even for those who do not attend the events, there is a greater awareness of who they are as part of the synod. They feel included, not the outsider. They know the Bishop sees himself as a supporter of the spouses and we have an awareness in the synod that it is important for family dynamics, thereby congregational life, to have a healthy clergy family.

Along with the luncheons, the retreats continued to build in the new synod. Some conferences began having events that included spouses. Efforts to keep the costs of the retreats low were helpful in encouraging attendance, though costs have inevitably risen. Efforts were also made to find retreat centers across the territory of the synod.

Over the past twenty-three years, an average of thirty-three spouses have attended the luncheons. While the average retreat size has been twenty-three, a total of ninety-seven spouses have attended one or more retreats. Friendships and support groups among clergy spouses formed over the years since the first clergy spouse retreat. Spouses participating in the retreats assumed more and more responsibility for the planning and leading of the retreats.

In reflecting upon her experience in supporting the spouses of clergy in the synod, especially those participating in the luncheons and retreat, Bozeman noted in an interview,

They are really a special group. We are blessed by these folks—both women and men—who are clergy spouses. We need to keep looking for ways in which they can be supported as part of the Virginia Synod family.

Dee Keister, St. Paul, Strasburg; Pamela Briehl, River of Life Parish, Shenandoah; and Tara and Anna Rose Bouknight, Trinity Ecumenical Parish, Moneta enjoy a luncheon for the spouses of rostered leaders sponsored by Roanoke College Church Relations in June 2006.

Spouse Retreat participants gathered on the Massanetta lawn.

CARE OF THE CALL/CARE OF THE SOUL

"Collegiality, support, care of one another, examination of the call, and the challenge to develop a spiritual discipline are all part of the events."[58] With these words from his annual report to the 1996 Synod Assembly, Bansemer expressed what he hoped would be the experiences of pastors and associates in ministry participating in a series of retreats he called "Care of the Call/Care of the Soul." The first of these retreats was held at the Williamsburg Christian Retreat Center, Toano, Virginia, October 30-November 1, 1995. Additional retreats were scheduled in May, September, and November 1996 and in May 1997.

These retreats were begun by Bansemer to address what he sensed was a need of pastors and associates in ministry to receive more of his and the synod staff's attention and support, particularly in the need for developing a stronger sense of collegiality and spiritual practices. Reflecting on what he felt was the significance of these retreats, Bansemer shared the following in an interview in 2012:

We—myself, Jim and Jean—sensed a need for more of our attention to be given to pastors. I tried Care of the Call/Care of the Soul retreats for meditation and reflection, for two or three days in different parts of the synod, for worship and fellowship.

The retreats were well attended. Following one of the retreats held in Shawsville, just outside of Salem, one pastor noted that he felt more connected to more of his fellow pastors. Another

---

58. Minutes, 9th Annual Synod Assembly, Virginia Synod/ELCA, 1996, p. 14.

pastor noted that she appreciated the time away to relax, pray, and be inspired with good worship and Bible study that she did not have to lead.

In his report to the 1997 Synod Assembly, Bansemer noted that among those things that made for a very good year in the synod were the efforts of the staff, with help from the Leadership Support Committee, assisting to offer the Care of the Call/Care of the Soul retreats.

Five Care of the Call/Care of the Soul retreats have covered the synod, giving opportunity for every pastor and associate in ministry to be with colleagues for prayer, reflection, small group work, and the sharing of faith with one another.[59]

RESTRUCTURING FOR MISSION AND MINISTRY

From the beginning of the new synod, leadership struggled with implementing the functions and forms of a new synod structure. There were new organizational structures to learn with redefined and added functions to implement. "Councils" in the former synod structure—Ministry, Missions, and Parish Life—became "Commissions" in the new—Ministry, Outreach, and Congregational Life. Managing Groups of the former councils—Professional Preparation, Professional Service, Campus Ministry; Home Missions, Social Action, Special Missions, World Missions, Inclusive Ministry, Ministry with Aging; and Educational Ministry, Evangelism, Lay Leadership, Stewardship, Worship, Youth Ministry, and Ministry with Disabled Persons became committees or task groups of the new commissions—Daily Life, Candidacy, Leadership Support; Evangelism, Global Mission, Social Action, Virginia Missions; and Children, Youth, Young Adults, Adults, and Senior Adults, respectively.

Synod Assembly: "Mission Possible.

---

59. Minutes, 10th Annual Synod Assembly, Virginia Synod/ELCA, 1997, p. 13.

In addition to the three new commissions and their sixteen related committees and task groups, five standing committees—Executive, Consultation, Discipline, Mutual Ministry, and Finance and Budget—were also mandated in the constitution and bylaws to accomplish the necessary functions assigned to the Synod Council. Within the first three years, 1988 to 1990, additional committees and task groups were added by assembly or council actions to the already complex structural and administrative realities facing the new leadership. These included the Environmental Accountability, Synod Mission Endowment Fund, and Inclusiveness and Minorities Ministry committees, as well as the Women's Issues, Program and Support, MISSION90, and Special Financial Appeals task groups. Commissions, committees, and task groups were given freedom and time by the Synod Council to insure that programs from the past that worked well and were popular would be continued, i.e. youth ministry events, candidacy convocations, and Power in the Spirit. It was also clear that there would be freedom and time for the commissions and their committees to be creative and plan new programs, especially those responsive to needs of congregations and program emphases within the new church.

On top of all these organizational units and their responsibilities, synods were also structurally related to Regional Centers for Mission. For Virginia, that meant a commitment to Region 9 with offices in Atlanta, Georgia. It also meant support of regional events held throughout the Southeast. All of the meetings of the coordinating council and event planning groups required more time and travel of an already overextended synod staff. Support of the new concept of regional centers also required financial support from an already depleted reservoir of financial resources.

Both Bansemer and the Synod Council knew that the demands of such a complicated structure of the synod could not be sustained. Budgets projected fewer financial resources available as giving to synod causes continued to be weak and the synod struggled to meet benevolence commitments to the ELCA. Of great personal concern to Bansemer and the Synod Council, the amount of time demanded of Brown, Mauney, and Bozeman to attend meetings of the various commissions, committees, and task groups steadily increased as new ideas and programs were discussed, planned, and implemented. Bansemer, Mauney, Brown, and Bozeman were constantly on the road and often away from office and home during these first years.

In his report to the 1990 Synod Assembly, Bansemer noted that changes in structures were already being made in the functioning of the regional centers.

We struggle with the function of the region, and are pleased that the cost has been contained, and the number of meetings reduced. Much study is underway to evaluate the structure of the ELCA, including the number of synods, the purpose of regions and the number of Commissions. The problem of cost effectiveness and fairness to dedicated leaders is forever difficult.[60]

---

60. Minutes, 3rd Annual Synod Assembly, Virginia Synod/ELCA, 1990, p. 138. See also Edgar Trexler, *High Expectations: Understanding the ELCA's Early Years, 1988–2002*, Augsburg Fortress Press, 2003, pp. 28-31 and 38.

In that same report, Bansemer notes, as he had in the previous bishop's reports, that his assistants—Mauney, Brown, and Bozeman—"continue to serve congregations in extra-mile service." The vice president of the synod, Leroy Hamlett, noted the following in his report to the 1991 Synod Assembly:

> As I am sure many of you realize, with the number of committees, commissions, task forces, and other special organizations of the Virginia Synod, as well as the myriad meeting dates and places, Bishop Bansemer, Keith Brown, Jean Bozeman, and Jim Mauney have been forced to "be continually on the road" with these meetings and other responsibilities.[61]

In November 1990, the Synod Council discussed a resolution of the ELCA Church Council which

> invited each synod to take the opportunity afforded by the completion of the review/configuration of the churchwide organization to engage in a review of its structure and operation, individually and in conversation with neighboring synods.[62]

The Synod Council wasted no time in doing just that, though no record is made of any discussion with a neighboring synod. By its January 1991 meeting, a preliminary proposal for restructuring the three commissions was presented to the council. The council gave general approval of the concept and directed the staff to prepare a detailed plan with the necessary changes to the synodical governing documents. Final approval was given to a restructuring plan at the March 1991 meeting of the Synod Council.

In the Report of the Vice President to the Assembly, Hamlett made clear his support for the assembly's action to approve the restructuring plan.

> As we convene for this assembly, it will mark the fourth anniversary of our existence as the Virginia Synod, Evangelical Lutheran Church in America. As was appropriate as we approach this anniversary, the Synod Council has been involved in a detailed review of our structure. This Synod Assembly will be afforded an opportunity to approve the restructuring plan. This restructuring plan would place responsibility for program in committees, to be reviewed by two coordinating cabinets. The committees would meet twice a year at the same time and place providing for coordination and common visioning. Furthermore, these changes would afford committees more time for in-depth program planning and will hopefully ease, at least temporarily, the over-extended nature of our staff.
>
> While the restructuring to be submitted to the Synod Assembly may not offer a permanent cure (I believe there will be need for additional staffing, either part time or full time, with the next three years), it will afford an opportunity for maximum efficient use of staff's time as well as a greater coordination among committees.[63]

The report of the Synod Council as recorded in the 1991 minutes of the assembly gives the following summary of the proposed restructuring of the synod:

    a. *Dissolve the Commissions.*

    b. *Establish Coordinating Cabinets for Congregational Life and Outreach with the following functions:*

        1. *Review schedules and work of committees to avoid overlap.*

---

61. Minutes, 4th Annual Synod Assembly, Virginia Synod/ELCA, 1991, p. 12.
62. Ibid., p. 65.
63. Ibid., pp. 11-12.

    2. *Budgeting.*
    3. *Reporting to Synod Council.*
    4. *Prepare an annual report for the Synod Assembly.*
    5. *Coordinating committee work.*
    6. *Others, as needed.*
c. Move the Ministry in Daily Life Committee from Ministry to Congregational Life.
d. Lodge program responsibility in the committees.
e. The Coordinating Cabinets and committees will meet twice a year, at the same time, for overnight meetings.
f. The Candidacy Committee and Leadership Support Committee will report directly to the Synod Council.
g. Present committees will be disbanded and the cabinets and new committee members recruited (some present members may be reappointed).
h. Expectation of/for members of committees and cabinets will be developed and a commitment to those expectations required.
i. Staff will not be committee members but will be resource persons.[64]

Three recommendations for approval of the restructuring proposals were placed by the Synod Council before the assembly for adoption of the necessary changes in the language of the bylaws and standing resolutions. All three recommendations were approved with minimal debate and only one minor amendment. Included in the adoption of the proposals was an effective beginning date of the new synod structure: September 1, 1991.

In his report to the 1991 assembly, Bansemer noted the completion of his first term as bishop.

Without so much as an inkling of regret, I must express my sincere thanks to you, the Virginia Synod, who have made it possible for me to serve in this capacity. Despite the many problems, I am forever grateful to you for this work. It takes a term as bishop to begin to understand the scope of the work, to know one's limitations and one's peculiar gifts for the tasks to be accomplished.[65]

The assembly affirmed Bansemer's work—his leadership through "turbulent swells of a new church being born"[66]—by electing him to a second four-year term as bishop on the first ballot. Of the 411 valid ballots cast, he received 349 or 84 percent, well beyond the 75 percent needed.

With a new organizational structure in place and the opportunity to serve as bishop for another four years, both the synod and its spiritual leader hoped for the promise of the future—especially, according to Bansemer,

as we prepare ourselves for the coming millennium, may we do so in the knowledge that none of us are able, in the end, to be worthy of God's constant love and attention. Nevertheless, God has chosen us, sustained us, and gives us the opportunity to serve through the sending of opportunities that are uniquely ours. Our Lord is not too proud to use us for holy work. May you and I miss fewer and fewer of these opportunities.[67]

---

64. Ibid., pp. 65-66.
65. Ibid., p. 87.
66. Ibid.
67. Ibid., p. 89.

"THAT CHRIST MAY BE SEEN—STRATEGY 2000"

In his 1994 Report of the Vice President to the Assembly, Hamlett noted, "my reflections are somewhat bittersweet." "Sweet" for him was the continued dedication and hard work of the bishop and the synod staff. "I am not sure many of us realize the tremendous number of hours given to the life of the Synod by these servants and the tremendous amount of stress that continues to relate to the Office of the Bishop."[68]

He also noted the significance of a multicultural event in the past year which he hoped would help those who attended share ways to make the synod "truly multicultural." He then added his positive assessment of seven pilot programs, five of which had been initiated as a result of the adoption at the 1993 assembly of the vision document written by Bansemer, "That Christ May Be Seen."

But it was the "bitter" that gave rise to Hamlett expressing his frustrations over three persistent problems that had plagued the synod from its beginning:

a. The financial support available for Synod Mission and Ministry continues flat. In our seven years since the founding of the Evangelical Lutheran Church in America, our yearly growth in funding to the Synod has been very minimal. This past year of 1993–1994 was the second of the last three years to have significant shortfall. An additional source of concern is that the preliminary Statements of Intent for 1994–1995 indicate that one-third of the congregations are at or above their "fair share" and two-thirds are below their "fair share."

b. A lack of ownership of Synod programs. The Synod Council has grappled for a number of years in an effort to determine what programs are most important to the congregations ... and have been unable to determine a clear sense of direction.

c. The over-extension of our professional synod staff. Many of us who served on the transition team for the Synod ten years ago reluctantly agreed to the decrease of staff from the level in the Virginia Synod, LCA days. The role of the region, in assisting this Synod, has been limited by financial constraints. The changing role of the Bishop, with greater amounts of time required for conflict and sexual abuse situations, has also heightened this overload. The Synod Council continues to view this situation with great concern and anticipates taking corrective action at its September meeting. Hopefully, growth in giving will support additional staffing.[69]

In his summary of the Synod Council's attempt to address these issues that he believed had hampered the implementation of a strong synod, Hamlett noted what he called three "short-term" responses:

1) Implement a three-year consultation process with congregations that would address their concerns and needed stronger financial support for the synod;

2) Appoint a Communications Task Group for improving communication between the synod and parishioners;

---

68. Minutes, 7th Annual Synod Assembly, Virginia Synod/ELCA, 1994, p. 13.
69. Ibid., pp. 13-14.

3) Meet with lay leadership of congregations (lay voting members from congregations) led by lay leadership of the synod during the Saturday afternoon session of the 1994 assembly.

As a result of the decision by the Synod Council to alter the program of the Synod Assembly on Saturday afternoon, oral reports from committees and task groups; auxiliaries, agencies, and institutions; Region 9 Center for Mission; and other ministries were "precluded."[70]

It is a fourth response of the Synod Council's actions that established a long-term response to these persistent issues. At its January 1994 meeting, the council established a Strategy 2000 Task Force whose task it would be to "look to the long-term implications of synodical programs and funding." The following were appointed to this long-range planning task force: Pastor Richard Carbaugh, Christ, Fredericksburg; Joe Leafe, First, Norfolk and member of the Synod Council; Pastor Martha Miller, Gravel Springs-St. John Parish, Winchester; Mark Reed, St. Mark, Luray; Kathryn Buchanan, treasurer; and Charles Williams, Ebenezer, Marion.

The task force met only once before the deadline of written reports were due for publication in time for the Synod Assembly scheduled early for May 13-15 at Roanoke College. The brief report provides understanding of its responsibility.

It will be the responsibility of "Strategy 2000" to take a look at how the Synod is relating to congregations; to examine the roles of the Synod, the Bishop and Synod staff members; and to identify and strengthen the connections of the Synod and Congregations.

The Task Force is committed to approaching its work as an inclusive process that is open to many different perspectives, that constantly seeks ways of sharing information and receiving feedback throughout the Virginia Synod, and that reflects good stewardship of synodical and congregational resources.

The Strategy 2000 Task Force will make its final report, with recommendations, to the 1995 Virginia Synod Assembly. In addition, interim reports will be provided to the Synod Council.[71]

In its report to the 1995 assembly, the task force noted use of an extensive questionnaire that was developed and distributed to over 600 members of the synod in the early summer of 1994. Interim reports were made to the Synod Council at its September and November 1994 meetings with a final report made at the January 1995 meeting.

The opening paragraphs of the final report are critical for understanding the six recommendations made to the Synod Council.

It is important to view the roles of the synod in a broad perspective, with the responsibility for implementation residing primarily in the synodical council. Although there are several roles for the synodical staff listed in the constitution under the role of the Office of the Bishop, it is the sense of this committee that the primary role of that office is to serve as spiritual leaders to clergy and congregations.

As the Bishop and staff develop healthy, supportive relationships among clergy, they are serving not only the clergy, but their individual places of mission as well. These relationships are formed and fostered through various forums for mutual support and training as well as individual staff contact with clergy and congregations.

---

70. Ibid., p. 103.
71. Ibid., p. 120.

Increasingly, the Bishop and staff are being drawn into the intricate operations of the organization and details of the administration which distracts them from their role as spiritual leaders that we all have agreed is paramount. This committee believes that it is the desire of the Bishop, his staff, and the members of the synod council that the Office of the Bishop be freed up, as far as possible, so that careful attention can be devoted to relationships with clergy and congregations.

This brings us back to our original premise that "synod" be understood in its broadest terms. The synodical organization functions best when synodical staff is freed up from direct involvement in all the committees, agencies and institutions to which we relate.[72]

The following is a summary of each of the six recommendations, specifically the action in each to address the findings stated in the opening paragraphs:

Recommendation #1: Conflict resolution and investigations are consuming large blocks of the bishop's time and, if reducing the demand of the bishop's time is a priority of the synod, the budget should make provisions for necessary professional assistance to meet this need.

Recommendation #2: The time of the bishop and staff in relating to agencies and task forces should be greatly reduced by council members serving in these liaison activities.

Recommendation #3: Council should encourage the gradual development of ownership and development of congregational life activities in local areas that support the purposes of congregational life and reduce synod-wide task forces.

Recommendation #4: Council should appoint a study group of stakeholders to carefully examine campus ministry, especially its costs and the wide disparity in the way it is done and not done at various institutions.

Recommendation #5: Council should carefully examine the relationship between the synod and agencies and institutions which it supports, with clear concern for financial support and other ways to maintain and even strengthen the relationship.

Recommendation #6: Council set as a high priority the development of the means by which members and congregations have a greater sense for ownership and responsibility of the synod's programs and services for congregations, including the development of guidelines for cost-sharing with congregations in the area of conflict counseling and cost-sharing for participants in synodical events in order to make such events as self-supporting as possible. In addition, council should contract for the professional development of the fund for mission.

In its conclusion of the report, the Strategy 2000 Task Force noted that not "all of the answers" to the many issues before the synod were contained within its report.

However, we believe that these are the first steps that the synod must take to begin the journey that will improve the synod's ability to respond to the rapidly changing needs, involve more people and develop more ownership of the ministry of the synod, provide a more effective allocation of all of the synod's resources, and, ultimately, that allow Christ to be seen in more ways, in more places, and by more people than is currently possible.[73]

---

72. Ibid., pp. 68-69.
73. Ibid., p. 70.

These words would prove to be prophetic. The steps in the journey to develop a comprehensive strategy for the future of the synod would take over three years of numerous meetings of many task groups, advisory committees, and a coordinating cabinet. In addition, significant time on the agenda would be given to study, discussion, and action on "Strategy 2000" reports at Synod Council meetings and retreats from 1996 to 1998. Reports and their conclusions as well as requests for actions would also dominate many meetings of other structural units of the synod during this time. Interim reports on the progress of these meetings, the decisions made, and the recommendations proposed were given time for discussion and action by the synod assemblies in 1996, 1997, and 1998. In his report to the 1997 assembly, Bansemer noted,

The Strategy 2000 report is before us for critique. It is the result of hundreds of hours of meetings and prayers. Still the task is not done. What is before us is not recommendations, but feedback of what we have heard you say.[74]

At a special meeting of the Synod Council in December 1996, a "draft report" was received and extensively modified by the council both in content and format. At its January 1997 meeting, final approval was given to the report and it was authorized for distribution throughout the synod before the May 30-June 1, 1997 Synod Assembly. The document had now taken the name "That Christ May Be Seen," the name of the vision statement authored by Bansemer in 1992 and approved by the council in January 1993.

More than a "strategy for mission" document, the report was, in fact, a summary of all the work done and all actions taken leading up to this point and time in the development of a "Virginia Synod Mission Strategy" that would finally be presented to the 1998 assembly as outlined in the document's timetable.

Bansemer was correct in his report that there were no specific, strategic recommendations in the document before the 1997 assembly. At the assembly, the "Strategy 2000" report would simply be presented; no debate or action would be requested by the Synod Council. Action would have to wait until the final report would be made to the 1998 assembly. Bansemer was also correct in that "Strategy 2000" as presented at the 1997 assembly was, indeed, a reflection of the long hours of listening, discussions, study, work, reflection, and prayer done by many "stakeholders" in the various groups and numerous meetings and retreats as noted above.

However, it is fair to note that Section D of the document was entitled "Recommendations" and included twenty-one "Propositions" with commentary that addressed the need for adopting a synodical mission statement, clarifying the synod's particular responsibilities in six areas of mission and ministry, and articulating what steps needed to be taken for implementation of each proposition.

The report was extensive—fifteen pages in the minutes of the 1997 assembly. These pages also included an addendum entitled "Financial Considerations" which leadership was to use in determining the "fiscal impact" of implementing each of the twenty-one propositions. Though not yet adopted by an assembly, the bishop and the Synod Council were already taking actions as recommended by

---

74. Minutes, 10th Annual Synod Assembly, Virginia Synod/ELCA, 1997, p. 14.

a working version of the document that Synod Council authorized in order to move forward with implementation of some of the more pressing issues before the synod, none more so than the need for additional staff and plans to extend geographically the Office of the Bishop.[75]

A THIRD FULL-TIME ASSISTANT AND OFFICE OF THE BISHOP IN THE EAST

The second of twenty-one propositions in the 1997 version of the proposed long-range plan, "That Christ May Be Seen—Strategy 2000," stated the following:

Proposition #2. THIRD FULL-TIME ASSISTANT. It is recommended that a third full-time assistant to the Bishop be called and deployed to the eastern part of Virginia with a job description including both program and presence no sooner than February 1, 1998.

Note: As a result of the Strategy 2000 discussion and past synodical experience, it has become clear that a third full-time assistant to the Bishop is needed. The need for more synodical staff presence as expressed by congregations, clergy and their families has been noted with care.

From the beginning of the new synod, Bansemer had made it clear that the synod was sorely understaffed. Almost every one of his reports to the annual synod assemblies noted his continuing concern for the growing and sometimes overwhelming demands being made on all the synod staff. The calling of Pastor Jean Bozeman in 1989 as a part-time third assistant to the bishop through a partnership generously funded by Lutheran Family Services of Virginia (LFS/VA) had proven helpful in the early formative years of the new synod when finances were limited. The other part of her time was to serve as director of the Office of Parish Services, a new and intentional strategy position of LFS/VA to connect with congregations in the synod. Early in this shared partnership of the two part-time positions, both the synod and LFS/VA recognized the need for both positions to become full-time. In April 1997, both partners took actions to make their respective part-time staff positions full-time.

The Synod Council's action that month was reported to the 1997 assembly in Section G, Special Items #6, Third Full-time Assistant, in a document entitled, "Report and Recommendation to the 1997 Synod Assembly—Addition of a third full-time Assistant to the Bishop of the Synod Council."[76] The four-page report gave the background, need, rationale, and other information on which the decision was made. It particularly noted the shared partnership with Lutheran Family Services, the changes anticipated in future funding sources for LFS/VA, and results of the comprehensive study of the synod's future life, mission, and ministry as reported in the long-range planning document, "Strategy 2000."

Also included in the minutes of the assembly was a copy of a resolution adopted in April 1997, "Regarding Strategy 2000 and Partnership with Virginia Synod," by the Executive Committee of Lutheran Family Services of Virginia. The resolution stated,

Whereas, the value of the Office of Parish Services as integral to the mission of Lutheran Family Services of Virginia has been demonstrated; and

---

75. Minutes, 8th Annual Synod Assembly, Virginia Synod/ELCA, 1995, pp. 68–70.
76. Minutes, 10th Annual Synod Assembly, Virginia Synod/ELCA, 1997, pp. 86–89.

Whereas, the Virginia Synod has indicated in mutual conversation with this agency and through the Strategy 2000 document that future needs of the Synod will require a full-time position to be funded by the Virginia Synod; and

Whereas, the visioning and strategic repositioning plans for Lutheran Family Services of Virginia will call for a full-time director of the Office for Parish Services with functions and responsibilities consistent with a new vision;

Therefore be it resolved, that Lutheran Family Services of Virginia will not fund the shared staff position for Assistant to the Bishop beyond the budget year 97/98 ending June 30, 1998.[77]

Bansemer made clear his support for adding a third full-time deployed staff assistant to the bishop in his report to the 1997 assembly.

This position has received the unanimous endorsement of the synod council and the unanimous endorsement of the Council of Deans. As an item of business it will come before us as a recommendation to ratify the decision of the Synod Council and adopt a budget that includes its funding.

Needless to say, I more than "endorse" this proposal. The reasons are clearly spelled out in the synod council report and I do not want to repeat the rationale here. However, I must report that I have been concerned for years about "ownership and responsibility" of our own staff time needs, and the workloads placed upon those who serve in the synod office.[78]

The agenda of the assembly placed the vote to ratify the addition of a third full-time staff person in the first meeting, Friday, May 30, 1997, 1:00-6:15 p.m. The motion from the Synod Council read, "That the Assembly ratify the decision of the Synod Council to increase the number of assistants to three full-time assistants to the bishop."[79]

Time was taken for questions and discussions. No amendments or other actions were made. The vote was taken by ballots distributed to the voting members. The results were announced followed the singing of a hymn: 343 for, 55 against, and 1 abstain. The addition of a third full-time assistant to the bishop was declared ratified.

The Rev. Jean Bozeman, upon nomination by the bishop, was called to this position by the Synod Council at its June 1, 1997 meeting immediately following the Synod Assembly. At the September 1997 meeting of the council, action was taken to deploy the third full-time staff position to the Peninsula area of the synod and to authorize the bishop and the Executive Committee to develop specific plans for that deployment. A temporary location of the Office of the Bishop-East was established at Gloria Dei Lutheran Church, Hampton. After a few months, the office moved to a more permanent location at St. Paul, Hampton. Bansemer noted in his report to the 1998 assembly,

We have had an eventful year. We have called and deployed the Rev. Dr. Jean Bozeman to the eastern part of the state to staff the Office of the Bishop-East. Her responsibilities are not limited to this part of our synod, but she will be the primary contact person for congregations and clergy in the area. She will be the primary vacancy counselor in the area, but will also have many synod-wide responsibilities including Power in the Spirit, Disaster Relief, Professional Leadership, clergy spouse retreats, and many other wide-ranging events.[80]

---

77. Ibid., pp. 88-89.
78. Ibid., p. 14.
79. Ibid., p. 88.
80. Minutes, 11th Annual Synod Assembly, Virginia Synod/ELCA, 1998, p. 12.

"STRATEGY 2000"

The calling of Bozeman as the third full-time assistant to the bishop and her deployment to the eastern part of the synod had demonstrated the value of the time and effort given to the development of a plan for the mission of the synod for the future. The final version of the long-range planning document, "That Christ May Be Seen—Strategy 2000," was placed before the 1998 assembly for debate and action. It received both.

In the Report of the Bishop to the Assembly, Bansemer wrote the following:

Six initiatives come before us at this assembly as part of the Strategy 2000 business agenda. The initiatives are not filled with detail, but rather point us in a direction to go. Strategy 2000 has already impacted the life of our synod. The launching of the Care of the Call/Care of the Soul retreats and the calling of a deployed staff person are two examples of paradigms.

When the votes are over at this assembly, we still won't be done, and changes will rightfully come before the assembly in the years to come. What all this means is that Strategy 2000 is more of a process than it is an event. It is a way to reach as much consensus as possible, "That Christ May Be Seen" as broadly as possible. Although we don't expect the document itself to come back before the assembly in years to come, surely its provisions will necessarily be altered.[81]

In her third year as the new vice president of the synod, Kathryn Buchanan echoed Bansemer's concerns for a broader, less "finished" view and more of an understanding that "Strategy 2000" is a "living document" pointing us to a greater good.

Wise people are those with good judgment who seek to make things better for the good of the whole. I ask you not to prejudge this document before you examine "ALL OF ITS PARTS." If we want to be fair to ourselves, we must leave the door open a little. We ought to enjoy reflecting, thinking, imagining, and searching for who we are and what we want to be as a Synod in the next millennium—the rest is up to God. The one responsible for making us who we are, the one who gives us the strength, the trust, and the courage to effect change.[82]

In anticipation of the debate and action on the adoption of the long-range planning document, "That Christ May Be Seen—Strategy 2000," the Synod Council authorized forums to be conducted as part of the assembly program. Forums for each of the six initiatives—Reaching Out, Trust Fund for Mission, Youth and Young Adult Ministry, Mission To and With Senior Adults, Developing a Data Bank of Resource Persons, and Coordination of Mission and Ministry Through Global Awareness, Social Ministry, and Communications—were scheduled for Saturday afternoon from 1:45 to 3:00 at different locations on the Roanoke College Campus. During the forums, the bishop met with clergy and associates in ministry to discuss the initiatives and any other items of concern.

The assembly reconvened following the forums and the first item of business was action of the "Strategy 2000" document. In Section I, Six New Initiatives—Laying New Tracks, ten amendments offering new emphases, programs, or causes for specific action, changing language to the text

---

81. Ibid., p. 13.
82. Ibid., p. 14.

of the original initiatives, or adding a new initiative were moved, seconded, and debated. Seven of the ten recommended actions were adopted, including an additional seventh initiative, which called for an intentional reaching out in mission to and with young children and infants, with three emphases calling for the appointment of a synodical task group to study the special needs of children. Intentionally promoting strong and stable marriages providing more stable and secure environments for infants and children to grow and thrive, the task group developed synodical guides for creating and fostering congregation-based daycare centers, preschools, and elementary schools.

In Section II, The Basics—The Tracks Already in Use, four amendments were made to add emphases or change language. Three were adopted and one defeated. Following the debate and votes on these amendments, the bishop ruled that the discussion and actions on "Strategy 2000" would be carried over to unfinished business.

"Strategy 2000" was the last item of business following adoption of the proposed budget for 1999 and before the report of the Transportation Committee during the sixth meeting of the assembly on Sunday, May 17, 1998. No amendments were offered to change Section III, Tracks Needing Further Study. An amendment to offer an eighth initiative, which called for reaching out in mission to middle-age adults, was defeated.[83] No further debate followed.

On behalf of the Synod Council, Bansemer took the initiative to place the following motion before the assembly:

That the Document, "That Christ May Be Seen" Strategy 2000 (as amended) be given general approval; that the Synod Council be directed to take the necessary steps for implementation; and that a progress report be given to the 1999 Synod Assembly.[84]

It had taken three and a half years to develop, revise, amend, and adopt the final draft of a long-range plan that would give direction to the synod in the last year of the twentieth century and in the future years of the new millennium just ahead. "That Christ May Be Seen—Strategy 2000" would prove to be among the most important of accomplishments of synod leadership, lay and ordained—especially the efforts of a bishop who was entering the fourth year of a six-year third term. Its adoption would be among the final actions of implementing the new Virginia Synod during the leadership of Bishop Richard F. Bansemer. Its directions for the future would sustain the synod and its moving forward with mission goals in the years to come.

THE NEED FOR CHURCH TO BE A SAFE PLACE

In his final Report of the Bishop to the Assembly in 1999, Bansemer recalls a particularly poignant observation shared with him by a colleague at the time of his election as the new bishop in May 1987.

When I was first elected bishop, a pastor of our synod told me that my work would be shaped by what came upon me, more than what I wished it to be. So it has been. I could not imagine in 1987 the changes that would come to us all.[85]

---

83. Ibid., pp. 75-78; Ibid., 92-93.
84. Ibid., p. 93.
85. Minutes, 12th Annual Synod Assembly, Virginia Synod/ELCA, 1999, p. 10.

Particularly hard for Bansemer to have imagined would be the number of clergy sexual misconduct cases that would demand so much of his time and energy. In a 2012 interview about the struggles he faced during his tenure as bishop, Bansemer shared, "Clergy misconduct was a heartbreaker, the heaviest part of my years as bishop. There were a lot of incidents, all them heart wrenching. I needed the wisdom of Solomon and the love of Jesus."

When pressed about how many incidents, Bansemer chose not to give a specific number, but acknowledged, in a 2012 interview,

There were more than a lot. I would say numerous and they were burdensome. They were very stressful, especially the ones that ended up in litigations. I was personally sued. No, I am not going to say how many times.

In the 1994 Report of the Bishop to the Assembly, Bansemer did share for the first and only time some specifics and the impact clergy misconduct was having upon the functioning of the Office of the Bishop and synod.

I do lament this: the urgent hinders the essential. The "urgent" are those sinful life-draining things that come unexpectedly to the desk of the bishop and into the life of the synod. These are things that cannot be ignored. These urgencies are most likely to be conflict in congregations and sexual abuse accusations against clergy.

Ten separate cases have been dealt with during the last term. Each of these cases can take weeks, if not months, of prayer time, emotional stress, and concern for all involved.

In a 2013 interview, Bansemer noted that the process of intervention in the early years of the synod was placed heavily upon the Office of the Bishop whenever sexual abuse and misconduct allegations of pastors were brought to his attention.

It was pretty much on me at first, as it needed to be given confidentiality and legal concerns. But the approach was changing with the ELCA having been clear about not tolerating misconduct. I discussed situations with the staff. Jean became particularly helpful in her presence with me at meetings with congregations. She was also helpful in relating the synod's pastoral care and concern to the abused party or wife of the pastor.

I also made a point of calling on legal counsel at ELCA headquarters in Chicago. I really appreciated help with the legal issues involved. Leroy Hamlett and Humes Franklin were helpful, as were Mark and Nancy Reed in the later years of my serving.

I appreciated the support of synod staff, especially their loyalty to me and the hard work they did to keep things going while I was consumed with meetings with councils and involved in depositions or legal proceedings. Keith, Jim, and Jean picked up so much of what I could not get to because of the demands of each situation. In that sense it was a real team effort.

From the beginning, the new synod had shown sensitivity to issues related to brokenness in human sexuality and especially its impact on women. In 1989, the Synod Council authorized the formation of a task group on synod structure for women with its purpose

to see how women's issues could best be handled with the synod structure. The synod council approved a recommendation from this group that an Advisory Task Group on Women be appointed by the Synod Council. Its purpose would be to evaluate the present situation, make recommendations through appropriate synod channels and to serve the synod as a resource and advocate for women's issues. Betty Kipps was appointed as chair of this Task Group.[86]

In its first report to the 1990 assembly, the advisory task group noted that among the first issues discussed at its first meeting was domestic violence. A recommendation was sent to the Commission for Outreach that a workshop on domestic violence be planned for pastors to attend and that a special bulletin insert be provided to congregations for use on a Sunday in October, "Domestic Violence Month." In 1991, the task group focused on development of a "Sexual Harassment Statement" for the synod modeled after the statement that had recently been adopted by the ELCA.

Since the ELCA churchwide organization had recently released a statement on sexual harassment to be used as a model for the Synods, the statement developed by the Task Group was an affirmation of that statement, with some additional suggestions for handling problems which might emerge. The statement was approved by the Synod Council, and mailed in January 1992 to all parishes and clergy in the Virginia Synod.

Because we feel that the issue of sexual harassment is a sensitive and important one, we do not feel that our work on this issue is complete. In conjunction with the Synod's Leadership Support committee, we are in the process of planning a series of workshops on the issue.[87]

By the time of its report to the 1993 assembly, the Advisory Task Group for Women's Issues had begun to address the issue of sexual abuse, including clergy sexual misconduct, advocating that the time had come for the church to take a leadership role. Kate Wood, chair of the task group, gave a summary of their efforts:

Our energy has primarily focused on working against sexual harassment and sexual abuse, two areas in which we believe that the church can and should take leadership. With the help of Bishop Bansemer, we are following up on the sexual harassment statement adopted by the Synod Council last year, to determine if the statement has been adopted by parishes of the synod ... working to become informed on the issue of clergy sexual misconduct, an issue of major importance to all churches and denominations.

The Rev. Jean Bozeman, through Lutheran Family Services, has gathered a group of professional counselors to serve as resources to help clergy minister to those who are victims of sexual abuse at home and elsewhere. Sexual harassment, clergy sexual misconduct, and sexual abuse are topics that make us supremely uncomfortable as church people. But it is the belief of the Advisory Task Group that the church needs to face its uncomfortable feelings and witness against these dehumanizing behaviors.[88]

Six workshops addressing the issues of sexual harassment and clergy sexual misconduct were conducted throughout the territory of the synod in the months of October, November, and December 1994. Led by Pastor Jean Bozeman, the workshops were entitled "Called to Integrity—Called to Be a Safe Place." Emphasis was placed upon understanding the professional conduct of ordained ministers and associates in ministry as outlined in the governing documents of the ELCA, "Vision and Expectations," "Ordained Ministers in the Evangelical Lutheran Church in America, 1990," and "Visions and Expectations, Associates in Ministry Candidates,

---

86. Minutes, 2nd Annual Synod Assembly, Virginia Synod/ELCA, 1989, p. 98.
87. Minutes, 5th Annual Synod Assembly, Virginia Synod/ELCA, 1992, p. 115.
88. Minutes, 6th Annual Synod Assembly, Virginia Synod/ELCA, 1993, p. 93.

Interim Document, 1990." Training was given in response to reports of sexual harassment and sexual abuse that may be made by a member to the pastor or member of the staff of a congregation. The process of responding to allegations made to the bishop was reviewed and clarified, making clear the intention of the synod, along with the support of the ELCA, not to tolerate any form of sexual harassment or sexual misconduct by pastors and other persons in leadership positions.

In an interview with Bozeman in 2013, she noted,

The workshops were well attended by pastors and well received. These were good conferences intended to educate pastors on how to handle issues of sexuality and how misconduct allegations would be dealt with by the church, especially in our synod. Lots of written resources were shared, intended to help pastors by making them more aware of the issues of sexual harassment and misconduct.

At the 1996 assembly, a resolution on clergy misconduct—Resolution 5.0—was received from the Committee on Reference and Counsel and placed before the assembly without comment or recommended action from the committee. No record is given of the author or origin of the resolution. The resolution reads as follows:

Whereas, clergy sexual misconduct is a manifestation of sin in the world, and a betrayal of trust which may cause significant hurt and pain for all involved;

Whereas, we of the ELCA believe in the Gospel of Jesus Christ which promises forgiveness and reconciliation to all who sin;

Therefore be it resolved that we uphold the ELCA's commitment to continue to take clergy sexual misconduct seriously;

Be it further resolved that the Virginia Synod continue to keep open means for reconciliation and to care and pray for victims, congregations, clergy, and bishop.

Be it further resolved that we commend to congregations the resource for members of the ELCA produced by the Division for Ministry entitled SAFE Connections by the Rev. Jan Erickson-Pearson, which discusses what parishioners can do to understand and prevent clergy sexual abuse, and that a similar publication be prepared for clergy, AIMS, and all other rostered persons.[89]

The Synod Council reported to the 1997 assembly that the Executive Committee of the council referred the resolution of the Virginia Synod on clergy misconduct to the Division for Ministry for response directly to the synod.

In the 2013 interview, Bansemer admitted that the "tidal waves" of clergy misconduct impacted his health. "I did suffer. Each incident impacted my life, my ministry. So many were hurt." In a concluding paragraph of his final report to the assembly, Bansemer wrote, "Though there has been heartbreak through the years, in every instance God sent people to be with people who needed someone to show them the incarnate love of Christ."

---

89. Minutes, 9th Annual Synod Assembly, Virginia Synod/ELCA, 1996, p. 94.

A FINAL ELECTION AND RETIREMENT

The 1993 assembly of the ELCA in Kansas City approved changes to churchwide and synodical constitutions increasing the years in a term of a synodical bishop from four to six. Bansemer would finish his second four-year term 1995. The next term of the bishop of the synod would be for six years.

The first ballot for bishop was conducted at the end of the first meeting of the eighth annual assembly of the Virginia Synod of the Evangelical Lutheran Church in America on Friday, May 19, 1995. Bansemer turned the "chair" of the assembly over to Vice President Hamlett, who explained that for the election of a bishop the first ballot served as the nominating ballot and 75 percent of the ballots cast were needed for election. Pastor Chip Gunsten, chaplain of this portion of the assembly, offered a prayer for trust and guidance.

The Report of the Committee on the Conduct of Elections was among the first items of business of the third meeting of the assembly following morning worship on Saturday.

Number of Ballots Cast	387
Number of Valid Ballots	381
Number of Votes Needed for Election	286

Bansemer received 257 votes (67 percent), twenty-nine votes short of the 75 percent needed. The remaining ninety-five votes were distributed among thirty-nine names. Declaring no election on the first ballot, Hamlett called for distribution of the second ballot following a prayer offered by Gunsten. The results of the second ballot for bishop were reported during the course of the third business meeting on Saturday morning.

Number of Ballots Cast	415
Number of Valid Ballots	415
Number of Votes Needed for Election	312

Bansemer received 283 votes (68 percent), twenty-nine votes short of the 75 percent needed for election on the second ballot. The remaining 132 votes were distributed among twenty-six of the thirty-nine names from the first ballot with twenty-one votes going to the next-highest nominee. Declaring no election on the second ballot, rules for election called for the names of the top seven vote receivers to be the only names eligible for election on the third ballot, which required two-thirds of the votes cast for election. Hamlett called for the distribution of the third ballot for bishop by listing the following names in order of the number of votes received.

Richard Bansemer

Jean Bozeman

James Mauney

James Cobb

Robert Humphrey

Gary Schroeder

J. Christopher Price

A motion was made that candidates for bishop be allowed to speak before the next ballot was cast. The motion was seconded and amended to read "nominees" instead of "candidates." The motion was defeated. The third ballot was cast following a prayer once again offered by Gunsten.

The results of the third ballot were reported by Robert Poole, chair of the Committee for the Conduct of Elections during the first part of the fourth meeting on Saturday afternoon, May 20.

Number of Ballots Cast	417
Number of Valid Ballots	416
Number of Votes Needed for Elections	278 (66%)

Bansemer received 280 votes, 67 percent of the votes cast. Having received the required number of votes cast, Hamlett declared Bansemer elected as bishop. The minutes note that Bansemer spoke to the assembly and asked his wife Mary Ann to join him. Elected for the third time as bishop, Bansemer "offered a prayer of acceptance and service."

† † †

Throughout his years as bishop, Bansemer revealed a heart of compassion for Christ and His Church—a heart that was strong for the gospel and caring of God's people. A self-described "spiritual pilgrim," he cherished times of solitude and reflection. To comfort his soul and renew his heart and mind, he wrote books of prayers and reflections on spiritual themes during his tenure as bishop. Yet, he had no choice but to be a public figure and attend to issues of administration of a new synod and the consequences of human brokenness. As a pilgrim he had to travel too many miles to attend too many meetings and spend too much time away from his wife, Mary Ann, and their home of peace and quiet on a mountaintop.

In the medium of words, he worked hard at preaching works of verbal art proclaiming God's love and forgiveness in Jesus Christ. Among his deepest desires was the building up of the body of Christ as a synod and within each of its congregations. Yet he had to enforce policies, follow constitutional guidelines, and administer the discipline of the church in circumstances of communal brokenness that he witnessed too closely too many times in his years as bishop. All of these were experienced by him and many others as times of "tearing down the body of Christ," often as the result of the betrayal of relationships because of the depths of human sin, particularly in the arena of human sexuality. In them all he offered guidance and spoke reassuring words to those hurt and suffering. These broken experiences of others—many close to him over his years as a friend to some, colleague to others, but bishop to all—cut Bansemer to the quick. There came a time when his heart could no longer bear all that was demanded of him.

In January 1999, Bansemer unexpectedly announced his intention to retire effective August 31, only four years into his six-year term. In his letter he said he would be "open to God's call in new ways." He noted that a new bishop "can see the vision and have major input in carrying out the synod's Strategy 2000."

In April, Bansemer had a heart attack. Two stents were implanted by angioplasty to open up the arteries of his heart.

In his last report to the assembly, Bansemer stated,

The years have been about people journeying together. They have been about people trying their best to let the light of Christ shine out from them, that Christ may be seen. They have been about people learning to care as much about mission as ministry.

To all the laity and clergy, deans, council members, and saints throughout the whole church, grace be to you for belonging to Jesus Christ, and for being bold enough to show it.

Richard F. Bansemer, Bishop[90]

---

90. Minutes, 12th Annual Synod Assembly, Virginia Synod/ELCA, 1999, p. 11.

CHAPTER 4

SUSTAINING THE VIRGINIA SYNOD

1999–2012 and Beyond

ELECTING THE NEXT BISHOP

Bishop Richard F. Bansemer's unexpected announcement in January 1999 of his intention to retire at the end of August changed the focus of that year's annual Synod Assembly. It would not be business as usual for the 485 registered voting members gathered for the twelfth annual assembly of the Virginia Synod of the Evangelical Lutheran Church in America (ELCA) to be held at Roanoke College, Salem, June 4-6. "That Christ May Be Seen—Strategy 2000" would not dominate the agenda as it had three previous assemblies. Now it would be the electing of the next bishop—a new bishop to lead the synod into the new millennium.

The Rev. Dr. Lowell G. Almen, secretary of the ELCA, was present to represent the ELCA and preside over the process of electing a bishop. Early in the first meeting of the assembly on Friday afternoon, Almen addressed the voting members regarding the importance of the Office of the Bishop and the process of casting ballots. Following his comments, Pastor William Boldin, chaplain of the assembly for the day, offered a prayer after which Bansemer called upon Leroy Hamlett, chair of the Committee on Elections, to distribute the first ballot—the nominating ballot—for bishop. The last item of business during the first meeting was the report of the results of the first ballot.

Number of Ballots Cast	442
Number of Valid Ballots	435
Number of Votes Needed for Election	327 (75%)

The votes were distributed among fifty names nominated:

James Mauney	158	Frederick Donahoe	2
Jean Bozeman	37	William Hall	2
James Utt	36	Paul Henrickson	2
J. Christopher Price	27	Robert Humphrey	2
Dwayne Westermann	22	Darla Kincaid	2

James Cobb	21	Paul Orso	2
Mark Graham	15	Thomas Prinz	2
Frank Senn	11	Harold Uhl	2
Thomas Bosserman	10	James Bangle	1
George Sims	10	Henry Boschen	1
Terry Clark	9	Dennis Bucholz	1
Frank Honeycutt	6	John Byerly	1
Douglas Stowe	5	Judy Cobb	1
Paul G. Gunsten	4	Thomas Frizzell	1
Gary Schroeder	4	C. Marcus Engdahl	1
Lawrence Shoberg	4	Robert Holley	1
John Herman	3	John Lilly	1
William Nabers	3	Steve Ridenhour	1
Richard Olson	3	Kenneth Ruppar	1
Edward Schaack	3	Wayne Shelor	1
Joseph Vought	3	Russell Siler	1
William Boldin	2	David Stacy	1
Duane Carlson	2	Terri Sternberg	1
Richard Carbaugh	2	William Stewart	1
David Delaney	2	Robert Ward	1

No election was declared and the assembly recessed for dinner. There was little doubt what would be the primary topic of discussion at dinner and throughout the evening before the second ballot would be cast early in the third meeting on Saturday morning.

Following a prayer offered by Pastor Lynn Bechdolt, chaplain of the assembly for the day, Bansemer called on Hamlett to distribute the second ballot for bishop, which had been reduced from fifty to fifteen names. The results of the second ballot were reported during the fourth meeting of the assembly on Saturday afternoon.

Number of Ballots Cast	466
Number of Valid Ballots	466
Number of Votes Needed for Election	350 (75%)

The votes were distributed among fifteen names:

James Mauney	220	William Nabers	4
James Utt	48	Joseph Vought	3
Dwayne Westermann	43	Henry Boschen	2
Terry Clark	36	Paul Gunsten	2
J. Christopher Price	36	Duane Carlson	1
James Cobb	35	David Delaney	1
Mark Graham	20	Paul Henrickson	1
Frank Senn	14		

Declaring no election, Bansemer called upon Almen, who asked the seven pastors with the highest votes on the second ballot to come forward to give a five-minute speech to the assembly. "O God, Our Help, in Ages Past," was sung as the seven pastors came forward.

After speeches were given and a prayer offered by Bechdolt, the third ballot for bishop was distributed. The results of the third ballot were announced within minutes.

Number of Ballots Cast	470		
Number of Valid Ballots	469		
Number of Votes Needed for Election	313 (66%)		
James Mauney	182	James Utt	46
Dwayne Westermann	81	James Cobb	32
J. Christopher Price	67	Terry Clark	15
Mark Graham	46		

Declaring no election, Bansemer called upon Almen to moderate the "question and answer" period of the three pastors who received the highest vote total on the third ballot. Questions were selected from those submitted by voting members of the assembly. Numbers were drawn to determine the order of response—Price, Westermann, Mauney—to each question asked of the three pastors.

Following the "question and answer" period, prayer was offered once more by Bechdolt and the fourth ballot was cast late on Saturday afternoon. The assembly recessed for dinner and gathered later for an evening service of Holy Communion with Ordination at St. Andrew's Roman Catholic Church, Roanoke.

The results of the fourth ballot were announced following worship and the report of the Committee on Minutes during the sixth meeting of the assembly on Sunday morning, June 6, 1999, the day a new bishop would be elected.

Bishop Jon Anderson, Southwest Minnesota Synod; Bishop Emeritus Richard Bansemer; and Bishop James Mauney prepare for worship at St. Andrew's Catholic Church, Roanoke.

Number of Ballots Cast	466
Number of Valid Ballots	465
Number of Votes Needed for Election	279 (60%)
James Mauney	224
Dwayne Westermann	149
J. Christopher Price	92

Declaring no election on the fourth ballot, Bansemer called for the distribution of the fifth ballot, which would have the names of the two pastors with the highest number of votes. Pastor Bill Kinser, preacher for the morning worship service, offered the prayer before the fifth ballot was distributed. A panel discussion on the theme of the assembly, "That Christ May Be Seen—Our Church in a Hungry World," was the only item of business before the results of the fifth ballot were announced by Hamlett.

Number of Ballots Cast	449
Number of Ballots Valid	449
Number of Votes Needed for Election	225 (Simple Majority)
James Mauney	282
Dwayne Westermann	167

Having received the required number of votes cast, Bansemer declared the Rev. James F. Mauney elected as bishop of the Virginia Synod of the Evangelical Lutheran Church in America. Bishop-elect Mauney was then introduced to the assembly along with his wife, Lynda. Mauney spoke to the assembly and offered a prayer.

Reflecting upon his election years later, Mauney shared in an interview,

I was willing to put my name forward, but I did not anticipate being elected—not with all the capable pastors I knew out there in the synod. If I were elected, so be it. Leading up to the assembly I kept asking myself what was I afraid of. I didn't want to look back and regret that I had ducked the call of the Spirit by not letting my name go forward. If elected, I would serve. If not, I could go back to the parish. I mean I loved being a parish pastor.

Mauney also recalls what he believes was for him a turning point in the balloting process.

When asked what I would do when a misconduct situation was made known to me, I quickly answered, "The first thing I will do is call Richard." There was a moment of light laughter to my response. Then I said I would call Phil Harris [ELCA legal counsel in Chicago], *and then I would call Jean and then I would try to get the facts and have a team approach to the situation.*

That response would prove to be an insight to Mauney's style of leadership and a key to accomplishing much of the work of the Office of the Bishop that he would face in sustaining the mission and ministry of the synod in the years ahead. Mauney would ask those known and well experienced in the work of the synod to serve on his staff. He would develop strong partnerships with the deans of the synod's eleven conferences. He would be intentional in developing teams of pastors and lay leaders as well as bringing together executives of institutions and ministries of the synod to form coalitions of partners in the broader work of sustaining the synod.

In its twelfth year, the synod was poised to move forward with implementing a strong mission strategy for the future led by a new bishop who would, as Bansemer had noted in the letter announcing his retirement, "see the vision and have major input in carrying out the synod's Strategy 2000." A new synod implemented by its first bishop would be sustained by its second.

A former assistant now elected bishop knew what would be expected of him and the office. Elected fifteen days short of his forty-seventh birthday, Mauney would bring new energy and fresh enthusiasm to the Office of the Bishop. His election confirmed his previous work on the synod staff and entrusted him with the synod's future direction.

BUILDING THE TEAM

Mauney moved quickly to build his team of assistants. He did not hesitate to turn to those he knew well and with whom he already had trusted working relationships. Within hours of his election, Mauney asked Keith Brown and Pastor Jean Bozeman to continue as assistants to the Office of the Bishop. Having worked closely with both during the past twelve years, he was confident of their ability to work well together and continue a strong team approach in leading and managing the synod. He also knew that both would provide the experienced leadership and the continuity of working relationships needed with key lay leaders. Their leadership would be necessary to build upon and sustain the mission and ministry the three of them had helped Bansemer and the Synod Council to achieve, especially in drafting and adopting of the long-range plan, "That Christ May Be Seen—Strategy 2000."

Brown would continue to oversee financial matters and manage synod office operations, providing a seamless transition in administrative functions and continued confidence in fiscal management. Brown would work closely with the Finance and Budget Committee, the Synod Missions Committee, and manage the synod office.

Bozeman would continue in the newly established Office of the Bishop-East, sustaining a key component of the long-range plan for providing a stronger presence of the synod in the Richmond, Peninsula, and Tidewater conferences. Mauney would call upon Bozeman to continue in assisting congregations in these conferences during the call process for new pastoral leadership and in providing guidance in times of conflict. She would also continue her work with the Worship, Christian Education, and Leadership Support committees. As with Bansemer, Bozeman would prove to be particularly helpful in assisting Mauney in the development of a team approach for responding to reports of clergy misconduct. Bozeman would also continue her work in rostered leaders wellness emphasis and lay leadership development, as well as planning and implementing faith formation events and programs for adults such as Power in the Spirit and Rostered Leaders Spouse retreats.

Mauney moved just as quickly to choose a pastor he knew well to take his place and be the third assistant to the bishop. The morning following his election he visited Pastor Paul Gerhard "Chip" Gunsten in his office at St. Philip in northeast Roanoke. In an August 2012 interview Gunsten recalled Mauney's opening line giving the reason for his visit: "I want to offer you an invitation to a call that will turn your world upside down if you accept it."

Mauney made the offer hoping that Gunsten would accept. After conversations and prayers with his wife, Kris, daughters Sarah and Anna, and a few conversations with some trusted friends and colleagues, Gunsten accepted Mauney's invitation to join the bishop's team before the end of the week.

PAUL GERHARD GUNSTEN—FROM PARISH PASTOR TO ASSISTANT TO THE BISHOP

Paul Gerhard "Chip" Gunsten's early years of growing in the faith took place in the "cradle" of Virginia Lutheranism—the Shenandoah Valley. He was baptized at Muhlenberg Lutheran Church, Harrisonburg, and he fondly remembered the family's participation in the life of the congregation during his formative years of faith. He was confirmed at Luther Memorial, Blacksburg, not long after his father accepted a position in the sports department at Virginia Tech. During his youth, he became a "summer camper" at the synod's Caroline Furnace Lutheran Camp in Fort Valley. He had the distinction of being its first CIT—counselor in training—a program to encourage campers to become future summer staff at the camp. The CIT program had been initiated by a summer program director at Caroline Furnace, Dwayne Westermann, with whom Gunsten had developed a close friendship while Westermann, a student at Virginia Tech, volunteered time as a youth worker at Luther Memorial.

The Rev. Paul G. "Chip" Gunsten

During the summers of his college years, also at Virginia Tech, Gunsten served as "water front director" at the camp and made many friends with fellow staff. Among the closest of these friends was Paul Henrickson, whom Gunsten would ask to serve with him on the summer staff at Koinonia, a large, year-round Lutheran camp and retreat center in the Delaware River Valley just north of New York City. Little did they know that years later both would be ordained colleagues in the Virginia Synod, serving together as part of a strong team of pastors who worked with Mauney in the early years of the new synod, planning and leading youth events, especially Winter Celebration, which witnessed dramatic increases in popularity and attendance during the early years of the new synod.

A graduate of Luther-Northwestern Seminary in St. Paul, Minnesota, Gunsten returned to his home synod upon receiving and accepting a call to become the associate pastor at Grace, Winchester, beginning in July 1985. In an interview years later, Gunsten expressed his belief that his return to Virginia to become a parish pastor and an assistant to the bishop was an act of God and the grace of the Lutheran church which had not given up on him.

Gunsten had become well known to Mauney first as a colleague in parish ministry at Grace and then as pastor of St. Philip, a congregation in need of strong pastoral leadership when the congregation called him as pastor in the spring of 1990. In addition to working well together on various synod tasks, the two developed a solid friendship and sense of partnership.

During his years as pastor of St. Philip, Mauney witnessed Gunsten's energy for ministry, positive leadership style, and pastoral skills in working with youth and adults. He was the right pastor at the right time for St. Philip. In his nine years as their pastor, Gunsten brought dramatic changes to a struggling congregation yearning to grow. The church grew in membership and worship attendance and expanded its education and fellowship programs for all ages. Following its move to new facilities built on a prime mission site on U.S. Route 11 northeast of Roanoke, the congregation developed a reputation for reaching out in service to the surrounding community, which included Hollins University where Gunsten was ordained in the campus chapel during the Virginia Synod/LCA convention in June 1985.

Mauney knew the dedication and down-to-earth character of his towering six-foot-seven colleague. Mauney also knew he was a well-loved pastor, respected colleague, and trusted friend to many pastors and members of congregations throughout the synod. From day one following his election, Mauney was confident Gunsten would be the right assistant at the right time. Gunsten would work with the Global Missions, Social Action, Stewardship of Life, Evangelism, and Candidacy committees of the synod, as well as with youth, pastors, and lay leaders in providing leadership for youth events and with the synod Lutheran Youth Organization.

†††

In his first written report to the Synod Assembly, Mauney shared the following about his team of assistants and the particular strengths they brought to the Office of the Bishop:

I love the Virginia Synod, its people, its clergy, its congregations, its institutions, its special history. I, therefore, have done my best to provide a strong team in the synod office for ministry and planning for the Virginia Synod and for serving the people of the synod. I am grateful that Mr. Keith Brown, our wise maintainer of constitution and synodical rolls and wizard of details and numbers, has remained on the synod staff so that our transition did not miss a beat in terms of the on-going very important administration of our synod. I give great thanks that the Rev. Jean Bozeman agreed to remain at the Office of the Bishop East where she provides ever-present help and support to our congregations and continues to undergird many ministries of our synod. It has been such a joy to have the Rev. Paul (Chip) Gunsten agree to serve in the synod as well! He, too, is a gift to us for he serves so pastorally, and he does all my previous areas of ministry better than I ever did already! All three provide me with outstanding, wise counsel in the many issues and events that arise in the life of the synod.[1]

In the same report, Mauney also notes with appreciation others who had served the synod and would continue to be part of the bishop's "team" in the synod office: Sue Dugas, Rosemary Thompson, Billie Hall, Debbie Worley, and Lenae Osmondson, administrative office staff, who "do the work of many and serve many in the synod." He also noted appreciation for the "mission-mindedness" of Pastor Hank Boschen, Division of Outreach/ELCA staff person, and Mr. Jim Taylor, who "truly personifies stewardship" as the staff person for stewardship from the ELCA. In addition, Mauney noted his appreciation for the officers of the synod: Kathryn Buchanan, vice president, "for her 13 years of experience as an officer of the synod"; Mark Reed, secretary, who "provides us excellent legal counsel as well"; and Martha Edwards, synod treasurer, who "brings a wealth of synodical leadership to her service!" Mauney also offered words of appreciation to the synod for electing "a superb Synod Council that works together well and who challenges us all to be about mission in the name of Christ!"[2]

---

1. Minutes, 13th Annual Synod Assembly, Virginia Synod/ELCA, 2000, p. 15.
2. Ibid.

THE INSTALLATION OF BISHOP JAMES F. MAUNEY

The Rev. James Foltz Mauney was installed as the second bishop of the Virginia Synod of the Evangelical Lutheran Church in America on Saturday, September 11, 1999, at First Presbyterian Church, Waynesboro, Virginia. Over 800 Lutherans from across Virginia, including more than one hundred youth, attended. Bishops of the North Carolina, South Carolina, and Florida-Bahamas synods of the ELCA and many other ecumenical guests were also present and assisted in various ways in the Service of Holy Communion with the Installation of a Bishop.

Bishop Mauney receives the pectoral cross from Bishop Bansemer.

The Rev. Dr. H. George Anderson, presiding bishop, Evangelical Lutheran Church in America, presided and preached. Kathryn Buchanan, vice president of the synod, served as the assisting minister. Mark Reed, secretary of the synod, presented Mauney for his installation and also presented for installation the assistants to the bishop and the deans of the conferences. Lectors were members of Bishop Mauney's family: Pastor J. Luther Mauney, Jr., cousin, first reading; Pastor H. Alvin Kuhn, uncle by marriage, second reading; and Pastor Marshall F. Mauney, father, gospel reading. Shari Shull, minister of music, Christ Lutheran Church, Staunton, served as the organist/music director, assisted by Lavelva Stevens, music director at Holy Trinity, Wytheville, providing musical leadership a second time for the installation of the synod's bishop. Numerous youth assisted in the service and over one hundred young people participated by singing popular songs from synod youth events as the offertory. A new Virginia Synod banner was designed by Andrew Bansemer. Peg Chapman, Gravel Springs-St. John, Winchester, made new communion pottery for the service. Vicki DeVilbiss, Celebration Art, provided the paraments for the day. Ruth Fendley, St. John, Roanoke, baked the bread. Pastor John McCandlish, Christ, Radford, served as coordinator for the worship.

Newly installed Bishop Mauney with Presiding Bishop H. George Anderson.

Virginia Synod † 117

It was especially meaningful for Mauney and the others present to have Anderson preside and preach given his long association with the Virginia Synod. As a professor of church history from 1958 to 1970, he had taught many of the pastors serving in Virginia, including Mauney, who graduated from Lutheran Theological Southern Seminary in Columbia, South Carolina, Class of 1978. Anderson had served with distinction as president of the seminary from 1970 to 1982 and continued giving lectures on the Lutheran Confessions and church history during his tenure as president. Throughout the church, Anderson was highly regarded as a scholar and teacher, theologian and ecumenist, author and church leader.

In his sermon, Anderson placed Mauney in a historic line of synod leadership. He recalled by name past leaders of the synod that he knew well and had served the synod with distinction.

Luther Mauney, Virgil Moyer, Richard Bansemer, variously gifted. Each of them God's answer to the particular time and place for the synod. A bishop needs many gifts. It's a big job. The bishop is God's steward. To be steward of God means to help people to use their gifts for God's purpose—to strengthen, guide, encourage and support the pastors and congregations. This is the day in which the whole church joins with you in recognizing the choice that you have made with the blessings we now pray that God will bestow on your next bishop.[3]

New to the installation service was the transfer of the synod's pectoral cross. Commissioned by the Synod Council in 1988 and given to Bansemer to wear during his tenure as bishop, the gold cross with an amethyst stone is a slightly smaller replica of the pectoral cross worn by the presiding bishop of the ELCA. Now it would be Bansemer who would pass the symbol of the office on to Mauney with these words printed in the installation service booklet:

Bishop Mauney, it is with joy that the synodical pectoral cross is placed around your neck to lay next to your heart. May your soul always cling to God; but remember it is God's right hand that holds you fast. An admonition: The golden cross, mined from the earth, purified in fire, is a reminder of Christ rising from the grave. Wear it to reflect his love for us, and to remind us all that grace happens because God is good.[4]

Reflecting on this particular moment in his installation, Mauney shared the following in an interview in 2012:

I can remember the tears in Richard's eyes as he placed the cross on me, not because of his joy for me, but because he knew better than anyone the burdens and demands that would be on my shoulders and in my hands in the years ahead. I was very touched by his emotions and concern for me.

---

3. "Bishop Anderson installs Mauney as next synod bishop, Sept. 11," *The Lutheran*, Virginia Synod Supplement, December 1999, front page.
4. Service Booklet, "Holy Communion and Service of Installation—Office of the Bishop, Virginia Synod/ELCA," First Presbyterian Church, Waynesboro, VA, Sept. 11, 1999, pp. 14-15.

Also included in the service were the Installation of Assistants to the Bishop and the Installation of Conference Deans.[5] The newly installed bishop presided at both. Secretary of the synod Mark Reed presented the assistants: Pastor Jean Bozeman, Mr. Keith Brown, and Pastor Paul G. Gunsten. Following their installation, Reed presented the following pastors appointed to serve as conference deans: William W. Boldin, Tidewater; John F. Byerly, Jr., Richmond; R. Nicholas Eichelberger, Page; Mark A. Graham, Southern; Arthur J. Henne, Southern Valley; Robert H. Jones, Northern Valley; H. Alvin Kuhn, Peninsula; John W. McCandlish, New River; Steven P. Ridenhour, Highlands; George L. Sims, Central Valley; and William T. Stewart, Germanna.

These "installations within an installation" were more than symbolic of changes in staff and leadership within the synod. Including both reflected what would be Mauney's emphasis on "team" and "partnership" in accomplishing the mission and ministry of the synod in the years to come.

It is also important to note a particular petition within The Prayers that followed the installations—a petition reflecting the new bishop's continuing commitment to the youth of the synod:

We remember with thanksgiving the stories of Joseph, of David, of Ruth, and Mary; youth who were used by you, O Lord, to be a blessing to the nations, to be models of faith, and to be pregnant with your Word. We give thanks for the youth of our synod, and we pray for all youth among us and in our communities who are in need of your Spirit's presence for their formation and their life. We pray that we might listen to the visions of faith that our youth proclaim; that we might be excited by their enthusiasm; that we might give thanks for their joy and be sensitive to their concerns and sorrows. We give thanks for the Lutheran Youth Organization, and for the ministry of congregations and synod with and among our youth.[6]

The offering from the service was designated to go to the synod's Youth-to-Youth Project to raise funds for the renovation of the Martin Luther Seminary Elementary School which serves the children and youth of the Islands District, companion synod of the Evangelical Lutheran Church in Papua New Guinea.

Following the service, a reception was held in the fellowship hall of First Baptist Church, just across the street.

Reflecting on his installation as bishop in his 2012 interview, Mauney recalled,

It was a great day at Waynesboro—all the people and all the youth. I saw myself being installed, not consecrated as some talk about it. I always had what I would call a "low order" view of the bishop, one who is a servant of servants, installed to serve pastors, have pastors come to Virginia to be stronger, deeper; build up ministries; honor and encourage healthy leadership and healthy congregations. To sustain the people where they are. I recognized the office was bigger than me.

---

5. Ibid., pp. 15-18.
6. Ibid., p. 19.

AMBASSADORS FOR CHRIST

"So we are ambassadors for Christ, since God is making his appeal through us" (2 Corinthians 5:20a, NRSV). These words of St. Paul gave title to Bishop Mauney's first written report to the 2000 Synod Assembly. To be certain, this was not some new idea Mauney had for a different vision of the synod. He quoted the verse during his turn for the "five-minute speech" given by the seven pastors who had received the highest numbers of votes on the second ballot for bishop. And whether or not it influenced Mauney when serving as an assistant, it is of interest to note that Bansemer had referenced the importance of being ambassadors for God's mission in Christ to the modern world in his 1992 report to the Synod Assembly.

For Mauney, "Ambassadors for Christ" gave focus to what would be his emphasis as the new bishop of the synod. In his first written report to the synod in assembly this focus is clearly articulated:

You elected a bishop who loves the Virginia Synod and the ELCA, loves the people of the synod, has a high respect for all the Ministerium of the synod, who believes every pastor should know two books through and through—the Bible and the Book of Concord—who believes most strongly in the external Word!, who believes that the church must be transformed into congregations that intentionally develop "ambassadors for Christ," who understands most emphatically that God is making an appeal through them to God's World because God loves the world, who believes that our institutions are our ambassadors, who believes in the ecumenical movement so that the world may believe that the Father has sent the Son! (John 17), who believes that we dare not lose touch with the poor, the weak, and the hungry, who has a great love for our children and youth and young adults!

"Ambassadors for Christ" became part of the synod's official letterhead and referenced constantly in issues of the synod's communication instruments, *Journey Together* and *Virginia Lutheran*. It has been in the theme title of every Synod Assembly beginning in 2001, "Ambassadors for Christ—Pardon Our Dust, Disciples Under Construction." Every written Report of the Bishop to the Assembly has highlighted the role of an ambassador as a way for every member to understand their role in a particular call to mission or emphasis in the life of the church. His report to the 2002 assembly offers insight into Mauney's maturing view of the role of "ambassadors for Christ" in the life of the synod:

An ambassador is one who is sent to represent the one who sends them. The ambassador lives among those who do not know the land or kingdom that the ambassador represents, but they catch a glimpse of what the ambassador's president or king must be like by what they hear and see in the ambassador. The ambassador personifies the king and the kingdom that sent the ambassador.

In 2 Corinthians, the use of the word "ambassador" is not so much a title as it is the active functioning to represent Christ! "We are representers of Christ! God making his appeal through us!"[7]

---

7. Minutes, 15th Annual Synod Assembly, Virginia Synod/ELCA, 2002, p. 11.

In a 2012 interview about his emphasis on "Ambassadors for Christ," he noted:

Ambassadors represent the life of the church and seemed to be the best image in scripture that would be consistent with the synod's doing mission. I thought we did not need to go from image to image, idea to idea or some new cause or effort each year. We had that, especially in the early years of the ELCA and synod with MISSION90 and other emphases of our own.

We were not shifting the primary focus from Mission 2000 and the initiatives. I wanted us to see ourselves as ambassadors—everyone sharing and teaching the faith, creating another layer of lay leadership in the synod. We never have enough lay leaders.

"Ambassadors for Christ" would become more than Mauney's mantra in his years as bishop. It would be his clear and consistent reminder to the pastors and members of the congregations of the synod to see themselves as the church, the body of Christ, engaged in mission where they were planted in their lives of faith—home, church, community, vocation—in those everyday places where God is making his appeal through us for Christ and his church.

The mission field is no longer thousands of miles away, the mission field is your home, your workplace, your neighborhood, your school! And the ambassador is no longer the missionary you send away, the ambassador is now YOU sent as a missionary/envoy to places very near and close to you!

Every good ambassador does two things:

1) the ambassador returns again and again to listen, learn, to be equipped, and enjoy bringing the life and presence of the one who sends them, the ambassador is RENEWED in this returning.

2) the ambassador goes to bring the light and life of the one who sent them into the world, the ambassador is RENEWED in this going and serving.

How is your congregation equipping you to be an ambassador for Christ?[8]

20/20 VISION GOALS

In addition to quoting 2 Corinthians 5:20a and introducing his mission and ministry focus for the synod if elected bishop, Mauney also shared a set of "20/20 Vision Goals" during his five-minute speech at the 1999 assembly. Using familiar optometric language for measuring eyesight, he articulated a set of goals measurable by "twenties" to be obtained by the year 2020.

The following listing of those goals was recorded in Mauney's written report to the 2002 Synod Assembly:

Let me offer some "20s" for our 2020 vision. By 2020 we will seek to have:

1) 20 year old young adults who are ambassadors for Christ, WILLING AND ABLE TO SHARE THE FAITH WITH OTHERS OUTSIDE THE WALLS OF THE CONGREGATION!

2) 20% growth in worship attendance in every congregation.

3) 200% growth in adult Christian education in every congregation.

4) 20 new mission starts.

5) 20 million dollars in our Trust Fund for Mission.

---

8. Ibid.

6) 20 candidates a year for full-time service in the Church.

7) 20 congregations a year participating in Healthy Congregation Seminar.

8) 20 x 2 congregations revitalized.

9) 20% as a congregational goal for giving to the wider Church.

10) 20% Lutheran students at Roanoke College.

11) 200 Lutheran youth a year participating in an intensive Christian leadership/formation track in their congregations as junior and seniors in high school.

12) 20 spiritual retreats happening around the synod each year.[9]

He acknowledged in a 2012 interview, "I got a little too carried away with the goals. I recognize that some were way too steep. But they were just that—a vision of goals with twenty years to accomplish them."

Over time, some goals were adjusted and new ones added that reflected new realities facing the synod. A set of 20/20 goals in the manual for the 2012 "Orientation for Rostered Leaders New to the Virginia Synod, ELCA" reflects these changes.

1) 20 year old young adults who are ambassadors for Christ, WILLING AND ABLE TO SHARE THE FAITH WITH OTHERS OUTSIDE THE WALLS OF THE CONGREGATION!

2) 20% growth in worship attendance in every congregation.

3) 200% growth in adult Christian education in every congregation.

4) 20% as a congregational goal for giving to the wider Church.

5) 20 new mission starts.

6) 20% of our members leave a Bequest for Ministry of the Church.

7) 20 new candidates a year for full-time service in the Church.

8) 20 congregations a year participating in Healthy Congregation Seminar.

9) 20% Lutheran students at Roanoke College.

10) 20 spiritual retreats happening around the synod each year.

11) 20 years of growing partnership with the Islands District of Papua New Guinea.

12) 20 servant/mission events happening around the synod each year.

13) 20% growth in minority membership in the churches of the synod.

14) 20 members of the Ministerium in active partnership with the Synod's African-American Outreach Team.

15) 20 minority persons actively encouraged to discern their vocational call, which may be to rostered service as a Pastor, Associate in Ministry, or Diaconal Minister.

It is beyond the scope of this work to provide an evaluation of each goal. However, it is hoped that one will be able to note the influence of the goals in shaping the direction of the synod, the fulfilling of "Strategy 2000" goals, and in defining the leadership of Bishop Mauney, the Synod Council, and the synod staff in developing, funding, and implementing the major emphases of the synod in the narrative that follows. Statistics on the life of the synod are provided throughout the narrative and particularly in the Appendix for further study and analysis of the goals.

---

9. Ibid.

VISITING AND LISTENING

Before taking office on September 1, 1999, Mauney was already busy making plans for his first months in office. In the early summer, he asked Bozeman to set a date for that summer and come to Salem to spend a day together talking and listening to each other about their vision and plans for the future. In an interview, Bozeman recalled,

He asked me to dream about what would be some helpful visions as we moved into this new place in the life of the synod and particularly my role. He indicated he would be doing the same. So I prepared a list and we met in August. The main thing that I remember about our conversations was that both of us highlighted a renewed emphasis on adult education and faith formation for children and families. Of course, both of these emphases were natural with my educational background, my emphasis as a seminary professor, and faith formation for children and families would continue some of the work we began with Lutheran Family Services.

Mauney encouraged Bozeman to focus her time on these visions and be creative and come back with some plans. She had been thinking about asking the Synod Council for a three-month sabbatical in the fall to do research, engage other leaders in the synod for input, and survey other synods who were focusing on adult catechesis programs and faith formation events for children and families. The council did not think the proposal for this work during a sabbatical sounded like a sabbatical, but rather granted her the time to concentrate her work over the next several months on the development of a new and creative adult educational emphasis in the synod. The report of the council to the 2000 assembly noted the following:

In order to move forward with one of Bishop Mauney's vision goals—the establishment of synod-sponsored Lay Schools of Theology, the bishop selected the Rev. Jean Bozeman for a special three-month full-time assignment to develop a model for a Lay School of Theology for use in the synod.[10]

In August, Mauney wrote a letter to all the pastors and lay leaders of the congregations of the synod asking them to give thought to their vision for the future of the synod. After taking office, the new bishop began visiting all of the pastors, active and retired, and every parish, large and small, in the synod over a nine-month period to hear their thoughts and concerns for the future of the synod.

What an inspiration to listen to lay leaders speak to their vision and love to the Lord's Church! The constant themes from lay and clergy were "Discipling", "Christian Formation", "Back to the Basics", "Get Solid in the Word", "Let's Be About Mission!", "Ministry to our Youth!", "Build up the Ministerium", "How to Be Faithful for the Future!" It has been a year of listening, studying, and visioning with the staff, executive committee, synod council, deans, synodical committees built upon 12 years as an assistant to the bishop of this synod.[11]

This visiting and listening would continue into Mauney's second year of leadership. In his report to the 2001 assembly, he noted the importance of continuing to build the unity of the synod through the vision that we are ambassadors for Christ, God making his appeal through us.

---

10. Minutes, 13th Annual Synod Assembly, Virginia Synod/ELCA, 2000, p. 69.
11. Ibid., p. 16.

It is why I have: Visited every active pastor; Been in every conference talking with lay leaders and clergy; Begun a Day of the Ministerium …; Lifted up the importance of the Pre-Lenten Retreat …;Worked as a team with 11 excellent deans of our conferences; Begun meetings of pastors and rostered lay leaders who share common ministries such as campus ministry, mission developing, large congregations, small congregations, etc.; Continued the luncheon for our retired pastors; Begun intentional prayer for rostered leaders and congregations for each conference and institution by our congregations during their Sunday morning worship; Attended first call retreat for new pastors; Sought to welcome new pastors to the synod through a two-day orientation in cooperation with several institutions; Continued the clergy spouse retreat …; Plan with synod staff to visit one half of the pastors serving in active ministry each year …; Gathered all the CEOs of institutions three times already and intend to gather together twice a year for networking, partnership, sharing of our ministries, planning, and cooperation. The faith and commitment of our CEOs to the life of the Church is most inspiring![12]

Left to right: Pastor Jean Bozeman, ELCA Presiding Bishop Mark Hanson, Pastor Harvey Atkinson, Bishop Jim Mauney, and Pastor Chip Gunsten prepare for Synod Assembly worship at St. Andrew's on June 4, 2011.

Within his report, Mauney announced three new initiatives in the life of the synod that resulted from these opportunities of visiting and listening. These initiatives focused on unifying the synod through the goals of "Strategy 2000" and the vision of the synod being "ambassadors for Christ."

We will have a full-time Synodical Director for Youth and Young Adults in place by September 2001. This position will be funded by the Office of the Bishop. We will seek to continue to endow this position for the future of this ministry that is so important to the people of the synod.[13]

The institutions of our synod, the Virginia Synod, and the ELCA Foundation have partnered to call a pastor to serve our congregations in lifting up planned giving. I am pleased to announce the establishment of The Mission Office for Planned Giving.

We are encouraging the use of a synod-wide "family systems" approach to dealing with conflict in the life of congregations within the synod. Our major partner in this approach is Lutheran Family Services of Virginia, which brings a strong background and understanding of family systems.

---

12. Minutes, 14th Annual Synod Assembly, Virginia Synod/ELCA, 2001, pp. 11-12.
13. Ibid., pp. 12-13.

SUSTAINING MINISTRY TO YOUTH—A SYNODICAL DIRECTOR FOR YOUTH AND YOUNG ADULT MINISTRIES

The Youth Ministry Committee hopes that the synod will be able to find ways to provide youth ministry the staff support it requires, as it has continued to be ranked as a ministry of high importance among the members of the synod.[14]

The report of the Youth Ministry Committee and the Lutheran Youth Organization to the 1995 assembly of the synod is not the first time hope had been expressed for the day when there would be a full-time synod staff member for youth ministry. The report is correct in noting that youth ministry has always ranked high in importance in the life of the synod throughout its history. Luther League was popular in congregations and supported by the synod as far back as the years of the synod and congregations in the United Lutheran Church in America (ULCA), 1918–1962. Then there were the difficult yet promising challenges and changes from the legacy of Luther League to the new emphases of youth ministry with and by youth in the early years of the Lutheran Church in America (LCA), 1962–1987.

Synod Youth Assembly, 2006

Synodical youth programs and events had always been popular. The Massanetta Summer Assembly attracted large numbers of teenagers to the traditional summer synod event for families with children of all ages. In the 1970s, Winter Celebration for high school youth began and became popular with youth returning to Massanetta for a wintertime gathering of exploring faith around a program developed and led by young pastors in the synod and adult chaperones. Changing the leadership style of Winter Celebration from an adult leadership and adult perspective to an emphasis on the inclusion of more youth and "peer faith relationship building" brought Winter Celebration even more popularity, especially with its emphasis on large group gatherings and presentations on a theme. Small group curricula were developed around each theme and written by a planning group composed primarily of youth leaders from across the synod.

In the 1980s, Lost and Found was created for seventh- through ninth-graders and Winter Celebration became exclusive to tenth- through twelfth-graders. In 1985, Lost and Found registration surpassed 300 and by 1990 was approaching 400 participants. It continued to push the ca-

---

14. Minutes, 8th Annual Synod Assembly, Virginia Synod/ELCA, 1995, p. 16.

pacity of the new site for youth events, Eagle Eyrie Conference Center, a large Virginia Baptist facility in the mountains northwest of Lynchburg. The practice of including sixth-graders in Lost and Found ended in 2000, when the synod created a new event for fifth- and sixth-graders entitled "Seventh Day," which has continued to draw between 150 to 300 participants since its beginning. In addition, ninth-graders were included in Winter Celebration starting in early 1990s and for a time they could choose to attend either Lost and Found or Winter Celebration. This was done to accommodate the varying configurations of congregational youth groups and confirmation classes across the synod as well as to make sure that neither event would strain the capacity of Eagle Eyrie.

In addition to all this growth in the popular youth events of the synod, there came the added responsibility to provide a synodical component for participation in the national Lutheran Youth Organization (LYO) that had been created with the formation of the ELCA in 1988.

Stacy Hudy, Muhlenberg, makes the Youth Assembly report to the 2004 Synod Assembly.

By the mid-1990s the need for more administrative attention was becoming increasingly obvious. "Alumni" of Winter Celebration and Youth Assembly and high school and college graduates who had attended creative leadership training events were returning to the synod as young adults and seeking to be involved and give back to the synod their time, talents, and energy in planning and leading youth events. Some former youth returned as young adult leaders wanting to do more in their home congregations. Those congregations began seeking more "on-site" consultation for their youth programs as their youth wanted to be involved in the life of their congregations. All of these forces began to combine in the early 1990s to generate conversations among those most involved in youth ministry in the life of the synod. As it also noted in its 1995 report, "An ongoing concern of the Youth Ministry Committee is the limited amount of time available to Pastor Mauney for attention to youth ministry due to responsibilities assigned to him."[15]

During his years as assistant to the bishop responsible for youth ministry, Mauney was well aware of these forces and the demands upon his time. He knew firsthand the importance of the coalitions of pastors, lay leaders, and gifted youth who were significant partners with him in hard

---

15. Ibid.

work and long hours of planning, implementing, and evaluating the key programs and events that kept the youth ministry programs in the Virginia Synod among the strongest in the ELCA.

In his five-minute speech during the balloting for the next bishop of the synod at the 1999 assembly, Mauney noted that he was committed to adding a full-time staff position for youth ministry and young adult ministries. He made it clear that he would be committed to the priority of sustaining and expanding the present youth ministry programs and reaching out to the synod's young adults to be engaged in the life of their church. He was well aware of and had participated in numerous discussions with other youth leaders in previous years about the importance of moving forward with this new staff position in the life of the synod. In his comments he made the case that the need for a full-time staff position had been present for many years and the future could not wait. He proposed raising $1 million to endow the position. Mauney was confident making both assertions knowing that the synod had adopted "Strategy 2000" calling for a "Synodical Director of Youth and Young Adult Ministries." Following his election and in the midst of all the other demands upon him as the newly elected bishop, he kept this goal before the Synod Council and made efforts along with other members of the council to raise the funds.

An opportunity for funding the position came early in the second year of Mauney's first term. Keith Brown, assistant to the bishop for administration and finance, announced his intention to retire. Mauney engaged the Synod Council in setting forth the terms for two new positions—a part-time position of ten hours a week in the areas of administration and finance effective June 30, 2001, which Brown would be offered, and a full-time synodical director for youth and young adults. The plans and descriptions of each position were recorded in the Report of the Synod Council to the 2001 Synod Assembly:

Mr. Keith Brown will be retiring June 30, 2001, but has expressed an interest in remaining in a part-time service of 10 hours a week in the area of finance and administration. His willingness to serve has allowed the synod a transition time of about four years for the synod to begin using a full-time Synod Director of Youth and Young Adult Ministry through the Office of the Bishop.

The Synodical Director would be directly under the call and direction of the Bishop. The Synodical Director for Youth and Young Adults Ministry will be the programmatic position that would seek to provide a strategy in youth and young adult ministry for forming "ambassadors for Christ." The Synodical Director will be the one to oversee the development of the strategies and their implementation in an ongoing way. The Synodical Director will be actively engaged with the congregations of the synod as a consultant and resource for youth and young adult ministry. The Director will be active in campus ministry and strategical planning for campus ministry. The Director will oversee the synodical youth events, the Lutheran Youth Organization, and the Youth Assembly. The Director will give staff support to the synodical youth ministry committee and synodical campus ministry committee. The Director will be a resource to the Synod Council and Executive Committee of the Synod.

Because of the Kairos moment of Mr. Brown's retirement and willingness to work part-time for the synod, the Office of the Bishop could be re-configured and the work re-distributed in a way that would allow for Mr. Brown's portfolio to be cared for through Assistants to the Bishop, the Bishop, and Support Staff. It would allow for a full-time position for the Synodical Director to be created.[16]

---

16. Minutes, 14th Annual Synod Assembly, Virginia Synod/ELCA, 2001, pp. 93-94.

DAVID K. DELANEY—FROM PARISH PASTOR TO DIRECTOR FOR YOUTH AND YOUNG ADULT MINISTRIES

Pastor Dave Delaney became involved in youth ministry in the Virginia Synod from the moment of his first call and arrival as associate pastor at St. Mark, Yorktown in 1983. Within his first year he was asked to serve as chaplain and director for Lost and Found. As youth, adults, and pastoral colleagues began recognizing his relational skills, musical talents, and leadership gifts, especially his attention to details, he became more involved first as a member of planning teams and then as one of the popular "up-front leaders" at the annual synod youth events—Winter Celebration, Lost and Found, Kairos, and Youth Assembly. After the formation of the ELCA and the beginning of the new Virginia Synod/ELCA he agreed to serve as chair of the synod's Youth Ministry Committee for seven years and again during two brief vacancies in the position.

The Rev. Dr. David K. Delaney

In 1990, he was asked by Mauney, then assistant to the bishop, to serve as the ongoing director for the Youth Assembly. He was asked to give leadership and work with other pastors, adult advisors, and youth in developing the synodical Lutheran Youth Organization and clarify its relationship to the well-established youth ministry programs and events of the synod. He was also asked to help in the synod's participation in the national expression, especially in identifying pastors and adults who could be involved in coordinating those congregations' youth groups who participated in what were becoming known as the "National Youth Gatherings" scheduled and planned every three years by the ELCA churchwide staff. In an interview, Delaney noted,

Throughout the '90s I had a lot of responsibility for generating youth and adult leadership, including recruitment of directors, chaplains, and small group leaders, so I was becoming increasingly familiar with the overall structure and mission of all the synod's youth events and other programs. In addition, I was providing on-site guidance and advice on youth ministry for several synodical congregations every year.

I remember in the mid-1990s, as attendance at the events continued to grow and the overall ministry of the synod with youth and young adults expanded, it became increasingly clear that we were going to need a staff person whose primary responsibility would be to provide leadership and administrative support for all the various youth events and other ministries.

A half-dozen of those who had been widely involved in the synod youth ministry gathered for conversation and began to describe what such a position would look like as well as asking how it might possibly be financed. I was taking notes for the study group and as the list of responsibilities and expectations lengthened I remember thinking, "I feel sorry for whoever ends up with this job!"

In 1989, Delaney was accepted into the Ph.D. program at the University of Virginia in the field of Christianity and Judaism in Antiquity, a concentration in the university's Religious Studies Department. Delaney was approved by the Synod Council for an "on leave from call for graduate

Lutheran Youth Organization board officers, 2011–2012 (left to right): Wayne Jones, multicultural representative, Lutheran Church of Our Saviour, Richmond; Will Southard, tenth-grade representative, Salem, Mt. Sidney; Amanda Downs, eleventh-grade representative, Grace and Glory, Palmyra; Grace Clough, president, Muhlenberg, Harrisonburg; and Emily Depew, outgoing 2010–2011 president, St. John, Abingdon.

study" status in order to remain on the roster of active ordained pastors. During his studies at UVA, he accepted a part-time call as associate pastor, St. Mark, Charlottesville, 1990–1992. Upon finishing his coursework he accepted a call in 1993 as associate pastor, St. John, Roanoke, returning to the roster of active ordained pastors. During his first years at St. John, he finished his dissertation and was awarded his Ph.D. in 1997.

In April 2001, Mauney first approached Delaney about the role of serving as the synod's first director of youth and young adult ministries after Brown had informed him of his intention to retire and after Mauney had discussed the matter with synod leadership. Delaney recalled in an interview,

I had not anticipated the invitation, so I expressed surprise, thinking that we might have wanted to have a wider pool of candidates—even beyond the synod—from which to choose someone who might be better suited for the variety of responsibilities and the visibility of a synod staff person, but Jim assured me that I was his first choice.

On Thursday, June 7, 2001, just before the start of the annual Synod Assembly, Mauney announced his decision and presented Delaney's name to the Synod Council. The council gave approval of Mauney's recommendation to call Delaney to serve as the Virginia Synod's first director of youth and young adult ministries. In the discussion on the recommendation and details of the call, the council included among the responsibilities of young adult ministries the work of the Campus Ministry Committee. After the vote, Mauney called to inform Delaney. Following a short period of deliberation and discernment he accepted the call.

At the same meeting, the Synod Council also gave approval to the terms of the call and its means of funding. The decision was announced at the Synod Assembly, but it was agreed that members of the council and staff would not reveal that a call had already been issued to Delaney, giving him time to respond and an opportunity to submit his letter of resignation to the council of St. John, which he did on Monday, June 11. Due to scheduled responsibilities through the summer, Delaney did not start in the new position until September 4, his first day in the synod office as the first director of youth and young adult ministries in the history of the Virginia Synod.

Having a director of youth and young adult ministries did more than just consolidate the administrative work of planning youth events. Now there was a specialist in the synod office who could work as a consultant for congregations and the various youth workers in congregations. More time could be given to developing additional youth workers and small group leaders for the numerous youth events. In an interview in 2013, Delaney noted,

Pastors and congregation youth leaders began calling on me to assist with questions of searching for staff, hiring, supervision, job description, compensation, facility and program safety, planning, crisis interventions, background checks, and available resources.

Delaney also noted the following achievements that were made possible by the creation of the specialized position of director of youth and young adult ministries:

1) The ability to dramatically widen the circle of those participating in youth ministry events and faith formation in general in congregations. For example, the 1983 Lost and Found event staff orientation consisted of approximately twenty-five adults sitting in a circle reviewing curriculum. Now staff for that event orientation includes as many as one hundred or more adults who are there to lead small groups and fulfill other important tasks for the event. More than 1,000 adults have been part of youth ministry leadership in various ways in the synod since the formation of the ELCA.

2) The steady increase in the involvement of young adults—eighteen-to-twenty-one-year olds—in leadership of the youth events. Lost and Found 2013 included more than thirty in this age group, and they consistently reported that the chance to engage in faith sharing and prayer with younger youth and participating as small group leaders was a significant experience in strengthening their own faith.

3) The LAUNCH event, initiated in July 2004, gathers youth just graduating from high school, and for five days, gives them opportunities with peers and adult leaders to discuss faith, lifestyles, and vocational discernment as they prepare for their next experiences in life. More than seventy-five youth have participated in this event since its beginning. Delaney shared in an interview, "It was the single thing that I most wanted to do when I started in the position as Director of Youth and Young Adult Ministries."

Kairos, 1994

4) The start of a summertime "servant event" for junior high youth, a neglected age group for structured and reflective service experiences. The event started in 2005 and has since been adopted by leaders from the Tidewater Conference.

5) The development of the "AmbassadorCast" podcast which, though very sporadic in its production schedule, has produced more than fifty episodes and is available on iTunes.

Delaney shared the following in response to a question during an interview about the impact of the rise of social media:

It is hard to believe that when I started in 2001, what we now know as the vast world of social media had barely been imagined. Starting in 1997 with "SixDegrees", then continuing with "Friendster" (2002), "MySpace" (2003), "Facebook" (2004), and others, social media sites that combined personal story-telling, "status updates," and easy messaging quickly began to be the norm for general communication and promotion among college students first, then high school youth, and even older junior high youth.

Members of the Synod Staff began to use these tools very soon after they were made available to publicize events, share pictures from the events, and stay in touch with one another in between events. Soon after that, we began to see references to the media experience in our events. The theme for Lost and Found 2007 was "MyFaith", a take-off on "MySpace." Still, there are many young people for whom sites such as Facebook are neither an interest nor a priority. Since the mid-2000s, text messaging via cell phone has maintained an even stronger presence in the lives of young people than online social media.

What this has meant for youth ministry at the synodical level is that the number of modes by which we must communicate has more than doubled in the last 20 years. Not knowing whether a young person will be most likely to respond to a message sent by U.S. Mail, email, Facebook post, text message, regular phone call, or something else has meant that all these modes must be used. As the church moves onward through the 21st century, the challenges associated with building relationships and retaining the attention and interest of the church's youth will likely grow rather than diminish.

SUSTAINING THE FINANCIAL BASE—THE MISSION OFFICE FOR PLANNED GIVING

The case can be made that the genesis for the Mission Office for Planned Giving had its beginnings in the establishment of the Trust Fund for Mission adopted at the 1989 assembly of the new synod in Williamsburg. Perhaps it is more accurate to say that it was the lack of sustained promotion and the disappointing response to calls for more planned gifts to the Fund that prompted the Synod Council to title Initiative #2, "Recommit Ourselves to the Trust Fund for Mission,"[17] one of the seven proposed initiatives of "Strategy 2000" adopted by the 1998 Synod Assembly. The initiative emphasized that recommitment to the Fund be accomplished by

- *Calling upon individual congregational members to give gifts and bequests to the Fund;*
- *Calling upon congregations to give a tithe of congregational endowment receipts to the Fund as they are received;*
- *Securing a part-time development person to be financed through the Fund.*[18]

In 2000, the Synod Council and new bishop committed time and energy to review each of the seven initiatives of "Strategy 2000." Concerning Initiative #2, the following action of the council was announced in its report to the assembly:

---

17. Minutes, 11th Annual Synod Assembly, Virginia Synod/ELCA, 1998, p. 95.
18. Ibid.

The Synod Council has taken action to form a Planned Giving Consortium, with the ELCA Foundation, the Synod, and the agencies and institutions of the synod as participants. The Consortium will hire a development director for the synod. The development director's portfolio will include the Synod's Trust Fund for Mission.[19]

Mauney's time given to visiting and listening to others, especially in his first two years as bishop, revealed his gift of building teams and coalitions of leaders to work with him and the Synod Council in achieving goals set forth in "Strategy 2000." This gift is seen especially in the development of the Planned Giving Consortium, a coalition of the chief executive officers of the synod's agencies and institutions, as well as leadership from the ELCA Foundation. In his gathering of these partners "who share in our ministries," he heard them also as "ambassadors for Christ" and integral to the synod's mission and ministries. He listened to their desire to work with the synod around the mantra articulated by Ron Herring, CEO, Lutheran Family Services of Virginia: "We can do far more together than any one of us can do alone."

Thus, the visions in 1998 and 2000 for securing a part-time director for planned giving became an exciting reality for calling a full-time director by combining resources brought by each member of the coalition. The office would represent the interests of all the partners participating in this new effort to generate present and future sources of funding through planned giving: the ELCA through the ELCA Foundation, the Virginia Synod, and the institutions and agencies related to the synod—Roanoke College, Lutheran Theological Southern Seminary, Lutheran Family Services of Virginia, National Lutheran Home, Virginia Lutheran Homes, the Lutheran Council of Tidewater, Caroline Furnace Lutheran Camp and Retreat Center, Hungry Mother Lutheran Retreat Center, and the Chaplain Service Prison Ministry of Virginia.

Funding for the Mission Office for Planned Giving would be the responsibility of all the partners with the ELCA Foundation providing 50 percent of the costs for compensation, office operations, and program materials. The Synod Council approved committing $10,000 each year from unrestricted income generated by the Synod Trust Fund for Mission. The remaining partners agreed to contribute to an annual "range of support" as each was able. The Foundation would provide the training of a pastor selected by the bishop and approved by the coalition.

GEORGE L. SIMS—FROM PARISH PASTOR TO DIRECTOR OF THE MISSION OFFICE FOR PLANNED GIVING

Mauney made the announcement of the synod's first director of the Mission Office for Planned Giving in his written report to the 2001 Synod Assembly, June 8-10, at Roanoke College.

The institutions of our synod, the Virginia Synod, and the ELCA Foundation have partnered to call a pastor to serve our congregations in lifting up planned giving. I am most pleased to announce the establishment

---

19. Minutes, 13th Annual Synod Assembly, Virginia Synod/ELCA, 2000, p. 62.

of the Mission Office for Planned Giving with our full-time person, the Rev. George Sims. This new mission office for planned giving will begin June 1, 2001. Pastor Sims has been chosen by the institutions of the Virginia Synod and the ELCA Foundation to provide a ministry to our members in encouraging and helping them to plan for the care of their families and loved ones through planned giving and to provide opportunities for our members to make a strong Christian witness to their families and loved ones by their planned giving.

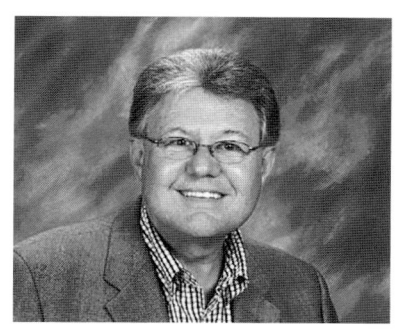

Twenty-two trillion dollars will be passed from our oldest generation to those who follow! I ask each of us to prayerfully consider how great an impact our Christian planned giving will make for the future mission of our congregations, synod, institutions, and wider Church.[20]

The Rev. George Sims

Officially, it was the ELCA Foundation, in consultation with the bishop and the executive officers of the agencies and institutions of the synod, that called Sims as "deployed staff to serve as a 'Planned Giving Specialist' on the territory of the synod."[21] At the time of the call, he was serving as pastor of Reformation, New Market. The bishop was confident in his choice of Sims and his recommendation to the Foundation and the officers of the agencies and institutions.

A 1975 graduate of Lutheran Theological Southern Seminary, Columbia, South Carolina, and ordained by the South Carolina Synod, Sims first served congregations in the North Carolina Synod before returning to serve congregations in South Carolina, his home synod. He came to the new Virginia Synod/ELCA in 1988 upon receiving a call to serve as pastor of Reformation, New Market. In 1991, Bishop Bansemer asked him to serve as dean of the Central Valley Conference. In an interview in 2012, Mauney recalled "getting to know George" as he traveled up and down the valley during his years as assistant to Bansemer. "He was seen by me and others as a competent pastor who was well known among pastors and respected among those with whom he served."

During his first year, Sims operated his office out of his home in Basye. His time, however, was spent in making contacts and visiting members and congregations and other groups throughout the territory of the synod, introducing himself and the work of the new Mission Office for Planned Giving. In 2002, his office moved to Grace, Winchester when his wife, Pastor Martha Miller Sims, received a call as pastor of Grace.

Throughout his years as director, Sims made numerous reports to the ELCA Foundation and the sponsoring agencies and institutions, as well as to Bishop Mauney, the Synod Council, and through written reports to the annual assembly of the synod. In 2005, Sims developed the Legacy for Ministry, composed of members who

---

20. Minutes, 14th Annual Synod Assembly, Virginia Synod/ELCA, 2001, pp. 12 and 13.
21. Ibid., p. 92.

have designated bequests through their wills or other estate plans ... Believing generosity begets generosity, a legacy society will be formally established during this year's assembly to celebrate the gospel at work in its many and various forms, encourage greater charitable giving throughout the church, acknowledge generosity of benefactors to any ministry, give thanks to donors, create a forum to allow donors to tell their stories and motivation for giving, bring people together to recognize and celebrate successes.[22]

In the report of his work to the 2006 assembly, Sims noted that 125 planned gifts had been recorded by the Mission Office. In 2007, he reported that as of March 30, giving units had planned 205 bequests for ministries of the church, including social ministry organizations, colleges, seminaries of the church, the Virginia Synod, and ministries of the ELCA (World Hunger, Domestic and International Disaster Response, Lutheran World Relief) and their congregations.

Events combined in 2011 that brought an end to the ministry of the Mission Office for Planned Giving. The ELCA Foundation headquartered at the Lutheran Center in Chicago experienced changes in executive-level leadership positions, impacting operations and relationships with Foundation partners. Significant reduction in mission support for ELCA during this time also generated losses of personnel and operations especially bringing into question continued support of deployed staff positions in regions and synods. It was also during this time that Sims was approached by National Lutheran Communities & Services (NLCS) in Rockville, Maryland, an ELCA-affiliated institution, and offered the position of director of philanthropy for the newly developed Village at Orchard Ridge being built in Winchester. He accepted the position effective October 1, 2011.

The Mission Office for Planned Giving operated for just over ten years—June 1, 2001 to September 30, 2011. In an interview reflecting on his ten years as director, Sims noted that he made hundreds of visits on behalf of the Foundation, synod, and supporting agencies and institutions of the synod.

Relationships were built with generous, faithful Lutherans. That's what the work was all about—building relationships and encouraging a planned gift for the church in the future. Many made plans; some did not immediately, but the seed was planted.

In his written report to the 2009 assembly, Mauney highlighted the fruit of Sims' work on behalf of the whole church with a play on words using the newly adopted ELCA slogan, "God's Work, Our Hands."

God's Word through Our Plans might be a way to speak of our planned giving together to pass on to generations to become a powerful witness of the Lord of life. We have received notice of 290 planned gifts made to the life of the Church that are a part of our Legacy Society for the synod. These gifts help congregations, institutions, foundations, and foreign missions, etc. for their present and future ministry. Pastor George Sims, the Executive Director for the Mission Office for Planned Giving, reported nearly $5 million given through planned giving this year with congregations receiving over 90% of those gifts. Our ability now

---

22. Minutes, 18th Annual Synod Assembly, Virginia Synod/ELCA, 2005, p. 157.

to create an opportunity and expectation to make planned gifts including the ongoing life of the church and institutions will be a powerful witness for our generation and a joyous source for thanksgiving for generations to come to whom these gifts will make such a difference![23]

In his final report to the 2011 Synod Assembly, Sims wrote,

"Go and do likewise" are words Jesus spoke to a lawyer who had prompted the telling of the parable of the Good Samaritan (Luke 10). There are opportunities to make a difference in the lives of others every day. One way, often overlooked because "no one asked," is to use a will to make a bequest to a ministry of the church, including a congregation or organization that shares your values and purpose in helping others. In the end, the task is usually simple and straightforward. The real benefit is that you can have a profound impact in the lives of others. To date 132 households of Virginia Synod have included bequests in their wills designating 320 ministries. In addition, 15 donors who have died have made significant impact in ministries through their estate plans. For every known gift studies indicate there are 7 to 8 times as many planned but not reported.[24]

LUTHERAN PARTNERS IN MISSION

The loss of the Mission Office for Planned Giving and the retirement of the Rev. Floyd Addison as coordinator of the annual United Lutheran Appeal (ULA) in 2011 prompted Mauney to do again what he does best—gather leaders to seek their advice and make plans for moving forward with the mission of the synod. He turned first to the Synod Council, who recognized that these developments provided an opportunity to look anew at the way these ministries could be accomplished in the synod. He also called upon the executive directors of the agencies and institutions of the synod as well as the deans of the synod's eleven conferences to seek their advice.

Following these discussions, Mauney appointed a task force to develop a proposal that could encompass the scope of this new effort. After months of careful study, the task force recommended the creation of a new full-time staff position in the life of the synod to connect the institutions of the synod to the congregation more fully through

1) Storytelling and offering hands-on service projects,

2) Encouraging annual financial support for the ministries affiliated with the Synod, and

3) Nurturing planned giving among the members of the congregations of the Virginia Synod as well as providing for an annual congregation-based giving opportunity by members to the various institutions and agencies of the synod.

Mauney shared the results of these conversations in his written report to the 2012 Synod Assembly:

With the planning of the CEOs of our synod's institutions and the deans of our conferences, we have combined the Mission Office for Planned Giving with the United Lutheran Appeal to create a new position.

---

23. Minutes, 22nd Annual Synod Assembly, Virginia Synod/ELCA, 2009, pp. 72-73.
24. Minutes, 24th Annual Synod Assembly, Virginia Synod/ELCA, 2011, p. 114.

The Search Team writes: a **L**utheran **P**artners in **M**ission Director. The Lutheran Partners in Mission Board is seeking a Director who will be responsible for coordinating the God's Work, Our Hands: Lutheran Partners in Mission (LPM) program of the Virginia Synod of the ELCA. The Director will be an employee of the Virginia Synod and report to the partner institutions through a Board of Directors comprised of their representatives.

This donor-centric position has two major areas of responsibility: 1) managing the LPM effort to engage congregations and individuals in mutual ministry with eight agencies and institutions, and 2) carrying out the ELCA's regional gift planning program by serving as a resource for congregations and their cultivation and gift solicitation efforts and its ministry of encouraging the making of a will for the care of loved ones and as a final witness of faith.[25]

With these actions, Lutheran Partners in Mission (LPM) was created as a new ministry of the Virginia Synod following the assembly. It began on July 1, 2012. Its purposes expanded to include encouraging volunteerism of members and congregations in the work of the agencies and institutions, and the encouraging of philanthropy—the planned financial support by individuals of the various agencies, institutions, or ministries of the Virginia Synod and ELCA. It should be noted that the ELCA Foundation was asked but elected not to participate in the new partnership. The Foundation's "Virginia Synod Portfolio" developed during the years of the operation of the Mission Office for Planned Giving was transferred to the Foundation's deployed staff serving in the Metropolitan Washington, DC Synod.

ELLEN I. HINLICKY—DIRECTOR, LUTHERAN PARTNERS IN MISSION

Ms. Ellen Hinlicky

Ellen I. Hinlicky was hired as the first director of Lutheran Partners in Mission. She had served previously as director of development for Virginia Lutheran Homes and as director of church relations at Roanoke College. Additionally, she served as parish administrator of the New River Parish in Blacksburg for five years, thus bringing both parish-based service and fundraising experience to the new position.

In her first report to the 2013 Synod Assembly, Hinlicky listed the following accomplishments:

- *Revised and updated the United Lutheran Appeal, with enhancements to encourage congregation and donor participation*
- *Assisted in the complete revision of the Virginia Synod website, which includes online giving options for individuals and congregations*
- *Raised awareness of giving opportunities throughout the Virginia Synod among its congregations, pastors and lay members through conference gatherings and congregational visits*

---

25. Minutes, 25th Annual Synod Assembly, Virginia Synod/ELCA, 2012, p. 6.

- Identified funding opportunities for congregations and Mission Partners through the Mission Investment Fund and Thrivent
- Promoted the Synod's Mission Partners through outreach to congregations, pastors and laypeople
- Assisted congregations in considering endowments, bequest policies and online giving options[26]

Hinlicky noted at the end of her first report that Lutheran Partners in Mission will have as its primary goal in its second year connecting members of the synod with Mission Partners through new and creative ways of giving and continuing to encourage generosity through legacy gift planning.

A summary of the ministry of Lutheran Partners in Mission was articulated by Hinlicky in a brochure she developed entitled, "Lutheran Partners in Mission—Empowering Ministry Outside the Church Doors":

Remember the game we all played as children with our fingers laced together? Here's the church, here's the steeple—open the doors, there's all the people!

It's true that as the thriving body of Christ, we gather together weekly and worship in our pews. As we lift our hearts and prayers, together we inspire our shared journey in faith. But much of what we are called to do as Christians takes place outside the church doors.

And that's why the Virginia Synod supports several faith-based non-profit organizations. Each one empowers believers to be the hands and feet of Christ in our local communities, or offers a place of comfort and care for senior living, or a place of respite and connection with God, or nurtures the next generation of pastoral and lay leadership. With the support of Virginia's Lutherans, these ministries ensure we live our collective call to go out into the world and care for others.

Lutheran Partners in Mission continues to serve the Virginia Synod's eight Mission Partners in a variety of ways: connecting congregations with church-related institutions through the United Lutheran Appeal and the Synodical Day of Service; offering consulting assistance to Mission Partner staff and to congregations; and assisting the bishop in fundraising for the synod.

SUSTAINING CONGREGATIONS AND LEADERS—HEALTHY CONGREGATIONS AND BRIDGEBUILDERS

The first day on the job convinced the new bishop there had to be a healthier way to deal with conflicts in the life of congregations and pastors. In a 2013 interview, Mauney reflected upon that defining moment:

I will never forget sitting in the center of the head table with leaders of a congregation in open conflict. Over 200 members were present. Everyone who stood up to speak focused all of their words and emotions at me and not at any of the leaders sitting with me. I remember feeling like I was sitting in front of the end of a funnel and all the anger and frustration going in the funnel was coming out right at me. I needed to think. What was I going to say? What could I do?

---

26. Minutes, 26th Annual Synod Assembly, Virginia Synod/ELCA, 2013, pp.102-103.

That experience, combined with his knowledge of the impact that conflicts had upon Bansemer, the staff, pastors, and congregations, motivated Mauney to turn to others he knew had the training, skills, and experiences in responding to what appeared to be a growing problem of congregational/clergy conflict crises. As was his style of leadership, Mauney gathered once again a team of trusted colleagues—experienced pastors, trained counselors, and knowledgeable executives—to meet with him to discuss a strategy for a more proactive response to unhealthy and divisive conflicts among congregations and pastors. Reflecting on his motivations for the first meeting, Mauney recalled,

At first I was just hoping to identify some recognized leaders in our synod to turn to and seek advice and hopefully encourage one of them to go with me to these meetings whenever I felt it was appropriate. That strategy changed after our first meeting.

To that meeting held in January 2000, just before the annual Pre-Lenten Retreat at the Roslyn Center, Richmond, Mauney invited the following: Pastor Tom Bosserman, Trinity, Newport News; Pastor Chris Price, Epiphany, Richmond; Pastor Jim Utt, Grace, Winchester; Pastor Daniel Jungkuntz, executive director, Peninsula Counseling Center, Newport News; Pastor Luther Mauney, retired chaplain, Medical College of Virginia; and Ron Herring, chief executive officer, Lutheran Family Services of Virginia.

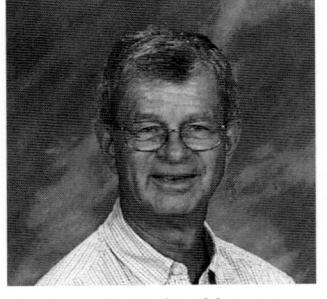

The Rev. Dr. Luther Mauney

The bishop stated his concerns for the impact that congregation/pastor conflicts were having upon the synod and the fallout such conflicts had upon pastors and their families as well as the negative impact on congregations and their life together. He also expressed concerns for the demands such situations placed not only on his office, but also on the synod staff, as their time and energies were needed to attend to other responsibilities and leadership for new ministries being considered in the life of the synod. Could there be another way?

The answers to that question and the discussion that followed generally acknowledged the best practices that were known and used among those present in their own settings of ministry. It was Ron Herring who first suggested there might be a different approach. He had heard positive reports from a colleague of a Lutheran social ministry organization in Iowa who had participated in a leadership training workshop based on "family systems thinking" led by Lutheran Pastor Peter Steinke. Herring offered to contact his colleague, find out more about the workshop and Steinke, and report back to the group at the next meeting.

That meeting was scheduled for March 10, 2000, and held at Grace, Waynesboro. Herring prepared a report that shared basic information about Healthy Congregations, an ecumenical and interfaith organization begun by Steinke that provided workshops for facilitators and trainers to serve as independent educators within their congregations and communities. The workshops train facilitators and provide consultation in understanding and implementing "family systems" theory and its application to the resolution of congregational conflict and development of healthy congregational leaders. Bridgebuilders, an affiliated program of Healthy Congregations, was a program also developed and offered by Steinke to train pastors and lay leaders to be facilitators intervening in congregations experiencing active conflict. After hearing and discussing Herring's report, it was the consensus of the group that the synod, through the Office of the Bishop, pursue further conversation with Herring about introducing Healthy Congregations and Bridgebuilders to the pastors and congregations of the synod.

Over the next several months, meetings were held between the synod and Lutheran Family Services (LFS) resulting in a "partnership" to sponsor and coordinate Healthy Congregations and Bridgebuilders workshops as the programs the synod would use in training facilitators, lay and ordained, for guiding pastors and lay leaders in healthier ways of dealing with congregational conflict. The Synod Council gave its approval of a "Letter of Agreement" with LFS, drafted by Herring, assisted by Mauney, and endorsed by the LFS board. The Synod Council also approved providing $10,000 from the Porter-Hess Fund in support of the partnership and the costs of the start-up operations of the new program. In the letter, LFS agreed to provide all administrative support of the program, including hiring, financing, and providing oversight of a coordinator of the program, and seeking further financial support through grants.

Dr. J. Luther Mauney, Jr. was invited by Herring to serve as coordinator of the new emphasis in the life of the synod. Luther Mauney brought with him a wealth of experience through his clinical pastoral training and familiarity with family systems theory. He had also served in various administrative capacities throughout his years as a leader, administrator, and teacher in the Clinical Pastoral Education and Chaplaincy programs at the Medical College of Virginia. L. Mauney was well known and respected by pastors and laity throughout the synod.

In his report to the 2001 Synod Assembly, Bishop Mauney wrote the following:

In May 2001, we trained facilitators to introduce the family systems approach to help congregations understand and deal with the dynamics of change and the healthy conflict that can arise from issues of change. In April 2001, we trained a dozen consultants to be of assistance to congregations encountering significant amounts of conflict. It is our desire to create a synod-wide understanding of family systems and healthy ways to deal with change and conflict.[27]

In the 2002 report to the Synod Assembly, Mauney began giving the numbers of those trained and the progression of the program into congregations.

We have trained almost two dozen facilitators and have begun introductory conference seminars and several congregational seminars. This is a very proactive program to promote health among our congregations and synod.

---

27. Minutes, 14th Annual Synod Assembly, Virginia Synod/ELCA, 2001, p. 12.

We have also selected Dr. Steinke to help train Bridgebuilder consultants who are available for congregations that are in unhealthy conflict. This program is to enable the Office of the Bishop to react to conditions in a congregation that require long term consultation and outside help.

By the end of 2004, seventy pastors had been trained as Healthy Congregations facilitators and an estimated 1,800 members of congregations had experienced at least one workshop.[28] Within one year, approximately 700 additional members of congregations in the synod participated in at least one or more Healthy Congregations workshops led by pastors trained as facilitators.[29]

L. Mauney proved to be the effective leader/coordinator needed for this new initiative in the life of the synod. It was his leadership that helped the synod move into the full embrace of the Healthy Congregations training of pastors and lay leaders for congregational workshops as the more proactive approach of dealing with conflict in congregations. This decision led to deactivating the more reactive approach of the Bridgebuilders program.

In an interview in 2013, L. Mauney noted, "We decided it would be best to be more proactive, developing congregational leaders' strengths to deal with potential problem areas. It was a deliberate decision and the congregational workshops were embraced."

In 2007, L. Mauney wrote a position paper entitled, "Healthy Congregations Initiative," in which he gives the perspective and rationale of Lutheran Family Services of Virginia committing to a strong partnership with the synod in establishing the Healthy Congregations and Bridgebuilders initiatives in the life of the synod:

LFS viewed this partnership as a natural application within the life of the Synod of its mission to promote healthy family relationships and to respond to family crisis situations. This also seemed like a natural partnership since the theory behind both the Healthy Congregations program and the Bridgebuilder program was based on family systems theory, which through application to life within the Synod would enhance the Synod's functioning as a family system.

Since the accountability for the conduct of the program was through LFS, agreements were drawn up to describe the scope of the expectations for the facilitators and consultants and the nature of their responsibilities. It was thought that housing the accountability of the program within LFS would provide important distance from the Bishop's Office to avoid triangulation and promote confidentiality. In order to fund the training of additional facilitators, a grant was obtained from the Price family (Hebron, Madison) which has been used to support scholarships and innovative dimensions of the program, in addition to funding the training of another group of Synodical facilitators.

Because the Healthy Congregations (HC) model assumed that the anxiety level in congregations would be low enough that they could function in an optimum learning mode, congregations who were in severe crises would not be encouraged to participate in this HC program, but rather in the Bridgebuilder program.

The organizational structure of the Healthy Congregations Initiative included the Steering Committee, comprised of members of the original planning committee; and a Review Committee, comprised of the Bishop, the LFS CEO, and one member each of the Synod Council, the LFS Board, and the Steering Committee. The Steering Committee met at least twice a year during the semi-annual retreats. The Review Committee

---

28. Minutes, 18th Annual Synod Assembly, Virginia Synod/ELCA, 2005, p. 16.
29. Minutes, 19th Annual Synod Assembly, Virginia Synod/ELCA, 2006, p. 13.

met yearly for the first three years. LFS provided the financial structure and the secretarial assistance. The Coordinator reported regularly to the Bishop, the LFS CEO, and through them to the Synod Council and the LFS Board.

L. Mauney's leadership as coordinator of the Healthy Congregations Initiative concluded in July 2009. During the years that he served as coordinator, LFS provided over $300,000 in financial support of all aspects of the program. In the position paper, he noted the significant results from the Healthy Congregations program in the life of the synod:

- *Over 2,000 lay leaders in 126 congregations have been involved in HC workshops.*
- *Twenty-two congregations have experienced Healthy Starts (assistance from Healthy Congregations principles) during the pastoral vacancy process.*
- *35 pastors and laity have been trained as congregational facilitators.*
- *Twenty pastors have participated in coaching groups.*
- *Thirteen continuing education semi-annual retreats for our facilitators have been held, with an average attendance of 31 persons.*
- *The concept of healthy congregations and healthy leadership is no longer a strange concept, but is something that is understood by a large part of the synod. We have been recognized nationally as a model for other synods.*

The Healthy Congregations effort generated other "healthy initiatives" in leadership development throughout the synod. Healthy Starts was developed to assist congregations during the time of pastoral vacancy to prepare lay leaders in guiding their congregation through a transitional time by applying Healthy Congregations principles and understanding emotional responses in times of anxiety. Coaching Groups were offered to equip pastors for the special challenges they face in providing healthy leadership. The purpose of what came to be known as Pastoral Leadership Consulting Groups was to deepen participants' theological and behavioral understanding of and capacity for leadership as it pertains to the pastoral office. Peer groups of seven to eight pastors were formed in geographic locations throughout the synod. Groups were formed by invitation from the bishop and under the guidance of a qualified facilitator who was trained and experienced in Bowen Family Systems Theory and its application to the pastoral leadership of a congregation. Each group was asked to commit to meeting for eight three-hour sessions during a twelve-month period.

In addition to these new "healthy initiatives," Bishop Mauney was concerned with providing continuing education opportunities for the pastors trained and serving as facilitators. It was also his concern to provide opportunities for introducing new pastors coming to the synod to the Healthy Congregations model of leadership in dealing with congregational conflict. Before he retired in July, L. Mauney gathered a group of Healthy Congregations facilitators to solicit feedback for the best way to continue the program emphasis. Reporting to the Healthy Congregations Steering Committee the feedback solicited from the facilitators, L. Mauney and the committee recommended that the Healthy Congregations program be absorbed into the Office of the Bishop with a new emphasis focused on "Healthy Leaders."

The new emphasis is to be on Healthy Leaders with a view toward the continuing education of Healthy Congregations facilitators, as well as rostered leaders' leadership training during Orientation, First Call, and Candidacy.[30]

The impact of the Healthy Congregations initiative and its emphasis on developing healthy congregational leadership, lay and rostered, would continue to fulfill Bishop Mauney's vision of sustaining pastors and congregations for effective leadership in the future years of the Virginia Synod/ELCA.

AMBASSADORS COMMUNITY FOR THEOLOGICAL STUDY (ACTS)

The action of the Synod Council in the fall of 1999 to grant Jean Bozeman a "special three-month, full-time assignment to develop a model for a Lay School of Theology for use in the synod"[31] reflected the council's support for the new bishop and his visions for the synod. The council's action also confirmed its confidence that Bozeman could do the job. Her skills as an educator and administrator at the highest levels of the church and her dedication as a continuing member of the new bishop's team gave the council every hope that the time given and her talents applied to the task would bear good fruit. The bishop and Synod Council would not be disappointed.

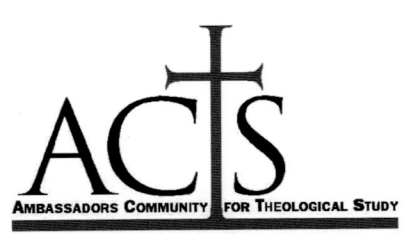

In an interview in 2013, Bozeman recalled,

During those three months of that first year, I began to sharpen the adult education focus. A number of geographically smaller synods had been doing intensives for adults but I struggled with how we could do those events with our spread-out geography.

Bozeman used surveys among pastors and adult leaders and educators in some of the congregations of the synod to gather their thoughts and ideas. She recalled having numerous conversations, phone calls, and correspondence with colleagues across the church. "I did a lot of reading and held conversations with synodical, churchwide, and ecumenical leaders to see what was happening around the U.S."

From this intensive time of research and reflection, Bozeman decided in 2000 that it was time to have a synodical task group of lay and ordained leaders to begin designing this new venture in lay adult theological education in the synod. The group met for the first time in June 2001 at the English Inn in Charlottesville to immerse themselves in the task of drafting a design.

Initially we planned to have 4 to 5 "Teaching Parish" sites around the synod. The Teaching Parish Sites would be hosts for adults to come together several times for each course. All sites would be linked electronically with the professor rotating each session so that all students would have both live and real time transmitted classes. Each Teaching Parish would be a host who offered meals and in-home lodging for overnight students. Well, with further research into this sophisticated technology, we learned that our vision was a bit too expensive.

---

30. Minutes, 23rd Annual Synod Assembly, Virginia Synod/ELCA, 2010, p. 105.
31. Minutes, 13th Annual Synod Assembly, Virginia Synod/ELCA, 2000, p. 69.

As recorded in the minutes of its meeting, time was given to discussing various models and getting feedback at meetings of the Christian Education Committee of the Congregational Life Cabinet. At one of the meetings of the committee in 2001, a report from the design task group to the committee generated further discussion on the proposed model and introduced a possible title—

Virginia Synod Academy for Ministry—the name given as a tentative title for a program designed to offer training and education to lay persons on a wide range of possible topics for multiple uses in congregations. Three congregational sites with the synod will serve as resource centers and modern technology will link each center, allowing for education and conference development using a new paradigm. The Rev. Dr. Jean Bozeman has led the development of this concept.[32]

In her comments on the development of the program during an interview, Bozeman shared the following:

The task group became a bit discouraged when we realized that our technologically based vision with five sites was way beyond our financial budget. The task group wanted to delay—not cancel—our launching at least a year. I was filled with energy and just felt we should not wait. I went back to the drawing board and pulled out the essentials and modified the plan moving to one site for the sessions, decreasing the number of class sessions but adding the element of small groups led by a local pastor. Actually, this was a tremendous bonus in building the community part of our name, which was another issue we dealt with as we tried to come up with just the right name for this new program. After many names were floated, like Virginia Synod Academy for Ministry, we found the right name to identify the program, its purpose, and its link to the synod's vision and sense of mission—Ambassadors for Christ. So the new name would be Ambassadors Community for Theological Study—ACTS.

The first ACTS class was held in September 2002 at Grace, Waynesboro. It was the first of twenty-three "core" courses offered at Grace by December 2013. The location and facilities of the congregation was an obvious choice for the site of the initial courses. Even before the advent of ACTS, the synod leadership looked to Grace, Waynesboro as the synod's geographical center to have committee meetings and hosting of the Synodical Convocation for Leaders each fall. It

Donna Gum, third from left, and coworkers, Grace, Waynesboro, make sure ACTS participants have food for the body as well as the soul.

---

32. Minutes, 14th Annual Synod Assembly, Virginia Synod/ELCA, 2001, p. 117.

should be noted that rather than seeing such a commitment to hosting synodical meetings as a burden, the Congregational Council and other lay leaders, especially with the leadership of Pastor Robert Humphrey, embraced their role as host for many synodical events, especially this new adult theological education emphasis.

In an interview in 2013, Bozeman noted,

Looking back, there is no question that a big measure of the stability and successful development of ACTS is due to having a home at Grace, Waynesboro, and to the steady gifts of many of their members, especially Donna Gum and Owen Keefer. Lots of thanks are due to Grace congregation and their support.

Owen Keefer, left, technology guru, Grace, Waynesboro, and Dave Raecke, Our Saviour, Warrenton, ACTS student and Steering Committee member, confer between sessions.

Reflecting on her anticipation of the first class, Bozeman shared the following in an interview:

I arrived early in Waynesboro and checked into the motel the weekend of the first event. Many of the students commuted, some as far as three hours away, but many stayed at the local motel. I went down to the lobby after dinner that night just as some of the participants had walked into the motel lobby. I did not know them by name but you can imagine the look of joy on my face as I saw people with the Book of Concord tucked under their arm and checking into their rooms.

Fifty-seven students from across the synod attended that first class. Dr. Timothy Wengert, Professor, Lutheran Theological Seminary at Philadelphia led a study on the Lutheran Confessions. Wengert was perfect for our first ACTS course. He was engaging with the students, fully knowledgeable about each of the confessional documents, and sharing his love for the Book of Concord.

The first ACTS class, Lutheran Confessions, was taught by the Rev. Dr. Timothy Wengert on September 21, 2002.

Reflecting on the impact that ACTS has had upon the life of the synod, Mauney gave the following assessment in an interview:

I gave Jean three months to research and think through an approach to create ambassadors for Christ who could teach in small congregations since I had heard many pastors say they needed lay teachers. I hoped that small congregations would send lay people to be trained to teach Bible and Lutheran Confessions. Jean did excellent work in her research and development of ACTS! I commend her in every way. She created a community of learning, fellowship, and a pool of leaders for the life of congregations, their leadership, the synod's leadership, and congregational ministry.

The ACTS Steering Committee on August 21, 2008 (left to right): Judy Timm, St. Michael, Virginia Beach; Pastor Jim Larsen, Apostles, Gloucester; David Raecke, Our Saviour, Warrenton; Pastor Scott Mims, Good Shepherd, Virginia Beach; Debbie Mintiens, Mt. Sidney, Salem; and Hank Thomlinson, St. Peter, Churchville.

In one of her reports to the Synod Council in 2007, Bozeman gave her assessment of the importance of ACTS in the life of the participants and the life of the synod:

ACTS has brought meaning and depth to participants in a way I could not have anticipated. I am continually thrilled and amazed with the level of new leadership that ACTS has raised up. I treasure the community that has been built. I am awed and humbled by the depth of faith and faith articulation that has come from ACTS participants. They are so excited to have begun a study journey.

In an interview, Bozeman added these comments to her evaluation of ACTS:

My first reflection on ACTS is what an incredible sense of community we have been able to establish through ACTS. It has been awesome. Then there is the leadership that has developed. In 2004, Elizabeth Smythe, Jim Stensvaag and Janet Gomez all were elected to the synod council. Each would credit ACTS with their increased roles in synodical life. Elizabeth with Power in the Spirit; Janet as secretary of the synod; and Jim became the director of Lutheran Council of Tidewater. Leadership within their own congregations was the primary goal of ACTS but it also became significant in providing leadership beyond the congregation as these three modeled.

A new phase of ACTS begins with a November 2008 travel/study tour of the Second Missionary Journeys of Paul. A great experience to Greece ensured that there would be further ACTS travels.

Virginia Synod † 145

FORMING FAITH AT HOME—ROOTS & WINGS

The successes of the Healthy Congregations program convinced the bishop that the application of Healthy Congregations principles and the emphasis of training pastors and lay leaders could be incorporated into a new ministry of the synod that would focus on creating healthy families. Mauney wrote the following in his report to the 2005 Synod Assembly:

In the midst of anxious times I give thanks for the 70 pastors trained as facilitators of Healthy Congregations and for the 1,800 participants who have experienced at least one workshop. But I now want this program to move from congregational health to family health, to help young couples thinking about marriage, young couples pregnant and anticipating their first child, young families with small children, single parents with small children becoming grounded in healthy family systems and faith formation called as parent to be an ambassador of Christ within the home.[33]

> Most certainly father and mother are apostles, bishops and priests to their children, for it is they who make them acquainted with the gospel. In short, there is no greater or nobler authority on earth than that of parents over their children, for this authority is both spiritual and temporal.
>
> - Martin Luther

Within the report, Mauney noted the strong financial support from congregations for the 2004 budget creating a surplus of $91,000 at the end of the fiscal year. A grant of $10,000 to Healthy Congregations was recommended by the bishop and Synod Council approved the funds to be used for "the beginning of healthy families."[34]

The bishop once again called upon Bozeman to take staff lead in working with L. Mauney, as well as including Lutheran Family Services, to advance this new initiative of the synod. Mauney asked that a team from Healthy Congregations and ACTS participants form a Healthy Families Ministry Team with the focus of developing a strong holistic approach and emphasis on the age group of prenatal to grade 5. The overall purpose of this initiative would be to grow healthy families with parents becoming ambassadors for Christ in their own homes, learning to nurture their own faith and developing faith practices at home for their children.

This was Bozeman's area of expertise, given all of her years of experience in teaching Christian Education at the seminary level and leading workshops on nurturing the faith of adults so as to pass on the faith to the next generation of children and youth. Bozeman's heart for the cause and set of skills to establish the new synodical program are revealed in an article she authored in 1997 for *Lutheran Partners*, the ELCA's periodical for rostered leaders.

---

33. Minutes, 18th Annual Synod Assembly, Virginia Synod/ELCA, 2005, p. 16.
34. Ibid., p. 17.

To keep the faith is also to nurture the faith. The primary place to nurture faith is none other than the home. In the home we have the daily experiences of life—not text book examples—for the growing recognition of God at work in our lives. The home should be a place of intentional, planned study and reflection in which we can articulate and experience faith and daily life. In another light, a focus on the household as the primary place for nurturing faith must recognize that families come in all shapes and dimensions. Even when children are not present in the household, this is still the primary place for nurturing the faith.

To get started, Bozeman invited pastors, rostered lay leaders, staff, and other lay leaders in family ministries or educational ministries in congregations from across the synod to an all-day meeting that would focus on taking the necessary steps in developing the new synodical ministry emphasis. Over twenty attended the meeting held at Grace, Waynesboro, on Friday, February 8, 2006. Most of those attending had participated in Healthy Congregations training or had attended ACTS courses. Time was given to brainstorming ideas, gathering information on already established "family ministry programs" designed for congregations, and the suggestion of the next steps. Task groups were appointed to examine and make reports on developmental concerns and learning characteristics of young children, "home-based" curricula available throughout the wider church, and discovering what some congregations in the synod were already doing in family or home-based ministry programs. All of the participants were asked to consider nominees for a steering committee with attention to diversity and representation from across the synod. Participants were also asked to give creative thought for a new name, with the concerns that it needed to be seen as not just another Healthy Congregations emphasis by the synod which could cause confusion, but rather a "clear, catchy, but not cutesy" name easy to use and focused on nurturing faith in the home and supported by the congregation.

Participants acknowledged that Bozeman's emphasis was a major paradigm shift from an institutionally focused, home-supported faith formation emphasis to a home-focused, institutionally supported emphasis for faith formation centered in the early childhood development years. Participants were also asked to consider the development of a website and how it should be related and accessible to the congregations of the synod and Christian Education leaders in congregations. It was agreed that Bozeman should coordinate with the bishop, staff, Synod Council, and other leadership groups giving emphasis to this new effort at the annual Synod Assembly, Power in the Spirit, ACTS, and other groups or settings in the life of the synod.

A report on some of the developments of the task groups was given to the Christian Education Team at its March 11, 2006 meeting. For example, from the website task group it was suggested that the words from Deuteronomy 6:6-7 would be on the link for the new ministry on the synod's website: "Keep these words I am commanding you today in your heart. Recite them to your children and talk about them when you are at home and when you are away, when you lie down and when you rise" (NRSV).

The Team also agreed with other task group's recommendation to suggest to the bishop and Synod Council that "Ambassadors for Christ—Faith in the Home" be the theme for the 2007 assembly. The Steering Committee would help with obtaining a keynote speaker, develop assembly workshops, provide information through brochures and presentations, and provide a theme banner.

Those who served on the Steering Committee to work with Bozeman and guide the work of the task groups over the course of developing this new ministry initiative were Jan Tobias, Zion, Waynesboro; Pastor Cathy Mims, Good Shepherd, Virginia Beach; Diaconal Minister Christy Van O'Linda, Epiphany, Richmond; Ellen Greene, Rejoice, Chesapeake; Associate in Ministry Jane Nicholson, First, Norfolk; Janet Gomez, Apostles, Gloucester; Wayne Burke, St. Peter's, Stafford; Patrick Hite, Grace, Waynesboro; Karen Smith, St. Peter's, Stafford; Glen Dewire, Our Saviour, Richmond; Pastor Jonathan Hamman, Rural Retreat Parish, Rural Retreat; Pastor Philip Bouknight, Floyd-Willis; and Pastor John Wertz, St. Michael, Blacksburg.

The first meeting of the committee was held on May 17, 2006. Bozeman suggested the possibility of the new ministry being called "Wings" based on the ideas of sheltering and giving wings to our children as found in Psalm 91 and Matthew 23:37. It was also suggested that the following quote from Martin Luther be incorporated into promoting the importance of parents in the formation of their children's faith:

Most certainly father and mother are apostles, bishops and priests to their children, for it is they who make them acquainted with the gospel. In short, there is no greater or nobler authority on earth than that of parents over their children, for this authority is both spiritual and temporal.

By the time the Steering Committee met in September 2006, "Wings" had become "Roots & Wings" and was described as "a developing ministry of the Virginia Synod particularly for families with children from birth through grade 5."

The Steering Committee also agreed to adopt the "Four Keys for Family Ministry Supported by the Church" as central to helping communicate to congregations, families, and pastors the guiding principles of this new educational initiative. According to the "Roots & Wings" brochure developed by the Steering Committee, "The Four Keys offer an effective, doable strategy for congregations wishing to develop a meaningful and faith-focused partnership between home and congregation."

The source of the "Four Keys" comes from the book *Frogs Without Legs Can't Hear*, written by David W. Anderson and Paul Hill and published by Augsburg Fortress (2003). The Four Keys are

1—*Caring Conversations*—*Caring conversations include more than simply telling our stories. At the heart of the communication recommended here is the sharing of faith, values, and the care of others. This can range from supportive listening, sharing the good news of Jesus Christ with one another, and simple praise and thanksgiving to challenging admonition, ethical discussions, and a call to action on behalf of all God's creatures and creation.*

2—*Family Devotional Life*
   a. Practice being in the presence of God
   b. Learn/experience the language of prayer and faith
   c. Attitude of thankfulness

3—*Family Service*
   a. Service on behalf of one's neighbor is the calling of all who follow Jesus Christ
   b. Service that is done as family establishes this as a value of the family. Family service projects have a life-long impact on children.

  c. *Service creates an emotional bond of those working together.*

  d. *Talking about the service, reflection, articulating learning gives the service meaning and vitality.*

 4—Family Rituals and Traditions

  a. *Rituals and Traditions are already a part of everything we do from the way we get up, greet one another, share meals, celebrate birthdays, etc.*

  b. *How do we more consciously name and identify what we are doing?*

  c. *How do we intentionally name the God moments and actions in our life?*

  d. *Joshua 4:6-7... When your children ask, "What do those stones mean to you?", how will our families be prepared to answer?*

  The Steering Committee was offered thirty minutes for a presentation before a plenary session of the 2007 assembly. It was also communicated that Dr. Roland D. Martinson, professor of Children, Youth, and Family Ministry, Luther Seminary, St. Paul, Minnesota, would be the keynote speaker on the theme of the assembly, "Ambassadors for Christ—Baptized Disciples," to be held June 8-10, 2007, at Roanoke College. Later in the summer, the Steering Committee would also have the opportunity to conduct workshops at Power in the Spirit.

  In his report to the 2007 assembly, Mauney wrote that the year *has given rise to Roots and Wings which looks to the parent and grandparent as a teacher, role model, and example of the faith just as Paul speaks of granny Lois and mother Eunice in II Timothy 1. As pulpit and altar should proclaim the same gospel, so home and congregation should reinforce a culture of faith.*[35]

  In the years that followed, the Steering Committee introduced Roots & Wings in six "pilot congregations" with members of the committee serving as consultants in the process: Emmanuel, Virginia Beach; Zion, Floyd, Floyd-Willis; Reformation, Newport News; St. Luke, Richmond; St. Mark, Luray; and St. Philip, Roanoke. Regional workshops were held in four locations across the synod—two in the spring in Blacksburg and in Charlottesville with attendees representing a total of twenty-seven congregations attending between the two, and two other workshops in the fall at St. Paul, Strasburg and Trinity, Newport News. A PowerPoint presentation introducing the fundamentals of Roots & Wings was well received at each of the workshops with participants asking for copies to show to their individual congregations. A synod-sponsored Roots & Wings website was created and a blog set up for the sharing of ideas and information between leaders in congregations.

The logo and title "Roots and Wings" are based on sheltering and nurturing as well giving wings to our children. The logo designed by Vickie DeVilbiss, Celebration Art, uses images from Psalm 91, Isaiah 40, and Matthew 23:37.

---

35. Minutes, 20th Annual Synod Assembly, Virginia Synod/ELCA, 2007, p. 11.

Workshops continued to be offered at synod assemblies, Power in the Spirit, and the Gathering of the Ministerium. Presentations were also made to new pastors at the annual new pastors' orientation program conducted each year by synod staff.

With Bozeman's retirement in 2011, the Steering Committee took on the responsibility of responding to requests for supporting resources from Roots & Wings congregations and for planning ways for further implementation in the congregations of the synod. Resources such as weekly bulletin inserts continued to be offered to participating congregations through the Office of the Bishop-East. Home-based faith formation planning calendars were edited by Ellen Greene and mailed out to sixty congregations through postal mail and email each month throughout the year. A version was also posted on the synod's website for Roots & Wings. Beyond these efforts there was little more the Steering Committee could do in terms of making plans for workshops and addressing other needs expressed by pastors and congregational leaders. Synod staff tried to share responsibility for continued support for all these areas of responsibilities in Bozeman's portfolio, but the need for a more intentional means of support was too great for Mauney to ignore.

PHYLLIS BLAIR MILTON—SYNODICAL MINISTER FOR CHRISTIAN FORMATION

The Rev. Dr. Phyllis Milton

Phyllis Blair Milton began her duties as synodical minister for Christian Formation on October 1, 2012. Milton was hired by the Synod Council upon recommendation by Bishop Mauney for the part-time position. Her primary responsibilities were defined as giving leadership and guidance to Christian Formation and working with the planning/steering committees for ACTS and Roots & Wings.

Milton earned a bachelor's degree in business from Morgan State, Baltimore, Maryland, in 1976. In the years that followed, she earned two master's degrees—Business Education, Georgia State in 1980, and Religious Education, Bethel Theological Seminary, Minneapolis, Minnesota, in 1993. She owned a Christian Education consulting ministry presenting workshops on multisensory teaching and learning and served as an adjunct faculty member teaching practical ministry courses for students at the diploma and graduate level at the John Leland Center for Theological Studies, Minneapolis. She earned a Doctor in Ministry (D.Min.) degree from Bethel Seminary in Minneapolis, Minnesota, in 2004. Her husband's Naval career brought them to Newport News, where she began a year of "personal discernment."

After becoming a member of Reformation, Newport News in 2007, Milton entered into a mentoring relationship with Pastor Jim Nickols, who recognized her gifts for ministry. In

September 2008, she applied for entrance into the candidacy process working with Pastor Chip Gunsten, assistant to the bishop. She was approved by the candidacy committee in 2009. She fulfilled her year of seminary study at Lutheran Theological Southern Seminary in 2010, then was approved as a candidate for ordination and assigned to the Virginia Synod. In October 2012, Milton was "contracted for services" as synodical minister for Faith Formation. In January 2013, she was hired as "vicar" at Gloria Dei, Hampton, providing assistance to Pastor Charles Bang and the leadership of the congregation's school.

Upon receiving a call to become an associate pastor at Gloria Dei, Milton was ordained by the Virginia Synod in May 2014.

In an interview, Milton shared the following concerning her work in the life of the synod:

ACTS and Roots & Wings are important ministries of the Synod, providing opportunities for individuals and congregations to participate in activities to grow and strengthen their faith. In ACTS we offer courses that teach the foundational doctrines of our faith, but also provide courses that allow participants to put their faith into practice through ministry in their communities and the world.

SUSTAINING THE COMPANION SYNOD RELATIONSHIP— CHANGES AND CHALLENGES

Seven years would pass before a Virginia Synod delegation would travel a second time to visit its companion synod, the Islands District of the Evangelical Lutheran Church in Papua New Guinea. The 1995 visit greatly improved communications and established strong relationships connecting the two Lutheran church bodies half a globe apart. Better communications and stronger relationships led to the synod hosting a delegation from the Islands District/ELC-PNG in June 1999. The visiting delegation was led by District President Roewec Roenuc, who came to be known as "Pastor Roy"; Benni Zarathan; Erik Tang; and Roselyn Meromar. Pastor Paul Pingel, chair of the Global Missions Committee (GMC), shared the following observations in his report to the 2000 Synod Assembly:

The Virginia Synod delegation is welcomed to the New Guinea Islands District on July 20, 2004. Shown are the Evangelical Lutheran Church of PNG representative and the Rev. Chip Gunsten.

The synod was blessed by the delegation's presence; Bishop Bansemer and many other people who visited with the PNG people were struck by their shrewd observations about our prosperity and how it dampens the effectiveness of our witness, the aging congregations with few youth participating in many welcoming celebrations, and questions of how "church" happens in Virginia, anxious both to learn and to share.[36]

The 2002 delegation from Virginia traveled with a new bishop to visit the Islands District and see the friends they had made during their visit in 1999 to Virginia. In the seven years, 1995 to 2002, changes in the Companion Synod Program redefined the meaning of "companion." Along with those changes came new challenges to sustaining the relationship.

The changes came as a result of the Division for Global Mission (DGM) "rethinking" the ELCA's "mission principle" at the beginning of the new millennium.

In tandem with the companion synod program, the Division for Global Mission entered the 21st-century lifting up the philosophy of "accompaniment," a "walking together in Jesus Christ of two or more churches in equal companionship in service in God's mission." The philosophy is a refinement of the mission principle of interdependence from the latter decades of the 20th century, as well as an obvious evolution from the mission philosophy of the mid-1900s of "sending" and "receiving" churches ... accompaniment emphasizes relationship before resources."[37]

This change in principle coincided with frustrations that followed the 1999 visit of Pastor Roy and others from the Islands District/ELC-PNG. Letters between the two companions expressed disappointment in the direction the companion relationship had gone. Apparent misunderstandings over resources to be shared and accountability of the use of the resources were met with no response from those in charge of projects funded by gifts from individuals, congregations, and groups in the Virginia Synod. It appeared that neither companion felt their concerns had been heard. The report of the GMC to the 2001 Synod Assembly acknowledged frustrations each companion had experienced in previous years.

Your Global Mission Committee learned the importance of what the ELCA calls "Accompaniment" in the year 2000. How important it is to listen to your friends in Christ, even if they are 12,000 miles away, and to be honest in your own communication with people you care about as fellow disciples. In the year 2000, your Global Mission Committee learned how important it is to balance the material needs of a Companion Church with the time that is necessary to let a friendship in Christ blossom and grow.[38]

It was apparent to DGM that other companion synods were also having issues with communication and the coordination of projects and their financial support with other districts in the ELC-PNG. To address the concerns and establish better understandings about "accompaniment" in the companion relationships, DGM invited ELC-PNG Bishop Kigasung to the church offices in Chicago in June 2000, to meet with the chairpersons of the four ELCA synods and personnel of DGM. Pingel wrote in the 2001 report of the GMC,

Bishop Kigasung reminded us how important it is for us in the United States not to come in and "fix things." Certainly, with our material riches and resources, part of our call is to help with the material needs

---

36. Minutes, 13th Annual Synod Assembly, Virginia Synod/ELCA, 2000, p. 98.
37. Edgar Trexler, *High Expectations: Understanding the ELCA's Early Years, 1988–2002*, Augsburg Fortress Press, 2003, p. 175.
38. Minutes, 14th Annual Synod Assembly, Virginia Synod/ELCA, 2001, p. 114.

of those who cannot otherwise afford them. The other part is the time to go with those resources. Time spent to build the relationship, and to "build up the body of Christ."[39]

Following the meeting with Kigasung, communications with President Roenuc (Pastor Roy) of the Islands District were reestablished. It was agreed that the synod and district would work harder on the companion relationship with emphasis on "walking together in Jesus"—the idea of accompaniment. Efforts were made to establish a new "Congregation-to-Congregation" program where individual congregations from Virginia and the Islands District would be "yoked" together to build a mutual relationship of communication and support. Over the next few years the Global Missions Committee (GMC) assisted fourteen congregations across the synod to establish such "congregation companion" relationships. A "Youth-to-Youth Project" was begun. The PNG Fishing Project led by the synod Lutheran Youth Organization established a goal of Lutheran youth of Virginia raising funds to buy four fishing boats for youth groups in four Islands District towns which would help the youth of those towns learn a trade and provide income. The GMC hoped that such an emphasis on this congregation-based relationship and the new youth project would build enthusiasm for a visit to the Islands District in the next three to four years. It would only take one year.

Late in 2001, Bishop Wesley Kigasung invited the four companion synods in the ELCA to send delegations in April 2002 to a global missions consultation at ELC-PNG headquarters in Lae. The delegation from Virginia would be led by Bishop Mauney, accompanied by his wife, Lynda, and include Pastor Paul Gunsten, assistant to the bishop; Pastor Paul Pingel, chair of the GMC; Pastor Ted Schultz, Shepherd of the Valley, Dayton, fluent in pidgin; and Susie Mahanes, committee member, Epiphany, Richmond. The consultation was held April 8-12 and the visit to the Islands District took place April 13-20 following the conference.

The 2002 visit brought new life and energy to the companion synod relationship as noted in the report of the GMC to the 2003 Synod Assembly. Virginia Synod youth raised funds to build elementary school classrooms located on the Martin Luther Seminary campus in Lae. Diane Giessler, new chair of the committee, noted that plans were being made for another trip to the Islands District/ELC-PNG in 2004. Hope was expressed in the report that the trip would be different from previous journeys in that representatives of congregations participating in the new "Congregation-to-Congregation" program would make the trip and spend significant time in an "immersion experience" on the sites of their sister congregations in PNG. News was shared in the report that President Roewec Roenuc (Pastor Roy) of the Islands District had been promoted to work in the headquarters of the ELC-PNG in Lae as the director of International Church Relations.

Other events contributed to a sense of the renewal of the companion relationship. The synod celebrated the graduation of Mary Tankulu from Roanoke College in 2002 and rejoiced that she returned to teach sociology at Martin Luther Seminary. Members of the GMC had attended a Region 9 Consultation in August 2003. Plans were announced to publish a newsletter, *The Bridge—Ministries That Span the Globe*. The GMC also considered the possibility of establishing a Godparent Scholarship Program to provide financial support to cover fees for school for children

---

39. Ibid.

in the Islands District. Strengthening of the Companion Synod relationship was evidenced in the gift from the synod to the Islands District to establish a communications center to provide better telephone coverage and e-mail capacity. Postage was also given to companion congregations to encourage communication with their Virginia Synod companion congregation.

A new era in the Companion Synod relationship had been established.

In May 2004, Pastor Jimmy Joe, ELC-PNG assistant to the bishop, visited the Virginia Synod. His visit was timely. Joe's primary responsibility was the coordination of the ELC-PNG and ELCA Companion Synod Program. His visit helped finalize plans of the July 2004 synod and companion congregation representatives from Virginia to the Islands District. Pastor Chip Gunsten, assistant to the bishop, would lead this delegation. Gunsten was accompanied by his wife, Kris; Diane Giessler and her husband, Richard, Zion, Floyd, Floyd-Willis; Karen Mayer, St. Michael, Blacksburg; Ann Mitchell, St. Mark, Willis, Floyd-Willis; and Judy St. Pierre, Trinity, Newport News. The visit was coordinated to begin with the delegation attending the annual celebration of the founding of the ELC-PNG in 1886. Bishop Wesley Kigasung recognized the presence of the Virginia delegation at the celebration held in a soccer stadium a short distance from the ELC-PNG headquarters in Lae. Mary Tankulu traveled with the delegation and made a visit to her home in Bialla in the West Province, an especially meaningful experience for Mary's parents to see her and her Virginia Synod friends. Members of the delegation visited their companion congregations: Nahavio in Kimbe, Soi in Bialla, Bethel in Kimbe, and Kavieng Lutheran.

In 2005, the Islands District president, Pastor Hynna Motec, and district youth leader, Dacca Wagai, visited during the annual assembly. It was Motec's first visit since his election three years earlier. Mauney noted in his report the importance of his visit for continuing to build the Companion Synod relationship. In anticipation of the visit of Motec and Wagai, Mauney had recommended, and the Synod Council approved, a gift of $5,000 in surplus funds following the 2004 fiscal year to cover the costs of their travel and expenses. Their visit was noted as particularly important due to the global missions theme of the 2006 assembly, "Ambassadors for Christ—God's Appeal Through Us as Global Partners." An additional $5,000 was also recommended and approved in support of the $30,000 goal of the two-year Youth-to-Youth Project for the construction of a new youth center and living quarters for the youth director of the Islands District. During the 2005 assembly, $8,500 was given through generous offerings to the Islands Distict to provide education scholarships for pastors' children. The report of the GMC to the 2006 assembly noted that "over 30 [Islands District] students ranging from primary grades, high school and seminary were supported with these funds."[40]

During the following years, the GMC developed scholarship guidelines for providing school fees for pastors' children in the Islands District schools. In the 2012 Companion Synod Report, Giessler noted the following concerning this effort of the GMC:

---

40. Minutes, 19th Annual Synod Assembly, Virginia Synod/ELCA, 2006, p. 114.

For the 2012 school year, approximately $14,000 was raised in various ways to pay school fees for 55 students. The cost of support increased due to the falling value of the U.S. dollar, older students attending high school or technical schools and rising tuition costs.

"Expected the unexpected," a phrase often used to refer to PNG, is true. It seems that the government has announced that school fees will be eliminated for grades K through 8 and high school fees reduced 50%. If it turns out to be a definite change to PNG's education program, then the Companion Synod Committee will be re-evaluating their scholarship guidelines to determine how the VA Synod can serve the education needs of our companions.[41]

The Global Missions Committee experienced other positive changes. The committee grew to fourteen members that represented eight of the synod's eleven conferences. The 2005 Power in the Spirit planning committee embraced the GMC's recommended theme, "Christ, the Kaleidoscope of Light Around the World." The Rev. Raphael Malpica, director of the Division for Global Mission, ELCA, was recruited for the key role of Bible study leader at the July 2-9 annual summer event hosted by Roanoke College. During the event, the GMC sponsored five "global missions" workshops for the participants. It was also during this time that the committee decided that there needed to be a division of labor—a committee chair and a coordinator of the Companion Synod Program. Pastor Philip Bouknight, Floyd-Willis, was elected chair of the GMC and Diane Giessler was appointed chair of the Companion Synod Program.

Visits between the two companions continued. In 2007, Diane Giessler, Zion, Floyd, Floyd-Willis; Mary Short, St. Paul, Shenandoah; and Karen Mayer, St. Michael, Blacksburg, visited ELC-PNG headquarters, the Islands District, and two seminaries in other districts of PNG. In 2008, Rose Kidabing, president of the women's organization of the Islands District, visited the synod. Also in 2008, three Virginia Synod youth—Matt Wertman, Grace, Waynesboro; Suzanne Rhodes, Christ, Richmond; and Danielle Martin, Apostles, Gloucester—were accompanied by Bishop Mauney, Diane Giessler, and Ann Mitchell, Holy Trinity, Lynchburg, on a visit to the companion Islands District.

After years of fundraising efforts, the Virginia Synodical Women's Organization of the Women of the Evangelical Lutheran Church in America (VSWO/WELCA) brought two women from the Islands District to visit the synod. In her written report to the 2012 assembly, Risse Snelgrove wrote the following:

Youth trip to Papua New Guinea: Matt Wertman, Grace, Waynesboro; Susanne Rhodes, Lutheran Church of Our Saviour, Richmond; Danielle Martin, Apostles, Gloucester; and Bishop Mauney.

---

41. Minutes, 25th Annual Synod Assembly, Virginia Synod/ELCA, 2012, p. 105.

There were so many highlights to our 2011 convention that it is hard to mention them all. However, the biggest highlight was hosting two guests from Papua New Guinea. Mary Irasua and Miriam Muyambe traveled thousands of miles to share their love, faith, culture, and smiles with the women of Virginia. We were only able to experience this memorable meeting of our two cultures due to the generous giving of the women of the synod. The VSWO Board thanks everyone who made this dream a reality.[42]

The website of the synod provides information about its Companion Synod relationship with the Islands District of the ELC-PNG. The Companion Synod Purpose Statement in the website describes well the journey together in these past years that has been experienced by both partners in this unique relationship of Christian love across the globe:

The Companion Synod relationship exists for the purpose of strengthening one another for life and mission within the body of Christ. It offers us the privilege of participating in the life of another church through prayer, study, communication and exchange of persons and resources. It opens our eyes to the global challenge that Christ offers us today and calls us to deepen our commitment and discipleship as individual persons and as a community of faith.

Visitors Mary Irasua and Miriam Muyambe from Papua New Guinea to the VSWO assembly on July 23, 2011.

BUILDING UP THE MINISTERIUM

Following his election in 1999, Mauney gave much of his time and energy visiting the active and retired pastors of the synod. In his first report to the 2000 Synod Assembly, he related the importance of having heard "numerous concerns for the future of the synod, among them, building up the ministerium."[43] In his second report to the 2001 assembly, he articulated a vision for sustaining the unity of the synod through the Ministerium:

I have begun a Day of the Ministerium which gathers all the rostered leaders for a day of worship, sharing of faith, inspiration, and fellowship. We lifted up the importance of the Pre-Lenten Retreat for our ministerium which is a three day event of worship, continuing education, and fellowship; continued the luncheon for our retired pastors in appreciation for their service and in continuing their collegiality and fellowship and up-building of one another; began intentional prayer for rostered leaders and congregations for each conference and institution by our congregations during their Sunday morning worship; attended the first call retreat for new pastors out of seminary in their first three

---

42. Ibid., p. 130.
43. Minutes, 13th Annual Synod Assembly, Virginia Synod/ELCA, 2000, p. 16.

years of service who are teamed with mentoring pastors; sought to welcome new pastors to the synod through a two-day orientation in cooperation with several institutions; continued the clergy spouse retreat as an effort to offer worship, study, fellowship as a retreat to build up and encourage clergy spouses.[44]

Mauney called for the first Day of the Ministerium to be October 27, 2000. Plans for the first day were developed by the bishop and synod staff in cooperation with the staff of the Church Relations Office at Roanoke College led by Kathryn K. Buchanan, who also served as treasurer of the synod at that time. All pastors and lay rostered leaders were invited to gather at Roanoke for a day of fellowship, worship, and support. Time was also given for pastors and rostered leaders to ask questions and discuss concerns before the synod and the ELCA. The second Day of the Ministerium, All Saints Day, November 1, 2001, and the third Day of the Ministerium, October 30, 2002, were also held at Roanoke College. The fourth Day of the Ministerium, October 28, 2003, was held at Epiphany, Richmond.

In its annual report to the 2004 assembly, the Leadership Support Committee noted that the Day of the Ministerium had become a part of its responsibility for fostering collegiality for all rostered leaders. In the same report, Pastor Bill Trexler, First, Norfolk, chair of the committee, wrote the following:

Our committee met twice since our previous synod assembly. In our first meeting Bishop Mauney shared his strong desire for strengthening the Ministerium. In our second meeting we evaluated existing activities, with input from an evaluation instrument completed by rostered leaders at the Pre-Lenten retreat. This evaluation indicated strong support for the current menu of events.[45]

While there may have been strong support for the current menu of events, 2003 was the last year of the Pre-Lenten Retreat that dates its origins back to the 1970s in the years of the Virginia Synod/LCA. It was also the last year of the Day of the Ministerium.

The report of the Leadership Support Committee to the 2005 assembly announced these changes for future gatherings of the Ministerium:

A highlight of the year was our first Conference on Ministry, October 25-27, 2004, at Roslyn Episcopal Retreat Center, Richmond. This event combined components of our previous Day of the Ministerium and Pre-Lenten Retreats. A record 108 persons registered for the event and the evaluations were very positive. The keynote speaker for the Conference on Ministry was Bishop Mark Hanson.[46]

The second Conference on Ministry was held on October 24-26, 2005, at the hotel and conference facilities at Natural Bridge, with over one hundred rostered leaders in attendance. However, this time the event was given the name "Gathering of the Ministerium." The keynote speaker was Dr. Fred Reisz, president, Lutheran Theological Southern Seminary, Columbia, South Carolina. The evaluations of the event were very positive according to the report of the Leadership Support Committee.[47] The third Gathering of the Ministerium was held October 23-25, 2006, at Natural Bridge with the Rev. Ruben Duran, director of New Evangelizing Congregation, ELCA Evangelical Outreach and Congregational Mission Unit, as the keynote speaker. Two workshops relating to leadership support were introduced as new "program components" to the annual gathering.

---

44. Minutes, 14th Annual Synod Assembly, Virginia Synod/ELCA, 2001, p. 12.
45. Minutes, 17th Annual Synod Assembly, Virginia Synod/ELCA, 2004, p. 114.
46. Minutes, 18th Annual Synod Assembly, Virginia Synod/ELCA, 2005, p. 124.
47. Minutes, 19th Annual Synod Assembly, Virginia Synod/ELCA, 2006, p. 115.

At the fourth Gathering of the Ministerium, held October 15-17, 2007, at Natural Bridge, the Leadership Support Committee expanded the offerings of the event by including additional worship times, greater use of small group time for discussion following plenary sessions, as well as time for recreational opportunities. Attendance continued to be strong and evaluations very positive. The Rev. Michael Burk, executive director for Worship and Liturgical Resources, ELCA, was the keynote speaker.

The fifth Gathering of the Ministerium in 2008 made the move to the Quality Inn and Suites Oceanfront in Virginia Beach. Attendance at the October 13-15 gathering remained over one hundred even though many traveled greater distances to the most eastern part of the synod. The format of the Gathering continued to offer a keynote speaker for plenary sessions followed by "breakout time" for small group discussions on the topic presented. Dr. Shauna Hannan, assistant professor of Homiletics, Lutheran Theological Southern Seminary, Columbia, South Carolina, was the presenter. Tuesday afternoons became designated as free time for participants to enjoy planned group activities ranging from sightseeing to recreational activities such as golf, or a time to explore individual interests or just take the time for rest or a walk on the beach.

By 2009, the annual Columbus Day Monday-through-Wednesday time frame became the set schedule of the Gathering. The theme for the sixth gathering was "God's Appeal Through Us as Teachers of the World" with the Rev. Dr. James Thomas, associate professor of Church and Ministry and director of African American Ministries, Luther Seminary, Minneapolis, Minnesota, as presenter. Evaluations of this Gathering indicated a favorable view of continuing the event at the Quality Inn in Virginia Beach. The site provided the best off-season rates and Virginia Beach was seen as an appealing destination, especially for those who had to travel greater distances. The schedule retained the emphasis on worship, opportunities for fellowship, the Tuesday afternoon free time, and the program times of plenary presentations by a noted theologian in the areas of each Gathering's theme. The themes were chosen by the Ministerium Team from suggestions received from the evaluations of those participating. Evaluations also favored the emphasis placed on small group gatherings for sharing responses among peers and discussions fol-

Left to right: Bishop Jim Mauney and Pastors Jim Baseler, Terry Edwards, and Scott Benson sharing music after the evening session at the Gathering of the Ministerium.

lowing presentations. Workshops led by colleagues providing resources and examples of congregations implementing programs often related to the theme of the event received favorable comments and continued to be offered.

† † †

The report of the new Ministerium Team to the 2010 Synod Assembly chaired by Pastor David Derrick, St. Philip, Roanoke, provided a summary of major changes and new developments in synodical structures and programs directly related to the support of rostered leadership.

In April 2009, Lutheran Family Services announced that they would no longer be funding the Healthy Congregations program. In May, Luther Mauney gathered Healthy Congregations facilitators to solicit feedback about the best way to continue the program emphasis. Utilizing this feedback, the Healthy Congregations Steering Committee then met and recommended that the Healthy Congregations program be absorbed into the Office of the Bishop. The new emphasis is to be on Healthy Leaders with a view toward the continuing education of Healthy Congregations facilitators, as well as rostered leaders leadership training during Orientation for New Pastor, First Call, and Candidacy.

Additionally our synodical Leadership Support Committee has functioned in a different yet related way in nurturing healthy leaders through the First Call Theological Education Retreat, Gathering of the Ministerium, Pre-retirement Seminar, Sabbatical Initiative, and Compensation Guidelines. We give great thanks to those that served the synod through both Healthy Congregations and Leadership Support.

During this past year these groups were disbanded with the vision for creating a new entity that would retain some of the elements of both groups, but be born anew as the Ministerium Team. In March 2010, the Ministerium Team gathered for the first time. With much enthusiasm and passion for the health of our rostered leaders the team began conversation as to how we might live out the vision of the synod and the Ministerium. We determined that we are in a unique place in the life of the church and synod where there is equal potential for division and/or diverse unity. The life of the Ministerium will live right in the middle of this tension. We are still connected to history, have uniquely Lutheran gifts to add to the body of Christ, and the experience of community is a core value to us. We will be a Ministerium who are competent, feel confident, bring

New pastors are welcomed into the synod at the 2003 Synod Assembly.

leadership, and who face the future without anxiety. We will support one another in this endeavor and will plan to realize this possibility.

Serving on the Ministerium Team: Jim Mauney, Chip Gunsten, Mike Maxey, Kathleen Miko, Mark Cooper, Cheryl Griffin, Jim Utt, Starr Mayer, Christy Huffman, and David Derrick.[48]

Among the first items of discussion of the new Ministerium Team was the development of a vision statement to guide the team in its work to support and advance the importance of developing the sense of unity and collegiality among the pastors, associates in ministry, and diaconal ministers of the synod. Throughout the discussions, Mauney and the team discovered that they wanted something more than just a vision statement. The idea of a living covenant developed over the course of the team's discussions in its first meetings. It was agreed that the language of the covenant would incorporate key principles of the vision that had guided the Leadership Development Committee, but the bishop and team wanted the covenant to be more than a written statement filed among the many documents of the synod. What developed in the course of these discussions was new language for this new covenant defining the responsibilities and relationships between peers in service to Christ. The covenant would call upon all the rostered leaders to affirm their importance to one other as colleagues, acknowledge core values of their calls to serve the Church, and clearly state expected behaviors of each rostered leader in upholding the actions of a Ministerium centered in Word and Sacrament and Service.

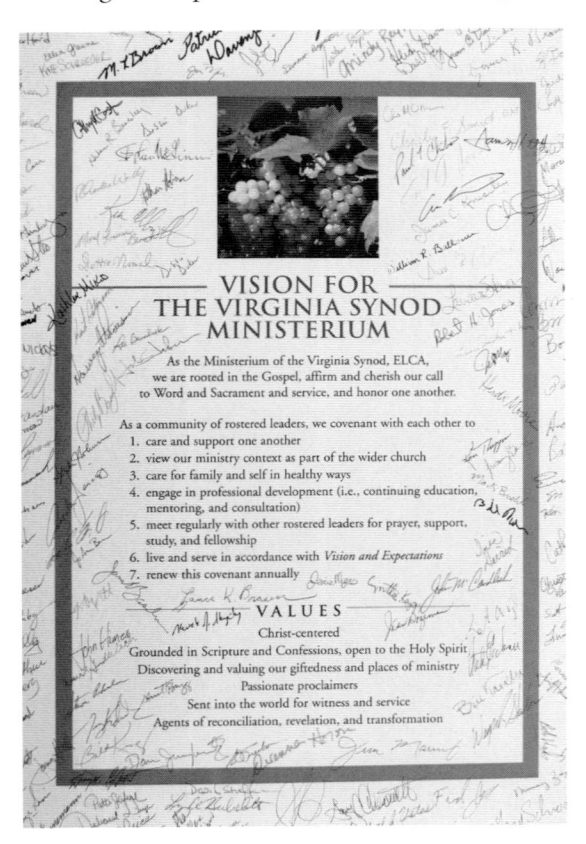

To emphasize the covenant's importance it was agreed among the team that time would be given to incorporate the reading of the document at every gathering of the Ministerium beginning in 2011 and those present at each gathering would be asked to sign their names. The team also encouraged the bishop to include the covenant as a guide for pastors to follow in making their annual written report to the bishop.

With the covenant established as the guiding document for the work of the Ministerium Team, Mauney turned to

---

48. Minutes, 23rd Annual Synod Assembly, Virginia Synod/ELCA, 2010, p. 105.

the team for help in restoring "the remarkable program of Healthy Congregations and Bridgebuilders that Dr. Luther Mauney developed."[49]

He also sought the assistance of the team in developing support programs for "healthy leaders." It would be contact with a candidate for diaconal ministry named Mindy Reynolds that would initiate restoring the remarkable program of Healthy Congregations and initiate new efforts in creating healthy leaders.

MINDY REYNOLDS—DIACONAL MINISTER FOR HEALTHY LEADERSHIP AND WELLNESS

In April 2010, Mindy Reynolds was approved for a call to become a diaconal minister by the North Carolina Synod/ELCA. She noted in the forms required to receive a call her preference to continue her work in the either the "Virginia or North Carolina area." Baptized Lutheran in New Milford, New Jersey, she received a Bachelor of Science in Nursing (BSN) and a Master of Science in Nursing (MSN) from Wagner College in New York in 1977 and 1983 respectively. In 1998, she earned a Master of Church Ministries at Duke Divinity School, Durham, North Carolina. During her thirty-six years of professional experience, she held a variety of clinical, administrative, teaching, and academic positions, including twenty years of employment with the Duke University Health System. While in North Carolina, she attended Good Shepherd Lutheran Church in Raleigh and completed her diaconal ministry candidacy process with the North Carolina Synod/ELCA.

Reynolds became engaged in parish/faith community nursing and health ministries at the local, regional, and national levels. She assisted in developing a joint master's program between the Duke School of Nursing and Divinity School and established a parish nursing practice program within the Duke University Health System. She served as a board member of the national Health Ministries Association from 2002 to 2004. She became familiar with Virginia through her completion of a certificate program in Interfaith Parish Nurse Education through Shenandoah University, Winchester, and through her work in the research, development, and assessment of approximately 3,300 active and retired clergy and spouses of the Virginia Conference of the United Methodist Church.

In the fall of 2010, she met with Pastor Paul Gunsten, assistant to the bishop, who had noted her openness to receive a call to the Virginia Synod. During a meeting in Waynesboro, Gunsten acknowledged that there may be an opportunity to serve on the synod staff as Bishop Mauney and the Synod Council were anticipating some staffing changes and future staffing needs. In an interview, Reynolds noted,

I went about life (after meeting with Gunsten) and on the Friday before Super Bowl Sunday, 2011, I received a phone call from Bishop Mauney, asking me if he could meet with me that Sunday afternoon. We met at Shoney's in Staunton and talked for an hour and a half. We scheduled a follow-up meeting a month later, and then a few more meetings after that—including one where he could meet Charlie, my husband. During that time Charlie served as the Executive Director for Wellness Ministries for the Virginia Conference of the United Methodist Church, and the Bishop saw opportunities where a possible sharing of ministry could take place between the two denominations.

---

49. Minutes, 25th Annual Synod Assembly, Virginia Synod/ELCA, 2012, p. 7.

By the summertime of 2011, the Bishop was serious about having me come on board as a lay employee—Coordinator for Healthy Leaders—for a one-year contract. I began in this role September 1, 2011 and an office was set up for me in Waynesboro. In April 2012, prior to a staff meeting, the Bishop approached me and asked how I liked my work. I told him I enjoyed it very much. He then proceeded to extend (through the Synod Council) an official call to me to become a diaconal minister. I did not have to give to him an answer right away, so I prayed and told him in May I would be honored to serve the Virginia Synod in a called capacity. Things went into high gear from there as the Bishop wanted me to be consecrated as a diaconal minister and installed as the Synod Minister for Healthy Leadership and Wellness at the upcoming Synod Assembly, which took place June 9, 2012. Reverend Gunsten was my sponsor.

In his written report to the 2012 Assembly, Mauney wrote the following acknowledging Reynolds' work after a few months on the job and before her call and consecration:

Mindy Reynolds is commissioned as a diaconal minister with the Rev. Chip Gunsten, sponsor, and the Rev. Charles Reynolds, Mindy's husband, executive director for Virginia Conference Wellness Ministries of the United Methodist Church.

The Synod Council hired Mindy Reynolds, a former nurse and now approved diaconal minister candidate, who is trained in family systems, Healthy Congregations and Bridgebuilders by Peter Steinke, who has a tremendous background in wellness ... we have been introducing her to congregational and rostered leaders through conference gatherings for leadership even while she has begun her planning for this synod. We will be having Dr. Steinke, the founder of Healthy Congregations, in Waynesboro, May 22 for our Healthy Congregations facilitators and May 23 for all. Mindy is planning for four coaching groups for pastors, a women's rostered leader retreat in the spring of 2013, renewing availability of Healthy Congregations workshops, especially for congregations in transitions. In this new year, four congregations are now using them.[50]

Within six months of Reynolds' consecration, Gunsten, who had first contacted her and sponsored her through the process of a call and her consecration to diaconal ministry, died unexpectedly. In an interview, Reynolds shared, "Upon the death of Chip in December 2012, the Bishop expanded my role, and I assumed a number of Chip's duties and responsibilities from that time forward."

Reynolds was asked to collaborate with the bishop, synod staff, and the Ministerium Team helping to strengthen the Ministerium. She provided staff leadership oversight for the annual Ministerium Gathering, working closely with the team. She also assisted with the annual First Call

---

50. Ibid.

Retreat, the annual Rostered Leaders Orientation, the annual Retired Rostered Leaders, Spouses and Guests Luncheon, and planning of a Women Rostered Leaders Retreat every two years.

In an interview in 2013, Mauney noted his appreciation for Reynolds' skills and hard work in helping to achieve the significant goals of creating healthy congregations and healthy leaders in the synod.

She has been most effective in helping to achieve the goal of having 65% of the eligible ELCA-Primary health-plan members and spouses in our synod complete the annual online Mayo Clinic Health Assessment. Congregations and the synod have saved lots of money through Mindy's efforts and encouragement. More importantly, I think we are a healthier synod of leaders and congregations.

RESPONSES TO THE ISSUES OF HUMAN SEXUALITY

Issues in the constellation of human sexuality called for attention throughout all the years of the new synod. In the years of implementing the new church, leadership on the churchwide and synodical levels did not avoid addressing these issues. The issues included the blessing of same-gender relationships, concerns for premarital sex among teens, cohabitation among singles, abortion practices, clergy sexual misconduct, the ordination of persons in open same-gender relationships, and the "coming out" of those already ordained and living with a same-gender partner.

"Irregular" ordinations, suspension of congregations supporting such ordinations, and congregations calling candidates who had not received approval for ordination became the most divisive of the issues that tore at the fiber of unity of the new church in all of its expressions—congregations, synods, and churchwide. Writing about one of the irregular ordinations of three "practicing homosexuals" at St. Paulus Lutheran Church in San Francisco, January 20, 1990, Edgar Trexler, editor of *The Lutheran*, observed the following about these ordinations and the other sexuality issues in his book about the early years of the ELCA:

The ordinations were the culmination of two years of rumors about gay ordinations. Not only was the service a first for the ELCA, it came at a time when the young church was vulnerable because the documents about approval of candidates and the expectations of clergy behavior from the predecessor churches were no longer in effect, and the new church's own documents were still being formulated and were untested. At the very least, the ordinations unleashed torrents of anger, fear, or support, depending where one stood on the issue. The immediate crisis passed, but the ordinations proved to be the opening salvo of sexuality issues that were to consume the ELCA at various times in its first 15 years.

In 1991, with surprising ease, the church managed to hammer out a social statement on abortion. In 1993 came the release of the first draft of a social statement on sexuality that created such an uproar that neither it nor a second draft was ever forwarded to a churchwide assembly. Also in 1993, the Conference of Bishops adopted a statement that there was basis neither "in Scripture nor tradition for the establishment" of blessings of same-gender unions. The expulsion of two San Francisco congregations from the ELCA in 1995 again caused tempers to flare. Between 1991 and 1997, three synod bishops and two ELCA clergy staff persons were forced to resign over sexual misconduct. Some parish pastors were removed by synod bishops when charges of sexual misconduct against them were substantiated. There were both heterosexual pastors' infidelities and homosexual pastors who declared their homosexual practice publicly. In 2001, the ELCA set a goal of deciding about the proper ordination of gays and lesbians by 2005, along with another statement on sexuality by 2007. The setting of the time line indicated that the ELCA sensed it was ready to deal with a tough issue.[51]

In his written report to the 1990 assembly, Bishop Bansemer noted the following in a section of the report that he entitled, "ISSUES":

If the first several sections of this report have been hastily perused, this section is likely to have more interest. Something in all of us likes to know where "the action" is.

As has been well reported, our church is engaged in many important studies which will eventually lead to statements. We can expect the church to speak to abortion, capital punishment, and ministry in the coming years.

The ordination of practicing homosexuals in California against the will of the church, both at the synod and churchwide level, has been well reported. The bishops of the ELCA have issued a reprimand to those persons who participated in this service, considering it as a threat to the unity of the church. Other investigations that may lead to discipline are in progress.

For Bansemer and the Synod Council, the primary human sexuality issue that dominated the formative years of the new synod would be the cases of clergy sexual misconduct and the resulting legal entanglements. The nature of the cases required confidentiality and the corporate response centered in the Office of the Bishop and in the realm of legal proceedings. Advice from churchwide legal staff and synodical leaders with law degrees proved valuable throughout the first years of the new synod. Bansemer, staff, and council did not just react to the impact of the several cases of misconduct. Positive and responsible actions were taken by Bansemer, the council, and his assistants to address the issues. Bansemer encouraged deans to have open discussions at conference pastors' gatherings. The staff identified churchwide resources, materials, and staff, and planned clergy workshops across the territory of the synod educating leaders about making congregations a "safe place" for all.

Few recommendations or resolutions addressing these and other sexuality issues came to the synod assemblies throughout the 1990s for debate and action. Discussions among voting members at synod assemblies in the early '90s noted the 1991 ELCA assembly adoption of resolutions "that this church welcome gays and lesbians to participate fully in the life of the church and that it is the position of this church to oppose verbal or physical harassment or assault of persons because of their sexual orientation." These actions were reaffirmed at the 1995 ELCA assembly.

In 1993, the release of the first draft of a social statement on human sexuality generated strong emotional responses throughout the church. The negative reaction was not only because of its contents but also because it had been released to the secular media before being distributed to bishops, pastors, and congregations of the ELCA. Both content and the manner of the release of the statement prevented a draft of the statement from ever being forwarded to a churchwide assembly.

---

[51]. Edgar Trexler, *High Expectations: Understanding the ELCA's Early Years, 1988–2002*, Augsburg Fortress Press, 2003, pp. 77-78.

However, the attention of the church went on high alert, especially to the issues of ordination of "practicing homosexuals" and the issues surrounding the "blessing of same-gender couples."

At the 1994 assembly, the Congregational Council of Grace, Waynesboro submitted a resolution through the Reference and Counsel Committee addressing the process of development and the contents of the first draft of the social statement, "The Church and Human Sexuality: A Lutheran Perspective." The committee offered a substitute resolution, which was adopted by the assembly commending the Congregational Council and reducing the number of the "Whereas" clauses and the "Resolved" statements, noting in the single "Whereas" clause of the substitute resolution that

the Division for Church in Society and the Church Council of the ELCA have significantly modified the process for developing a social statement on human sexuality. Developments in the process that have arisen from the broad and intense reaction to the first draft statement.[52]

Three "Resolves" adopted in the substitute resolution directed the Virginia Synod/ELCA to:

... state its genuine encouragement for careful study and prayerful deliberation on the topic of human sexuality;

... affirm the modifications made in the process of developing a social statement; and

... that this resolution be forwarded by the Virginia Synod Council to the ELCA Church Council and the ELCA's Division for Church and Society.[53]

The 1995 assembly adopted a resolution that asked the Social Action Committee of the synod to study and report back to the 1996 assembly if there were a need to

establish a synodical "gay and lesbian" task force to foster moral deliberation with, and provide advocacy for, persons in our synod congregations of gay and lesbian orientation; and that this synod seek ways to convey the Gospel message of unconditional love and welcome to all persons of gay or lesbian orientation.[54]

The resolution was adopted and the Social Ministry Committee made its report to the 1996 assembly recommending that such a task group not be appointed; rather, that a special subcommittee be formed by the committee to address the concerns of the original resolution in the coming months and years.[55] The committee also reported on its work in this area of concern at the 1997 assembly. That report noted the committee had included more time on its agendas for discussion of these issues and received input from persons invited to attend the meetings of the committee who had particular awareness and knowledge of issues for gays, lesbians, and their families. The report concluded, noting that it had decided to

- Include information about Lutherans Concerned and its programs for congregations that will welcome gays and lesbians called Reconciled in Christ as well as copies of the March 1996 letter from Bishop Anderson and the Conference of Bishops in its display at the 1997 Synod Assembly.

- Request that, as part of the agenda of the 1997 Synod Assembly, there be time for a small group forum on the church and gay/lesbian issues led by Pastors Jan Tobias and Daphne Burt Carbaugh entitled "Can We Talk?"

- Seek to establish a subcommittee of the Social Action Committee to focus on gay/lesbian issues.[56]

---

52. Minutes, 7th Annual Synod Assembly, Virginia Synod/ELCA, 1994, pp. 77-79.
53. Ibid., pp. 78-79.
54. Minutes, 8th Annual Synod Assembly, Virginia Synod/ELCA, 1995, pp. 77-79.
55. Minutes, 9th Annual Synod Assembly, Virginia Synod/ELCA, 1996, pp. 82-83.
56. Minutes, 10th Annual Synod Assembly, Virginia Synod/ELCA, 1997, p. 85.

In the Virginia Synod, no resolutions or actions were placed before the 1998 assembly. In the ELCA, work had continued in units and divisions of the churchwide structure. A report to the 1999 Churchwide Assembly

outlined steps the units had taken to generate discussion on homosexuality, including a new resource for congregations. Titled "Talking Together as Christians about Homosexuality" (ELCA Division for Church in Society), the report covered biblical, scientific, ethical and other perspectives.

The 1999 Churchwide Assembly decided not to speed up work on the issue, defeating a motion to suspend temporarily disciplinary action against noncelibate gay and lesbian pastors. The action disappointed gay and lesbian advocates, but it also indicated that the issue was back on the front burner and that it might be dealt with in the future in a temperate way.[57]

The 1999 assembly of the synod was dominated by the election of a new bishop, finalizing details of the synod's new long-range plan, "That Christ May Be Seen—Strategy 2000," with presentations and workshops on the theme of the assembly, "The Church in a Hungry World."

Beginning with the 2000 Synod Assembly, the debate on matters of human sexuality would dominate much of the time, attention, and energy of the voting members. It is beyond the scope of this narrative to examine in detail or try to summarize fairly every recommendation, resolution, substitution, and amendment addressing the issues of human sexuality that came before the Synod Assembly from 2000 to 2008.

During the course of the nine assemblies of the synod from 2000 to 2008, nineteen resolutions or motions were placed before the assemblies addressing or proposing means of addressing issues of human sexuality. These issues before the church primarily ranged from debate over the biblical understanding of homosexuality, the ordination of gay and lesbian individuals in open relationships, and the recognition, blessing, or marriage of persons in same-gender relationships. Some resolutions called for the synod to end debate or "take no further action." The resolutions came from various sources: congregational councils, individual voting members or groups of voting members, and individual pastors or groups of pastors.

The 2001 assembly took action to help facilitate conversations about human sexuality during this time. As noted in his report to the 2003 assembly, Mauney wrote,

The 2001 assembly charged the Synod Council to appoint a task group to facilitate conversation within congregations regarding the blessing of same-gender unions and the ordination of non-celibate homosexual candidates for the ordained ministry.

I appointed five people I believe to be very good in group process to facilitate conversation within congregations: Pastor Thomas Bosserman, Trinity, Newport News; Pastor Richard Goeres, St. Paul, Strasburg; Michael Maxey, President, Roanoke College, College Church, Salem; Starr Mayer, St. Stephen, Williamsburg; Pastor Dorothy Nimal, St. Luke, Richmond. After meeting several times over the past months, we will be offering to disperse at the assembly a booklet that we suggest can be used to begin the conversation. While some congregations have had much conversation and study, many congregations have not.

---

57. Edgar Trexler, *High Expectations: Understanding the ELCA's Early Years, 1988–2002*, Augsburg Fortress Press, 2003, pp. 98-99.

RESPONSE TO THE 2009 ELCA SOCIAL STATEMENT, "HUMAN SEXUALITY—GIFT AND TRUST"

Voting members to the June 2009 Synod Assembly gave significant time and attention to the proposed social statement addressing human sexuality that would be among the major items of business at the Eleventh Churchwide Assembly of the Evangelical Lutheran Church in America, August 17-23, 2009, in Minneapolis, Minnesota. The motion to enter into a "Quasi-Committee of the Whole"[58] and conduct a secret ballot "sense vote" of the voting members of the synod was approved. The vote was 227 in support of the social statement and 163 against.

According to the minutes of the Synod Assembly, a total of fourteen additional resolutions and four recommendations were placed before the voting members of the synod. The Committee of Reference and Counsel recommended that many of the resolutions be considered *en bloc*—together—given their similarity of intent. One final vote was taken to accept or reject the sexuality statement to go before the ELCA Churchwide Assembly in August. The results were: 220 yes, 170 no, and 6 abstain. The various votes on the recommended changes, motions to withdraw, and resolutions to reconsider or amend or delay action at the Churchwide Assembly reflected what the statement itself acknowledged about the range of responses to the social statement—a lack of consensus in the church.

A memorial—a written statement of facts presented to a governing body in the form of or along with a petition—from the 2009 Synod Assembly to the August ELCA assembly was adopted addressing more specifically the concerns of its authors for changes in the proposed "implementing resolutions" consequent to the adoption of the social statement and as outlined in the Report and Recommendation on Ministry Policies. The complete text of the synod's resolution is recorded as "Item 21.Virginia Synod (9A) [2009 Memorial], printed on pages 154-155 in the Reports and Records: Assembly Minutes, Evangelical Lutheran Church in America, 2009." Eight "Whereas" statements set forth the foundational arguments for the three "Resolves" which enunciate the synod's thanks for the work of the Task Force on the proposed social statement, a petition to reject the recommended changes to current ministry policies, and a petition to reaffirm the ELCA's current standards for pastors and other rostered leaders as expressed in "Visions and Expectations" and "Definitions and Guidelines for Discipline."

Thirty-six synods submitted similar memorials to the Churchwide Assembly addressing the Report and Recommendation on Ministry Policies. Action of the assembly placed all of these memorials *en bloc* and approved the recommendation that "the action of the 2009 Churchwide Assembly of the Evangelical Lutheran Church in America [be] the response of the Churchwide Assembly to the memorials of these synods."[59]

The range of responses shown in the various votes of the synod were consistent with that section of the statement acknowledging that a "consensus in the church did not exist on how to regard same-gender committed relationships." That section follows in this narrative.

---

58. According to Robert's Rules of Order, "Quasi-Committee of the Whole" allows for votes on matters that have come before a meeting to be taken which are not final decisions of the meeting and are reported for final consideration under the regular rules of the meeting; also allows for the presiding officer of the meeting to remain in the chair and preside over the committee's session. When a meeting resolves into a committee, discussion can be much freer.
59. Reports and Records: Assembly Minutes, 11th Churchwide Assembly, ELCA, 2009, pp. 169-170.

Lifelong, Monogamous, Same-gender Relationships

Within the last decades, this church has begun to understand and experience in new ways the need of same-gender-oriented individuals to seek relationships of lifelong companionship and commitment as well as public accountability and legal support for those commitments. At the same time, public debates and deliberations have continued regarding understandings of human sexuality in medicine, social science, and corresponding public policy about same-gender relationships.

We in the ELCA recognize that many of our sisters and brothers in same-gender relationships sincerely desire the support of other Christians for living faithfully in all aspects of their lives, including their sexual fidelity. In response, we have drawn deeply on our Lutheran theological heritage and Scripture. This has led, however, to differing and conscience-bound understandings about the place of such relationships within the Christian community. We have come to various conclusions concerning how to regard lifelong, monogamous, same-gender relationships, including whether and how to recognize publicly their lifelong commitments.

While Lutherans hold various convictions regarding lifelong, monogamous, same-gender relationships, this church is united on many critical issues. It opposes all forms of verbal or physical harassment and assault based on sexual orientation. It supports legislation and policies to protect civil rights and to prohibit discrimination in housing, employment, and public services. It has called upon congregations and members to welcome, care for, and support same-gender couples and their families and to advocate for their legal protection.

The ELCA recognizes that it has a pastoral responsibility to all children of God. This includes a pastoral responsibility to those who are same-gender in their orientation and to those who are seeking counsel about their sexual self-understanding. All are encouraged to avail themselves of the means of grace and pastoral care.

This church also acknowledges that consensus does not exist concerning how to regard same-gender committed relationships, even after many years of thoughtful, respectful, and faithful study and conversation. We do not have agreement on whether this church should honor these relationships and uplift, shelter, and protect them or on precisely how it is appropriate to do so.

In response, this church draws on the foundational Lutheran understanding that the baptized are called to discern God's love in service to the neighbor. In our Christian freedom, we therefore seek responsible actions that serve others and do so with humility and deep respect for the conscience-bound beliefs of others. We understand that, in this discernment about ethics and church practice, faithful people can and will come to different conclusions about the meaning of Scripture and about what constitutes responsible action. We further believe that this church, on the basis of "the bound conscience," will include these different understandings and practices within its life as it seeks to live out its mission and ministry in the world.

This church recognizes that, with conviction and integrity:

- On the basis of conscience-bound belief, some are convinced that same-gender sexual behavior is sinful, contrary to biblical teaching and their understanding of natural law. They believe same-gender sexual behavior carries the grave danger of unrepentant sin. They therefore conclude that the neighbor and the community are best served by calling people in same-gender sexual relationships to repentance for that behavior and to a celibate lifestyle. Such decisions are intended to be accompanied by pastoral response and community support.

- On the basis of conscience-bound belief, some are convinced that homosexuality and even lifelong, monogamous, homosexual relationships reflect a broken world in which some relationships do not pattern themselves after the creation God intended. While they acknowledge that such relationships may be lived out with mutuality and care, they do not believe that the neighbor or community are best served by publicly recognizing such relationships as traditional marriage.

- On the basis of conscience-bound belief, some are convinced that the scriptural witness does not address the context of sexual orientation and lifelong loving and committed relationships that we experience today. They believe that the neighbor and community are best served when same-gender relationships are honored and held to high standards and public accountability, but they do not equate these relationships with marriage. They do, however, affirm the need for community support and the role of pastoral care and may wish to surround lifelong, monogamous relationships or covenant unions with prayer.

- On the basis of conscience-bound belief, some are convinced that the scriptural witness does not address the context of sexual orientation and committed relationships that we experience today. They believe that the neighbor and community are best served when same-gender relationships are lived out with lifelong and monogamous commitments that are held to the same rigorous standards, sexual ethics, and status as heterosexual marriage. They surround such couples and their lifelong commitments with prayer to live in ways that glorify God, find strength for the challenges that will be faced, and serve others. They believe same-gender couples should avail themselves of social and legal support for themselves, their children, and other dependents and seek the highest legal accountability available for their relationships.

The proposed social statement was adopted by the exact number required to achieve a two-thirds majority which is required for adoption of all social statements.

With adoption of the social statement, attention moved to discussion of the fifteen implementing resolutions related to the statement with particular concerns expressed for providing pastoral guidance and liturgical resources to congregations and pastors. The more contentious debates and votes taken at the assembly addressed proposed Recommendations on Ministry Policies resulting from the adoption of the statement. Motions to amend by deletion or substitution the four recommended policies were debated and defeated. A motion to limit the number of speakers allowed for discussion before the assembly of each policy recommendation was also defeated.

The following motions were adopted after extensive debates, offering of substitute motions, amendments, and initial attempts to limit debate:

1—Resolved, that in the implementation of any resolutions on ministry policies, the ELCA commit itself to bear one another's burdens, love the neighbor, and respect the bound consciences of all. (Yes-771; No-230)[60]

2—Resolved, that the ELCA commit itself to finding ways to allow congregations that choose to do so to recognize, support, and hold publicly accountable lifelong, monogamous, same-gender relationships. (Yes-619; No-402)[61]

3—Resolved, that the ELCA commit itself to finding a way for people in such publicly accountable, lifelong, monogamous, same-gender relationships to serve as rostered leaders of this church. (Yes-559; No-451)[62]

---

60. Ibid., p. 348.
61. Ibid., p. 352.
62. Ibid., p. 366.

4—Resolved, that the Evangelical Lutheran Church in America call upon its members to commit themselves to respect the bound consciences of those with whom they disagree regarding decisions on the call and rostering of individuals in publicly accountable, lifelong, monogamous, same-gender relationships, in this church and with churches ecumenically and globally; and be it further

Resolved, that this church, because of its commitment to respect the bound consciences of all, declare its intent to allow structure flexibility in decision-making regarding the approving or disapproving in candidacy and the extending or not extending of a call to rostered service of a person who is otherwise qualified and who is living or contemplates living in a publicly accountable, lifelong, monogamous, same-gender relationship; and be it further

Resolved, that the Evangelical Lutheran Church in America make provision in its policies to eliminate the prohibition of rostered service members who are in publicly accountable, lifelong, monogamous, same-gender relationships; and be it further

Resolved, that the Evangelical Lutheran Church in America make provision in its policies to recognize the convictions of members who believe that this church should not call or roster people in publicly accountable, lifelong, monogamous, same-gender relationships; and be it further

Resolved, that the appropriate churchwide unit(s) be directed to develop, in consultation with the Conference of Bishops, and the Church Council be directed to approve, appropriate guidelines for a process by which congregations, synods, and the churchwide organization could hold people publicly accountable who are in or contemplate being in lifelong, monogamous, same-gender relationships and who seek to be on the rosters of this church; and be it further

Resolved, that the Committee on Appeals be directed to develop, in consultation with the Conference of Bishops, and the Church Council be directed to approve, appropriate amendments to "Definition and Guidelines for Discipline" and the Vocation and Education program unit be directed to draft, in consultation with the Conference of Bishops, and the Church Council be directed to approve, appropriate amendments to the "Vision and Expectations" documents and the Candidacy Manual to accomplish the intent of this resolution; and be it further

Resolved, that the additional policies be developed, as necessary, so that those whom this church holds responsible for making decisions about fitness for rostered ministry in general and for call to a particular specific ELCA ministry may discern, and have guidance in discerning, the fitness for ministry of a member living in a publicly accountable, lifelong, monogamous, same-gender relationship, and be it further

Resolved, that this church continue to trust its established processes and those to whom it has given the responsibility to discern who should and should not be rostered or called to public ministry in this church. (Yes-667; No-307)[63]

In his report to the 2010 Synod Assembly, Bishop Mauney noted the impact of the decisions upon the synod.

This year included the 2009 Churchwide Decisions. And while the initiatives on ending Malaria and AIDS, the full communion decision with the United Methodist Church, and the 10th Anniversary of the Agreement on Justification by Faith with the Roman Catholic Church might have caused some worthwhile excitement, the decisions on human sexuality have been the source of most attention.

We do not have a consensus on the new ministry policies adopted at the churchwide assembly, but I have admired how our congregations and leaders have remained in union with one another. Those who have

---

63. Ibid., pp. 372-373.

been in favor of the new policies have been very respectful of others, and those who have disagreed with the new policies have remained a part of a loyal opposition within the church. We remain a synod with peoples holding four of the different views lifted up by the Social Statement on Human Sexuality, yet remaining together. In reviewing the sense motions at last year's assembly, I was surprised to be reminded that while the ELCA churchwide assembly approved the recognition, support, and holding publicly accountable lifelong monogamous relationships with a 59% approval, the Virginia Synod approved the policy with a 61% vote.

While there have been many conversations around the synod, the Office of the Bishop has worked with 25 congregations in terms of visits, meetings, and conversations in an ongoing way. Since August, we have had three congregations who have voted twice to leave the ELCA:

Apostles, Chesapeake to Lutheran Church in Mission for Christ

St. John, Roanoke to Lutheran Church in Mission for Christ

Morning Star, Hepners to become Independent

At the January 16, 2010, meeting of the Synod Council [we] received the record of the second vote of these and gave the Council's approval for leaving the ELCA.

We are greatly saddened by their leaving, and our fellowship in Christ is diminished by their absence. We keep them in our prayer, and we hope for reunion in the years to come.

At this time in the Virginia Synod, St. Paul Lutheran in Timberville parish has now had a 2/3 first vote to leave.

The finances of congregations and the finances of the synod and churchwide have seen a strong downturn in this past year. Perhaps the economic recession and the churchwide decisions have caused a double impact upon the drop in giving.[64]

In the remaining pages of his report Mauney presented a more positive view of the synod, noting fulfillment of its mission support to the ELCA and financial commitments to the synod's related institutions, as well as generous fulfillments of financial support to the Gulf Coast Relief and specific to Peace, Slidell, Louisiana, and Pastor Barbara Simmers. He then expressed his deep appreciation for all who serve in unselfish ways the mission and ministry of the synod. He sounded a final note of hope for the future of the synod by thanking the members of the synod for the "privilege to worship together, walk together, serve together, and to be together the Virginia Synod, Ambassadors for Christ: reaching out, sharing the good news of Jesus Christ."[65]

Three more congregations voted to "disaffiliate" with the synod in 2011—Lebanon, Lebanon Church; Reformation, Culpepper; and United, Crockett. "Disaffiliated" had become the more precise legal term to designate congregations that had voted twice with a two-thirds majority and been approved by the Synod Council to leave the Virginia Synod and the ELCA. During the year, Mauney met with the pastors of each of the eleven conferences. Following each conference gathering, he offered time to meet individually with pastors that requested his time. In an interview in 2014 reflecting on the continuing fallout of the 2009 assembly decisions, Mauney shared,

I grew to love the synod that much more during 2011. It was another year of listening and more pastoral care of those who were struggling—pastors and lay leaders. I grew in love of the congregations, leaders, and pastors because of the level of commitment and, I would say, their loyalty to their relationships to one another

---

64. Minutes, 23rd Annual Synod Assembly, Virginia Synod/ELCA, 2010, pp. 10-15.
65. Ibid., p. 15.

and their congregations. It was the depth of their struggle and that we all were struggling mightily together, hanging in there with love for each other and making a commitment to stay together.

One resolution addressing concerns of the actions of the 2009 Churchwide Assembly was placed before the 2011 assembly of the synod. Entitled "Welcoming Traditional Lutherans,"[66] a significant time of debate was allotted and numerous motions were made to postpone action and substitute or amend language in the original resolution. A substitute resolution entitled, "Welcoming All Lutherans" was finally approved, including amendment of two "Whereas" statements and one "Resolve." The adopted resolution reads as follows:

WHEREAS, the 2009 Churchwide Assembly's Decisions on Ministry Policies have caused great consternation and distress to many Lutherans with differing views on marriage, family and sexuality, and

WHEREAS, some Lutheran congregations, rostered leaders, and lay persons are now questioning their welcome and place in the ELCA; therefore be it

RESOLVED, that the Virginia Synod will be a place of welcome for all Lutheran congregations, all rostered leaders, and all Lutheran lay persons.[67]

In 2012, a resolution from the Congregational Council of the Lutheran Church of Our Savior, North Chesterfield was placed before the Synod Assembly entitled, "New Category for Membership in Congregations." The resolution called for the Synod Assembly to

memorialize the ELCA Churchwide Assembly to make constitutional changes allowing a new category of congregation membership for those members who disagree by faith or conscience with decisions of the ELCA churchwide organization.[68]

The Committee on Reference and Council placed the resolution before the assembly "without comment." An amendment to change the timing of implementation was defeated, and the resolution was adopted by voice vote.

MOVING ON IN MISSION AND MINISTRY

In his written report to the 2012 assembly, Mauney made no mention of concerns regarding the decisions of the 2009 ELCA assembly, adoption of the social statement, or the loss of members, mission support, or congregations. The continued emphasis of visiting and being out in the synod is noted in his expression of thanks for the forty-two congregations that allowed the synod staff to be present on Sunday mornings for preaching and for the eleven congregations who hosted conference gatherings with the staff and the leaders and pastors of the eleven conferences. No comment is made in his report or that of the Synod Council of the five congregations that voted for different reasons to "dissolve" in 2012: Grace, Spotsylvania; Messiah, Virginia Beach; Furnace Hill, Smyth County; Corinth, Wythe County; and Rejoice, Chesapeake. In 2012, it was time to be positive and look to the future after three years of conflict and struggle.

In his report, Mauney looked to the immediate future, not the immediate past, and introduced plans for major mission and ministry efforts in the years ahead.

---

66. Minutes, 24th Annual Synod Assembly, Virginia Synod/ELCA, 2011, pp. 83-85.
67. Ibid.
68. Minutes, 25th Annual Synod Assembly, Virginia Synod/ELCA, 2012, p. 91.

As we enter into these five years that lead to 2017 and the 500th anniversary of the Lutheran Reformation, the 300th Anniversary of Hebron Lutheran, our oldest organized congregation, and the 175th anniversary of Roanoke College, we are going to lift up five emphases as we continue to seek to be Ambassadors for Christ in these coming five years:

THE EMPHASES IN OUR LIFE TOGETHER AS THE VIRGINIA SYNOD 2011–2017

As ambassadors for Christ, the things we want to focus on for the coming six years:

Tending to the Spirit of the Body of Christ—Bishop Mauney lead

Leading with excellence—Pastor Gunsten lead

Treasuring Christian Formation—Pastor Delaney lead

Caring for the most vulnerable—Bishop Mauney lead

Knowing our neighborhood to do God's Mission—Pastor Gunsten[69]

Throughout his report, optimism abounds and his focus returns to an agenda of hope and healing, caring for congregations and pastors, addressing issues of poverty and hunger, and focusing mission on the needs of local communities. The year would be one of transition toward a brighter time focused on mission and ministry.

The unexpected death of Pastor Gunsten in December would change the staffing needs of the Office of the Bishop, but in Pastor Gunsten's honor, Mauney and the remaining members of the staff would not lose heart but rather continue a faithful journey together toward the years ahead and be reminded of the words of this prayer:

O God, you have called your servants to ventures of which we cannot see the ending, by paths as yet untrodden, through perils unknown. Give us faith to go out with good courage, not knowing where we go, but only that your hand is leading us and your love supporting us through Jesus Christ our Lord. Amen.

In one of his written reports to the assembly, Bishop Mauney shared these words of wisdom from theologian Reinhold Niebuhr, framed and sitting on his office desk:

Nothing that is worth doing can be achieved in a lifetime;

Therefore we must be saved by hope.

Nothing which is true or beautiful or good makes complete sense in an

immediate context of history.

Therefore we must be saved by faith.

Nothing we do, however virtuous, can be accomplished alone,

Therefore, we must be saved by love.

The quote came after the final paragraph of the report expressing thanks to the people of the Virginia Synod for what Mauney called "this privilege to serve among you and to journey in faith with you as bishop."

Niebuhr's words and Mauney's comments serve well the purpose of concluding a history of the members, congregations, pastors, and leaders of the Virginia Synod of the Evangelical Lutheran Church in America who journeyed together in faith and love throughout its first twenty-five years of strong and faithful witness to the gospel of Jesus Christ.

---

69. Minutes, 26th Annual Synod Assembly, Virginia Synod/ELCA, 2013, p. 5.

CHAPTER 5

EXTENDING THE MISSION OF THE VIRGINIA SYNOD

Related Institutions, Agencies, Auxiliaries, Camps, Ministries, Ecumenical Relationships, and Organizations

ROANOKE COLLEGE

In the past twenty-five years, Roanoke College enrollment has grown from 1,550 to 2,060 students and the college has risen from a perception as a regional up-and-coming school to number four among national up-and-coming colleges. The student body comes from twenty-five nations and thirty-eight states and the faculty has increased from 105 to 126. A goal is to become one of the top one hundred national liberal arts colleges.

Strong growth has occurred in the campus footprint and infrastructure as the number of buildings almost doubled—from forty to seventy-three. The Colket Student Center, Fintel Library, West Hall (former county courthouse), residence halls, a stadium, and a track and tennis complex are among the new and renovation projects of the last quarter-century.

The Lutheran presence has grown with the establishment of the Pickle Dean of the Chapel endowment, several professorships of Lutheran theology and studies, creation of the Robert Benne Center for Religion and Society, the service of Chaplain Paul Henrickson throughout twenty-five years, and expansion of the Center for Community Service in the chaplain's office. The college has been host to Synod Assemblies, Power in the Spirit, Kairos, and other youth events and conventions of the Synodical Women's Organization. The Office of the Bishop and Virginia Synod headquarters has been on campus throughout this period. The chaplain has had active association with Lutheran, Catholic, Baptist, and other campus ministry groups as well as leadership in Habitat housing construction during freshman orientation and on spring and fall break trips.

College presidents Norman Fintel, David Gring, and Sabine O'Hara have worked to strengthen the Lutheran roots and Michael Maxey, president since 2007, continued this focus to showcase Roanoke as an affiliated ELCA college and the second oldest Lutheran college in the nation.

The college received a Phi Beta Kappa charter and the campus was recognized as the eighteenth most beautiful college campus in the nation. Its curriculum has moved from general education to intellectual inquiry. The college operating budget has expanded more than six times from $15.2 million to $93.1 million. Its endowment rose from $23 million to $120 million.

"Roanoke Rising" is the theme of a $200-million, four-year capital campaign to build a major campus center for athletics, academics, and community, scholarships, student support, and smaller projects. About $140 million had been raised before mid-2013.

Six varsity athletic teams have been added and Roanoke teams have won seventy Old Dominion Athletic Conference championships since 1987. Roanoke students won two NCAA national championships. Nineteen varsity teams are in the Athletic Department.

Presidents
Norman Fintel, 1975–1989
David Gring, 1989–2004
Sabine O'Hara, 2004–2007
Michael Maxey, 2007–

LUTHERAN THEOLOGICAL SOUTHERN SEMINARY

Since 1987, Lutheran Theological Southern Seminary has seen a great deal of change but with a steadfast commitment to prepare faithful women and men for ministry in the church and world. In this time, over 600 seminarians have been formed by the faculty and community at the seminary and sent to churches and other places of ministry around the globe.

Located in Columbia, South Carolina, the seminary campus has grown and been modernized with two complexes of student apartments and the addition of a large auditorium education center.

The seminary transformed during this time period from a small, regional seminary with almost exclusively Lutheran students to a more diverse, nationally and internationally known ecumenical Lutheran seminary. Though the school has attracted top students from around the world from various Christian backgrounds, it remains a strong and vital hub of Lutheran theology in the South—its largest population of students comes from the South—and it is primarily supported by people and congregations within the six ELCA synods in the Southeastern United States.

As the seminary and theological education across the country evolved at the turn of the twenty-first century, Southern Seminary moved boldly into the future by merging with a sister Lutheran institution, Lenoir-Rhyne University, of Hickory, North Carolina, on July 1, 2012. The merger was the first of its kind in Lutheran higher education. The new multiple-campus organization provided both institutions with increased efficiencies, greater reach to serve a larger number of students, and increased depth in a number of different areas of study and ministry.

Presidents
Dr. Mack C. Branham, 1982–1992
Dr. J. Frederick Reisz, Jr., 1992–2006
Dr. Marcus J. Miller, 2006–2012
Dr. Clayton J. Schmitt, provost, 2012–

NATIONAL LUTHERAN COMMUNITIES & SERVICES

In 1987, the National Lutheran Home had been at its new 300-bed skilled nursing facility in Rockville, Maryland, for seven years. The move from its original location at 18th and Douglas Streets, NE, Washington, DC happened in 1980.

With the establishment of the Evangelical Lutheran Church in America, the National Lutheran Home began serving all three local synods of the ELCA—Virginia, Metropolitan Washington, DC, and Delaware-Maryland—on January 1, 1988. In the fall of 1990, the one-hundred-year anniversary was celebrated. From 1990 to 2008, the ministry was always known as the National Lutheran Home, a one-site location.

Starting in 2008, the dreams of expanding the ministry to provide for seniors in Virginia became a reality. The Board of Trustees voted to create a parent entity to help guide the Virginia project. The National Lutheran Home became known as the National Lutheran Home & Village at Rockville and the parent entity assumed the organization's founding name, the National Lutheran Home for the Aged. A marketing office was then opened in downtown Winchester to bring awareness to the new continuing care retirement community (CCRC), The Village at Orchard Ridge–A National Lutheran Community.

In 2009, 132 acres of land off Route 50 in Winchester was purchased for the development of The Village at Orchard Ridge. That same year, the board appointed its first CEO, Larry Bradshaw, to oversee the growing needs of the organization.

The 120th anniversary in 2010 marked new names to better reflect the current and future services the ministry would offer: The National Lutheran Home & Village at Rockville became The Village at Rockville–A National Lutheran Community. The parent entity, National Lutheran Home for the Aged, became known as National Lutheran Communities & Services.

In 2011, an enhanced mission statement was adopted by the boards of trustees to more accurately reflect the activities of the ministry, while taking great care to preserve the guiding principles of the 1890 iteration:

To fulfill its Christian ministry, National Lutheran Communities & Services provides an array of options for seniors, including residential living along with home and health care services which are designed to meet individual needs.

The Village at Orchard Ridge broke ground in May 2011. That August, National Lutheran Communities & Services enhanced its mission of reaching seniors from varying socioeconomic backgrounds with the purchase of The Legacy at North Augusta in Staunton (formerly known as Bentley Commons). In September 2011, plans were announced for a community-integrated retirement concept called The Village at Crystal Spring–A National Lutheran Community in Annapolis, Maryland.

By 2012, the National Lutheran family had grown from one retirement community to three, with plans for a fourth. The Village at Orchard Ridge was finalizing phase one of construction to open in early 2013, while The Legacy at North Augusta received licensure to add assisted living services.

CHAPLAIN SERVICE OF THE CHURCHES OF VIRGINIA

Chaplain Service Prison Ministry of Virginia, Inc. was founded in 1920 by seven denominations: Methodists, Baptists, Episcopalians, Presbyterians, Lutherans, Society of Friends, and Disciples. Eight executive directors (now presidents) have served and several name changes have occurred over the ninety-two years of the ministry organization.

The purpose of Chaplain Service is to provide Christian worship, religious education, pastoral counseling, and pastoral care in the state prisons and juvenile correctional centers. We accomplish this by providing chaplains who serve in the state prisons. The chaplains also serve as the overall religious program coordinators at their facilities, advocating for the rights of offenders of *all* faiths and ensuring adequate meeting time, space, materials, and volunteers for each faith group.

During the past twenty-five years, we have seen a tremendous increase in the number of prisoners and prisons in Virginia. In the mid-1980s, there were about 12,000 prisoners. Today there are approximately 30,000 state prisoners and forty-plus state prisons. Currently, we provide thirty part-time chaplains who serve in thirty state prison facilities. We dream of the day in the near future when we will be able to provide full-time chaplains in all of Virginia's adult and juvenile correctional centers.

Chaplain Service has been blessed to be a recipient of generous donations from the Virginia Synod of the ELCA over its entire twenty-five-year history. Praise God!

LUTHERAN FAMILY SERVICES OF VIRGINIA

The story of Lutheran Family Services of Virginia is one of a deepening and expanding community of care. In the last twenty-five years, we have grown into a $22-million, 400-plus-employee organization serving vulnerable children, families, and adults in fifteen locations.

The last twenty-five years are a part of a rich history of service. Our story begins with the Rev. William S. McClanahan, who founded an orphanage in 1888 supported by the Lutheran church in seven states and that served more than 1,000 children through the 1970s.

In the early 1980s, it was clear to the leaders of the Lutheran Children's Home of the South that they needed to create a new way of serving children and families. As happened to many other orphanages, the Children's Home ceased operation and its ministry took a new shape. The Board of Trustees created two new entities: Lutheran Family Services opened group homes in locations around the state and began offering foster care services to localities, and Minnick Education Center in Roanoke opened to provide behavioral and academic services and support to students and their families.

The 1990s saw Lutheran Family Services expand in services as well as reach. The agency began an adoption program and built an administrative office in Roanoke. Our education services also expanded with a new Minnick Education Center opening in Wytheville in 2000 followed by a third school in Harrisonburg in 2005. In 2008, a new Lutheran Family Services office housed in Grace Lutheran Church in Winchester began a fruitful partnership. Minnick Education Centers, the Lutheran Children's Home of the South, and Lutheran Family Services became one organization under the Lutheran Family Services of Virginia name in 2009.

Our circle of caring has become much wider in the last four years. A generous bequest enabled the agency to start offering services to older adults; our purchase of an agency that provided services to adults with intellectual and developmental disabilities brought new and exciting opportunities.

Today we continue to help restore life's rich promise to the most fragile of our sisters and brothers by offering adoption and foster care, community-based services, services to adults with disabilities, educational services to children with complex needs, and support and services to older adults and those who are grieving. We serve with grateful hearts.

Officers
Ron Herring, executive director, 1978–2005
Julie Swanson, president, 2005–

CAROLINE FURNACE LUTHERAN CAMP AND RETREAT CENTER

Caroline Furnace Lutheran Camp and Retreat Center, dating from 1958, was incorporated on December 31, 1987. Pastor V.A. "Buck" Moyer, the founder of the camp, was honored when the lodge was renamed Moyer Lodge and the Buck Moyer Endowment was established in 1992.

A new water treatment system and toilets in each cabin were completed in a Royal Flush Campaign in 2002. An office and staff residence were added on the camp side of the property in 2003. A wilderness building at the original site of the Furnace master property was renamed the Marston Activity Center for the original resident in 2005.

The fiftieth anniversary of the purchase of the camp property was celebrated in 2007 and the fiftieth anniversary of the first camp sessions was marked in 2008. The Upper Room meeting facility and sixteen-shower/bath house were dedicated in 2009. The dining room was enlarged in 2012 and new spaces were named "Neal Nooks" in honor of Pastor Richard Neal, who with Pastor Moyer was instrumental in establishing Caroline Furnace.

In 2001, the board of Caroline Furnace established a Master of the Furnace Award for those who have "aided this ministry with time, sweat, prayer and resources and instilled the same in others." These are Masters of the Furnace, selected annually since 2001: Dr. Richard Barry Westin, Maurice "Mo" Dugard, Frank Funkhouser, Bishop Emeritus Virgil A. Moyer, George Kegley, David Nestleroth, Judi Hangen, and the Rev. Richard "Dick" Neal.

Directors

Rev. Wayne Williams, 1972–1990

Rev. Kenn Nilsen, 1991–1999

Rev. David Horn, 1999–2000

Rev. Wayne Shelor, 2000–2012

VIRGINIA LUTHERAN HOMES

Virginia Lutheran Homes, Inc. (VLH) was created in May 1967, under its former name, Virginia Synod Lutheran Homes. In 1973, VLH opened its first facility, the Virginia Synod Lutheran Home, in Roanoke (renamed Brandon Oaks Health Center in 1993). In the 1980s, the VLH family expanded into new locations with the addition of Luther Manor in Virginia Beach and Luther Crest in New Market, communities providing rent-subsidized apartment living and supportive services.

In 1987, VLH made the decision to proceed with an expansion of its Roanoke site and create a continuing care retirement community (CCRC) that would offer a full range of living accommodations for the elderly, ranging from independent living units to a nursing care facility, incorporated under a "life-care" contract. In 1991, VLH opened Laurel Meadows, a nursing home in Carroll County also serving Floyd and Patrick counties. This was operated by VLH until 1995, when it was sold to HCMF, a large healthcare company. This reduced VLH operating losses.

Construction began in 1991 and by February 1993, the new Brandon Oaks (CCRC) was opened, consisting of independent living units, assisted living units, and the Health Center. In 2003, a new Brandon Oaks Nursing and Rehab Center was opened across the street, replacing the old Health Center.

In 2007 and 2008 at Brandon Oaks, we added the Dogwood Apartments and a new assisted living wing. We also opened the Community Center, which holds a second dining option called the Grille, a country store, pool, salon, fitness center, and massage therapy. In July 2011, we opened the Pines, one of the first retirement facilities in the Valley to offer "green living." Scheduled to be complete in 2014 will be an expansion of our current Nursing & Rehabilitation Center, offering a state-of-the-art therapy and rehabilitation wing. Virginia Lutheran Homes serves 550 residents in our three locations.

VLH has had a full-time chaplain since 1993, when Dr. Charles Easley became the first full-time chaplain, called by the Virginia Synod. Chaplain Bob Ward has been with VLH for sixteen years, and in 2012 we welcomed our second chaplain, Kathleen Miko. The Chaplaincy Outreach Program began in 2004 and now provides a monthly presence at both Luther Manor and Luther Crest.

Our mission is to value and serve seniors by achieving and enhancing the best possible quality experience for our residents. From 1999 to 2012, we have had twelve Lutheran internships, providing a unique and in-depth ministry experience to those preparing for a life of pastoral service. Additionally, local auxiliaries for both Luther Manor and Luther Crest provide support to enhance the well-being and lives of the residents. For much of the past twenty-five years, VLH has served close to a total of 500 residents.

Our future plans and dreams include further expansion and renovation as needed, and at some point we are hopeful to be able to offer in-home services (a "virtual CCRC").

Officers

Rev. Carl Plack, executive director, 1967

Brandol West, administrator, 1973

Rev. Robert Fellows, executive director, president, 1974–1990

Rev. Janet Ramsey, administrator/chaplain, 1985

Rev. Floyd Addison, president, 1990–2000

Dale Ankney, president, 2000–2006

Jim Doyle, interim president, 2006

George "Skip" Zubrod, president, 2006–2011

Heather Neff, president, 2012–

LUTHERAN COUNCIL OF TIDEWATER

The Lutheran Council of Tidewater (LCT), a Pan-Lutheran social ministry organization recognized by both the ELCA and LCMS (Lutheran Church Missouri Synod), was established in 1972 and dissolved in 2011.

The LCT was instrumental in forming the Southeast Foodbank of Virginia and chaplaincies in several area hospitals and continued the chaplaincy at Lake Taylor Transitional Hospital until the LCT dissolved. Additionally, the LCT provided chaplaincy services for troubled youth at the Norfolk Detention Home for many years. Although not involved in starting it, the LCT was also active in the area jail ministries.

Other LCT youth programs included annual retreats for middle school and high school students. Additionally, in the past, the LCT provided a scholarship for kids to attend the Lutheran camp at Caroline Furnace.

Programs providing assistance to families included Partners-in-Hope, a program designed to provide "friends" to families who had left an abusive situation, and a job bank. The LCT provided, along with Lutheran Family Services, assistance to Katrina evacuees who relocated to the Tidewater area, and operated the Human Warmth and Care Fund, assisting the less fortunate in paying heating bills during the winter season.

The LCT also coordinated efforts to encourage joint ventures of the area churches through the annual Reformation Celebration and also a German Christmas service.

Executive Directors

Rev. Arne Kristo, 1972–1981

Rev. Gary Danielson, 1981–1994

Rev. W. Arthur Lewis, 1995–1997

Samuel F. Ross, 1998–2003

Thomas A. Litchford, 2004–2006

Dr. James Stensvaag, 2006–2010

HUNGRY MOTHER LUTHERAN RETREAT CENTER

The Hungry Mother Lutheran Retreat Center near Marion, dating from the 1950s, was the first outdoor ministry established by Virginia Lutherans. Camping and programming were established over the course of the first few years. Unfortunately the synod, of which it was a part, reorganized and much of the retreat center's intended base was lost. At that time the synod extended to Chattanooga, Tennessee, but now stops at the Virginia state line in Bristol, which is a mere forty-five miles away.

The retreat center limped along in critical condition for much of the 1960s and eventually was closed altogether in the 1970s. In the 1980s, a group of local pastors who recognized the value in the retreat center revived it and began camping and programming for local area children.

Today, the Hungry Mother Lutheran Retreat Center is a fifty-eight-acre site in the mountains near Marion in Southwest Virginia. Our mission is to provide intentional community in God's creation. We spread God's grace by giving our sisters and brothers an opportunity to sense the presence of God in nature. We seek to practice Christ-like hospitality and welcome all who wish to visit us.

VIRGINIA SYNODICAL WOMEN

The Virginia Synodical Women's Organization (VSWO) looks back on a busy quarter-century of service on many fronts at home and abroad. The list of VSWO projects is diverse. The eight women who have led the VSWO reported more than a dozen programs and projects meeting many needs.

Banner for the Virginia Synodical Women's Organization.

The VSWO sponsored many retreats for members. They created and distributed a variety of booklets on "Prayers from the Heart," Lenten devotions, poems, stories, and faith experiences. They supported the Minnick Education Center in Roanoke County with funds to furnish a resource center, sponsored the new library, and donated books, school supplies, and box-tops and labels for education.

Over the years, the women made hundreds of quilts for Lutheran World Relief and they sent a truckload of quilts to an African American community in South Carolina after Hurricane Floyd and to the Pine Ridge Reservation in South Dakota. They sent $985 to the women in the Islands District of Papua New Guinea, Virginia's Companion Synod, to help them as they hosted their national women's convention, and another $2,500 to help build a headquarters building for the district. Several VSWO women visited Papua New Guinea and some of their members came to Virginia.

The VSWO established a scholarship at Roanoke College for a young woman of the synod and they started the Sophie Wilson Scholarship for women attending a convention for the first time. Love offerings have supported many deserving non-Lutheran organizations. Funds in a savings account were invested in Lutheran Brotherhood (now Thrivent Financial) as an endowment fund. The interest is used to help defray expenses of VSWO conventions.

At the triennial convention of Women of the ELCA, the VSWO was recognized for giving over $3,000 for the twentieth anniversary of the national organization. The executive director of Women of the ELCA (WELCA) attended the 2004 VSWO convention.

Members of the VSWO have been active in Women of the ELCA. In 1989, Sophie Wilson was selected as a "One in Christ" participant. Barbara Atkinson was one of two women to represent WELCA at a "Stirring the Waters" Conference in Switzerland, sponsored by the Lutheran World Federation. In 2008, Anjanette Hodges was elected to a three-year term as treasurer of WELCA. Jody Smiley was appointed to the board of WELCA in 2011.

The VSWO launched a website in 2007. In 2009, the organization started a Young Women Guest Program to invite younger women to conventions.

Presidents of WELCA in the ELCA Years
Anne Minnick, 1989–1991
Sophie Wilson, 1991–1993
Judy Ann Fray, 1993–1997
Judy Casteele, 1997–2001
Janice Brown, 2001–2003
Joyce Kipps, 2003–2007
Jody Smiley, 2007–2011
Risse Snelgrove, 2011–

The presidents of the Virginia Synodical Women's Organization (left to right): Joyce Kipps, Anne Minnick, Judy Ann Fray, Janice Brown, Sophie Wilson, Jody Smiley, Judy Casteele, and Risse Snelgrove.

VIRGINIA LUTHERAN MEN IN MISSION

Virginia Lutheran Men in Mission (VLMM), a group of committed men, have raised more than $90,000 for mission congregations through the Committee of 100+, enjoyed annual gatherings, and worked on several other projects in the last quarter-century.

Following the Men's Brotherhood in a previous synod organization, the VLMM held its first retreat at the Roslyn Center in Richmond in May 1993. Dolph Moller of Christ the King, Richmond was chairman of the steering committee and he has led in arranging the gatherings ever since.

Taking St. John, Singers Glen apart for rebuilding at Caroline Furnace, a project of Virginia Lutheran Men in Mission.

When Bishop Richard Bansemer asked VLMM to consider undertaking a project to raise funds for the support of mission congregations in 1998, the organization turned to a model men's committee in the South Carolina Synod. Moller, who has also served as synod treasurer, took the lead in starting a Virginia Synod Committee of 100+ and he has actively promoted this program since. The membership goal, not reached yet, is for one hundred men and other supporters throughout the synod to contribute $100 annually.

In this outreach ministry, a total of over $90,000 has been contributed to more than fifteen new and developing congregations and they have used the funds for such expenses as newsletters, bulletins, publicity, musical keyboards for worship, and rental payments. In recent years, this support has been given to the Bedford Mission and Living Waters at Kilmarnock.

Pastors K. Roy and Kenn Nilsen led a group of volunteers who dismantled the old St. John Church, Singers Glen in Rockingham County. The church, an old 1870 frame-on-log structure, was dismantled board by board. They hauled it to Caroline Furnace Camp and rebuilt it as a chapel.

The men, led by Herb Peterson, project coordinator, equipped a disaster relief trailer with four showers, two washer/dryer units, and a generator for use in a disaster relief situation. VLMM raised $14,000 for the project. The vehicle was blessed by Bishop Jim Mauney and turned over to Lutheran Family Services for storage at Minnick Education Center in Roanoke County. Julie Swanson, LFS chief executive, and her husband, Bruce Swanson, drove the vehicle to New Jersey for use by workers in Hurricane Sandy relief work. LFS has used grants and

Herb Peterson, Lutheran Church of Our Saviour, Richmond, and Fred Arbogast, Peace, Charlottesville, beside the Disaster Response trailer, which is a joint program with Virginia Lutheran Men in Mission and Lutheran Family Services of Virginia.

donations to assist tornado and earthquake victims.

Other projects completed by VLMM include distributing Master Builder Bibles for study groups across the synod and providing appliances for twelve families in Franklin whose homes were damaged by a flood in 2002.

Presenters and chaplains at the annual gatherings have included Bishop Jim Mauney; Pastors Chip Gunsten and Jean Bozeman, assistants to the bishop; Doug Haugen, executive director of the ELCA Men in Mission; Tim Crout, Region 9 representative on the national board; and Pastors Duane Steele, John Bengston, Doug Stowe, David Nelson, Ken Ruppar, Timothy Waltonen, and Andrew Bansemer. VLMM has worked closely with the national Lutheran Men in Mission. Their officers have participated in VLMM gatherings.

VLMM Presidents
Fred Fluckinger
Jim Burnish
Jim Costie
Orville Wolters
John Schallhorn
John Lasher

REGION 9 CENTER FOR MISSION

In 1988, with the start of the ELCA, a new organizational and structural concept was incorporated into the synod and churchwide constitutions. The purpose and goal was to foster partnership and interdependence between synods and with the churchwide organization. The ELCA was grouped geographically into nine regions.

Virginia Synod was part of Region 9, which also included South Carolina, North Carolina, Southeastern, Florida-Bahamas, and Caribbean synods. During 1987, each synod named representatives to a Regional Coordinating Council charged with the initial task of selecting a regional coordinator and establishing an office location.

The Region 9 Council, in cooperation with the bishops of Region 9, voted to call Dorothy L. Jeffcoat as the first coordinator and to locate the offices in Atlanta, Georgia, in space available with the Southeastern Synod. Jeffcoat served from 1988 to 2001, when she retired after twelve years as coordinator. The Rev. Chris Price served on the interview team for the council.

The regions and regional coordinators had a unique and sometimes a confusing role. They were to foster partnerships between the synods and the churchwide organization. They were located in the regions and the ministry focus was with the synods. Beginning in 1988, they (and a support staff) were salaried by the ELCA but by 1993 there was a pattern of decreasing support. In the early documents of Region 9, it was described as a "bridge" and a "catalyst."

From the very beginning, the Virginia Synod was an active partner and participant in Region 9. Rev. Chris Price was the first chair of the steering committee and others like Sue Clark, Leroy Hamlett, and Jim Mauney were strong advocates for and supporters of the regional concept. Perhaps it was their clear vision of the possibilities and partnerships, as well as the strength of their leadership and commitment, which put them, from the beginning, in leadership roles within the region. Among those from the Virginia Synod in key roles were: Katherine Reier, Paul Milholland, Leroy Hamlett, Kathryn Buchanan, Jackie Bourque, and Pastor Ken Lane.

A very important group in Region 9 was the Regional Resource Planning Group of representatives from synods who met twice a year with churchwide representatives from congregational life (Division for Congregational Ministry) and the church publishing house (Augsburg-Fortress). Most often synods sent a staff person to this gathering. Virginia Synod sent Jim Mauney and Sue Clark.

They learned about new congregational resources and events and how to help congregations use them most effectively. They shared resource ideas between synods and requested resources from the churchwide office and from Augsburg-Fortress. A published curriculum about Lutheran heritage was a direct result of requests from this group.

The group was a regular advocate for Spanish-language resources, especially in support of Puerto Rico and areas of the Florida-Bahamas Synod. To help raise awareness and learn about needs, the Resource Planning Group met in Puerto Rico.

Other people from the Virginia Synod provided leadership for a variety of regional partnerships and activities: regional Youth Gatherings were held every third year. Jim Mauney was among those involved in the planning. Chip Gunsten was on the planning team for an event at Roanoke College. The synods decided to rotate Youth Gatherings among the three Lutheran colleges on its territory. Bishops School was a weeklong summer program for selected high school youth. Jim Mauney was among those who spent a week on the staff for this event.

Staff, committee chairs, and committee or task group members participated in forums or consultations which brought them together with churchwide staff for training, sharing ideas, and cooperative planning in areas like outreach, ministry, evangelism, advocacy, stewardship, and global mission.

In 1991, one of the most significant actions for preserving regional history and heritage was establishing the regional archives and naming them for Dr. James R. Crumley, Jr., the last bishop of the Lutheran Church in America (LCA) and a son of the Virginia Synod/ULCA. Coordinator Jeffcoat worked with leaders like Dr. Raymond Bost and Dr. Carl Ficken, Southern Seminary had a treasure of inaccessible archival records, and some synods of Region 9 needed space to store historical records, and so a natural collaborative ministry and service emerged in a regional archives. Keith Brown has been a regular participant and member of this board. By 1998, with shared funding, the group was able to employ archivist Jeanette Bergeron and enhance the archival space and storage at Southern Seminary. Recognizing the need to help congregations with their task of recordkeeping and history preservation, the group started the Congregational Heritage Workshops and archival fundraising.

An interesting decision in Region 9 was the location of the office. The initial regional office was placed in Atlanta, Georgia, in 1987, but the cost of travel from outer points of the region, changes in churchwide financial support, and other factors led to a move of the office to Columbia, South Carolina, in 1991.

As structural and financial issues took their toll on other regional coordinators and as bishops called for more and more time on ministry issues, the region diminished as a bridge for partnership and interdependence. Coordinator Jeffcoat retired and Dr. Gerald S. Troutman, Division for Ministry staff, resigned and took another position. Region 9 called the Rev. Harvey Huntley, Jr. as both Region 9 coordinator and Division for Ministry staff. After twelve years of leadership by Jeffcoat and Troutman, Region 9 was in a transition. ELCA regions experienced a variety of ups and downs.

Region 9 began serious discussions in 1999 about a transformation into a different way of working. Instead of a bridge between synods and churchwide for partnership and interdependence, the focus seemed to be shifting to a bridge between synods (bishops and staff primarily) as a result of the decrease in financial support for the regions from the churchwide offices with increasing amounts borne by the synods.

After the Rev. Harvey Huntley, Jr. became coordinator in 2001, the Bishop's School for high school youth to focus on theological education expanded to a six-day week through a Lilly Foundation grant. The region focused on unmet needs of rostered leaders. Huntley reported that the region "fosters friendly engagement with its partners that fosters dialogue, sharing of resources and cooperation among ELCA expressions." He said the region's purpose is "to assist its six synods in shouldering their responsibilities." The region continues the "process of being transformed into a multicultural mission field by the movement of U.S. citizens and immigrants into the Southeast," according to Huntley.

A Career Crossroads discernment weekend was held for adults to clarify how their God-given gifts can be used in the church and the world. A Thrivent Financial for Lutherans grant was awarded for a Life Directions event. Servant Summer was an eight-week work experience for young adults, starting with an orientation week at Signal Knob Retreat Center at Strasburg through a Thrivent grant. They "reflected on ways God calls each to serve and express their faith in daily life."

In an ELCA restructuring in 2006, Huntley took on the additional title of coordinator for ministry leadership in Region 9. An event was planned for lay rostered leader formation. The region contracted with Southern Seminary to coordinate lifelong learning through a lay school of religion.

Huntley reported that the ELCA invited Region 9 to launch a candidacy pilot project focused on identifying candidates with gifts for mission. A planning team developed approval essay questions which will be used across the ELCA. Huntley said he provides staff and services in campus ministry at more than forty schools in the region.

Contributed by Dorothy Jeffcoat, Coordinator, Region 9 Center for Mission, 1988–2001

LUTHERAN CAMPUS MINISTRY

Structure and Funding

The structure of Lutheran Campus Ministry in Virginia underwent significant change between 1988 and 2013, reflecting trends in the larger society in general and Lutheranism in particular. The constant during that period was an ongoing desire to provide a Lutheran ministry on campus, rather than simply a ministry to Lutheran students.

Prior to the merger which formed the ELCA, budgets of campus ministry agencies in the Virginia Synod showed many funding streams. A full-time ministry might receive funds from the American Lutheran Church (ALC) District, the Virginia Synod/Lutheran Church in America (LCA); the LCA national budget; the Lutheran Church-Missouri Synod District (LC-MS); and local congregations. This pattern reflected the historical desire of major Lutheran denominations in the United States to join together in cooperation rather than competition. Campus ministry in Virginia reflected the strong national system of campus (National Lutheran Campus Ministry, or NLCM) which existed under the auspices of the Lutheran Council in the United States of America (LCUSA). Staff who served a campus ministry in Virginia served on behalf of the three major denominations of American Lutheranism.

The national structure began to change about 1988 due, most obviously, to the merger which formed the ELCA and the accelerating movement to the right of the Lutheran Church-Missouri Synod. The merger of the LCA, ALC, and AELC (drawn from the moderate wing of the LC-MS) moved NLCM under the functional oversight of the ELCA. While NLCM continued to have some autonomy, it was increasingly seen as a fiscal and theological child of the new denomination.

At a time when the LC-MS was increasingly conservative, this put strain on cooperative relationships with that denomination. This tension became most obvious when a staffing position became vacant. The ELCA, as a matter of conscience, required that qualified female pastors be considered. The LC-MS, also as matter of conscience, increasingly refused to allow female candidates to be considered in sites which they funded. Because of the demographics of Lutheranism in Virginia (the LCA historically being far and away the largest Lutheran body) this tension was not as significant as in some other synods. The identity and funding of campus ministry agencies was in large part driven by the ELCA following the merger.

The Virginia Synod's commitment to campus ministry during this period was exemplary. Over this twenty-five-year period funding for campus ministry declined in Virginia, but at a much slower pace than elsewhere in the ELCA. Across the ELCA (and indeed in all major denominations) this was a period of sharply decreased giving to national and regional judicatories. Ministries such as campus ministry, which relied on benevolence funding, were hard-hit during this period. In the face of this larger trend, Virginia continued its support for campus ministry longer and at a higher level than most synods in the ELCA. This is particularly notable given that after the merger the four full-time campus ministry agencies in the state of Virginia remained in the Virginia Synod, while approximately 25 percent of the congregations and support base for synodical programs moved to the newly formed Metropolitan Washington, DC Synod. Losing 25 percent of its funding, the synod initially maintained previous levels of support for campus ministry.

Support for campus ministry remained strong in the synod, but steadily declining benevolence resources necessitated cutbacks. In 1988, there were four full-time sites in Virginia; by 2013, there remained only one half-time site. In the early part of this period, synodical and national grants supported almost all the salaries of full-time staff, but by the end that was no longer true. Synodical funding for campus ministry became flat over the latter half of this period, while national funding declined precipitously. By 2013, most campus ministries relied on local fundraising efforts and local congregational support to maintain themselves.

Campus Ministry Sites

Campus ministry in Virginia during this period is best understood as a series of concentric circles. At the center were four full-time agencies located at Blacksburg (Virginia Tech), Charlottesville (University of Virginia), Harrisonburg (James Madison University), and Richmond (Virginian Commonwealth University and University of Richmond). These agencies served smaller institutions in their geographical area, but generally focused their ministries on a major university. These agencies and their staff were expected to give leadership to regional student ministry and retreats. They served as resources for congregations engaged in campus ministry.

The second ring consisted of congregations which received a small stipend to support programs or to purchase staff time of a local congregation for the purpose of campus ministry. The list of sites receiving this support and the level of support fluctuated over this period but support was given to congregations in Winchester, Lynchburg, Virginia Beach, Fredericksburg, Farmville, Lexington, and Norfolk.

Finally, there was a list of Cooperating Congregations in Campus Ministry which had access to program resources produced by the ELCA and were listed as the contact site for Lutheran students seeking a congregation near to their campus. Most of these congregations were related to small colleges or community colleges.

Just as a matter of nomenclature and clarification: Roanoke College had a wonderfully effective chaplain, Paul Henrickson, during this period. But in the ELCA the term "campus ministry" is usually associated with public institutions and major private universities, while ministry at church colleges is usually referred to as chaplaincy.

Blacksburg
Rev. Bill King, 1984–2013
Rev. Lisa Kline, 1994–1995
Rev. Joanna Stallings, 1996–

Campus ministry at Virginia Tech began as an independent agency housed at Cooper House, the site of PC-USA campus ministry. While not formally a unified ministry, the two ministries shared a number of programs, particularly those targeted for the campus community at large. In 1991, Luther Memorial built a campus center (made possible in part by a grant from synodical sources). It became clear that campus ministry would be best served by relocating to that center. The independent agency was dissolved and Pastor King was called by the congregation. In 1993, Pastor King was asked by the ELCA churchwide office to serve as a deployed director for campus ministry in Region 9. From this time until 2012, he served half-time on the national staff in a variety of capacities and served LCM-VT half-time. Pastors Kline and Stallings were called to serve half-time in campus ministry and half-time as congregational pastors.

Charlottesville
Rev. John Hougen, 1980–1986
Marcia Becker, lay associate, 1984–1986
Rev. Jim Pence, 1992–1993
Rev. Jan Tobias, 1993–1998
Rev. Bruce Wollenberg, 1997–2007
Rev. Sandra Wisco, 2008–

This ministry for the University of Virginia has been at St. Mark Lutheran Church since its beginning. It began the period with a full-time staff person. Since 1997, it has been served by the pastor of the congregation, assisted by lay volunteers. When Pastor Tobias left there was not enough funding to call a successor.

Harrisonburg
Rev. Lance Braun, 1976–1987
Rev. Bob Chell, 1987–1993
Rev. Janet Marvar, 1994–1996
Rev. Martha Miller Sims, 1998–2002
Rev. Kathleen Haines, 2003–2009

At the beginning of this period, Lutheran Campus Ministry to James Madison University was located at Muhlenberg congregation, but the campus pastor was not, strictly speaking, part of the Muhlenberg staff. During Pastor Sims' tenure, that changed, and she had dual responsibilities for campus ministry and Christian Education/youth in the parish. Pastor Haines was a PC-USA pastor who served an ecumenical ministry which involved Lutheran, Episcopal, and Presbyterian pastors. Following her departure, Muhlenberg chose to incorporate campus ministry within its structure.

<u>Richmond</u>
Rev. Lance Braun, 1985–1988
Rev. David Benson, 1989–1990
Rev. Mary Peterson, 1992–1995

The Richmond agency serving Virginia Commonwealth University and the University of Richmond is noteworthy for two reasons. First, it was the only Virginia campus ministry agency explicitly chartered as a Metro ministry (i.e., mandated to serve multiple universities within a metropolitan area), and secondly, it was the only ministry to have significant LC-MS partnership. The ministry, sited at First English Lutheran Church, found it difficult to serve such a geographically dispersed and diverse constituency and the theological tensions noted earlier also undermined its effectiveness. The agency ceased to exist after Pastor Peterson's tenure.

Ministry

For much of this period, the campus ministry agencies in Virginia were among the strongest in the region, supplying a significant portion of the student leadership for Lutheran Student Movement (LSM) both nationally and regionally. Agency staff were extremely cooperative and worked together to host regional retreats and service trips. In the latter years, regional organizations such as LSM and the national campus ministry structure began to weaken. Campus ministry became less a child of the synod and the churchwide system and more a function of the congregation near to a given campus. This decentralization made for experimentation across the synod but also for a sense of isolation among the ministries. Lutheran Campus Ministry has historically been rooted in gathering a worshiping community around Word and Sacrament. The great strength of LCM has been the depth of its reflection on the Christian tradition. It has not been as effective in evangelism and in envisioning new models of ministry. The challenge for LCM going forward, in the Virginia Synod and nationally, is to retain its strong core while cultivating new ways of offering a Lutheran witness on campus.

Contributed by Pastor Bill King, Director of Campus Ministry

ECUMENICAL RELATIONSHIPS

The ecumenical movement of the church is rooted not in a sense that we might achieve unity, but that we can live into a unity that has already occurred through Jesus Christ. Our constitution clearly calls the ELCA to "manifest the unity given to the people of God by living together in the love of Christ and by joining with other Christians in prayer and action to express and preserve the unity which the Spirit gives."

The ecumenical work is what the Full Communion Agreement between the ELCA and the Episcopal Church, USA declares as being "Called to Common Mission."

Prior to the formation and well into the first twenty-five years of the ELCA, the ecumenical work has been evident on a national and international scale through the many bilateral dialogues: Lutheran-Reformed since 1962; Lutheran-Roman Catholic since 1967; Lutheran-Episcopal since 1969; and Lutheran-Methodist since 1977. Forms of dialogue also have taken place with the Baptist, Orthodox, and Evangelical/Conservative traditions. These have been frank discussions concerning fundamental doctrines sacred to differing traditions in order to find intersections of consensus or agreement and, where disagreements emerge, to make an effort toward mutual affirmation of those differences and a commitment toward ongoing conversation.

And, of course, there have been the long-standing ecumenical intersections so important in the neighborhoods. Genuine affection, cooperation, and understanding were built through community Thanksgiving, Easter Sunrise, and National Day of Prayer services; Vacation Bible Schools; lay and clergy prayer and study groups; and social concern projects to care for the most vulnerable in the community.

It has been called a time of "Ecumenical Spring," a season when developing relationships, building trust, and initiating many "firsts" moved the churches to seek an end of what had for generations been a comfortable status quo within a seemingly divided Christ because of the segregation of Christian faith traditions. A new sense that these divisions could no longer work in a broken world drove the movement to ever new transformations.

The document "Baptism, Eucharist, and Ministry" was a seminal effort in this quest of realizing the unity God has given to the church. It was adopted in 1983 by the Faith and Order Commission, an arm of the World Council of Churches that serves as a forum for theological discussion of those issues which have played an important role in the divisions between the churches. It gave broader conversation and opportunity for agreement or consensus around a larger ecumenical table than the bilateral dialogues could ever have. "BEM" was seen by the ELCA as a continuing resource and study guide to explore the three fundamental areas of the churches' life and faith: Baptism, Holy Communion, and Ordained Ministry.

The ecumenical movement was very evident in the life of the Virginia Synod on the eve of the formation of the ELCA in 1988. As director of ecumenical relations, the Rev. John D. Keister actively involved himself and the Ecumenical Relations Managing Group in the emerging work. He developed relationships with other churches and ecumenical organizations in Virginia and on the national scene and offered opportunities for the people of the synod to grow in their understanding of the church's unity and to commit to it. In 1985, Pastor Keister attended both an ecumenical training seminar sponsored by the LCA and the National Workshop on Christian Unity. Seminars throughout Virginia discussed the meaning of possible mutual recognition of ministry, full intercommunion, and common mission with the Presbyterian and Reformed traditions. At the 1985 LARC (Lutheran, Anglican, Roman

Catholic) Conference, the Rev. Dr. William H. Lazareth spoke to over 200 laity and clergy in Virginia about the "Mutual Recognition of Ministry: Problems and Promises." The custom of inviting ecumenical guests to the Virginia Synod conventions (later called "assemblies") became a hallmark of Virginia Lutheran hospitality.

Two other Virginians of note came to prominence on the national ecumenical scene. Mrs. Olif Staley was for years a noted ecumenist on Virginia soil and served much of the 1980s as the LCA representative at the National Council of Churches General Assemblies. Also, the Rev. Thomas A. Prinz, asked by Pastor Keister to serve on his committee during the first Virginia Synod Convention appearance in 1978, left the Orkney Springs Parish to serve in New York City as the LCA's assistant director for ecumenical relations from 1982 to 1988.

The optimism and effort of this Ecumenical Spring continued after the formation of the ELCA in 1988. The title "Director of Ecumenical Relations" became "Ecumenical Representative" while the bishop received the title "Chief Ecumenical Officer" and the group's name became the "Ecumenical Relations Committee." The Rev. Conrad J. Christianson, Jr. assumed the leadership role and continued the synod's efforts of making visible the unity of the church through teaching, working with ecumenical organizations such as the LARC Conference and the Virginia Council of Churches (including the Faith and Order Commission), and attending both the National Workshop on Christian Unity and the North American Academy of Ecumenists. He and his committee also sought to deepen the Lutheran-Episcopal relationship and affirm and encourage ecumenical involvement on the local level.

The origin and work of the LARCUM Conference (Lutheran/Anglican/Roman Catholic/United Methodist) in Virginia needs special mention. The seeds were sown in 1970 in a cooperative effort between several Richmond city congregations that formed Stuart Circle Parish as a way of building necessary relationships for the sake of the community's needs. Current Stuart Circle Parish member churches are the Roman Catholic Cathedral of the Sacred Heart, First English Lutheran, Grace Covenant Presbyterian, St. James's Episcopal, and St. John's United Church of Christ.

Early in Stuart Circle Parish's life, the Rev. John Byerly of First English Lutheran Church joined in conversation with Father Walter Sullivan of the Cathedral of the Sacred Heart (who later became the bishop of the Roman

Bishop Emeritus Bansemer, center, talks with the Rev. Chis Agner, left, Episcopal Diocese of Virginia, and the Rev. Paul Phillips, right, Episcopal Diocese of Southern Virginia.

Catholic Diocese of Richmond) to see how they could expand the ecumenical conversation and cooperation to include the whole state. The first gathering of Lutherans, Anglicans, and Roman Catholics took place in 1974. With continued statewide dialogues, various gatherings, the building of an increasing base of both lay and clergy ecumenists, and the approval of an interim Eucharistic sharing between Episcopalians and Lutherans, the Virginia LARC Planning Commission was formed in 1984. Lutherans, Episcopalians, and Roman Catholics from across the state, both lay and rostered leaders, gathered annually around a specific topic that generally came out of the various bilateral dialogues and networked with each other to further develop connections in the local communities.

In 1989, the bishops in the state of Virginia from seven jurisdictions (Virginia Synod/ELCA; Metropolitan Washington, DC Synod/ELCA; Episcopal Diocese of Virginia; Episcopal Diocese of Southern Virginia; Episcopal Diocese of Southwest Virginia; the Roman Catholic Diocese of Richmond; and the Roman Catholic Diocese of Arlington) gave permission to draft a covenant of agreement. In June 1990, a preliminary document authored by Pastor Tom Prinz (Metropolitan Washington, DC Synod), Father Raymond Barton (Catholic Diocese of Richmond), and the Rev. Donald Gross (Episcopal Diocese of Southern Virginia) was ready for the bishops' consideration. Then, at the November 1990 LARC Conference in Lynchburg, Bishop Richard Bansemer of the Virginia Synod, nine other bishops of the other six jurisdictions, along with all of the participants at the conference, signed the agreement, "A Call into Covenant." The bishops stated in their declaration,

relying on the faithful love of the Triune God, we commit ourselves to celebrate the unity already achieved through years of Lutheran-Anglican-Roman Catholic conversations and to strengthen the visible unity of the Body of Christ in Virginia.

The Lutheran World Federation published the agreement worldwide, and it became a model taken up in North Carolina, Pennsylvania, and other parts of the nation. Since the original signing, every bishop who has become a part of any judicatory of the cooperating traditions in Virginia has signed the covenant.

In 2006, LARC became LARCUM with the addition of the Virginia Conference of the United Methodist Church through the effort of their bishop, the Rev. Charlene P. Kammerer. She had been connected with a LARCUM group when she was bishop in North Carolina and was anxious to form a similar relationship in Virginia.

This covenant makes visible the unity of the churches involved wherever the twenty points of the covenant are practiced. As the agreement states, "We will:"

1) *Pray for each other, particularly at the principal Sunday celebration;*

2) *Sponsor seasonal prayer services, especially during the Week of Prayer for Christian Unity;*

3) *Encourage shared lectionary studies;*

4) *Promote pulpit exchanges in accord with the respective guidelines of each tradition;*

5) *Encourage cooperation among member churches in providing premarital preparation for ecumenical marriages;*

6) *Encourage shared religious formational and educational events, e.g. youth ministry, vacation Bible school, living room dialogue;*

7) *Develop joint efforts in evangelism and social justice;*

8) *Develop covenants among our congregations, institutions and chaplaincies;*

9) *Support statewide, regional and local LARCUM Conferences, and establish annually a joint meeting of our ecumenical bodies;*

10) *Encourage each diocese and synod to develop supportive prayer services and covenanting models for its congregations through their respective ecumenical and liturgical committees;*

11) *Urge congregations to study the existing dialogues among our churches;*

12) *Develop covenants among schools and academies for shared programs;*

13) *Ask congregations to develop and reflect on their cooperative ministries to discover areas of convergence among our four churches;*

14) *Sponsor shared retreats and formational events for clergy and parish leadership;*

15) *Develop campus ministry covenants among Catholic Campus Ministry, Canterbury Association, Lutheran Student Union, and Wesley Foundation, and support covenants at existing ecumenical ministries and with college chaplains;*

16) *Seek ways to coordinate program and planning at the district/synodical/diocesan/conference level;*

17) *Collaborate at the judicatory level on justice issues and social concerns;*

18) *Review and evaluate this Covenant annually at a meeting of the state LARCUM Committee representatives with Bishops;*

19) *Establish goals annually which advance this Covenant;*

20) *Celebrate the renewal of this Covenant annually at the statewide LARCUM conference.*

Trinity Ecumenical Parish, Moneta is a shining example of the church's visible unity in Virginia. Following three years of work, this parish was organized/chartered in June 1991. It consists of three congregations (Episcopal, Lutheran, and Presbyterian) so that the links to the three traditions are maintained, yet it functions as one congregation. Trinity also includes active participants who do not belong to the three denominations. Using different models, other parishes have come on the scene, including the Bland Area Lutheran-Presbyterian Parish and Good Shepherd Congregation in Galax. Campus ecumenical ministries have flourished over the years as well. Among them have been James Madison University and William and Mary College along with a host of locally supported ecumenical ministries to schools of higher education.

Through the work of the bilateral dialogues, full communion partnerships have developed not as attempts at merger but rather as a desire for greater visible unity while respecting denominational differences. For the ELCA, the basis for this recognition is rooted in Article VII of the Augsburg Confession that states "the true unity of the church" is present where the gospel is rightly preached and the sacraments rightly administered. Upon this foundation, these agreements include:

- A common confessing of the Christian faith;
- A mutual recognition of Baptism and a sharing of the Lord's Supper, allowing for joint worship and an exchangeability of members;
- A mutual recognition and availability of ordained ministers to the service of all, subject to the disciplinary regulations of other denominations;
- A common commitment to evangelism, witness, and service;
- A means of common decision-making on critical common issues of faith and life;
- A mutual lifting of any condemnations that exist between churches.

Though the "Concordat of Agreement" between the Episcopal Church, USA and the ELCA failed to pass at the 1997 ELCA Churchwide Assembly, similar full communion agreements were approved that year with the Presbyterian Church (USA), the Reformed Church, and the United Church of Christ. The agreement, "Called to Common Mission," was ratified by the ELCA in 1999 and the Episcopal Church, USA in 2000. The Moravian Church became a full communion partner with the ELCA in 1999 and the United Methodist Church a full communion partner in 2009. As evidenced by the Episcopal Church's full communion agreement with the Moravians and an interim Eucharistic sharing with the United Methodist Church, the ELCA serves as a bridge for continued dialogue among various traditions and a vision for what unity can look like.

The fruits of the Lutheran and Roman Catholic bilateral dialogue were no less foundational and significant. In 1999, both the Roman Catholic Church's Pontifical Council for Promoting Christian Unity and the Lutheran World Federation approved the "Joint Declaration on the Doctrine of Justification." Along with the lifting of condemnations issued by both traditions since the sixteenth century, it states that the churches now share "a common understanding of our justification by God's grace through faith in Jesus Christ." This goes a long way to resolve the very conflict that was at the heart of Martin Luther's call for reform.

A discussion of the ecumenical life of Lutherans in Virginia would not be complete without a discussion of the Virginia Council of Churches (VCC). The Virginia Synod has been a prominent participant since the VCC organized on July 6, 1944, as thirty-one representatives from fourteen denominations gathered at the John Marshall Hotel in Richmond. Their goals were to declare publicly their commitment to Christian unity and formalize their relationships with one another so that by coming together the mission of Christ would be fully lived out in Virginia. From the beginning, the VCC has provided links between its member churches and issues of justice and need. Among the many programs connected to the VCC have been Weekday Religious Education, Refugee Resettlement, Migrant Ministry, Naomi Project, Elizabeth Project, Campus Ministry Forum, and Disaster Response. The VCC also worked with the Virginia Indian tribes to attain national recognition as tribes and has partnered with the Virginia Interfaith Center for Public Policy since the 1990s to further embrace a role as advocate in public policy decisions on the legislative level. The VCC's Faith and Order Commission has been a central and regular place for dialogue in the state.

The Rev. J. Luther Mauney, a former president of the Virginia Synod/LCA, was president of the VCC in the early 1960s, and his nephew, Bishop James F. Mauney, served as president in the early years of the new millennium. A number of Virginia Lutherans have received the VCC's Faith in Action Award in the last twenty-five years, including Bishop James F. Mauney, the Rev. Joseph M. Vought, and Trinity Ecumenical Parish. The Rev. Conrad J. Christianson, Jr. received the Lifetime Ecumenist Award in 2006. Bishop Mauney has been a tireless advocate for both the work of the VCC and Christian unity in general. He built strong relationships with many judicatory leaders and bishops, served as leader in a number of denominational retreats, and attended numerous state and local meetings of other traditions.

The Rev. Joseph Vought gave his first report as ecumenical representative to the Synod Assembly in 1999 by describing the advancements in the ecumenical movement along with the growing spirit and "wealth of ecumenical involvement across our Synod: community ministerium groups, joint work for social ministry, … ecumenical Bible Studies, Vacation Bible schools and ecumenical worship."

A Lutheran-Episcopal Day at the General Assembly "was well attended by pastors and laity." Discussion also continued concerning the full communion partners, and involvement in the LARC Conference and VCC remained vital to the synod's connections with ecumenical organizations.

In 2009, the Rev. Eric Moehring began his tenure as the ecumenical representative of the Virginia Synod. His work has been to build upon the efforts of his predecessors in education; relationship-building; maintaining a presence within the LARCUM Conference, the VCC, and the various full communion partners; and ever attempting to integrate the ecumenical spirit into the life and work of a new set of laity and rostered leaders in the Virginia Synod. The development of local ecumenical groups in the communities, especially among the LARCUM partners, that fostered worship, education, study, youth ministry, and social action remained a high priority.

As these twenty-five years have come to a close, it has become harder to "do ecumenism." Internal disagreements have not only affected and divided denominations, but also ecumenical alliances. There is also the sense of fatigue that comes as the newness of a "movement" wears off and the routine takes over. First-time ecumenical celebrations and advancements that made the front page in the past rarely made the back page as the ELCA reached the completion of its first quarter-century mark. The busyness of members and rostered leaders that stretch their time, energy, and pocketbooks in their own places make it difficult to add one more item. Skepticism of and disappointment in "what is church" by an increasingly post-Christendom and post-modern world make it difficult for churches to even survive, let alone cooperate with other faith traditions.

But as we look toward the next twenty-five years of the Virginia Synod/ELCA, this may be the very arena in which the ecumenical movement might regain creditability and momentum, and become a central platform to the way we do ministry in the future. The ecumenical quest for visible unity, genuine affection, worthwhile gathering, a common effort in fulfilling the missional call to make disciples, and living out the message of the inter-cooperation of the many rather than the few for the sake of those in most need may just light a fire in the body of believers and also in those who only see a divided, uncaring church. It is a time to again work diligently to "manifest the unity given to the people of God" (ELCA Constitution).

Contributed by Pastor Eric J. Moehring, Ecumenical Representative of the Virginia Synod, 2009–

CHAPTER 6

CONGREGATIONS OF THE VIRGINIA SYNOD

VIRGINIA SYNOD OF THE EVANGELICAL LUTHERAN CHURCH IN AMERICA

In the two previous editions of the histories of the Virginia Synod, sketches of congregations included noted historic county designations. In this edition, congregations are arranged according to their conference affiliation. Unlike the extended format suggested for the previous historical sketches, instructions to congregations from the synod office were simple—note the most significant events in the life of the congregation from 1988 to 2012, including a listing of the pastors serving the congregation during that time. Sketches have been edited. Congregations not responding are listed by name only.

CENTRAL VALLEY CONFERENCE
Martin Luther, Bergton

By 1987, the Martin Luther congregation had been settled into its present building for thirty years, and stood on its own, as it does today. The church continues to have ecumenical relationships with other churches in the area, and in 2008 a community food pantry began with the combined support of eleven other churches from the Mennonite, Church of the Brethren, United Methodist, and other traditions. In 1994, the need for handicapped access to the building was addressed and a master plan was developed in 2011 to create access and enhance the building's range of functions by adding a defined parking lot, a fellowship hall, an office, and restrooms. Two interns have served at Martin Luther: Stephen M. Anderson, 1987–1988, and Arlo "Pete" Peterson, 1988–1989.

Pastors
Rev. Michael A. Lippard, 1989–1991
Rev. Susan Hove, 1992–1997
Rev. Terry Edwards, 1998–2008
Rev. Sarah Trone Garriott, 2008–2013
Rev. Barbara W. Krumm, 2014–

Bethany, Columbia Furnace

Bethel, Edinburg

Pastor John F. Taylor, Jr. served as minister to Bethel, Zion, and St. Jacob's from 1981 until 1991 when Bethel decided to separate from the Edinburg Parish and become independent. In 1992, Pastor Lynn Bechdolt served at Bethel until 1998. Pastor Kenn Nilsen began as a part-time minister in 1999 and has remained Bethel's minister to the present. A new social hall was erected at Bethel in early 2000. Bethel currently has an active adult Sunday School class and a class for third-through-fifth-graders. We have thirty-five to forty members who attend worship on a regular basis. Bethel is involved in community fundraisers for Response, Inc., a shelter for abused women and children, and sponsors a needy family at Response each Christmas. Bethel's women's group also is involved with monthly meals and activities, as well as sponsoring a ward at the Western State Hospital each Christmas.

Pastors
Rev. John F. Taylor, Jr., 1981–1991
Rev. Lynn Bechdolt, 1992–1998
Rev. Kenn Nilsen, 1999–

St. Jacob's/Zion, Edinburg

In 1988, St. Jacob's was celebrating its 150th anniversary and one of the major projects was to put siding on the sanctuary. Pastor John Taylor, Jr. served Edinburg Parish, which consisted of three congregations: St. Jacob's, Bethel, and Zion. Susan Hove served as vicar in 1989–1990. In 1991, Bethel was asked by the synod to become independent and in June of that year the parish was reshaped to consist of St. Jacob's and Zion. In April 1990, St. Jacob's voted to build a two-story addition to the original sanctuary and basement, which was dedicated on July 21, 1991. In 1999, when Pastor Taylor retired, Pastor Jeffrey Marble served the congregation until 2003. A lengthy vacancy followed, after which Pastor Katie Gosswein accepted a call in November 2006. In recent years, the congregation's members have built a beautiful picnic shelter and provided volunteers for the Spring Forward program at Zion. St. Jacob's has maintained an active presence in the former town of Conicville, faithfully offering worship opportunities, Sunday School, Vacation Bible School, and various community outreach ministries throughout the years.

Pastors
Rev. John Taylor, Jr., 1981–1999
Rev. Jeffrey Marble, 1999–2003
Rev. Katie Gosswein, 2006–

St. Mark's, Forestville, Quicksburg

St. Mark's is a member of the Quicksburg Lutheran Parish along with St. Martin, New Market. The parish at the time of the founding of the ELCA included Mt. Zion, New Market, which left the parish on January 1, 1989, as a part of a realignment. On September 13, 1998, St. Mark's celebrated its 125th anniversary in a service in which Bishop Richard F. Bansemer was the preacher. The year 1998 was also marked by capital improvements to the 125-year-old facility as cushions were added to the pews and new windows were installed. Later, new siding was installed on the exterior. In 2012, the carpet was replaced. St. Mark's has been blessed with many good lay leaders.

Pastors
Rev. Jeffrey Sonafelt, 1987–1988
Rev. Richard M. Bland, Ph.D., 1989–1994
Rev. Joseph E. Summerville III, 1996–1997
Rev. Janet Marvar, interim, 1997–1998
Rev. N. Austin Gray, 1998–2001
Rev. George R. Feldman, 2002–2010
Rev. James B. Davis, Ph.D., 2011–

Faith, Fort Valley

In 1987, Faith, Fort Valley was active in proclaiming the Word of God and serving neighbors. Two congregations, St. David, a Lutheran Church in America congregation, and Mt. Zion, a former American Lutheran Church congregation, had successfully merged in 1965 to form Faith and moved into a new building on land donated by the Carl Galladay family in 1974. In 1993, Faith Lutheran Preschool was started under the direction of Ginger Neal, a member of the congregation. The preschool, which celebrated its twentieth year in 2013, operates three mornings a week and has the capacity for twenty preschoolers. A new addition was dedicated in 2001 which doubled the size of the church to accommodate a social hall, kitchen, and large classroom space especially designed for the preschool. In February 2005, the Fort Valley Senior Center opened, meeting in the social hall two days a week. The center is the result of a collaboration with the Shenandoah Area Agency on Aging and the congregation.

Pastors
Rev. Crockett Huddle, 1979–1991
Rev. James Heneberger, 1993–1997
Rev. James Ritchie, 1998–2001
Rev. Shelby DePriest, 2002–

St. Paul, Jerome

In 1987, we were pleased to retire the debt of the parsonage, and on January 31, 1988, a note-burning ceremony was held. A new chalice for Holy Communion was purchased in 1990, in honor of Pastor Springer and commemorating the twentieth anniversary of women's ordination in the Lutheran Church. During 1996, the new *With One Voice* hymnals were purchased by members and dedicated in memory or in honor of loved ones. In 2002, we celebrated our 175th anniversary with former Pastors Carl Pattison and Thomas Prinz preaching at two of our services. Bishop James Mauney preached at our Homecoming Service. In 2003, we refurbished eight stained glass windows and installed engraved memorial plaques. In 2004, a Congregational Mission Statement was adopted. Construction of a pavilion was completed in 2006 and a dedication service was held on July 30. In 2007, the restoration of the historic rock wall around the church property was completed and dedicated on June 29, 2008. Three pastors have served the parish in these twenty-five years.

Pastors

Rev. Susan Springer, 1985–1993
Rev. Harold Burnette, 1994–2009
Rev. Kathryn Schroeder, 2009–2012

Mt. Calvary, Mt. Jackson

Mt. Calvary, organized in 1844, was part of a three-church parish until it became independent about 1950. In 1989, the congregation sold its parsonage and bought a house, which was remodeled. In 2011, a choir of eleven members introduced handbells and hand chimes into the church's music ministry, using instruments borrowed from Emanuel, Woodstock and Reformation, New Market. A fundraising event collected money to buy thirty-seven bells and thirty-seven chimes. The choir adopted the name "Hands of Harmony."

Pastors

Rev. William A. Ballance, Jr., 1978–1987
Rev. James Braswell, Jr., 1988–1990
Rev. Sidney Roden, 1991–2002
Rev. Scott Paradise, 2003–2009
Rev. Matthew Diehl, 2010–

Solomon, Mt. Jackson

Solomon, Mt. Jackson, dating from 1793, once was paired with St. Mary in the Forestville Parish. In recent years, air conditioning was installed and improvements made to the kitchen.

Pastors

Rev. Scott Benson, 1991–2000
Susan Lance, licensed lay minister, 2002–

St. James, Hudson Crossroads, Mt. Jackson

In 2002, St. James went from once-a-month communion to twice-a-month and on every fifth Sunday as well as on special Sundays. A large service book and a processional cross were dedicated in 2002, and a Paschal candle was dedicated and the congregation's first community motorcycle blessing and picnic were held in 2006. Also in 2006, Pastor Rick Krasneck, with the help of two congregations with expenses, went to Slidell, Louisiana, on a mission trip to help rebuild homes destroyed by Hurricane Katrina. St. James' first ecumenical service with St. John United Methodist Church in Edinburg was in 2006. On September 16, 2007, St. James celebrated its 165th homecoming and anniversary as a church with Bishop James Mauney preaching. In January 2010, Pastor Rick Krasneck decided to retire from the church parish, but months later, the congregation invited Pastor Krasneck to contract for services and this was signed by Bishop Mauney.

Pastors
Rev. William Ballance, Jr., 1987–1997
Rev. William Burr, 1999–2000
Rev. Rick Krasneck, 2002–

St. Mary's Pine, Mt. Jackson

When the ELCA was forming in 1987–1989, St. Mary's Pine Lutheran Church was already 227 years old, and worshipping in its third building. In 1989, St. Mary's Pine had its first female pastor, the Rev. Lucille Dorband, who led the congregation in the celebration of its 225th year in 1985. The congregation would have three more pastors, including two more women. In 2004, the congregation took on a major building program, adding a fellowship hall with a stage, two classrooms, a pastor's study, a commercial kitchen, and larger, handicapped-accessible bathrooms. In 2006, the congregation called Pastor Van Stee to serve as pastor. They also voted to adopt the new hymnal of the ELCA, *Evangelical Lutheran Worship*. For the first time ever, air conditioning was added to the nave, making afternoon and evening services in the summer possible. It is by God's amazing grace that we have had more than two and a half centuries of ministry in the Mt. Jackson area, and we are blessed to be a part of the ELCA.

Pastors
Rev. Lucille S. Dorband, 1981–1988
Rev. Scott Benson, 1990–2000
Rev. Tara Magoon, 2001–2005
Rev. Karen Shumate Van Stee, 2005–

St. Matthew, Toms Brook

In 1987, the Toms Brook Parish served by the Rev. Jeffrey D. May dissolved and St. Matthew voted in 1988 to form the Mt. Olive Lutheran Parish with St. Stephen Lutheran Church, west of Strasburg on the Back Road. Since this partnership was formed, St. Matthew has maintained services on every Sunday, with Sunday School at 10 a.m. and Church Service at 11 a.m. Pastor James R. Daley, the first pastor of the new parish in 1988, served until 1994, when he accepted a call to Shenandoah. In 1995, the Rev. James E. Baseler accepted a call to be pastor of St. Matthew and continued to serve until his retirement in January 2012. In 1999, a forty-by-twenty-four-foot picnic shelter was built. In 2006, we began using the *Evangelical Lutheran Worship* hymnal. In 2007, St. Matthew came together with other congregations from the Central Valley Conference to form Shenandoah Valley Lutheran Ministries (SVLM), which began Luke's Backpack, the feeding ministry for children in Shenandoah County. In the spring of 2012, St. Matthew voted to join the North Mountain Parish, which is comprised of St. Stephen (prior Mt. Olive Parish) and St. Peter (twenty-five years ago, Toms Brook Parish). With this new parish we were able to call the Rev. Jonathan and the Rev. Deanna Boynton, who started on June 17, 2012.

Pastors

Rev. Jeffrey D. May, 1984–1987

Rev. James Daley, 1988–1994

Rev. James E. Baseler, 1995–2012

Rev. Jonathan M. Boynton, 2012–2014

Rev. Deanna S. Boynton, 2012–

Mt. Zion, New Market

Mt. Zion belonged to the Quicksburg Lutheran Parish from 1934 to 1988, when our congregation voted to become independent on January 1, 1989. At the end of 1988, we built a new parsonage in New Market. In 2003–2004, we celebrated our 150th anniversary with a cookbook and a history. During the fall and winter months, we cut wood for those in need. In August 2005, a long-range planning team was appointed to develop a plan for our congregation, resulting in a vision and a mission statement. Out of these statements, long-range plans were developed and we decided to build a new social hall and kitchen. On September 30, 2007, we voted to build a building. On March 30, 2008, a groundbreaking service was led by Bishop James Mauney, and the building was completed by September 2008, with members doing much of the work. In 2009, we started our "Time Out for God" evenings and have continued this summer intergenerational Bible study and fellowship. In 2009, the cemetery headstones were individually hand-cleaned and the outdoor shrine was restored by redoing the rock walls, adding a prayer bench, and installing electricity and water.

Pastors

Rev. Jeff Sonafelt, 1989–1996

Rev. Amy Crump, 1997–

Rev. Jeff May, 2004–2008

Rev. Debbie Dukes, 2008–

Reformation, New Market

Reformation Evangelical Lutheran Church has been a proud partner in the ELCA for twenty-five years. In 1990, Reformation celebrated its bicentennial. On August 2, 1992, the congregation celebrated a groundbreaking for a new addition to the building that included office space, a music room, a conference room, numerous Sunday School classrooms, and space for the preschool. It was completed and dedicated on Sunday, June 6, 1993. During the years 1995–2002, stained glass windows were installed in the worship area, narthex, and overflow area. In 2004, the congregation purchased and installed a Shantz organ, adding a new dimension to our worship experience. In 2007, the congregation established an endowment in excess of $1.3 million that is used to fund current ministry projects and will fund future ministry projects for years to come. The youth of our congregation have been active participants in Virginia Synod youth ministry and regularly attend national Youth Gatherings. In 2007, the congregation gave three gifts of $46,000 each to ELCA Domestic Disaster Relief, the ELCA World Hunger Appeal, and the National Lutheran Home.

Pastors
Rev. C.B. Troutman, 1970–1987
Rev. George L. Sims, 1988–2001
Rev. Paul St. Clair, 2002–2005
Rev. Jeffrey R. Sonafelt, 2006–

Prince of Peace, Orkney Springs/Basye

In 1987, Prince of Peace was a vibrant place for ministry within the communities of Basye, Orkney Springs, and the Bryce Resort and also in a close relationship with its next-door neighbor, Shrine Mont Episcopal Retreat Center. In 1991, the church ended its mission status and amicably separated from nearby Morning Star Lutheran Church. The Rev. John Koehnlein, who had served both congregations, resigned that year. Prince of Peace then called its first full-time pastor, the Rev. G. William Nabers. During his seventeen-year tenure, the congregation's relationship with the community at Bryce Resort was strengthened and the church campus was expanded considerably. In 2002, the church building grew with the addition of Stidley Hall, which included an up-to-date kitchen, handicapped-accessible bathrooms, and an office suite, mostly done by hand by members of the church. In 2008, a picnic pavilion was completed and dedicated to the memory of members Mary and Hank Canaday. The ordination and installation of the Rev. David C. Drebes was held on October 10, 2010. In 2011, the sanctuary was enhanced with the remodeling of the chancel. Bishop Mauney led a dedication of the chancel.

Pastors
Rev. John Koehnlein, 1983–1991
Rev. G. William Nabers, 1993–2010
Rev. Dianna Horton, interim, 2010
Rev. David C. Drebes, 2010–

St. Martin, New Market, Quicksburg

St. Martin is a member of the Quicksburg Lutheran Parish, along with St. Mark's, Forestville. The parish at the time of the founding of the ELCA included Mt. Zion, New Market, which left the parish on January 1, 1989, as a part of a realignment suggested by the synod. One of our lay leaders, Helen Neese, was a member of the Synod Council at the time of the founding of the ELCA and the founding of the Virginia Synod of the ELCA. On April 29, 1990, St. Martin celebrated its one-hundredth anniversary with worship and a fellowship meal. Several improvements to the facility have been done in the twenty-five years since the founding of the ELCA. In 2012, the parking lot was paved and lined to make the parking easier for members and guests.

Pastors

Rev. Jeffrey Sonafelt, 1987–1988

Rev. Richard M. Bland, Ph.D., 1989–1994

Rev. Joseph E. Summerville III, 1996–1997

Rev. Janet Marvar, interim, 1997–1998

Rev. N. Austin Gray, 1998–2001

Rev. George R. Feldman, 2002–2010

Rev. James B. Davis, Ph.D., 2011–

St. Paul, Strasburg

The congregation rededicated its building on January 11, 1987, after an extensive renovation which included reversing the sanctuary and adding an enlarged narthex and a balcony with a new Andover pipe organ. On August 11, 1988, the Congregational Council voted to establish a childcare center. The congregation agreed on August 27, 1989, to renovate a rental property as church administrative offices. After using interns for three years, the congregation voted on April 22, 1990, to call Darla J. Kincaid as associate minister; she resigned to accept another call in 1996. In 1997, the congregation celebrated its 250th anniversary with a variety of activities. Pastor Richard Goeres was called as pastor in 2001. In 2002, the Congregational Council voted to hire a "resource person for Christian education and youth ministry." Sonya Williams-Giersch was hired on November 14, 2002. She was designated minister of congregational life on June 12, 2003, and was called as an associate in ministry on November 19, 2005. In February 2003, an adjacent duplex structure was demolished to provide more parking. The congregation voted on May 25 to replace the flat roof on the parish house with a pitched roof. In 2004, the congregation voted to relocate the childcare center from the church to a new building on King Street. The program is currently serving sixty-one children. In 2009, the All Saints Chapel was turned into a multipurpose room including access to the sanctuary for overflow seating, contemporary worship, and meetings.

Pastors

Rev. William H. Hall II, 1980–2000

Rev. Darla J. Kincaid, associate, 1990–1996

Rev. Robert K. Bohm, interim, 2000–2001
Rev. Richard J. Goeres, 2001–2009
Sonya Williams-Giersch, AIM, 2005–2011
Rev. Russell O. Siler, interim, 2009–2011
Rev. Timothy Waltonen, interim, 2011–2013
Rev. William Nabers, 2014–

St. Stephen, Strasburg

In 1988, St. Stephen voted to join the Mt. Olive Lutheran Parish. Pastor James R. Daley became the first pastor of the new parish in 1988 and served until 1994, when he accepted a call to Shenandoah. In 1995, the Rev. James E. Baseler accepted a call to St. Stephen and the Mt. Olive Lutheran Parish and continued to serve until his retirement in January 2012. The *With One Voice* hymnals were also purchased in the late 1990s, and in 2006, we began using the *Evangelical Lutheran Worship* hymnal. In 2007, St. Stephen came together with other congregations from the Central Valley Conference to form Shenandoah Valley Lutheran Ministries (SVLM). This came from the discernment that stronger social ministry can be done together as a group of churches. From this, Luke's Backpack, the feeding ministry for children in Shenandoah County, was formed. Twelve members have taken part in the ACTS class and three members went to Israel with the Virginia Synod. St. Stephen is passionate about its young people going to camp. Many scholarships to camp have sent our young people to Caroline Furnace Lutheran Camp during their middle school years. In the spring of 2012, St. Stephen voted to join the North Mountain Parish, which is comprised of St. Matthew (prior Mt. Olive Parish) and St. Peter, Toms Brook. With this new parish we were able to call the Rev. Jonathan and the Rev. Deanna Boynton, who started on June 17, 2012.

Pastors
Rev. James Daley, 1988–1994
Rev. James E. Baseler, 1995–2012
Rev. Deanna S. Boynton, 2012–
Rev. Jonathan M. Boynton, 2012–2014

Rader, Timberville

Rader was once a part of a four-point parish but we continue today as a two-point parish, partnered with St. Paul, Timberville. In 1990, Rader celebrated its 225th anniversary with Bishop V. A. Moyer presiding at the service of worship. In 1990, a gift of land enabled a building renovation and addition creating a new narthex with an elevator, and an education wing that included a pastor's office, library, kitchenette, nursery, and four classrooms. In 1995, Rader hosted a gathering of the Henkel Family National Association. In the late 1990s, an outdoor children's playground was erected. In early 2002, there was an expansion of the church cemetery. In 2007, 150 new *Lutheran Book of Worship* volumes were dedicated. In 2009, an extensive restoration project greatly enhanced both the oldest and current church cemeteries. Rader provides annual support of Camp Caroline Furnace, weekday religious education, the area food bank, the Samaritan's Purse Christmas Project, and the sponsorship of a child through World Vision.

Pastors
Rev. John Yeich, 1979–1993
Rev. Jeffrey May, 1993–1998
Rev. Mark Briehl, 1998–2006
Rev. Kathleen Miko, 2007–2012
Rev. Kirk Shipley, interim, 2012–

St. John, Timberville

St. Paul, Timberville

In 1990, we celebrated our one-hundredth anniversary with Bishop Richard Bansemer participating. An anniversary book, *Celebrating Our First 100 Years of Memories*, was published. On June 12, 1994, a groundbreaking was held for an addition to the church. The fellowship hall with kitchen and restrooms was dedicated on June 9, 1995, with Bishop Bansemer as speaker. In 1997, the congregation contributed funds and labor to renovate a cabin at Camp Caroline Furnace. In 2007, a pavilion was built behind the church. Our outreach program consists of help for local families with financial needs, a food pantry, school backpack program, delivery of Meals on Wheels, helping make one hundred or more quilts each year for Lutheran World Relief, and making lap robes for local care facilities and cancer centers, as well as baby blankets.

Pastors
Rev. John D. Yeich, 1979–1993
Rev. Jeffrey May, 1993–1998
Rev. Mark S. Briehl, 1998–2006
Rev. Kathleen Miko, 2007–2012
Rev. Kirk J. Shipley, interim, 2012–

St. Peter, Toms Brook

In 1987, the Toms Brook Parish dissolved and the Rev. Jeffrey D. May left the call. The Rev. George Feldman came in late 1987 and served as the pastor at St. Peter until 2002. In this time we called our own pastor rather than being part of a parish. We were blessed with a strong youth ministry and youth choir during this era. In November 2005, we called Patrice Arthur to lead our congregation as a Theological Entrance for Emerging Ministry (TEEM) candidate through the ELCA. She was ordained as our pastor in 2010 and later that year tragically passed away. During her time as our pastor we saw a sense of vibrant ministry in our congregation and our community. The Rev. Dianna Horton, our interim pastor, 2010–2012, was integral in our transitions of ministry. In 2007, St. Peter came together with other congregations from the Central Valley

Conference to form Shenandoah Valley Lutheran Ministries (SVLM). St. Peter is currently very active in supporting the ministries of SVLM in addition to shopping for the Empty Stocking Fund. In the spring of 2012, St. Peter voted to join the North Mountain Parish, comprised of St. Matthew (twenty-five years prior, Toms Brook Parish) and St. Stephen, Strasburg. With this new parish we were able to call the Rev. Jonathan and the Rev. Deanna Boynton, who started on June 17, 2012.

Pastors
Rev. Jeffrey May, 1984–1987
Rev. George Feldman, 1987–2002
Patrice T. Arthur, Theological Entrance for Emerging Ministry (TEEM), 2005–2009
Patrice T. Arthur, 2010
Rev. Dianna Horton, interim, 2010–2012
Rev. Jonathan M. Boynton, 2012–2014
Rev. Deanna S. Boynton, 2012–

Emanuel, Woodstock

In the past twenty-five years, Emanuel, Woodstock has experienced growth in many ways. The addition of an 8:30 a.m. service with Holy Communion each week began under the direction of Pastor David Fritch. From its inception, attendance has more than tripled. Under the guidance of Pastor Lance Braun, Emanuel assisted in celebrating the Town of Woodstock's 250th anniversary with a float. Pastor Braun served as the town crier who began the parade. From a facilities perspective, the past twenty-five years have seen a remarkable overhaul of church offices and Sunday School rooms, as well as the repainting of the sanctuary and social hall. Beginning in 1996, each of the Sunday School rooms was remodeled and the bathrooms were renovated. Also in 1996, the church organ was completely remodeled and dedicated and a new copper steeple was added. A new stage curtain and heating and cooling units for each of the Sunday School rooms were added, as well as the choir room and kitchen. A handicapped ramp was built. In addition, the church office has been remodeled to ensure ease of access. In 2011, we had a yearlong celebration of our 250th year, which culminated with Bishop James Mauney preaching and presiding over worship. In August 2012, Emanuel highlighted the 300th year of the Muhlenberg Legacy with the church hosting a service which featured the robe that the Rev. John Peter Gabriel Muhlenberg wore, now on display at Philadelphia Seminary.

Pastors
Rev. David Fritch, 1983–1993
Rev. Lance K. Braun, 1994–2004
Rev. Marion Cobb, 2006–2007
Rev. Nathan Robinson, 2008–

Mt. Zion, Woodstock

In 1987, a big change took place for the congregation when Mt. Zion separated from a two-church parish to become a single congregation. An 8 a.m. service, in addition to the 11 a.m. service, began in 1994 and Holy Communion at both services every Sunday started in 2001. A new mission statement was created in 2003, stating: "Empowered by the spirit, Mt. Zion equips people to serve in Jesus' name." A church library was organized in 2006 and a nature garden was dedicated in 2007 in memory of Pfc. Thomas Wilson, a member of Mt. Zion who served in the Army in Afghanistan. The congregation's 125th anniversary was celebrated on November 4, 2009, with an old-time worship service with music led by an antique pump organ, members in period dress, a meal, and display of material from the archives room established in 2008. Since 2011, Mt. Zion has served as Shenandoah County's central distribution center for Luke's Backpack, a growing program providing backpacks of weekend food supplies for needy schoolchildren. With God's grace, Mt. Zion remains true to its mission and strong in service.

Pastors
Rev. Michael L. Heckathorn, 1982–1988
Rev. Murray A. Ziegenfuss, 1988–1998
Rev. Scott J. Maxwell, 1999–2001
Rev. Timothy D. Orrell, 2002–2007
Rev. Timothy R. Nilsen, 2007–

Patmos, Woodstock

St. Luke, Woodstock

The congregation has held bluegrass services on the second Saturday of each month and participates in the weekend backpack feeding program of Shenandoah Valley Lutheran Ministries, Luke's Backpack.

Pastors
Rev. Mary Louise Brown, 2006–

GERMANNA CONFERENCE
St. Thomas, Bealeton

On December 8, 1991, a small group of folks led by Pastor D. Ray Hatcher held a worship service at Grace Miller Elementary School in Bealeton. A charter was signed on November 15, 1992, and St. Thomas Lutheran Church was organized on April 25, 1993. Hatcher accepted a call as the first pastor and he was installed on October 31, 1993. Membership grew to nearly one hundred by May 16, 1996, when Hatcher resigned to accept another call. The congregation then called seminary graduate Jay Plummer, who was installed as pastor on June 22, 1997. On August 2, 1999, Pastor Plummer left St. Thomas to enter the Navy chaplaincy.

During much of this pastoral vacancy, retired ELCA pastor Kenneth Hauge supplied, leading worship and preaching, and on December 12, 1999, St. Thomas and Pastor Hauge entered into a formal contract for a part-time, open-ended interim pastor position. On September 5, 2004, Pastor David Penman was called to begin a full-time pastorate at St. Thomas. Discussions with the leadership of the Bealeton Presbyterian Church led to the decision to hold joint worship services at the church. A formal agreement to continue joint worship and explore further yoking between St. Thomas Lutheran and Bealeton Presbyterian was drawn up on August 28, 2005. The subsidiary entity known as PALS (Presbyterian and Lutheran Services) Church was formed in December 2007 by a formal agreement, approved by the Virginia Synod/ELCA and National Capital Presbytery, PC (USA). Worship services used Lutheran liturgy, but were later modified to a blended format more inclusive of the Presbyterian worship format. Pastor Penman was certified by the NCP to serve the yoked ministry. Each congregation respected its own constitution, and maintained its own membership roster and treasury. A governing board, comprised of St. Thomas Council members and BPC Session elders, was formed to manage the yoked ministry. In July 2008, Pastor Penman accepted another call, and Pastor Ken Hauge was called by PALS to provide pastoral services. On November 16, 2008, PALS Church entered into a formal contract with Pastor Hauge as a provisional (interim, or transitional) pastor. Under the Formula of Agreement partnership between the NCP and ELCA, he was certified as a minister member of the National Capital Presbytery to serve Bealeton Presbyterian as a part of PALS Church. A ministry handbook has been developed, blending, as well as possible, respect for each congregation's constitution with respect to governance of the ministry.

Pastors

Rev. D. Ray Hatcher, 1993–1996

Rev. Jay Plummer, 1997–1999

Rev. Kenneth Hauge, interim, 1999–2004, 2008–

Rev. David Penman, 2004–2008

Peace, Charlottesville

Peace Lutheran Church was a mission congregation of the Eastern District of the American Lutheran Church (ALC). The first worship service was held on February 12, 1984, in the general purpose room of Hollymead Middle School. Worship and Sunday School were held there for some time and then in other sites. The first service in the present permanent building was held on Christmas Eve 1994. A yearlong celebration of the twenty-fifth anniversary of the first worship service ran through 2009. An addition, which included a new kitchen, several classrooms, an elevator, and a youth room, was dedicated on December 2, 2012. The congregation has been served by the Rev. Ronald K. Chelton, founding pastor, now deceased; the Rev. William Stewart; the Rev. Greg Briehl, associate pastor; and the Rev. John Herman David Hively was an intern in 2007–2008. The congregation is presently served by the Rev. Viktoria H. Parvin, interim pastor, under a one-year contract, and the Rev. Paul St. Clair, under a part-time contract as pastor-on-call. In a Southwest Virginia community outreach, several members visited Nora, an impoverished area in Dickenson County, several times with a home repair and care ministry. This was a local mission effort begun by Peace and St. Mark Lutheran Church focused on home repairs for needy families. The congregation supplied financial and other resources and members visited Haiti, Honduras, India, and Togo for advancement of the gospel and meeting the needs of the poor and neglected.

Pastors
Rev. Ronald K. Chelton, 1983–1987
Rev. William Stewart, 1988–2000
Rev. Gregory Briehl, associate, 1998–2006
Rev. John Herman, 2002–2012
Rev. Paul St. Clair, 2010–
Rev. Vikoria Parvin, interim, 2012–

St. Mark, Charlottesville

The twentieth-century segment of this time period at St. Mark, Charlottesville, begins with a 1988 church renovation project that included expanding the narthex, installing an elevator, and refurbishing the offices and Student Room. During these years, we hosted a statewide ecumenical conference of Lutheran, Anglican, and Roman Catholic leaders; we also sponsored a refugee family of five from Bosnia. A Stephen Ministry was developed and teams began preparing and serving Sunday evening meals at the Salvation Army. As we enter the twenty-first century, St. Mark has emphasized our mission to community outreach that includes: PACEM (People and Congregations Engaged in Ministry), sixty area congregations—of which St. Mark is a part—that provide our homeless neighbors a safe and welcoming place to eat and sleep during the winter months; IMPACT (Interfaith Movement Promoting Action by Congregations Together), twenty-seven area congregations—for which St. Mark has provided office space—that together identify areas of community concern and try to alleviate the concern; and mission trips—a mission team (together with Peace Lutheran Church) went to Dickenson County in southwest Virginia in the fall of 2012 to donate clothing and food, work on housing construction and repairs, and conduct care ministry. The St. Mark Preschool and Lutheran Campus Ministry at the University of Virginia also continue to be a part of our mission.

Pastors
Rev. Robert Holley, 1987–1997
Rev. Jan Tobias, 1993–1999
Rev. Bruce Wollenberg, 1998–2006
Rev. William Stewart, interim, 2006–2008
Rev. Sandra Wisco, 2008–

St. Luke, Culpeper

At the formation of the ELCA in 1987, the church was led by Pastor Elmer Bosserman, who had recently inspired the church to open an elementary school to serve all people. Pastor Bosserman retired in 1988 and was succeeded by Pastor Alfred Fogleman. During his pastorate, the church renovated a farmhouse for use as the parsonage and received a donation of land for four sports fields in 1990. Pastor Fogleman retired in 1999 and was followed by Pastors James Foré and Debbie Fry, who served an interim term of four years with a special emphasis on the growth of youth and family ministry as a part of the body of Christ. In August 2004, Pastor Angela Jennings was called and provided strong leadership for the school and congregation until 2009. In that year, Pastor Ken Martin began serving as the interim pastor in a period of renewed spirit and mission. In 2010, the congregation and school separated into distinct entities, allowing each to focus on its own unique mission and ministry. In December 2012, the congregation called Kate Costa, a recent seminary graduate, to serve as pastor. She was ordained in January 2013, at St. Luke. Bishop James Mauney presided and Pastor Andy Ballentine served as the preacher. The congregation continues to actively "share God's love and serve all people" by supporting many community organizations. The congregation recently dedicated "The Upper Room," a new prayer room in honor of Mrs. Evelyn Estes, a longtime member and organist of the congregation. We give thanks to God for our lively history of the past twenty-five years, and pray God's blessing upon many more anniversaries to come as part of the body of Christ.

Pastors
Rev. Elmer Bosserman, 1978–1987
Rev. Al Fogleman, 1988–1999
Rev. James Foré, 1999–2003
Rev. Debbie Fry, 1999–2003
Rev. Angela Jennings, 2004–2009
Rev. Kenneth Martin, interim, 2009
Rev. Kate Costa, 2013–

Grace and Glory, Palmyra

In 2001, Lutherans in Fluvanna County met to discuss establishing a Lutheran congregation in the second fastest-growing county in Virginia, which did not have a Lutheran church. The first service of the Grace and Glory congregation was held on February 11, 2001, with about fifty-three attending in a synod-authorized worshipping community, meeting in the aerobics room of a fitness center. The new congregation was led by retired ELCA Pastor Bill Stewart. On Easter 2001, Grace and Glory received forty-five individuals as its first members. In 2003, a vote of the congregation authorized the purchase of ten acres of land on Route 53 in Fluvanna County. At the 2004 Synod Assembly, Grace and Glory was officially recognized as a mission congregation and the congregation began worshipping in the "cafetorium" of Fluvanna Middle School. In 2006, Grace and Glory extended a call to its first full-time pastor. Pastor Ken Albright began his service on August 1, 2006, and was installed on August 27, 2006. From 2008 through 2011, a successful capital campaign was conducted for the construction of our first worship center. On August 24, 2011, a groundbreaking ceremony was held to begin construction; on August 24, 2012, the congregation held its first worship service in the new center. A dedication service was conducted by Bishop James Mauney and Pastor Albright on September 23, 2012.

Pastors

Rev. Bill Stewart, part-time developer, 2001–2006

Rev. Ken Albright, 2006–

Christ, Fredericksburg

Our mission over these twenty-five years has included a ministry to the University of Mary Washington campus, quilters who have made over 2,000 quilts distributed locally and through Lutheran World Relief, a Food Pantry, faithful contributions to World Hunger needs, becoming a governing congregation for Micah Ministries for the homeless, membership on the InterFaith Community Council, as well as opening our facility to numerous non-profit community groups. A covenant was established with St. George's Episcopal Church in 1996 to live into and out of the covenants being established with the ELCA. Our leadership has included the continuing ministry of the Rev. Richard M. Carbaugh since 1981. In 2010, the congregation began a ministry with seminary interns Katharina Johnson, Ruth Moberg Foster, and Anne A. Jones. Three members of the congregation were ordained during this time: the Rev. Robert Chapman, 1997; the Rev. Lyla Harold, 2001; and the Rev. Lou Florio, 2007. In 1989, a new education wing was dedicated to better serve our Sunday School, music ministry, and community groups. An Endowment Fund was established in 1998 and a new organ was dedicated in 2001. In 2007, a new capital campaign was begun to provide for a renovation and addition to renew office space, improve accessibility, and further the mission of Christ Lutheran. At the close of these twenty-five years, the congregation was preparing to vote on laying a new foundation for the next twenty-five years.

Pastors

Rev. Richard M. Carbaugh, 1981–

Rev. David Derrick, associate, 1997

Rev. Stephen Bohannon, associate, 2001

Rev. Laura Sinche-Vitucci, associate, 2005–

Resurrection, Fredericksburg

Resurrection, Fredericksburg, was the first mission congregation started in the Virginia Synod after the founding of the ELCA in 1988. The mission developer and first pastor was Pastor Jeff Ruby. The charter was signed in April 1989, with fifty-two adults and thirty-four children. In concert with the ELCA Division for Outreach, a three-and-a-half-acre parcel on Route 3 was purchased for future building. The congregation worshipped at the Seventh Day Adventist gymnasium for seven years. The first major hurdle came for the young congregation when Pastor Ruby resigned in February 1992, to accept a call in Phoenix, Arizona. Pastor Al Rider was installed in October 1992. The congregation sold its three-and-a-half-acre parcel and purchased a seven-acre parcel, further west on Route 3. This property is historically significant since it was part of the setting for the First Day of Battle (May 1, 1863) for the Battle of Chancellorsville. The congregation faced a second major hurdle with the resignation of Pastor Rider after only twenty-three months of his pastorate. Pastor Paul Conradt-Eberlin was installed as pastor in August 1995. The congregation was energized to proceed with plans to build and a new worship facility was dedicated in April 1997. The 8,000-square-foot worship facility includes a sanctuary with seating for 224, a fellowship hall to seat ninety, plus classrooms, a kitchen, and offices. A fast-growth grant from the ELCA provided for a full-time pastoral assistant. Pastor Conradt-Eberlin resigned in March 2000 to become a mission developer in Richmond. Pastors Jim and Carol Kniseley were installed as co-pastors on February 11, 2001. The congregation grew in membership and attendance, peaking at 817 members and 300 in attendance in 2009. The building expansion was dedicated in April 2009 and includes 21,000 square feet on three levels. The spring of 2013 found Resurrection in a place that is both anxious and hopeful. The anxiety comes from having a mortgage of $2.4 million in a time of economic uncertainty. The hope comes from the increase in worship attendance (216 at the end of 2012), increase in membership (447 at the end of 2012), and growth in such areas as youth, the preschool with fifty children, young families, and volunteerism.

Pastors
Rev. Jeff Ruby, 1989–1992
Rev. Al Rider, 1992–1994
Rev. Paul Conradt-Eberlin, 1995–2000
Revs. Jim and Carol Kniseley, co-pastors, 2001–

Hebron, Madison

Hebron Lutheran Church, located in Madison County in the Robinson River Valley, has a long history and has been served since its formation by faithful Lutherans. The old church will celebrate its 300th anniversary in 2017. Thus far during these 300 years, there have been thirty-three ministers. The Rev. Karen Taylor was the first female pastor, serving from 2005 to 2009. The old Tannenburg organ, installed in 1802, has served the congregation well. It sat through extremes of temperature for years and still attracts professional organists who are eager to play it. It will soon undergo tuning and repair for the second time in the last fifty years. Hebron Church has always been involved in the community. Some of its outreach activities include making quilts for Lutheran World Relief, helping staff the thrift shop at Madison Emergency Services, providing food for the Loaves and Fishes program, collecting food for the food pantry, and providing gifts for needy families at Christmas. Hebron is a vibrant congregation that looks forward to continuing service to our community and the world.

Pastors

Rev. James E. Baseler, 1981–1995
Rev. James Larsen, 1996–2004
Rev. Karen Taylor, 2005–2009
Rev. Patti Covington, 2011–

Good Shepherd, Orange

Good Shepherd, Orange was organized in 1975 and the congregation met in a Presbyterian chapel until ground was broken for a new church in 1987. Good Shepherd and Mt. Nebo in Madison County have been in a two-church parish from the beginning. The congregation was a founding member of a Christian Emergency Council. In its early years, Good Shepherd bought a tractor, carpet, stove, and playground equipment; painted the interior; installed a roof; and completed major tree work. Among its community service projects, the congregation supplied lunch for Build Virginia, hosted Happy Camp, held a toy and clothing bonanza, and gave school supplies. Good Shepherd celebrated a mortgage-burning on Sunday, January 25, 2009. The mortgage was paid off seven years ahead of schedule. It supports a food pantry, free clinic, and English as a Second Language classes for refugees. A copying machine was purchased and contemporary worship was scheduled on Saturdays.

Pastors

Rev. Robert Ward, 1987–1990
Rev. Tom Mammoser, interim, 1990–1991, 1995–1996
Rev. Larrie Humbert, 1991–1995
Rev. Kenneth Price, interim, 1996–1998
Rev. David Brooks, 1998–2001
Rev. Waldron Rosheim, interim, 2001–2002
Rev. Patricia Nabers, 2003–

Mt. Nebo, Rochelle

In 1988, vinyl siding was put on the church and the trim and roof were painted. In 1989, a new Allen organ and a memorabilia cabinet were purchased with donations from members of the congregation and funds from the Memorial Fund. In 1993, a new pulpit Bible was donated by two daughters of the Rev. M.M. Kipps, a son of the congregation. A Paschal candle stand, oil Paschal candle, and oil altar candles were given to the church in 1995. In 1998, the Rev. David Brooks was ordained on July 12. Pew cushions were given to the church in 2007. The restrooms were renovated to make them more handicapped-accessible in 2009. In 2010, the fence around the property was replaced with vinyl fencing and the perpetual care endowment for the cemetery was clarified. Major bequests for the cemetery were received in 2012. For a number of years, the congregation was the highest in per-member giving in the synod to the United Lutheran Appeal.

<u>Pastors</u>
Rev. Robert Ward, 1987–1990
Rev. Tom Mammoser, interim, 1990–1991, 1995–1996
Rev. Larrie Humbert, 1991–1995
Rev. Kenneth Price, interim, 1996–1998
Rev. David Brooks, 1998–2001
Rev. Waldron Rosheim, interim, 2001–2002
Rev. Timothy Waltonen, interim, 2001–2003
Rev. Patricia Nabers, 2003–

St. Peter's, Stafford

St. Peter's Lutheran Church, Stafford, was developed by Pastor Frederick A. Donahoe and our first worship service was held in the Stafford County Courthouse on April 1, 1979. Pastor Fred ministered to the congregation from 1979 to 2001. During that time, we built a church, built two additions to our building, bought a new organ, and adopted a sister Russian church. Thankful Thursday fellowship suppers began in 1993 and continue to be an important fellowship event today. In 1999, a contemporary worship service was started and there was a fast-growing Christian Education and youth program. In January 2002, Pastor C. Richard Duncan accepted the call and shepherded this congregation until he retired in 2010. A new altar, senior choir loft, and praise band loft were built to allow for a better worship experience, dramas, musicals, and cantatas. We dedicated a large space in our church and invested in commercial refrigerators and freezers for the St. Peter's Community Food Pantry that was started in 1985. In 2008, St. Peter's held its first church camping trip at Prince William Forest Park, another tradition which continues today. In 2011, we held our first annual Pet Blessing and our first annual drive-through nativity. In September 2012, the Rev. Paul Toelke became the pastor of St. Peter's Lutheran Church. We look forward to starting new traditions and sharing many years of history with Pastor Paul.

Pastors
Rev. Frederick A. Donahoe, 1979–2001
Rev. C. Richard Duncan, 2002–2010
Rev. John Erickson, 2003–2006
Rev. Paul Toelke, 2012–

Our Saviour, Warrenton

Our Saviour, Warrenton started in 1959, dedicated a new church building on Dumfries Road in September 1986. In July 1988, the parsonage in Broken Hills was sold. A beautiful Luther Seal stained glass window was placed in the back of the sanctuary in memory of Ida Miller Hicks, who died in November 1982. The Rev. John Lillie, one of several supply pastors in 1990–1991, began serving the congregation in 1991. His prior employment with the Lutheran Office of Governmental Affairs in Washington, DC gave him fresh new ideas in leadership. Worship and Sunday School attendance increased. Nine stained glass windows were installed in the sanctuary in 1995. Also in 1995, the congregation broke ground for the addition of a new fellowship hall and youth, education, and women's meeting rooms. In 1998, an outdoor worship area was added behind the church as an Eagle Scout project. Between June 2003 and 2004, Our Saviour was served by two interim pastors, the Rev. Waldron Rosheim and the Rev. Fred Donahoe, who brought years of experience and knowledge that contributed to our growth. In calling Pastors Debbie Frye and James Foré as co-pastors, we acquired our first husband and wife team. In 2004, we commissioned our first Christian caregivers as an extension of our pastoral ministry. In July 2005, the Our Saviour Youth Group made its first trip to Hurley, Dickenson County to repair housing and support the people of that community. In November 2006, a Saturday evening contemporary worship service began. The year 2007 was exciting when we purchased a new Allen Renaissance Quantum 325 three-manual and pedal classical organ. During 2007, we also commissioned Eucharistic ministers to increase the opportunities for our homebound members to receive sacramental bread and wine. Deanna Scheffel from Our Saviour responded to God's call to ministry. She attended Southern Seminary and was ordained as the Rev. Deanna Scheffel Boynton on June 9, 2012. Pastor Debbie Frye and Pastor James Foré resigned effective on February 29, 2012. In 2012, Our Saviour was served by an interim pastor, the Rev. Lance K. Braun. We look back with thanksgiving for the ministry that has happened and is happening at Our Saviour Lutheran Church, and for the presence of the Holy Spirit leading and guiding us. We continue to look forward in hope, faith, and joy to the many ways God will continue to call God's people together, here in this place.

Pastors
Rev. James K. Rill, 1979–1990
Rev. John Lillie, 1991–2003
Rev. Waldron Rosheim, interim, 2003
Rev. Fred Donahoe, interim, 2004
Rev. Deborah Frye 2004–2012
Rev. James Foré, 2004–2012
Rev. Lance Braun, interim, 2012–

HIGHLAND CONFERENCE
St. John, Abingdon

St. John, Abingdon traces its beginnings to September 1961, when the Rev. Edwin Troutman announced a meeting to plan a new Lutheran church in Washington County. Sixty-four persons came to plan the first worship for October 1, 1961, and forty-five came to that service in the chapel of the Henderson Funeral Home. The congregation was named St. John and the Rev. Roger Kluttz was installed as the first pastor. He was followed by Pastors Wayne Williams, Robert Anderson, and Eric Moehring, who served from 1981 to 1988. In 1987, St. John celebrated its twenty-fifth anniversary. Special services were held at Mock's Chapel and later at Luther Chapel. In 1989, Pastor Frank Honeycutt began, serving until 2003. A new sanctuary and building additions were completed in April 1998. A Festival Service of Dedication was held to celebrate the beginning of worship services in the new space. In September 1998, the Lutheran Church Child Development Ministry opened its doors to forty-five three- and-four-year-olds. In 2003, the Rev. Melissa Chappell was called as interim pastor and Pastor Kent Peterson accepted a call in 2004. In August 2006, eight St. John youth and adults traveled to Guatemala. After Pastor Peterson resigned, the Rev. Jim Bangle served as vice pastor during the pastoral vacancy. In April 2011, the Rev. G. Scott Homesley accepted the call as pastor. The congregation observed its fiftieth anniversary in January 2012.

Pastors
Rev. Eric Moehring, 1981–1988
Rev. Frank Honeycutt, 1989–2003
Rev. Melissa Chappell, interim, 2003
Rev. Kent Peterson, 2004–2010
Rev. Jim Bangle, vice pastor, 2010
Rev. G. Scott Homesley, 2012–

St. Matthew, Red Oak, and Sharon, Bland

For much of the last quarter-century, St. Matthew, Bland has been aligned with Red Oak and Sharon, Ceres in a three-church parish. At one time, Central, Burke's Garden was in that parish. A fellowship hall was constructed at Red Oak. Occasional worship has been led by Lutheran supply pastors, in addition to Presbyterian services.

Pastors
Rev. J. Allen Snyder, 1988
Rev. Joel Thornton, Presbyterian
Rev. Murray Ziegenfuss, 1998–2001

Immanuel, Bluefield, West Virginia

Immanuel, Bluefield, West Virginia established the Hamilton Memorial Education Scholarship in 1991 and the Kahle Memorial Education Scholarship in 1997. The church basement was renovated and air conditioning was added in 1998. The congregation formed a yoke with Central, Burke's Garden in nearby Tazewell County, creating the Immanuel-Central Parish, in 2007. The parish became an intern site in 2009. Immanuel celebrated its 125th anniversary on September 16-23, 2012.

Pastors
Rev. Robert B. Lineberger, 1986–1989
Rev. Larry L. MacKey, 1990–1994
Rev. David Stacy, 1995–1998
Rev. Meredith P. Williams, 2000–2006
Rev. Terry Edwards, 2008–

Interns
Brian Campbell, 2009–2010
Lavonne Johnson-Holt, 2010–2011
Peter Suwak, 2011–2012
Barbara Krumm, 2012–2013

Redeemer, Bristol

During the early 2000s, the Redeemer, Bristol Parish's combination fellowship hall/gymnasium underwent extensive renovation. In 2003, Redeemer Parish celebrated its one-hundredth anniversary. To commemorate the anniversary, we hosted several former pastors of Redeemer, including the Rev. James Crumley, former bishop of the Lutheran Church in America and a native of East Tennessee. The Rev. Kate Proctor Costa, daughter of the congregation, was ordained in 2012. For many years, Redeemer had donated the use of its former caretaker's house to HELP House, a ministry of supervised visitation for non-custodial parents, run jointly by Lutheran Family Services of Tennessee and the Tri-Cities Area Lutherans in Mission. In the 2010s, our focus has been on transforming our congregation from a membership model to a discipleship model. Led by Pastor Gary Chenoweth, we have made good progress, and we are continuing to work toward that goal.

Pastors
Rev. C.W. Howell, 1970–1988
Rev. Glenn L. London, Jr., 1988–2000
Rev. Gary C. Chenoweth, 2002–2012

Central, Burke's Garden

Central, Burke's Garden, Tazewell County, one of the older congregations in Southwest Virginia, was organized in 1828 but records were not kept for a number of years. Several pastors held services part-time. In 2000, the sanctuary ceiling was replaced and lowered. Weekly worship services were reestablished in 2006. In 2007, Central formed a yoke with Immanuel, Bluefield, West Virginia, creating the Immanuel-Central Parish. Pastor Terry Edwards, the first full-time pastor in years, was called in 2008. Burke's Garden began serving as an intern site in 2009. A Hammond organ was replaced with a Yamaha digital keyboard in 2010 and a sound system was installed in 2011.

Pastor
Rev. Terry Edwards, 2008–

St. James, Chilhowie

In the last quarter-century, the most significant development in the life of St. James, Chilhowie came in 2006, when congregational voting resulted in approval for the formation of the Mt. Rogers Lutheran Parish, which includes Faith at Whitetop, St. Matthew at Konnarock, and St. James as a three-church parish. Plans were formed for the Lay Liturgist Program, which included nine lay members from the new parish who were trained and then commissioned by Bishop James Mauney to preach and preside at communion in the parish churches. Three of the lay liturgists are from St. James.

Pastors
Rev. George R. Feldman, 1983–1988
Rev. Edward Schaack, vice pastor, 1988–1989
Rev. Wallace E. Morton, Sr., 1989–1992
Rev. Charlotte Strecker-Baseler, 1992–1996
Rev. Melissa Chappell, 1996–2003
Rev. Martin Saarinen, interim, 2003–2004
Rev. W. Eugene Copenhaver, vice pastor, 2004
Rev. Joseph Shumate, interim, 2005–2007
Rev. Candis O'Meara, 2007–2013

Zion, Cripple Creek

Zion once was aligned with Bethany, St. Peter and Rosenbaum Chapel in the Cripple Creek Parish until the other three formed United Lutheran. Services are held monthly with supply pastors, and the church has an annual homecoming service.

Pastor
Gary Kelly, lay minister, 1983–1997

St. Matthew, Konnarock

St. Matthew, Konnarock was paired with Faith, Whitetop in the Konnarock-Helton Parish for some time until they joined St. James, Chilhowie in the Mt. Rogers Parish, served mainly by nine lay liturgists. The congregation remodeled the parsonage as a rental property and placed a new roof on the church. The lay liturgists commissioned by Bishop Jim Mauney are: Mark Merz, Sara Kegley, Kristine Hughes, May Hill, Cindy Anders, Sharon Compton, Barbara Jones-Butcher, Pam Badin, and Angela Dunn.

<u>Pastors</u>
Rev. William See, 1987–1988
Rev. John Cooper, 1989
Will Robertson, lay pastor, 1998–2006
Rev. Joe Shumate, supply, 2006–2007
Rev. Candis O'Meara, 2007–2013

Ebenezer, Marion

In 1987, Ebenezer, under the twenty-year leadership of the Rev. James H. Bangle, continued to serve God and the community in many ways: they raised funds and volunteered to restore the Lincoln Theater, mailed packages to troops, raised funds for a shelter home, helped build houses for Habitat for Humanity, collected food for food pantries, raised money for Smyth County Free Clinic, helped fund and feed community lunches, gave "Buddy Bears" to police for children in stressful situations, contributed to World Hunger Lutheran World Relief, supported Lutheran Family Services, helped with a local thrift store for the benefit of abused women, and adopted a needy family every Christmas. Members were very active in volunteering in hospitals, nursing homes, the theater, the thrift store, Relay for Life, and swim meets. In 1996, we launched a building program to add offices, classrooms, a youth room, a parlor and meeting room, a columbarium, and an elevator, plus the renovation of old classrooms, the kitchen, and the fellowship hall. A 200th anniversary celebration was held each month and a history minute was read before each service. The service was led by retired bishop James R. Crumley, Jr. A time capsule was buried in the front lawn of the church, to be opened in 2049. Pastor Bangle retired on July 31, 2007, after thirty-one years of service. A reception was held and a scholarship established at Southern Seminary in his honor. Later services were led by a former Navy chaplain, the Rev. Steve Dew, Interim Pastor Bob Maier, and Pastor Joe Shumate. Ebenezer called newly ordained Pastor Andrew Bansemer to serve our congregation and he was installed on July 19, 2009. Sheri, his wife, helped start Micah's Back Pack which sends over eighty food-filled backpacks home with kids each Friday after school. The program is funded by businesses, grants, and gifts from others and members, and is housed at Ebenezer.

<u>Pastors</u>
Rev. James Bangle, 1976–2007
Rev. Joe Shumate, interim, 2008
Rev. Steve Dew, supply
Rev. Bob Maier, interim, 2009–
Rev. Andrew Bansemer, 2009–

St. Paul and Grace, Rural Retreat

The journey of the past twenty-five years began with the election of our pastor, Richard Bansemer, who served our church from 1978 to 1987, as the first bishop of the Virginia Synod/ELCA. Following Pastor Bansemer's election to serve as bishop, the parish did not have a pastor until Pastor Larry Bollinger was called. His ministry was highlighted by a focus on social ministry. Parish members traveled to Haiti and completed other projects locally. In 1997, Grace celebrated 125 years of ministry in the Rural Retreat community. After Pastor Bollinger was called to North Carolina, Pastor T. Joseph Shumate, retired from the Walker Mountain Parish, supplied as interim pastor and a call was extended to him in 1999. In 2001, St. Paul celebrated 225 years of ministry in Crockett. The parish celebrated the ministry of longtime organist Kathryn Dodson from 1950 to 2002. Pastor Joe retired again in December 2004. The congregation was fortunate to have the services of lay speakers Bishop Emeritus Richard Bansemer and retired Pastor Paul Huddle during the pastoral vacancy. In 2005, Pastor Jonathan Hamman was called. In 2009, St. Paul added a fellowship hall to the back end of the church building, acknowledging the recent growth in membership and attendance. Also in 2009, Grace celebrated the one-hundredth anniversary of the original church building.

Pastors
Rev. Richard Bansemer, 1978–1987
Rev. Larry Bollinger, 1989–1998
Rev. T. Joseph Shumate, 1999–2004
Rev. Jonathan Hamman, 2005–

Pleasant Hill, Smyth County

Pleasant Hill at Groseclose, Smyth County has been served mainly by a series of interns in the former Attoway-Kimberlin Parish for the last quarter-century. They were supervised by Pastor Ed Schaack until he retired in 2006. Pastor Jonathan Hamman has supervised them in recent years. The interns were Pat McGlothlin, Sam Stowe, Charlotte Streckler-Baseler, Paul Pingel, Martha Miller, Barbara Hanson, Terry Edwards, James Foré, Cece Haxton, Sharon Wiggins, Tom Darr, Alex Hoffner, Dianna Horton, Pat Nabers, Liv Lamson-Andrews, Lucy Schottelkorb, Brian Chaffee, Mac Carpenter, Mac Day, and Lubo Batka, supply.

Holy Advent, Lebanon, and St. Luke, Walker Mountain Parish, Wythe County

Walker Mountain Parish, organized in 1977 by Pastor Joe Shumate, is comprised of Holy Advent, Lebanon, and St. Luke congregations. Holy Advent was organized in 1915, Lebanon in 1851, and St. Luke in 1888. The Rev. Joe Shumate was called to serve in 1977 and he retired in 1996. Since then we have been served by Pastors Amy Oehlschlaeger, Magda Forgacova, and Harvey Atkinson, our current pastor. For most of the past twenty-five years, the parish has worked with the Binns-Counts Community Center located in Nora, Dickenson County, located in the midst of a very depressed coal-mining region of Southwestern Virginia. We send school supplies, Christmas gifts, and a wide variety of new and gently used items such as clothing and household supplies and furniture to support the local community. In more recent years we have become active in supporting the Agape Food Pantry, the Community Food Kitchen, and the Lil' Maroon Packs backpack program, all located in Wytheville.

Pastors

Rev. Joe Shumate, 1977–1996

Rev. Amy Oehlschlaeger, 1996–1999

Rev. Magda Forgacova, 2000–2001

Harvey Atkinson, licensed lay minister, 2001–2005

Rev. Harvey Atkinson, 2005–

Faith, Whitetop

Pastor Walter Messick served as pastor from 1977 to 1989 when Faith, Whitetop and St. Matthew, Konnarock were the Konnarock-Helton Parish. That parish dissolved and Pastor Messick served only Faith for a time. Pastor John Strecker-Baseler followed at Faith from 1992 to 1996. Following his departure, Faith, Whitetop survived from 1996 to 1999 with members offering sermons and worshiping for three years without a pastor. In 1999, a wonderful opportunity came when Wil Robertson was commissioned to serve as lay pastor at St. Matthew, Konnarock. Both St. Matthew and Faith began cooperative planning and sharing, permitting Wil to serve both mountain congregations. In 2006, the Rev. Joe Shumate served as the supply pastor for St. James, Chilhowie; Faith, Whitetop; and St. Matthew, Konnarock, and through his guidance the Mt. Rogers Lutheran Parish was formed. Recognizing the difficulties in serving a three-point call, Pastor Joe encouraged lay people to participate in the ACTS program for a two-year training period. With the commitment of all three churches, nine lay liturgists were commissioned by Bishop James Mauney to serve within the parish, providing Word and Sacrament in a church each Sunday when the pastor would be in two other churches. Through Pastor Joe's encouragement and direction and with the support of the lay liturgists, in late 2007 our parish called Pastor Candis O'Meara, who navigated the demands of three churches, the hardy mountain folks, and the very crooked mountain roads very well.

Pastors

Rev. Walter Messick, 1977–1989

Rev. George Ziegenfuss, 1990–1991

Rev. John Strecker-Baseler, 1992–1996

Wil Robertson, lay pastor, 1999–2006

Rev. Joe Shumate, supply pastor, 2006–2007

Rev. Candis O'Meara, 2007–2014

Christ, Wise

The Rev. Edwin Troutman was the pastor of Christ Lutheran Church in Wise until 1987. In 1988, the Rev. Harold Burnette became our pastor and stayed until 1994. During his tenure, the church building was remodeled. After the departure of Pastor Burnette in the spring of 1994, Christ, Wise was served by three interns from Trinity Seminary in Columbus: Ted Koehl, 1994–1995; Mike Ward, 1995–1996; and Stacey Anderson, 1996–1997. When the relationship with Trinity Seminary ended, Michael Samerdyke became the lay worship leader of Christ, Wise in November 1997 and he has led since. During the 1990s, Christ, Wise offered an after-school tutoring program to academically challenged students. The biggest recent development has been the building of a fellowship hall from 2006 to 2009, which greatly expanded the size of the building.

Pastors

Rev. Edwin Troutman, 1980–1987

Rev. Harold Burnette, 1988–1994

Michael Samerdyke, licensed lay minister, 1997–

Holy Trinity, Wytheville

In 1987, Holy Trinity called the Rev. Roger Kluttz. In 1992, the Luther Hall wing was added with six classrooms, a nursery, a parlor, and handicapped-accessible restrooms. The St. John Conference Room was also refurbished. An Allen organ was purchased in 1990, and Martha Ballard returned to serve as administrative assistant. In 1993, Lavelva Stevens, associate in ministry (AIM), was called as music director, and the Rev. Roger Kluttz retired. Holy Trinity called the Rev. Steven P. Ridenhour as pastor in 1994. In 1995, an Adult Retreat began with the Rev. Jean Bozeman as the first keynote presenter. Leaders have included Bishop Richard Bansemer, Bishop Jim Mauney, and Pastor Chip Gunsten. In 1996, the congregation began taking servant trips to Haiti, Atlanta, West Virginia, the Gulf Coast, and Joplin, Missouri. The Agape Food Pantry began in Holy Trinity's basement in 1998. Annually, Holy Trinity provides housing for servant groups traveling through the area. In 1999, the Rev. James Armentrout joined the staff as a part-time youth pastor. Throughout these years, the youth have participated in synod youth events and the ELCA national Youth Gathering in New Orleans, St. Louis, and Atlanta, and in summer church camp programs. Holy Trinity celebrated its 125th anniversary in 2001 with Bishop James Mauney preaching on the November 24 anniversary weekend, the conclusion of a yearlong celebration in which former pastors and sons of the congregation preached. These included Pastors Roger Kluttz, William Van O'Linda, Kenneth Price, and Glenn London, and sons of the congregation, Pastors Richard Umberger, Joseph Shumate, Carl Pattison, and David Hendrix. From 2000 to 2010, the renovation of the Moeller pipe organ, sanctuary balcony, fellowship hall, youth room, restrooms, kitchen, and offices, as well as the addition of restrooms, showers, a hospitality room, and the installation of a playground and an elevator were completed. Interns from Gettysburg

Seminary serving at Holy Trinity have included Maureen Seifried, Andrew Schottelkorb, Virgil Cain, Jason Northridge, Jason Felici, and Jonathan Myers. Sister Kim Szogi from the ELCA Deaconess Community served a nine-month internship. Harvey Atkinson, a member of Holy Trinity and a graduate of Gettysburg Seminary, is pastor of the Walker Mountain Parish in Wythe County.

<u>Pastors</u>
Rev. Roger Kluttz, 1987–1993
Rev. Steve Ridenhour, 1994–
Rev. James Armentrout, youth pastor, 1999–2003

<u>Interns</u>
Brian Campbell, 2009–2010
Lavonne Johnson-Holt, 2010–2011
Peter Suwak, 2011–2012

NEW RIVER CONFERENCE
Luther Memorial, Blacksburg

Luther Memorial, located on the edge of the Virginia Tech campus in Blacksburg, celebrated its one-hundredth anniversary on February 23, 1986, with the dedication of a new pipe organ. In 1991, a Campus Center was constructed to support Lutheran Campus Ministry at Virginia Tech. In 1996, the congregation purchased a brick house on Price's Fork Road, next to the church, and established the Von Bora Haus, to be used as emergency housing for people in need. The congregation of Luther Memorial voted to become a Reconciling to Christ church in February 2003, one of two in the Virginia Synod, St. Mark, Charlottesville being the other. In 2007, Luther Memorial made a major commitment to creation care by using recycled paper, utilizing commercial composting of waste, and making renovations and equipment changes designed to reduce energy usage. Luther Memorial joined other congregations in 2010 to host To Our House, a thermal shelter for homeless men in the New River Valley.

<u>Pastors</u>
Rev. Gary Schroeder, 1987–2012
Rev. Lisa Klein, associate, 1996–1998
Rev. Bill King, campus pastor, 1997–2012
Rev. Joanna Stallings, associate, 1998–
Rev. Bill King, senior pastor, 2013–

New Mt. Zion, Blacksburg

A picnic shelter was added to the church in the late 1980s. Renovations to the church were done in the mid-to-late-1990s, including enlarging the chancel and adding a restroom, a handicapped ramp, and six stained glass windows representing the seasons of the church year of Advent, Christmas, Epiphany, Lent, Easter, and Pentecost. The windows were dedicated in

2001. Additional renovations include removing carpet and refinishing the existing hardwood floors and replacing the drop ceiling with exposed beams and tongue-and-groove boards. A one-hundred-year anniversary celebration was held in September 2004. A new baptismal font was also dedicated. In April 2011, New Mt. Zion Lutheran Church and Shiloh Lutheran Church voted to separate as a parish, but cooperation and a shared pastorate continue as always.

Pastors

Rev. Robert T. Hughes, 1989–1992

Rev. Gary Rhinesmith, 1993–1997

Rev. Robin Henrickson, 1997–2002

Rev. Shirley Larson, interim, 2003

Rev. Dr. Paul Hinlicky, 2004–2008

Rev. Magdalena Sevcikova, 2009–2010

Rev. Richard F. Banesmer, 2010

Shiloh, Blacksburg

Among several events that have taken place in the last twenty-five years at Shiloh, near Blacksburg, a new addition to the church was constructed in 1991. Much of the work was done by members of the congregation. In September 2001, the congregation celebrated its 125th anniversary! A handicapped ramp was also completed and dedicated that year. In 2006, a playground was added. In April 2011, Shiloh Lutheran and New Mt. Zion Lutheran voted to separate as a parish, but cooperation and a shared pastorate continue as always, but without a two-church parish designation. Nine stained glass windows were completed and dedicated in 2013.

Pastors

Rev. Robert T. Hughes, 1989–1992

Rev. Gary Rhinesmith, 1993–1997

Rev. Robin L. Henrickson, 1997–2002

Rev. Shirley Larson, interim, 2003

Rev. Paul Hinlicky, 2004–2008

Rev. Magdalena Sevcikova, 2009–2010

Rev. Richard F. Bansemer, 2010–

St. Michael, Blacksburg

As proclaimed in our mission statement, St. Michael Lutheran Church in Blacksburg is a community of believers guided by the Holy Spirit and called to care for all God's people in need, to hear God's love through Word and Sacrament, to respond to God's grace with thankful hearts, to invite others into Christ's community, to serve God in daily life and to tell the story of God's love for all. Over the last twenty-five years, St. Michael has lived out this calling through expanded worship opportunities, new facilities, and community partnerships which help people in need. In 1987, the congregation offered one worship service at 11 a.m. on Sunday. Today, St

Michael offers Sunday worship at 9 and 11 a.m. and 6:30 p.m. to make it easier for people to find a worship time that works in their lives. In 1987, the congregation's ministry was supported by a sanctuary and a fellowship hall. Today, a classroom addition completed in 2009 provides additional space which allows St. Michael to offer two Mother's Morning Out programs and provide meeting rooms to community groups. In 1987, the congregation participated in the SHARE food cooperative to help provide affordable food to people in the community. Today, St. Michael partners with over 150 local community groups to operate Micah's Caring Initiative, providing over 240 weekend meals to hungry students in Blacksburg; operates a community garden, providing fresh produce for local food pantries; delivers meals to low-income seniors; and offers dinner to the community on Thanksgiving Day. Ongoing helping ministries initiated or expanded during the past twenty-five years include the Christmas shoebox project for Head Start students on the Pine Ridge Reservation; a Justice and Mercy Fund, which assists an average of twenty families each month with living expenses; a fall collection of school supplies for area elementary schools; and a middle school mission trip. The ministry is supported by several part-time lay ministry professionals.

Pastors
Rev. Jake Mayer, 1986–1998
Rev. Linda Mitchell, 1998–2003
Rev. John Wertz, Jr., 2004–

Our Saviour, Christiansburg

Following the organization of Our Saviour Lutheran in 1983 as a congregation of the Lutheran Church in America, OSLC dedicated a sanctuary, fellowship hall, kitchen, and classroom space in December 1988. The organizing pastor resigned in 1989. Our Saviour called the Rev. Mark S. Briehl and he served from September 1990 until October 1998. The Rev. Frederick "Fred" A. Hodges was called, beginning in May 2000 through the present. In thirty years of ministry, OSLC spent five years in an old sanctuary of a Baptist church which inspired the congregation to share its building with a fledgling Roman Catholic congregation for approximately ten years and Pentecostal congregation in transition from one building to another for nine months. OSLC began an outreach ministry in the New River Valley Juvenile Detention Home and this continued for over twenty-five years with monthly visits to the home. In March 2009, OSLC broke ground for an addition to nearly double the square footage under the roof. The addition was dedicated in September 2009 by the Rev. Fred Hodges and the Rev. Paul "Chip" Gunsten. It includes a fellowship hall, kitchen, handicapped-accessible bathrooms, choir room, and a geothermal heating and air conditioning system. The previous fellowship hall and kitchen were renovated into a classroom, youth lounge, library/parlor, and sacristy.

Pastors
Rev. Mark Briehl, 1990–1998
Rev. Frederick Hodges, 2000–2014

Zion, Floyd, Floyd-Willis

In 1988, Zion, Floyd, in the Floyd-Willis Parish, was actively reaching out to serve community needs. Zion sponsored "Lunch Bunch," transporting nursing home residents and homebound members each month to the church fellowship hall and providing a hot lunch and entertainment. Zion had an extra monthly offering to fund "Community Care," a program set up to help people in need of assistance for food and shelter, and it has continued to this day. Zion used to be the only church in Floyd that held an Ash Wednesday service, and it was well known for its outstanding choir that the community at large came to hear, especially on Christmas Eve, when it was the only service held. In 1989, Zion received a large bequest from the Moses Estate; $30,000 was used to perpetuate Zion's cemetery that dates back to the 1790s. Soldiers from every war are buried there and it is believed to be the second-oldest cemetery in Floyd County. Some of the Moses funds were used to pave the Zion parking lot. From a Ruth Holman bequest, a scholarship fund was established to help Zion students attend college. During the summers of 1988, 1989, and 1990, Pastor Richard Giessler led weeklong youth confirmation retreats at Nags Head, North Carolina. The youth held many fundraisers, such as car washes and selling donuts, to make this possible. Deb Boynton, a daughter of the parish, left for Southern Seminary in Columbia, South Carolina, to begin her studies for the ministry and in 1994 was given financial assistance from Zion. In 1995, an outdoor pavilion with a stage was constructed in Zion's historic Oak Grove (trees thought to be almost 300 years old) and the summer outdoor ministry of musical and theatrical performances was launched as an outreach program and to establish visibility in the community. Proceeds from free-will offerings totaling $60,000 have been given to local charities, such as the volunteer rescue squad, fire department, and women's resource center. Eighteen years later, it is still going strong on summer Saturday nights. In 2000, Zion built an addition of a kitchen, three bathrooms, Sunday School, choir and nursery rooms, pastor's study, office, rear deck, an enlarged fellowship hall and gave the sanctuary and narthex a facelift. In 2008, Zion replaced the carpeting in the fellowship hall with hardwood floors and new tables and chairs. The fellowship hall has been home to Girl Scout troops, the Circle of Friends for intellectually disabled folks, an area senior citizen's Friendship Café group, and the Heartsong Singers, a community choir that ministers to people in hospice. In 2011, Zion added a freestanding communion table constructed by members Michael Daiber and Peter Vandenberg, and in 2012 replaced the carpeting in the sanctuary. The Rev. Paul Pingel, the synod's global mission chair, traveled on a mission trip in 2000 and 2002 to the New Guinea Islands District of Papua New Guinea, the Virginia Synod's partner in the ELCA Companion Synod Program. Diane Giessler joined the synod Global Mission Committee in 2000, served as its chair for six years, and traveled to Papua New Guinea in 1995, 2004, 2007, and 2008. In 2007, she was appointed coordinator of the synod's Companion Synod Program with the Islands District. Youth from Zion were led on summer Youthworks, Inc. mission trips to New Orleans in 2003; Lynn, Massachusetts, in 2004; Windsor, Ontario, in 2005; and in 2006, to Port Charlotte, Florida.

with Lutheran Disaster Relief. In recent years, Zion began participating in joint summer Vacation Bible School and Advent services with the Presbyterian Church of Floyd. Zion has also held a full Christian Seder on Maundy Thursday since 2007. Zion has helped to launch and staff Angels in the Attic ministry, a local thrift store that gives its profits back to community needs. Bishop Jim Mauney was the guest preacher for the celebration of Zion's 200th anniversary on May 10, 2013.

Pastors

Rev. Richard A. Giessler, 1986–1993

Rev. Paul H. Pingel, 1993–2003

Rev. Philip A. Bouknight, 2004–2007

Rev. Linda S. Mitchell Motley, 2010–

St. Mark, Willis, Floyd-Willis

St. Mark has been a beacon of faith in the small Willis community for many years. Its tall steeple and red door are readily seen from the main Route 221 that passes in front of the white frame church. St. Mark, established in 1879, is said to be the oldest church building to hold continuous services in Floyd County. St. Mark shares a pastor with its sister congregation, Zion, in Floyd. In 1988, a handicapped ramp was built with help from AAL funds toward the project. In 1995, the first annual chicken barbeque dinner was held that included a variety of desserts made by the ladies of St. Mark. The proceeds were given to church members and/or people in the community that were in need. In 1998, a picnic pavilion was built in memory of Don Henley, a longstanding member of St. Mark who had this dream. Ralph Yopp led this building project. In 2005, a new organ was dedicated through the generosity of the Fullbright and Rutrough families. In 2010, a storm with high winds blew the steeple off the church. Jim Garland, David Harman, and Jim Coulehan led others to rebuild and install it. Since 2010 to present, an annual free Thanksgiving meal has been offered to the community as an outreach program. A new floor was installed in St. Mark's fellowship hall in 2011. When the old flooring was removed, a big rock was found beneath it, so large it would have been almost impossible to remove (1st Peter 2:4-9). Pastor Linda Motley began a prayer shawl ministry in 2011. She taught many ladies of the church to knit. Between seventy-five and one hundred shawls have been knitted and distributed to those in need of comfort. For more than a decade, St. Mark has hosted a community Bible study each week.

Pastors

Rev. Richard A. Giessler, 1986–1993

Rev. Paul H. Pingel, 1993–2003

Rev. Philip A. Bouknight, 2003–2007

Rev. Linda S. Mitchell Motley, 2010–

Good Shepherd, Galax

The Church of the Good Shepherd, Galax became a joint mission of the Virginia Synod/ELCA and the Episcopal Diocese of Southwestern Virginia in 1987 as a result of talks between Bishop Richard Bansemer and Episcopal Bishop Heath Light. Good Shepherd, formerly a parish of the Episcopal Diocese, also became a mission of the Virginia Synod. It was served part-time by the Rev. Standrod T. Carmichael, who retired in 1991. The Rev. Robert G. Walker, D.D., a retired Lutheran pastor, was appointed pastor-in-charge and he was installed by both bishops in 1991, nine years before full communion was established between the ELCA and the Episcopal Church. Good Shepherd was a pioneer in this ecumenical field. Community and church growth has been slow because the Galax area has little history of liturgical services and the former furniture and textile economy slowed to only one operation after four closed. After attendance had reached thirty per Sunday, Walker retired and the Rev. Harold E. Morgan III was called as rector/pastor on a half-time basis. He and his wife, also an Episcopal priest, lived in Bluefield, West Virginia, where she served a parish. The congregation bought a site on Route 58, west of Galax, and built a church that was dedicated in 2005. Morgan accepted a call from another parish in 2006 and the Rev. Helen Beasley, an Episcopalian, was called in 2007 and she served three-fourths time until retirement in 2013. The parish sends delegates to synod and diocese conventions and it makes financial contributions to both bodies, operating as a single church.

Pastors

Rev. Standrod T. Carmichael, 1987–1991

Rev. Robert G. Walker, 1991–1999

Rev. Harold E. Morgan III, 2001–2006

Rev. Helen Beasley, 2007–2013

Gladesboro, Carroll County

Gladesboro, the only Lutheran church in Carroll County, was organized by Pastor John Christopher Repass in 1855. In 1978, Pastor Duane Steele began serving Gladesboro, before the ELCA was formed in 1987, and he continued for thirty-two years until his retirement in 2010. This was a unique pastorate because Pastor Steele was sightless. The members rallied behind him in providing transportation and other means of support. Pastor Steele's musical talents enabled him to introduce both the *Lutheran Book of Worship* and *Evangelical Lutheran Worship* to the congregation. He reached out to the community in many ways—in ecumenical events in Hillsville and the county and as president of the Ministerial Association. In March 1988, a twenty-five-minute documentary video, *Blind Shepherd of the Hills*, gave the Gladesboro Church family the chance to share with a larger audience how the congregation and Pastor Steele served Christ together. Following Pastor Steele's retirement in 2010, the congregation has been served by Interim Pastor Joseph Shumate. Holy Communion is celebrated each Sunday. Gladesboro has contributed five sons and a daughter to the Lutheran ministry. They are: the Rev. John Davis Utt, ordained in 1908; the Rev. Aaron F.

Tobler, ordained in 1915; the Rev. Claude Jackson "Jack" Martin, ordained in 1953; the Rev. James "Jim" Howard Utt, D.Min., D.D., ordained in 1976; the Rev. John Gary Largen, D.Min., ordained in 1980; and the Rev. JoAnn Kinzer Bunn, ordained in 1981. As a result of a year's work, a history of Gladesboro Lutheran Church was published in the fall of 2013, giving the story of Christian ministry by these dedicated brothers and sisters in Christ in the beautiful hills of Carroll County.

Pastors

Rev. Duane Steele, 1978–2010

Rev. Joseph Shumate, interim, 2010–

Redeemer, Pearisburg

Redeemer, Pearisburg was once paired with Luther Memorial, Pembroke in a Giles parish, but only Redeemer survives. Youth activities were featured in the late 1980s and early 1990s. A bell tower was dedicated in 1991, using a bell cast in 1892 which once hung in St. Paul's, Newport, before it closed in 1975. A celebration of 150 years of Lutheranism in Giles County was held in 1993 and a Heritage Service featured worshipers in early dress. Ceiling fans and a water filter system were installed and a furnace was replaced. A fiftieth anniversary celebration was held in 2011, and air conditioning was installed. A visiting worshiper provided a stained glass Luther Seal for a window in the narthex. A Good Neighbor Fund was established to help people in emergencies and provide continued support for local service organizations.

Pastors

Rev. Dennis Gillespie, 1988–1995

Rev. Walter Vierling, supply, 1996–1998

Rev. Diana Jackson, 1998–2005

Rev. Linda Motley, interim, 2005–2009

Rev. Martin Saarinen, supply, 2009–2011

Rev. Grady Beaver, supply, 2011–

Trinity, Pulaski

Beginning in 1987, the congregation sponsored Remy Nelson, a young man from St. Marc, Haiti, who graduated in International Relations from Roanoke College, received his M.Div. degree from Philadelphia Seminary, and was ordained at Redeemer Lutheran Church, Ft. Lauderdale, Florida, in 1999. He has been serving in hospital chaplaincy since 2003 and he became a United States citizen circa 2005. We celebrated the signing of the Joint Declaration on the Doctrine of Justification with members of St. Edwards Catholic Church on October 31, 1999, with a joint procession from Trinity to St. Edwards, ending with a celebrative service of Word and prayer. Our 125th anniversary offering allowed us to send $1,000 to Bedford Lutheran as a mission encouragement gift and $1,000 to our local New River Community Action Emergency Needs program. Trinity celebrated its one-hundredth anniversary in 1988.

The anniversary theme was "O God Our Help… Our Hope…" The guest preacher for the anniversary worship service was Bishop Richard Bansemer. For our 125th anniversary in 2013, former Pastors Steve P. Ridenhour and Gene Copenhaver participated. The anniversary theme was "Be Thou My Vision."

Pastors
Rev. Steve P. Ridenhour, 1984–1994
Rev. Terrie L. Sternberg, 1995–

Christ, Radford

During these twenty-five years, Christ Lutheran has been active in worship and mission. In April 1991, a new church ramp was dedicated along with a centennial birthday celebration in July of that year. In 2008, the Parish House was removed to make way for additional parking. More recently, the congregation voted to repair the original Italian stained glass windows and to improve the building's green footprint with replacement windows in the parish hall and a high-efficiency heat/air conditioning system in the sanctuary. Christ Lutheran participated in numerous local and national outreach programs from the Radford Food Pantry to hosting delegates from Papua New Guinea. Throughout the years, Christ Lutheran also enjoyed participation in many ecumenical programs with neighboring congregations, from VBS to youth ministry, campus ministry at Radford University, and Logos programs. Currently in the works is a dedication for the new Memorial Garden and plans to renovate the narthex. In 2012, Christ Lutheran initiated an intentional effort to revision our mission and ministry in the Radford area, with an emphasis on inclusive hospitality, faith development, and growth in Christian discipleship.

Pastors
Rev. John McCandlish, 1987–2008
Rev. Stephen Shackelford, 2011
Rev. Conrad A. Braaten, interim, 2012–2014

NORTHERN VALLEY CONFERENCE
Good Shepherd, Front Royal

For over twenty-five years, Good Shepherd has been actively involved as individual members and as a congregation in offering time, talents, financial resources, and church space in servant ministry to the needs of others in the local community and the world. The congregation began a monthly folk-style service and occasional contemporary worship led by a praise band. In 1989, Good Shepherd joined other congregations in the Northern Valley Conference in witnessing training and door-to-door visitation, starting with a sermon by Pastor James Capers, co-director of witness and evangelism for the ELCA. Youth from the church prepared food for the homeless in Washington, DC, participated in summer servant camps based at Hungry Mother Lutheran Camp, and joined in synod and ELCA youth events. They joined four other churches in forming an Ecumenical Youth Fellowship. Good Shepherd celebrated its fiftieth anniversary in 1992 and its sixtieth anniversary, led by Bishop James Mauney, in 2002. Prayer services for peace were held during the Persian Gulf War. A higher education scholarship fund was established with an anonymous bequest of $35,000, and a synod loan financing construction of a fellowship hall was repaid; asbestos abatement work replaced all floor tiles. Dr. Bonnie Dult, nursing professor at Shenandoah University, became the first parish nurse in the congregation, and in 2006, Mary Louise Brown, a former member, was ordained at Good Shepherd. Pastor Robert Jones was recognized for thirty years of service to the congregation in 2012. After a shortfall in financial support, the congregation voted to tithe all undesignated receipts to churchwide mission and ministry.

Pastor

Rev. Robert Jones, 1982–

Gravel Springs, Star Tannery

The Gravel Springs Lutheran Parish, once a five-church parish, was reduced to the two churches that now comprise the Gravel Springs-St. John's Lutheran Parish. The parish is stronger than ever due to the interest and day-to-day operations of the synod. When the ELCA began, our congregations began to witness a change in broadening our religious base by ministers giving us updates and news of events from the Virginia Synod. Each pastor has made it a priority to encourage us to become involved. On November 21, 1999, Gravel Springs Lutheran Church celebrated its 150th anniversary with a special celebration banquet, followed by a special service the next day. In 2003, when our parish was in need of guidance and direction, Bishop Mauney and Pastor Paul "Chip" Gunsten offered support and recommendations to reunite our congregations in faith and love and their advice led to an amicable compromise. On Sunday, July 31, 2011, a reception was held at Gravel Springs Lutheran Church in celebration of Interim Pastor Lance Braun's forty years of service in the ministry. Bishop Mauney gave a brief history of Pastor Braun's work. Our most recent parish celebration, held at St. John's on Sunday, January 29, 2012, was the installation of the Rev. Sonya Williams-Giersch, former associate in ministry (AIM), as the new pastor of the parish. The installation was presided over by the Rev. Bob Jones, Good Shepherd, Front Royal, dean of the Northern Valley Conference.

Pastors

Rev. Warren C. Heintzelman, Jr., 1985–1993

Rev. Martha Miller Sims, 1994–1998

Rev. Lynn A. Bechdolt, 1999–2002

Rev. William L. Rosenow, 2003

Rev. Lance K. Braun, interim, 2005–2011

Rev. Sonya Williams-Giersch, 2012–

Trinity, Stephens City

Trinity, Stephens City was organized in 1765 and it joined St. Paul to form Stephens City Parish in 1902. Trinity became a single church parish in 1989. Stained glass windows were refurbished in 1994 and again in 2007. Sewing for the Savior, a group who make quilts to celebrate special life events or for cancer or dialysis patients or the Red Cross, began work. Members began a monthly community meal and they started restoration of the cemetery and a monthly men's breakfast.

Pastors

Rev. Frank Honeycutt, 1985–1988

Rev. William F. Hogan, 1989–1993

Rev. Susan Springer, 1993–1995

Rev. John Ericson, 1997–2002

Rev. Elizabeth Yates, 2003–2010

Rev. Cameron Keyser, 2011–

Bethel, Winchester

Bethel, a congregation tracing its origin back to 1820, dedicated its fifth building in 1980 while Pastor Conrad Christianson, Jr., was serving his twenty-nine-year tenure from 1966 until his retirement in 1995. Until 1964, the congregation was part of the Gravel Springs Parish. In 1994, a new roof and general refurbishing were completed. A new pipe organ was dedicated in 1995, the 175th anniversary of the congregation. Pastor D. Rhodes Wooly was called in 1996. Members voted substantial assistance for construction of a chaplain's residence for the MaaSae Girls Lutheran Secondary School in Tanzania. Refurbishing of the church parlor, dedicated as the Christianson Room, began in a capital improvement campaign. Conrad Christianson was named pastor emeritus. In 2004, the Rev. Scott Maxwell was called as a second pastor for leadership and administration. A new vision and mission was discerned for the congregation, and in 2005, a Mission Expansion Team was formed to consider additional Sunday School space, a youth center, and addition to worship space. A Global Mission Team was formed to oversee Bethel's growing involvement in Tanzania, the Philippines, and India. A youth director was hired to begin ministry to youth in grades six to twelve. After Wooly and Maxwell took calls to other churches, Pastors David Young and Heidi David-Young began ministry at Bethel in 2010. In 2011, the congregation adopted a vision statement, "A community growing deeper in faith and wider in love."

Pastors

Rev. Conrad Christianson, Jr., 1966–1995

Rev. Rhodes Wooly, 1996–2009

Rev. Scott Maxwell, 2004–2009

Rev. David Young, senior pastor, 2010–

Rev. Heidi David-Young, associate, 2010–2013

Grace, Winchester

In its twenty-five years in the ELCA, the congregation adopted three different long-range plans which have helped the congregation move forward in mission. "Heritage for the Future" led the congregation to purchase a large building located next to the back of the property and renovate the space to expand its preschool operations and Sunday School classrooms. "Growing in Grace" led the congregation to renovate the sanctuary and expand the versatility of and accessibility to the sanctuary. A new Schantz organ was installed and an elevator for easier access to the sanctuary. The plan also called for the purchase and renovation of the G&M Music building next door to the church to become the Grace Ministries Outreach Center, a space for community outreach, faith formation classrooms, and a second fellowship hall. With this property the congregation started an after-school program, TEAM Grace, in partnership with Winchester Public Schools, and provided space for English as a Second Language classes in partnership with Northern Shenandoah Valley Adult Education. Offices and meeting space were also provided for opening a regional office of Lutheran Family Services of Virginia and the office of the Virginia Synod Mission Office for Planned Giving. Grace celebrated its 250th anniversary throughout 2003, inviting former pastors to return throughout the year to preach. *This Heritage*, a history of Grace written by Pastor William E. Eisenberg (1944) in celebration of the congregation's 200th anniversary in 1953, was expanded and republished. In 2007, the congregation called its first full-time director of music/organist, Daniel P. Hannemann, associate in ministry. GraceVision, adopted in 2009, called for intentional leadership and participation of lay people in all aspects of the ministry of the congregation. During this time, the historic east wall of the original Lutheran Church in Mount Hebron Cemetery was restored and the Memorial Garden landscaped. This included the installation of an outdoor prayer labyrinth to incorporate a Luther's Rose for the center. Throughout these twenty-five years, Grace was blessed with pastoral leadership: James Utt, Paul "Chip" Gunsten, Mark Fitzsimmons, Rudy Keyl, Jeffrey May, and Martha Miller Sims. The congregation has also been blessed with a strong lay leadership and competent lay staff members. Pastors Utt and Sims and lay leaders Jerry Kerr and Lisa Behr provided a vision and the leadership on the board of National Lutheran Communities & Services, which opened a new continuing care retirement community (CCRC) in Winchester, The Village at Orchard Ridge, in 2013.

<u>Pastors</u>
Rev. James Utt, 1982–2013
Rev. Paul "Chip" Gunsten, associate, 1985–1990
Rev. Mark Fitzsimmons, associate, 1991–1996
Rev. Rudolph Keyl, Jr., pastoral associate, 1994–2010
Rev. Jeffrey May, co-pastor, 1998–2001
Rev. Martha Miller Sims, co-pastor, 2002–
Rev. Jonathan M. Boynton, 2014–

St. John's, Winchester

The parish was renamed in 1989 as the Gravel Springs-St. John's Lutheran Parish. A celebration of the 200th anniversary of the founding of the congregation was held in 1996. Bishop Richard Bansemer delivered the sermon at the formal banquet. Two decades of facility improvements began in 1998 when a family offered a new public address system in remembrance of their loved ones. The next year, a custom-built digital organ was acquired, thanks to a bequest from the estate of the church's organist and Sunday School teacher of fifty years. In 2006, using donations provided by a member through his family's trust fund, new roofs were placed on both the church and the adjoining social hall. After that, the interior of the nave was painted, thanks to a bequest from the estate of a member who had given flowers for the altar for close to forty years. The social hall underwent a two-year renovation, and a new driveway entrance sign was erected to complement the newly repaved and relined parking lot. The congregation's 210th anniversary celebration was held in 2006 with the blessings of Bishop James Mauney and Bishop Rick Foss of the Eastern North Dakota Synod. The Sunday School marked its 150th year of instruction in 2009. In 2010, the parish shared in the celebration of the fortieth anniversary of the ordination of Pastor Lance Karl Braun. On January 29, 2012, our parish celebrated the installation of Pastor Sonya Williams-Giersch. A reception welcomed our new pastor and her husband, Richard, and Gabrielle, her daughter.

Pastors

Rev. Warren C. Heintzelman, Jr., 1985–1993
Rev. Martha Miller Sims, 1994–1998
Rev. Lynn A. Bechdolt, 1999–2002
Rev. William L. Rosenow, 2003
Rev. Lance K. Braun, interim, 2005–2011
Rev. Sonya Williams-Giersch, 2012–

PAGE CONFERENCE
Beth Eden, Luray

Beth Eden has been organized with Grace, Luray as the Stony Man Parish since the mid-1960s. Beth Eden celebrated its one-hundredth anniversary in 1996. The congregation made the parsonage handicapped-accessible and paved the parking lot. The choir has joined the choir from a Seventh Day Adventist Church for a Christmas musical program.

Pastors

Rev. Kenneth Bowman, 1985–1994
Rev. Linda Anderson, 1995–1998
Rev. Sharon Wiggins, 1999–2002
Rev. James R. Daley, 2004–2013

Bethlehem, Luray

Bethlehem was part of the two-church Blue Ridge Parish with Morning Star until they separated in 1995. The congregation observed its 150th anniversary with a homecoming and visits from former pastors in 2001. The Rev. Eddy Walker of the United Church of Christ has served as interim pastor since the death of the Rev. Ruth Rinker in 2012.

Pastors
Rev. Ruth Rinker, 1999–2012
Rev. Eddy Walker, interim, 2012–

Grace, Luray

Grace, Luray and Beth Eden, Luray have been in the Stony Man Parish since the mid-1960s. Grace marked its 125th anniversary as a Lutheran congregation in 2002.

Pastors
Rev. Kenneth Bowman, 1985–1994
Rev. Linda Anderson, 1995–1998
Rev. Sharon Wiggins, 1999–2002
Rev. James R. Daley, 2004–

Morning Star, Luray

Morning Star, Luray, formed in 1873, was part of a two-church parish with Bethlehem until they voted to separate in 1995. The congregation celebrated its 125th anniversary, a new organ was purchased, and a cookbook was published in 1998. In 2003, the cemetery road was hard-surfaced, protective glass was placed on the stained glass windows, and the Sunday School wing was air conditioned. A new steeple and new entrance were then installed. The congregation received a bequest of thirty-eight acres of mountain land behind the church in 2004. Members wore period clothing and Pastor Jeff Marble dressed as Pastor John Stirewalt, founder of the congregation.

Pastors
Rev. Jeffrey Marble, 1986–1991
Rev. Frederick Smith, 1992–1995
Rev. Barbara Hansen, 1995–2002
Rev. Jeffrey Marble, 2003–

St. Mark, Luray

St. Mark, Luray, dating from 1876, has been served by Pastor Nicholas Eichelberger since 1988. Air conditioning was installed in the church parsonage, glass doors were installed at the nave entrance, and a piano was purchased for the fellowship hall. A preschool was established in 1995 and a house next door to the church was purchased. Weekly ecumenical services were established and a baptistery was installed in the nave. A bronze plaque was mounted in front of the church and the original steeple was removed because of water damage. Protective covering was installed on the stained glass windows and a new roof was installed on the education building. The Child Care Center added before-and-after-school care and a Loaves and Fishes Backpack Ministry was established for Luray Elementary School.

Pastor

Rev. Nicholas Eichelberger, 1988–

St. Paul, Shenandoah

The congregation of St. Paul, Shenandoah helped to organize the Shenandoah Elementary School backpack food ministry, provide handyman/repair visits at Grace House women's shelter in Shenandoah, raise funds for people burned out of homes or facing daunting medical expenses, offer a storytime/outreach ministry to kids at the local food and clothing pantry, and share prayers, Bibles, and faith-forming materials at the Page County Fair, among other means. In 2006, St. Paul partnered with St. Luke, Stanley and St. Peter, Shenandoah to form River of Life Partnership. This is a cooperative venturing for outreach, faith formation, worship, and service. Along with a host of ministers called by baptism, two pastors serve as called ordained ministers. Significant partnering activities include: county fair booth ministry; a work trip to Slidell, Louisiana, following Hurricane Katrina; an annual Bible School for all ages; youth activities; and special worship services. Improvements to building and grounds include remodeling/updating the parsonage and a succession planting of new trees in the old oak grove on the church grounds.

Pastors

Rev. Henry Liskey, 1984–1994

Rev. Jeffrey Sonafelt, 1996–1999

Rev. Dorothy Nimal, 2000–2004

Rev. Patricia Covington, 2006–2011, River of Life Partnership

Rev. Mark Briehl, 2006–, River of Life Partnership

Rev. Phyllis Diamond, 2012–, River of Life Partnership

St. Peter, Shenandoah

The congregation of St. Peter, Shenandoah shared God's love these past twenty-five years by organizing an annual wood-cutting and delivery ministry; hosting community meals like Breakfast for Vets and occasional pancake suppers; hosting and helping organize ecumenical services at Thanksgiving, Christmas, and Easter; visiting members who are shut-in; and sharing prayers, Bibles, and faith-forming materials at the Page County Fair, among other means. In 2006, St. Peter partnered with St. Luke, Stanley and St. Paul, Shenandoah to form River of Life Partnership. This is a cooperative venturing for outreach, faith formation, worship, and service. Along with a host of ministers called by baptism, two pastors serve as called ordained ministers. Significant partnering activities include: county fair booth ministry; a work trip to Slidell, Louisiana, following

Hurricane Katrina; an annual Bible School for all ages; youth activities; and special worship services. Improvements to building and grounds include installing an elevator with four-level access, repairs and upgrades in the kitchen and social hall, and improvements in the parsonage.

Pastors

Rev. Bill Boldin, 1987–1993

Rev. James Daley, 1994–2005

Rev. Patricia Covington, 2006–2011, River of Life Partnership

Rev. Mark Briehl, 2006–, River of Life Partnership

Rev. Phyllis Diamond, 2012–, River of Life Partnership

St. Luke, Stanley

The congregation of St. Luke, Stanley shared God's love by making and giving prayer shawls; sharing prayers, Bibles, and faith-forming materials at the Page County Fair; assisting with the Stanley Elementary School backpack food ministry; supporting Choices, the local women's shelter; and offering a prayer/greeting card ministry connecting members with area residents. In 2006, St. Luke partnered with St. Paul, Shenandoah and St. Peter, Shenandoah to form River of Life Partnership. Along with a host of ministers called by baptism, two pastors serve as called ordained ministers. The congregations shared in significant ministry partnership opportunities. Improvements to building and grounds include installing an access ramp and landscaped entrance and installing an audio/video center in the social hall.

Pastors

Rev. JoAnn Bunn, 1985–1989

Rev. Aldon Purdham, 1990–1993

Rev. David Stouter, 1993–1996

Rev. Gary Chenoweth, 1997–2002

Rev. Elizabeth Yates, 2002–2004

Rev. Patricia Covington, 2006–2011, River of Life Partnership

Rev. Mark Briehl, 2006–, River of Life Partnership

Rev. Phyllis Diamond, 2012–, River of Life Partnership

PENINSULA CONFERENCE

Apostles, Gloucester

Apostles Lutheran Church began in 1981 as a satellite of St. Mark Lutheran Church in Yorktown. In September 1983, the congregation became chartered. As an independent Lutheran congregation, it purchased land and broke ground for a church building in May 1984. The congregation worshiped in an Episcopal chapel for almost three years until the first service in its new building on Palm Sunday 1987. On May 13, 1988, Apostles Lutheran Church became a congregation of the Virginia Synod of the ELCA. The Rev. Theodore M. Schulz was called as Apostles' first ELCA pastor in October 1988. Construction of fellowship and classroom space in the church basement was completed and dedicated in 1990. Pastor Schulz left Apostles to accept a call to Shepherd of the Valley Church in Bridgewater on November 1, 1996. The Rev. Charles H. Mayer served as vice pastor during the pastoral vacancy. The Rev. R. Paul Schafer was called by Apostles and began on November 9, 1997. Ground was broken for a new sanctuary on April 21, 2002. On Palm Sunday, April 13, 2003, the congregation worshipped for the first time in the new building and it was dedicated on September 14, 2003. Pastor Paul Schafer left Apostles to accept a call to St. Mark Lutheran Church in Wheeling, West Virginia, on May 1, 2004. The Rev. James R. Larsen was called as pastor of Apostles and began July 1, 2005. In January 2006, Apostles men began working one day each month for the Gloucester Housing Partnership to help improve substandard housing for the needy in the community. In response to the great need following Hurricane Katrina, Apostles sent the first of three work teams to New Orleans in the spring of 2006; following teams went in 2007 and 2008.

Pastors

Rev. Theodore M. Schulz, 1988–1996

Rev. Charles H. Mayer, vice pastor, 1997

Rev. R. Paul Schafer, 1997–2004

Rev. James R. Larsen, 2005–

Gloria Dei, Hampton

In June 1987, Pastor Mark Briehl was called to serve at Gloria Dei. Brian Larson joined our music ministry as cantor in November. The fall of 1987 saw a record enrollment of 415 students in our Gloria Dei School. On September 18, 1988, we dedicated our new church and organ with over 500 people in worship. In 1990, we celebrated our twenty-fifth year as a congregation. Gloria Dei celebrated its thirtieth year of ministry in 1995. We moved third-, fourth-, and fifth-graders into our new facilities on the Harris Creek Road campus. In 1997, the seeds were planted for what ultimately would become an adult daycare facility, Sunrise House, and the introduction of small group discipleship ministries. The year 1999 saw participation in the small group discipleship ministries exceeding one hundred members. The year 1999 was one of record highs from the school—over 1,800 hours of community service, over $16,000 collected for the American Heart Association (Jump Rope for Heart program), and an enrollment of 625 students. In 2000, our youth participated for the first time in the ELCA's national convention in St. Louis. In August, Dr. Martin Sunderland was installed as director of parish music. In February 2002, Pastor Edmund Freeborn brought a wealth of experience, knowledge, and pastoral energy with his call. We ended 2002 with the December groundbreaking for our atrium/connector space. In 2005, we celebrated our fortieth anniversary, purchased 18.5 acres of land, and dedicated the Koinonia atrium space. In May 2006, Pastor Kopp established our Gloria Dei Academy and its associated Pastoral Internship Program. As part of our Academy, Vicars Nathan Robinson and Garrett Bugg joined the Clinical Pastoral Education Program and Pastor Wayne Harrison started as director of Sunrise House. In 2007, we called Pastor Garrett Bugg as assistant pastor. On July 31, 2009, the Rev. L. Douglas Stowe, our senior pastor for over forty years, died following a series of setbacks that eroded his health. In April 2011, we called Senior Pastor Charles Bang, who had served the Buffalo, New York area for almost thirty years. We are currently planning our fiftieth anniversary celebration as Gloria Dei Lutheran Church in 2015.

Pastors

Rev. L. Douglas Stowe, 1969–2009

Rev. Mark S. Briehl, 1987–1990

Rev. Timothy W. Spring, associate, 1993

Rev. Edmund T. Freeborn III, 2002–2010

Rev. Garrett Bugg, assistant, 2007–2009

Rev. Charles Bang, 2011–

St. Paul's, Hampton

In 1987, St. Paul's, Hampton celebrated thirty-five years of ministry, and we celebrated our sixtieth anniversary in 2013. During these twenty-five years, St. Paul's has continued steadfast in its mission to love and serve God and all God's children. St. Paul's has shared its ministry locally and to the larger church through many programs: Hampton Ecumenical Lodgings and Provisions (HELP), Thrivent Builds/Habitat for Humanity, Lutheran Family Services, Lutheran World Relief/Equal Exchange, United Lutheran Appeal, Alcoholics Anonymous, the Peninsula Pastoral Counseling Center, and humanitarian aid packages to Afghanistan, Iraq, and Slovakia. Our newest missions include the ELCA's Malaria Project, providing birthing kits for mothers in developing countries, and Bread for the World. During the past twenty-five years, we have continued to increase accessibility and improve our physical plant. Ramps, hand rails, and handicapped-accessible bathrooms were added. In 2001, we received the ELCA Accessibility Award. Our volunteer efforts to maintain our grounds resulted in St. Paul's receiving the 2007 Hampton Clean Business Award. Our "crowning" achievement came in 2000, when the steeple was replaced, ending a thirty-year problem with leaks into the sanctuary. St. Paul's made a commitment to making a joyful noise with a complete upgrade of our organ and piano, and an improved sound system, beginning in 2007. We have added hearing assistance devices, large-print hymnals and bulletins, and other improvements to meet the changing needs of our congregants. Our Christian education program has adapted with the creation of a special needs curriculum in 2010 and a multigenerational Sunday School and confirmation class beginning in 2011. We look forward to many more years of shared ministry and service.

Pastors

Rev. Harvey Alvin Kuhn, 1984–1990

Rev. Paul Milholland, 1991–1995

Rev. William Gerald Weeks, 1996–1998

Rev. Jack Behlendorf, interim, 1998–1999

Rev. Christine Farrow, 1999–

Living Water, Kilmarnock

Living Water, Kilmarnock held its first worship service in 2003 after Pastor Chip Gunsten, assistant to the synod bishop, said the synod would like to start a new congregation in Northumberland County, about seventy miles from the nearest ELCA congregation. The first mission, called a synodically authorized worshiping community, held services led by retired Pastor Donald McClean at a Masonic lodge in Warsaw. Worship was moved to Kilmarnock, central to the area from which interest responses came. The congregation met in a chapel behind Grace Episcopal Church, advertised as "the ELCA New Mission to the Northern Neck." Realizing that Saturday services did not invite growth, especially for young people with children, the congregation leased a small office building and worship began there in April 2006, led by Pastor Robert Maier of Richmond. As growth continued, the ELCA approved a change in status to "a church under development." Members approved the purchase of the Center for the Arts building on a five-acre tract in Kilmarnock, with the help of a loan from the ELCA Mission Investment Fund. Members of the Church of New Visions, a new congregation beginning in Living Water's old location, came to worship. The congregation extended its first call to Pastor John Ericson of Hampton. The church began using audio/visual equipment with images on two screens, a breakfast was offered to children in Sunday School, and it worked with the Northern Neck Food Bank to allow installation of a high tunnel to grow vegetables. Ministry has grown, especially in helping to combat hunger locally, and volunteers are working harder than ever as members continue to find the strength to serve as disciples, doing what Jesus would do, fulfilling the purpose of mission.

Pastor
Rev. John Ericson, 2011–2014

Reformation, Newport News

Reformation awakened in 1987 having attained the age of twenty-six years filled with families and children, which led to an addition to the original building to add classroom and fellowship space. The congregation became Reformation Lutheran Church and Childcare in September 1998, as the congregation began a childcare ministry that continues to the present. A concert series, started in 2004 to provide our community with access to a broad spectrum of the musical arts, was named for Mildred McDaniels, who was a forty-year member of the congregation, active in the Worship and Music Ministry for many years. In 2011, Reformation celebrated its fiftieth anniversary with the same liturgy (from *Service Book and Hymnal*) that was used fifty years earlier for the congregation's first service in 1961. The congregation remains active by its focus on Word and Sacrament ministry, with a weekly celebration of the Eucharist. In addition, Christian Education, youth ministry, a prayer group, and fellowship events round out the congregation's life.

Pastors
Rev. Curtis H. Brandt, 1987
Rev. Harold J. Harter, 1988–1995
Rev. Darla J. Kincaid, 1996–2001
Rev. James P. Nickols, 2003–2009
Rev. Cheryl Ann Griffin, associate, 2005–2008
Rev. David Gunderlach, associate pastor for family ministry, 2007–2014
Rev. John Ericson, 2014

Trinity, Newport News

Trinity, Newport News, founded in December 1898, was originally located in downtown Newport News. A new church building was dedicated in 1958. During the 1980s and 1990s, the congregation and the youth became active with social ministry, including PORT (shelter for the homeless), Harvest of Hope, Habitat for Humanity, Respite Day Care, volunteering at a local soup kitchen, and collecting food for the food bank. In 1993, Trinity became a Stephen Ministry Congregation. In December 1997, the congregation began a yearlong celebration of one hundred years of ministry. Musical programs were presented monthly. The year culminated with a big celebration of history at the James River Country Club and a one-hundredth anniversary service attended by many former members. Trinity Lutheran School, established in 1961 with a preschool and kindergarten program, is presently a K-8 school which hopes to soon be accredited in the International Baccalaureate Program. The school is an integral part of the ministry and mission of Trinity. An addition was made to the building in 1999 for kindergarten rooms and a new school library. For the last several years, Trinity congregation has met with the Mennonite congregations in the Newport News area for an annual service of music and fellowship. As the congregation moves further into the twenty-first century, many new programs and worship opportunities are being introduced to the congregation under the leadership of Pastor Guy.

Pastors
Rev. Thomas L. Bosserman, 1972–2005
Rev. J. Christopher Price, associate, 1979–1983
Rev. A.G. "Chip" Austin, associate, 1984–1999
Rev. Jeffrey R. Sonafelt, associate, 1999–2005
Rev. Richard Olsen, interim, 2005
Rev. James Vigen, interim, 2006–2007
Rev. Frederick Guy, 2007–
Rev. Cheryl Griffin, associate, 2008–2013

Our Saviour, Norge

Our Saviour, Norge traces its beginnings to a settlement of Lutherans of Norwegian and Danish descent, who came from the Midwest in 1898, responding to advertisements of vacant, fertile land. They formed Zion Lutheran and in 1904 built a church still standing as Our Saviour today. Bethany, a second Scandinavian congregation, merged with Zion to form Our Saviour in 1932. An addition was constructed and a parish hall was added in 1986, followed by an accessibility ramp and an education addition to the parish hall in 1994. The church has three cemeteries—one immediately behind the church, one at the former Bethany Church, and the original one located on Riverview Road. Our Saviour changed its synodical affiliation in 1958 to the Virginia Synod of the United Lutheran Church in America and to the ELCA after the 1988 merger.

<u>Pastors</u>
Rev. Thord K. Einarsen, 1980–2000
Rev. Jack Behlendorf, interim, 2000–2002
Rev. Donald Chudd, 2002–2009
Rev. James Nickols, 2010–

St. Stephen, Williamsburg

The church building of St. Stephen, Williamsburg has undergone three renovations/expansion projects in the past twenty-five years, enhancing our service to the congregation as well as outreach to the community. Serving those in need has been a strong part of our ministry. In 1998, St. Stephen entered into a sister congregation partnership with Mongai Lutheran Parish in Tanzania. Pastor Andy Ballentine and other members of our congregation have visited Mongai to bring greetings and support from St. Stephen. A number of members have provided significant support for students in Tanzania through Godparents for Tanzania. In 2012, the congregation raised money to support Rogathe John "Roggy" Tippe in his studies toward a BS in Wildlife Management at Soloine University in Tanzania. The Vacation Bible School, Faith Formation children, and congregation also purchased more than 200 solar lights for "G4TZ"-sponsored students. The congregation celebrated its fiftieth anniversary in 2007. Over the past twenty-five years, eight members of the Lutheran Student Association (students from the College of William and Mary) and three members of the congregation have been ordained as ELCA pastors.

<u>Pastors</u>
Rev. Benton Lutz, 1973–1991
Rev. Lawrence Shoberg, 1992–2000
Rev. John Vought, interim, 2000–2001
Rev. Andy Ballentine, 2001–
Rev. Cheryl Griffin, 2013–

St. Mark, Yorktown

The Rev. Robert A. Anderson was sent by the Board of American Missions of the Lutheran Church in America as a mission developer to York County in July 1967, and the congregation was organized on May 19, 1968. The first building was constructed in 1975 and expanded in 1978. A new sanctuary was built in 1983. When the ELCA was formed, Pastor David Delaney served for two years, followed by Pastors Wayne R. Shelor and Gary M. Erdos. The refurbished Austin pipe organ was dedicated on November 17, 1991, with a special recital by Dr. Donald G. Moe, assistant professor of music at Roanoke College. Under the leadership of the Rev. Gary M. Erdos, the church has grown in membership and physically. The sanctuary was renovated in 2000. A groundbreaking ceremony for Phase 1 of construction was held on March 18, 2001. The new narthex, kitchen, office suites, Sunday School rooms, nursery, and conference room and renovation of the older building were completed to include a chapel, choir room, and Sunday School. Pastor Erdos accepted a call to Trinity English Lutheran Church in Fort Wayne, Indiana, in August 2012.

Pastors

Rev. David K. Delaney, 1985–1989

Rev. Wayne R. Shelor, 1990–1997

Rev. Gary M. Erdos, 1998–2012

Rev. Larry Laine, interim, 2012–2014

Rev. Joel Neubauer, 2014–

RICHMOND CONFERENCE
Lakeside, Littleton, North Carolina

Four couples met in May 1992 to discuss options in pursuing the development of a Lutheran church in the Lake Gaston area of North Carolina, near the Virginia border, and a month later, twenty Lutherans met with the Rev. Boyce Whitener to explore the possibility of establishing a church near the lake. Their first service was held at St. Alban's Episcopal Church in Littleton, North Carolina, in September 1992. Pastor Aldon Purdham began as a mission developer for Lakeside Lutheran and the first service was held in August 1993 in a rescue squad building and later in a fire department hall. In February 1994, forty-three adults and five children became charter members of Lakeside. The congregation was incorporated and it acquired a building site in 1995. Pastor Dennis Hahle began as pastor developer, the congregation voted to affiliate with the Virginia Synod, and a congregational unit joined the Virginia Synodical Women's Organization in 1996. Lakeside became an organized member of the Virginia Synod/ELCA in November 1996. The next year, an early service was added and the congregation approved a site plan and drawings for a multipurpose building. A pavilion was completed, and the first outdoor service, a groundbreaking service, and the first service in the first unit were held in 1999. Membership had grown to 160, and there were twelve associate members. Vacation Bible School with seven participating churches and the dedication of a cemetery followed; membership grew to 226 with twenty-three associate members and a tenth anniversary celebration was held in 2002. A mortgage retirement celebration came in 2003, multimedia equipment was installed, and a landscaping project with a watering system was completed. The congregation purchased thirty-seven handbells, filled its first intern position with Vicar Carolyn Simonds, began a neighborhood visitation program, and planned for a cemetery, bell tower, and biblical garden. In 2009, the congregation approved hiring an architect to design a multipurpose addition, but this was on hold through 2012. In 2010, the congregation voted to remain firmly in relationship with the ELCA. Charlotte Moss, a parish nurse, began work.

Pastors

Rev. Aldon Purdham, mission developer, 1993–1994

Rev. Richard Eisemann, interim, 1994–1996

Rev. Dennis Hahle, pastor developer, 1996–2001

Rev. Rich Olson, interim, 2001–2002

Rev. Fred Eichner, 2002–2011

Messiah, Mechanicsville

Development of Messiah, Mechanicsville as a Lutheran Church in America congregation began with worship in a firehouse in 1966 and its first building was dedicated on All Saints Sunday 1968. Messiah became part of the ELCA with its merger in 1988. On August 11, 1991, ground was broken for new worship space, a $420,000 renovation. The new space and a spacious multipurpose narthex were dedicated on May 10, 1992. In April 1996, stained glass windows were added to the sanctuary, designed and created by local artists with input from a team of congregation members. Sacramental and biblical themes are noted throughout. Several other major property and building enhancements have occurred since 2007. Messiah joined with Creator Episcopal and Redeemer Roman Catholic Church to start Mechanicsville Churches Emergency Functions (MCEF) over thirty-five years ago. MCEF currently has over thirty local congregations, providing local assistance including food, clothes, and other necessities to local residents in need. Messiah Lutheran School, opened in 1995, currently offers infant care, preschool, and after-school care for elementary students. Today, Messiah actively shares in the work and ministry of Central Virginia Friends of L'Arche, the Hanover Adult Center, Inc., Hanover Habitat for Humanity, Hanover Humane Society, Lutheran Family Services of Virginia, and MCEF, among others. In 2012, it began to host a stand on-site for Village Markets, a Lutheran free trade organization. Three past members have gone into ordained ministry: the Rev. Kelly Derrick, the Rev. Patti Arthur, and the Rev. Brett Wilson. The ordination of Pastor Lou Florio on December 8, 2007, was the first held at Messiah. Sue Gilnet, RN became Messiah's first trained parish nurse on December 6, 2009.

Pastors

Rev. Gary R. Rhinesmith, 1986–1993

Rev. Stephen L. Moose, 1994–2005

Rev. Lou Florio, 2007–

Our Redeemer, Petersburg

In 1987, $150,000 was received from the estate of John Nemetz, a longtime member of the congregation, establishing the Nemetz Fund for capital improvements. Fortieth, fiftieth, and sixtieth anniversaries were observed in 1989, 1999, and 2009. Special programs were planned with guest clergy as speakers. Youth attended the national Youth Gatherings in 2003, 2006, 2009, and 2012. Twenty-five years of ministry was celebrated with Pastor William Batterman in 1993. In 2005, in response to Hurricane Katrina, quilts were made and sent to hurricane victims in Louisiana, and the church developed its first website. In 2009, we became active in our local Neighborhood Watch group, hosting their annual National Night Out on the front yard of the church. A 2012 senior ladies group was organized. Pastor David Shaffer retired July 25, 2010. Seminarian Paul T. Christian was called to be our pastor in May 2011. He was ordained on June 4 at the Virginia Synod Assembly by Bishop James Mauney and installed by the Rev. Jean Bozeman, assistant to the bishop. In 2012, new carpet was purchased for the sanctuary and a new roof was placed there.

Pastors

Rev. William Batterman, 1983–1993

Rev. James Brady, 1995–1998

Rev. Timothy F. Waltonen, interim, 1998–2001

Rev. David Shaffer, 2001–2010

Rev. Paul T. Christian, 2011–

Christ, Richmond

January 1988 brought many changes to Christ, Richmond. Pastor James Mauney resigned as pastor to become an assistant to the bishop in the Virginia Synod. Pastor Eric Moehring was installed on September 11, 1988. In 1992, the mortgage was paid off, making way for a major two-level construction project that tied together two separate buildings with offices, a large gathering area, choir and youth rooms, and a library, plus a large kitchen added to the fellowship hall, all dedicated on October 23, 1994. A 2007 building renewal project replaced old roofs, HVAC systems, and windows, along with refreshing the educational wing, worship area, and fellowship hall. In 1992, we filled 6,000 requests for food assistance through our food pantry. In 2002, we led in forming the community-based LAMB's Basket, now filling over 250 requests each week. Since 1993, we have hosted the homeless through CARITAS. Since 1995, members have gone on mission trips to Appalachia and the Gulf Coast. Lakeside HealthCARE, a cooperative program of parish nurses providing health resources, was started by our parish nurse in 2008. In 1989, a Zimmer pipe organ was installed at a cost of $88,000. On Palm Sunday 1989, lay assistants first served at Holy Communion; on November 28, 1993, we offered two Sunday services, a practice discontinued in 1979. We began to offer Holy Communion every Sunday at every service on All Saints Sunday 2001. In 1990, Christ Church and the Episcopal Church of the Epiphany gathered for the first Lenten journey together, from Ash Wednesday through the five following Wednesday evenings and ending with a Good Friday service. The Rev. Kim Triplett, a daughter of the congregation, was ordained at Synod Assembly on June 7, 2008. We called our first associate pastor, the Rev. Kristin Hunsinger, who was ordained at Synod Assembly on June 6, 2009. Among her responsibilities are youth, education, and young adults. A large brick sign was placed on Woodman Road in 2008, offering a visible presence for a church building set back in the woods.

Pastors

Rev. James F. Mauney, 1981–1988

Rev. J. Christopher Price, interim, 1988

Rev. Eric J. Moehring, 1988–

Rev. Kristin Hunsinger, associate, 2009–

Christ the King, Richmond

Christ the King Lutheran was organized in March 1965 by Pastor Walter Huffman as a congregation of the American Lutheran Church. By 1988, as the Evangelical Lutheran Church in America was forming, the congregation had grown steadily and was being served by Pastor Bruce Wilder. In that year, the church conducted a significant building expansion to enlarge the sanctuary and to add a narthex as a gathering space. Pastor Wilder left in 1989 to serve a Lutheran congregation in New Mexico, and the following year Christ the King called Pastor Jeffrey May to be their next pastor. Pastor May served at Christ the King for two years before accepting a call to the Timberville Parish. Pastor Roger Bruns was then called to serve the congregation as its sixth pastor. During the next ten years, Christ the King experienced considerable growth, making the decision in 1995 to transform one of their two services into a contemporary service that was band-led and which incorporated a significant number of recently composed praise-and-worship songs, and by 1999, to begin a capital campaign to build a new sanctuary space. Pastor Bruns departed in 2002, and the congregation was served for fifteen months by Interim Pastors Karl and Kristin Jacobsen, who helped oversee the building campaign and the construction process. In September 2003, the congregation dedicated the new sanctuary addition. In April 2004, Pastor Stephen Bohannon began his ministry at Christ the King, and the combination of new worship space and renewed pastoral presence led to another period of significant growth for the congregation. We give thanks to God for blessing this place and its people so richly, and we rededicate ourselves to serving this community with the gospel as we seek to live up to the One by which we are known and named: Jesus Christ the King.

Pastors

Rev. Bruce Wilder, 1988–1989

Rev. Jeffrey May, 1990–1992

Rev. Roger Bruns, 1992–2002

Rev. Karl and Rev. Kristin Jacobsen, interim, 2002–2004

Rev. Stephen Bohannon, 2004–2014

Rev. Randy Lohr, 2009–

Epiphany, Richmond

Since 1987, Epiphany has grown from an annual Sunday service attendance of 238 to 396 for 2011. As a result of this growth, the need for expansion was quickly realized. Three building campaigns, in 1992, 2001, and 2006, resulted in expanded seating in the sanctuary, a new fellowship hall, a new chapel, balcony seating, chancel renovation, and a columbarium. With this expansion, Epiphany began a number of new ministries. In ministry to those outside our congregation, Epiphany began participation in spring/fall work weekends at Camp Caroline Furnace in 1987, student campus ministry in 1988, support for the Virginia Institute of Pastoral Care in 1990, CARITAS in 1993, Habitat for Humanity in 2002, LAMB's Basket in 2008, HHOPE in 2010, youth mission trips to Myrtle Beach for home renovations in 2010, and a youth trip to ELCA Youth Gathering in 2011. Epiphany saw the need to increase the ministry staff. To support the congregation in all these missions, a director of music was employed in 1997, a coordinator of volunteers in 1998, an associate pastor in 2002, a diaconal minister in 2004, and an administrative assistant in 2007. Three vicars were also included in the congregation's life: William Ridenhour in 1996, Scott Maxwell in 1997, and Dottie Nimal in 1998. In November 2004, a new constitution was approved and a three-part ministry team/council model established. This model consisted of (1) ministry teams composed of volunteer members of the congregation working in various ministries (evangelism, finance, and property) that are the daily life of the church, (2) the congregational council elected to provide leadership for future goals, and (3) clerical staff who provide spiritual guidance and liaison between the ministry teams and church council.

Pastors

Rev. J. Christopher Price, 1983–2012

Rev. Mark England, associate, 1999–2008

Christine V. Huffman, diaconal minister, 2004

Rev. Thomas Bosserman, visitation pastor, 2008

Rev. Philip W. Martin, Jr., associate, 2009; senior pastor, 2014–

First English, Richmond

The congregation, founded in 1869 as St. Mark's Lutheran Church and reconstituted in 1876 as First English to emphasize its commitment to worship in the language of this country, welcomed the birth of the new ELCA twenty-five years ago. In 1987, it made part of the education building available for the Read Center (an adult literacy program); in 1988, SPARC (a music program for youth) began using the facility on Saturdays. During the 1990s, First English continued to be very active in Stuart Circle Parish, founded in the 1970s as an ecumenical venture of the five churches—Episcopal, Lutheran, Presbyterian, Roman Catholic, and United Church of Christ—in its immediate neighborhood. A new organ was installed in June 2003 and formally dedicated on January 25, 2004. During 2004, it was decided to make music one of the main features of outreach. Linus Ellis, organist and choir director since 2000, was called as an associate in ministry (AIM) in March 2005, after required training. As the one-hundredth anniversary (May 21, 2011) of the dedication of the church's present building on Monument Avenue approached, a capital campaign to support major renovations on the building was conducted, beginning in 2006. The one-hundredth anniversary was observed on four Sundays in May 2011, each featuring a guest preacher and special program afterwards, culminating in a rededication service which took place on Sunday, May 22, with Bishop Jim Mauney participating. As First English enters its second century of service on Monument Avenue, the congregation is engaged in a visioning process, looking towards the year 2020 as an immediate goal, to determine how it might best continue to fulfill its mission to proclaim the gospel of Jesus Christ and continue to be a presence for good in the city of Richmond and beyond.

Pastors and AIM

Rev. John F. Byerly, Jr., 1973–1988

Rev. Cynthia Happel Bullock, associate/interim, 1987–1991

Rev. Richard Olson, 1989–1999

Rev. Mary Peterson, associate, 1992–1996

Rev. Larry Shoberg, interim, 2000–2001

Rev. John Schweitzer, 2001–

Linus Ellis, AIM, 2005–

Our Saviour, Richmond

Our Saviour, organized in 1979, dedicated its first worship space at 9601 Hull Street Road, Richmond in 1988. Pastor Joe Vought had been installed in 1987. The mission congregation became self-supporting in 1991 and an addition enlarging the sanctuary and constructing an education wing was dedicated. The congregation began preschool ministry in 1991 and welcomed its first intern in 1993. Pastor Vought accepted another call in 1997 and Pastor Ken Ruppar was installed in 1998. Pastor Ruppar was elected to a six-year term on the ELCA council in 2001. A bell choir was formed and the Nichols Scholarship Fund was established to help with college expenses for members, with preference for students in nursing or seminary education. The congregation celebrated its twenty-fifth anniversary in 2004. Our Saviour began sharing worship space with the Ethiopian Orthodox Tewahedo Beata LeMariam Church on Saturdays.

Pastors

Rev. Joe Vought, 1987–1997

Rev. Ken Ruppar, 1998–2014

St. Luke, Richmond

St. Luke, Richmond has been active in worship and service the past twenty-five years. In 1987, a new long-range plan was adopted. In 1988, Pastor Bill Kinser, founding pastor, and Louise Jacobson, director of music, retired after serving for more than thirty years. In 1989, our "Bold Vision, Bolder Witness" capital campaign was launched which led to ground breaking in November 1991 for a new nave, expanded east wing, and building renovation. Stained glass windows were installed in 1995 and 2003. In 1999, a new Allen Renaissance 350 three-manual electronic pipe organ was purchased and installed with funds raised by special appeal. Renovations continued in 2004 with a new floor in the nave, narthex, and fellowship hall. Our last renovation in 2010 included installation of new pews. In 1991, our first Stephen Ministry Class was prepared and this group continues with the ministry today. In 1994, we dedicated a Memorial Garden and it was upgraded and rededicated in 2007. A new playground was constructed and dedicated in 1996. A library and parlor were dedicated to Pastor Bill and Ernestine Kinser in 1998. A Mission Endowment Fund was established in 1999. Our Music Ministry was expanded to include a bell choir in 2000. In 2003, our congregation sponsored nineteen young adults to the national Youth Gathering in Atlanta. We sent youth to all of the national Youth Gatherings in the past twelve years. In 2006, we dedicated a new Children's Worship Center. On November 9, 2008, we celebrated the fiftieth anniversary of our first worship service. Bishop Jim Mauney and former pastors came to an anniversary service on February 22, 2009. Two of our members were ordained: Rachael Dietz in 2006, and Keith Long in 2012. On June 24, 2012, we hosted "St. Luke Past, Present and Future." Five children were baptized on October 21, 2012, a first for St. Luke and our pastor.

Pastors

Rev. William Kinser, 1958–1988

Rev. Kenneth Crumpton, interim, 1988–1989

Rev. John Bengston, 1989–1997

Rev. Luther Mauney, interim, 1997–1998

Rev. John Byerly, interim, 1997–1998

Rev. Robert Maier, 1998–2003

Rev. Donna Ruggles, interim, 2003–2004

Rev. Dorothy Nimal, 2004–2011

Rev. Frederick Marcoux, 2012–

SOUTHERN CONFERENCE
Bedford Mission

The Bedford Mission is currently a congregation under development, sponsored by the Virginia Synod. This outreach to Bedford County was initiated in late 2004 by Pastor Steve Schulz, retired from Holy Trinity, Lynchburg. Worship services were initially held on Sunday afternoons, starting in February 2005 in an old Episcopal Church building in downtown Bedford. Shortly thereafter the site's owners, Bedford Christian Church (Disciples of Christ), sold the building to a private arts foundation in Bedford and moved to a new facility nearby. This allowed the community to begin worshiping on Sunday mornings. The worship site was renamed the Bower Center for the Arts, with art galleries, studios, and a performance hall. Six acres have been purchased near Bedford's prominent National D-Day Memorial as a future worship site. The initial information meeting for the Bedford Mission was held at the Bedford Public Library on December 8, 2004. Pastor Steve Schulz convened its first worship service on the afternoon of February 13, 2005, with his wife Judy serving as musician.

Pastors

Rev. Stephen Schulz, mission developer, 2005–

Rev. Jonathan Myers, 2013–

Sister Jennie Myers, deaconess, 2013–

Glade Creek, Blue Ridge

Glade Creek, Blue Ridge, the oldest congregation in the Roanoke Valley, was organized in 1828. In the present church, erected in 1941, a Sunday School classroom and men's choir room were refurbished and consolidated into the Good Samaritan Memorial Room, containing pastors' plaques and memorabilia, in the 1980s. While the Rev. Robert Maier was pastor, a computer and copier were purchased and a gas boiler was installed in the early 1990s. New carpet, altar paraments, and pew cushions were purchased. The fellowship hall stage was rebuilt, pastor's office refurbished, and a microphone and communion items were dedicated. After 2000, a security alarm was installed, and an electronic organ and outdoor fireplace were dedicated. A home was purchased for a Youth House, new windows were purchased, and the narthex was refurbished. Six handicapped parking spaces were added and the parking lot was repaved. Trees were planted on the church grounds. Family Night gatherings began on the second Fridays of the month and the Youth House was sold. In 2012, the congregation decided to call a part-time pastor and the Rev. John McCandlish, former supply pastor, began service.

Pastors

Rev. Robert J. Maier, 1981–1998

Rev. Cynthia Long Lasher, 1999–2003

Rev. Keith A. Olivier, 2004–2006

Rev. Karin Howard, interim, 2007

Rev. Stephen P. Shackelford, 2008–2010

Rev. John W. McCandlish, supply, 2011–2012; pastor, 2013–

Wheatland, Buchanan

Wheatland Church is located in rural Botetourt County. In November 1991, a new digital organ was dedicated. Every three years since 2000, the congregation has sponsored trips for youth and leaders to attend the national Lutheran Youth Gathering. On September 18, 2005, a new addition with an elevator was dedicated, allowing for full accessibility. A museum room, established by a member, contains pictures of pastors and their years of service as well as historical artifacts of the church. Sharing God's Grace, a monthly luncheon, has been an outreach program for the community. A meal is provided, followed by a speaker or games of Bingo. Donations are used for continued outreach programs. In 2012, the council approved a "reverse offering." Each person attending on the designated Sunday was given $20 to use for outreach. Four weeks later, members shared how their offering was used. The congregation adopted the *With One Voice* and *Evangelical Lutheran Worship* hymnals. A number of worship-enhancing items have been dedicated and placed into use, including banners, altar appointments, and communion ware.

Pastors

Rev. John McCandlish, 1980–1988
Rev. Daniel Whitener, Jr., 1989–1993
Rev. Jeff Marble, 1994–1998
Rev. Cecie Haxton, 1998–2013

Ascension, Danville

In its twenty-five years as part of the ELCA and the Virginia Synod, Ascension Lutheran has continued in its mission to share the gospel with its neighbors in Danville. In 2007, the congregation marked the fiftieth year of using Christmas ornaments, called "Chrismons," as one vehicle for that ministry. The quarter-century also was marked by a number of renovations in the church fabric. The organ was rebuilt in 1993, the sanctuary was redecorated in 1999, and a set of needlepoint kneelers with Chrismon designs was completed in 2003. The congregation's outreach to the community has extended beyond the Chrismon tree with ministries ranging from a parking lot party at Halloween to handing out water to walkers on West Main Street. In the last nineteen months, the congregation has established a relationship with Grace and Main, a local ministry to the homeless. Ascension and Grace and Main have worked together to provide summer lunches to children and to celebrate a joint supper once a month.

Pastors

Rev. Richard Fritz, 1983–1995
Rev. Thomas Warme, interim, 1995
Rev. Caldwell Day, 1995–2001
Rev. Jonathan Hamman, 2001–2005
Rev. Meredith Williams, 2006–

Bethlehem, Lynchburg

In 1986, Pastor John Herman began service as the fourth pastor of Bethlehem, Lynchburg. In 1987, a Walker pipe organ was installed and the sanctuary was renovated. In 1992, Cauble Hall was renovated and the former sanctuary is now Cauble Fellowship Hall, honoring the late Pastor Frank P. Cauble, developer and first pastor of Bethlehem from 1958 to 1970. In 1993, an education wing was dedicated in honor of Pastor J.S. Koiner, Jr., who served at Bethlehem from 1970 to 1978. In 1997, Rosemary Backer became the first intern at Bethlehem. In 1999, Pastor Rosemary Backer was installed as associate pastor and she served until 2006. A picnic pavilion was dedicated in 1999 and a New Song contemporary service started. New leadership structure implemented in 2001 was based on the Mission 2006 program. Pastor Hank Boschen served as interim pastor. A major sanctuary renovation was completed in 2007.

Pastor Matthew Diehl served as pastor from 2008 to 2010. Pastor Floyd Addison has been vice and interim pastor since 2010 and Pastor Boschen joined him as interim again in 2012. A house on the church property serves as a community clothing distribution ministry center. Bethlehem works with several community ministries that assist people in need of food and shelter.

Pastors

Rev. John Herman, 1986–2002

Rev. Rosemary Backer, associate, 1999–2006

Rev. Hank Boschen, interim, 2006–2007

Rev. Matthew Diehl, 2008–2010

Rev. Floyd Addison, vice pastor, interim, 2010–2013

Rev. Hank Boschen, interim, 2012–

Holy Trinity, Lynchburg

The years 1988 through 2012 were a time of transformation and expansion for the congregation of Holy Trinity, Lynchburg, as it added staff and broadened its mission and ministry in a variety of ways. The addition of the first parish nurse in the Virginia Synod, a full-time church musician, and designated staff for youth and campus ministries helped launch growth in all areas of parish life. The congregation's worship and music ministries expanded greatly with the 1990 installation of a Taylor & Boody pipe organ handcrafted in Staunton which helped launch a time of worship and liturgical renewal which is ongoing. Christian Education was another of the congregation's priorities, with particular growth in Sunday and weekday adult education programming. Several visiting theologians made weekend appearances, including biblical scholars Bruce Metzger, Renita Weems, and Marcus Borg, and musician Alice Parker. Opportunities for children and youth education also multiplied. Youth ministries expanded considerably. In 1988, a sister congregation partnership exchange with the youth of Luther Church in Holzminden, Germany, was established. This relationship celebrated its twenty-fifth anniversary when the ninth group of Holy Trinity youth visited Germany. The congregation's mission is lived out very concretely in its outreach ministries. Holy Trinity houses the Rivermont Area Emergency Food Pantry, which has grown from a single closet to a $60,000 per year ministry in cooperation with eight other congregations. The congregation sponsored or co-sponsored and built eight Habitat for Humanity houses over twenty-five years. The congregation also supports more than twenty-five other local ministries. In 2002–2003, Holy Trinity celebrated its centennial with a yearlong series of events. Several former pastors and Virginia Synod Bishop James F. Mauney, who was a member of the congregation in his childhood, returned for the festivities. The congregation grew in its support of synodical and ELCA ministries, including launching the Virginia Synod Fund for Leaders in Mission, participation in the Papua New Guinea Companion Synod exchanges, and as a partner in establishing the Bedford Mission congregation. A number of improvements were made to the church and grounds in the last quarter-century, including the construction of a columbarium on the upper lawn and the addition and replacement of cooling units and boilers.

Pastors
Rev. Stephen J. Schulz, 1974–2000
Rev. Frederick P. Guy, 1986–1989
Rev. Dennis S. Roberts, 1991–
Rev. James L. Armentrout, 2003–2010

Holy Trinity, Martinsville

Holy Trinity, Martinsville is deeply involved in community service and ecumenical ministry in an industrial city in Southside Virginia. The congregation, served by Pastor Lynn Bechdolt since 2002, sold a portion of land for a group home for intellectually disabled women. Game nights are held periodically with Cottage Place residents and with neighborhood children. Six years ago, Holy Trinity was the founding congregation supporting an ecumenical ministry for a food pantry and assistance to the community. Interfaith meetings have been held with Muslims, Jews, and other neighbors. Contributions have been made to disaster appeals, the Heifer Project, and the malaria program in Malawi in conjunction with St. Philip, Roanoke. A handicapped ramp was built with support of Thrivent Financial for Lutherans, a brick sign was placed in front of the church, a curtain and cross were placed in the sanctuary, and a permanent outdoor cross and a bench in memory of a member were installed. The church has a playground used more by neighborhood children than its own. Due to budget constraints, the congregation has pioneered in the use of computerized music for worship.

Pastors
Rev. Robert T. Hughes, 1980–1989
Rev. John Ericson, 1990–1997
Rev. David Stacey, 1998–2001
Rev. Darina Kushirova Brehuvova, interim, 2001–2002
Rev. Lynn Bechdolt, 2002–

Trinity Ecumenical Parish, Moneta

Appalachian Power Co. constructed a hydroelectric dam on the Roanoke River at Smith Mountain in rural Southern Virginia in the 1960s, creating a 22,000-acre lake with a large residential community attracting people from all over the country, some looking for a church home. A group of lay people formed a steering committee with equal representation of the ELCA, the Episcopal Church, and the Presbyterian Church in the United States. They signed and celebrated a Covenant Agreement in June 1991, creating Trinity Ecumenical Parish and its three constituent congregations: Trinity Lutheran, Trinity Episcopal, and Trinity Presbyterian churches. Trinity Ecumenical Parish opened the doors of its first facility in April 1997. On the first Sunday, 325 worshipers overflowed the 300 seats in the new sanctuary. A major expansion program was completed in 2003 with seating for 450 in the sanctuary and a total facility of about 28,000 square feet. In its ministry and mission, Trinity Ecumenical Parish is truly a work in progress and we are very much accustomed to growth and change and transition. At the present time there are two worship services each Sunday. The early service, 8 a.m., is an ecumenical liturgy with Holy Communion every Sunday. The main service at 10:30 a.m. rotates on a monthly basis among the three traditions—Lutheran, Episcopal, and Presbyterian—and the Sacrament is normally included on the first Sunday of each month. Trinity Ecumenical Parish is currently served by the Rev. Dr. Gary Scheidt, a teaching elder in the Presbyterian Church USA, and by the Rev. Philip Bouknight of the ELCA.

Pastors
Rev. Gary Scheidt, 1994–2014
Rev. Philip Bouknight, 2007–

Christ, Roanoke

Since the beginning of the ELCA in 1987, Christ, Roanoke has maintained its dedication to serve in the name of Christ. Pastor Mark Radecke was at the helm in 1987 and shared the pastorate with successive associates Bruce Osterhout, Linda Mitchell, and Robin Henrickson. Nancy Delaney began her ministry of excellence in music and continues to provide quality leadership in worship as the choir director and organist. Ministries of the church that continued to grow during that time included the Aftercare Social Group that lifts up the needs of adults living in poverty-based assisted housing. Noah's Landing Daycare has a history of over twenty-five years of providing Christian-based preschool care. Pastor Radecke became the chaplain of Susquehanna University in Pennsylvania in 1997 and the church was served by the Rev. Dr. William Kinser as interim pastor. Pastor Rod Broker followed in a two-year pastorate that saw the addition of a contemporary service for awhile. After his departure, the Rev. Dr. Paul Hinlicky helped lead the church as interim pastor until Pastor David Skole began his tenure in 2001. In the years that have followed, Christ Church has had continued growth in its ministries and the addition of outreach through missionary sponsorship, regular mission trips of service with youth and adults, and the expansion of synod-wide involvement. We have been blessed with the opportunity of being part of the development of four interns from Southern Seminary from 2005 to 2010. During that time, a contemporary worship service was added as a vital part of our worship life in our congregational leadership with Pastor David and ministries have continued to grow and flourish.

Pastors
Rev. Mark Radecke, associate, 1978–1986; senior pastor, 1986–1997
Rev. Bruce Osterhout, associate, 1986–1990
Rev. Linda Mitchell, associate, 1990–1993
Rev. Robin Henrickson, associate, 1997
Rev. William Kinser, interim, 1997–1998
Rev. Rodney Broker, 1998–2000
Rev. Paul Hinlicky, interim, 2001
Rev. David Skole, senior pastor, 2001–
Rev. Cynthia Keyser, 2010–

St. Mark's, Roanoke

In the last quarter-century, St. Mark's, Roanoke has continued its long tradition of social ministry, serving more of its neighbors in the community and beyond in a variety of ways. Depending on the economy and the weather, the number of people served by a food pantry and clothes closet has increased. About twenty volunteers work in these operations twice a month. A new ministry, started in 2008, is David's Kingdom, a preschool daycare center serving about eighteen boys and girls in reserved space in the first floor of the church. The children have playground equipment at the adjoining Guinther House grounds of the church. A columbarium, pergola, and fountain were installed and extensive landscaping was completed on the grounds beside the church. In 2012, the Guinther House was renovated, involving roof repair, air conditioning installation, floor refinishing, and interior improvement. St. Mark's has been host to a Meals on Wheels route office for years. An extensive expansion and refurbishing of the church's physical plant was completed in 1993, providing a new office wing, an elevator, a library, larger space for the food pantry and clothes closet, and more Sunday School space on the third floor. In 2011, the church's music ministry was enhanced, choir members were added, and a bell choir reestablished under the leadership of Steven Lawrence, music director. St. Mark's, organized in 1869, is the oldest Lutheran congregation in the city of Roanoke. Its 140th anniversary was marked with a special service in 2009.

Pastors

Rev. Charles Easley, 1986–1993
Rev. Larry Dooley, 1988–1989
Rev. John Hawn, 1994–1999
Rev. Tracey Bartholomew, 2000–2003
Rev. Tim Anderson, 2000–2008
Rev. Paul Hinlicky, 2002–2006
Rev. John McCandlish, interim, 2009–2010
Rev. James Armentrout, 2010–

St. Philip, Roanoke

The past twenty-five years have been an exciting time of growth and discovery for the congregation at St. Philip. When the Rev. Paul "Chip" Gunsten was installed as the fourth pastor on June 17, 1990, St. Philip began having two worship services using the Chicago Folk Service at 8:30 and the *Lutheran Book of Worship* at 11:00. In 1992, the congregation voted to sell its former Peters Creek/Deer Branch property and purchase the Murray property, a seven-and-a-half-acre site on Williamson Road, to build our present facility. On July 4, 1993, we celebrated the move into our new church on Williamson Road. The altar was brought from the old church as well as the cross that now hangs in the narthex of the church. In 1994, St. Philip hosted our first blood drive for the American Red Cross on June 6, 1994. The St. Philip blood drive is now the largest in the Roanoke Valley. In 2000, we began celebrating Holy Communion every

Sunday at our two services. We established a parsonage as the David Derrick family moved into the house on the church property. In 2001, the building was expanded to include 1,400 square feet of multipurpose space to be added for additional classrooms. We continued to look beyond our own doors in ministry and mission as we hosted Bishop Joseph Bvumbwe of the Evangelical Lutheran Church in Malawi in January 2007. In 2007, St. Philip looked with joy and hope to continued growth in ministry as we called our first associate pastor for youth and family ministry, the Rev. Kelly Derrick. In 2008, St. Philip celebrated fifty years of ministry with over 450 attending worship. In the past several years, feeding ministries have been added to the life of the congregation, including meals to the community during the holidays and an active backpack feeding program for the local elementary schools.

Pastors

Rev. William Singleton, 1982–1989

Rev. Paul "Chip" Gunsten, 1990–1999

Rev. David Derrick, 2000–

Rev. Kelly Derrick, 2007–

Trinity, Roanoke

In 1987, members of Trinity, Roanoke founded a thrift shop clothing ministry using a former parish house next to the church. This ministry celebrated its twenty-fifth anniversary in 2012. On October 7, 1990, a new Rodgers organ was dedicated in memory of Ernst and Mary Steude. In 1993, the annual Chicken Barbeque Festival was launched, with proceeds going to local charities. New carpet and pew cushions were installed in the nave in 1995. A new parking lot was dedicated in memory of Paul C. Dress, Sr. and Margaret Obenchain in 1996. On February 2, 1997, Trinity celebrated the fiftieth anniversary of its worship services. The Rev. Russell Eckert Trinity's pastor from 1959 to 1966, delivered the sermon. Bishop Richard Bansemer preached on July 13, 1997, the fiftieth anniversary of our charter. In 1997, the Helping Hands ministry began, using volunteers to assist persons in financial emergencies related to rent, utilities, food medication, and transportation. In 1998, the nave was renovated by refinishing pews, repainting walls, and laying new floor tile. In 2003, adjoining property was purchased and a major renovation of the church's fellowship hall, kitchen, and classrooms was completed. In 2005, a Faith & Arts ministry was formed for teaching and doing crafts. It has sponsored annual craft and bake sale events, developed an active prayer shawl ministry, and produced gifts for first-time worshippers at Trinity and for special occasions. In September 2007, a community-based Senior Center program started with monthly meals and programs. On February 8, 2009, the first worship service was held with major changes in the chancel, including a freestanding altar and a new choir loft.

Pastors

Rev. Terry Clark, 1984–1988

Rev. Kenneth P. Lane, Jr., 1988–

College, Salem

After the founding of the ELCA, the congregation undertook renovations to the worship space, including installation of a new audio system and air conditioning in 1988. Charles Shenberger, retired assistant to the synod president, became the first church administrator in 1989, followed in 1992 by Dana Cox, who served until 1995. In that year, the role was expanded to become director of stewardship and finance, a position held by Glen Rosendahl. College also called its first of three directors of Christian Education. Pastor Dwayne Westermann, who was called in 1987, took his first of two sabbaticals for study and renewal, including work in Tanzania in 1995. In 1996, the congregation moved to the weekly celebration (every service, every Sunday) of the Holy Eucharist. The position of organist/choir director was expanded to become director of church music, with Dr. Lee Roesti serving until 1999. Pastor Bob Ward resigned to accept a call as chaplain of Brandon Oaks. A hand bell choir was created, bringing to six the number of active choirs at College Lutheran, highlighting College as a musical congregation in 1998. College established its first parish health ministry with Gloria Moe serving as the first parish nurse in 1999. Aaron Garber became the first full-time director of music/artist-in-residence in 2000, serving in this ministry until 2011. College Lutheran voted in 2002 to approve a $2-million building expansion. It celebrated its 150th anniversary throughout the year with events and activities. The new building was completed and dedicated on Reformation Sunday, October 31, 2004. Pastor Westermann retired in 2006, having served College Lutheran for nineteen years. In 2007, the congregation adopted a mission statement, "We Celebrate God's Grace and Share His Love in Christ." In 2008, College Lutheran called a new pastoral team with its first female pastor, the Rev. Wynemah K. Hinlicky, and first clergy couple, with her husband, the Rev. William S. Wiecher, as co-pastor. The congregation supported in mission a pastor in the Islands District of Papua New Guinea, funding the education of four children in 2011. The congregation opened the doors of the church to host Family Promise, a ministry of care to the homeless, and a new sound system was installed. The congregation called Karen Adams to serve as director of music and sponsored the Lutheran Elementary School in Martin, Slovakia, through Sunday School offerings.

Pastors

Rev. Dwayne Westermann, 1987–2006

Rev. Bob Ward, associate pastor, 1990–1996

Rev. William S. Wiecher, 2008–2012

Rev. Wynemah K. Hinlicky, 2008–

St. Timothy, Vinton

St. Timothy began as a mission congregation of the Lutheran Church in America (LCA) and the building was constructed in 1974. Since its beginning, St. Timothy has remained a small but active congregation. Much of the facilities and improvements, such as a kitchen and outdoor picnic shelter (which serves as an outdoor worship site in the summer) were constructed and furnished by our hardworking men and women of the parish. For over fourteen years, the church participated in a hunger food project called SHARE, wherein our community was served with low-cost food. In 2011, St. Timothy celebrated forty years of ministry in Vinton. The church is well known for its "Angel" display at Christmas time. Many of our charter members still faithfully come each week to worship and to serve the Lord. St. Timothy remains a "small but mighty" church of Christ.

Pastors

Rev. Robert Busch, 1979–1988

Rev. Pat McLaughlin, 1989–1990

Rev. Janet Ramsey, 1990–1992

Rev. Harold Uhl, 1993–1998

Rev. Amy Oehlschlaeger, 1999–2005

Rev. Judy Tavela, 2006–

SOUTHERN VALLEY CONFERENCE
St. Peter, Churchville

Since 1988, many improvements have been made to enhance the worship life of our church and its service to the community. Among these were the redecorating of the sanctuary with changes to the chancel, including a hanging cross, Holy Spirit light, dossal curtain, and new communion appointments of a chalice, paten, host box, cruets, and linens. On Sunday, November 4, 1990, we celebrated our 200th anniversary with a special service and guests. In 2004, we celebrated a groundbreaking for a new fellowship hall, which was dedicated on June 12, 2005. In 2007, a Viscount Prestige organ was purchased to add to our music. In 2011, St. Peter's Cemetery Registry was completed by Boy Scout Troop 388 as part of an Eagle Scout project. In 2011, Katie's Snacks, a program that provides healthy food on weekends for eligible children grades K-5 at Churchville Elementary School, began, a vast undertaking for our small church. Neighboring churches, civic groups, and individuals have since joined in to help. Our members do the buying and applying for grants, and the packing is done at our church. Numbers of recipients vary, but they have been as many as eighty-five a week.

Pastors

Rev. Gregory John Briehl, 1987–1996

Rev. Paul Eric Walters, 1997–2004

Rev. Cecil Bradfield, interim, 2005–2007

Rev. Kenneth Price, vice pastor, 2007–2008

Rev. Kim Triplett, 2008–

Shepherd of the Valley, Dayton

Shepherd of the Valley, Dayton was started as a mission church in 1982 by the former American Lutheran Church at the old Dale Enterprise School about four miles west of Harrisonburg. In 1994, the congregation sold the school building and 2.1 acres of land and moved to Bridgewater, where it worshiped in the Eureka Masonic Lodge. In 2003, the congregation bought the former college chapel in Dayton used by Shenandoah College and Conservatory of Music until it moved to Winchester in 1960. Shenandoah University alumni hold an annual reunion, hymn sing, and memorial service each April in Shepherd of the Valley Church. Shepherd of the Valley celebrated its twenty-fifth anniversary in September 2007 with a sermon by Bishop Jim Mauney. A focus of its ministry has been Hispanic outreach. A big Cargill poultry plant in Dayton employs a large population of Hispanic people. The congregation also helps to preserve Dayton's musical heritage in partnership with Shenandoah University. Community concerts are held there and the congregation has supported Habitat for Humanity, Bridgewater Area Food Pantry, worship service at Camelot Nursing Home, English as a Second Language classes for Latino neighbors, and other projects.

Pastors

Rev. William C. See, 1985–1987

Rev. Arnold H. Holgersen, 1987–1995

Rev. Cecil Bradfield, interim, 1995–1996

Rev. Theodore M. Schulz, 1996–

St. James, Fishersville

Muhlenberg, Harrisonburg

Harrisonburg and Muhlenberg Lutheran Church were very different places in 1987, when the ELCA came into being. With "valley" Germanic roots and the blessings of strong pastoral leadership, Muhlenberg began as a preaching-point in 1849 and moved into the decade of the 1990s concurrently with the growth of James Madison University as a major state school, an increased volume of traffic on Interstate 81, and a renewal of the downtown as a business and tourist destination. Following the resignation of Pastor John Derrick in 1991, Muhlenberg turned to the leadership of the Rev. Dr. K. Roy Nilsen, former assistant to the bishop of the Maryland Synod of the American Lutheran Church. Pastor "K-Roy" began building a strong lay leadership with mission focused on social ministry. The congregation provided office space for the valley Refugee Resettlement Program in the building and sponsored refugee families. In 1998, the congregation called the Rev. Martha Miller Sims as associate pastor with an emphasis on campus ministry and Christian Education/youth. Muhlenberg's commitment to campus ministry, begun in 1929, continued. Youth activity has grown: youth groups begin in elementary school and culminate in the high school J-Crew, planning and raising money for a summer group activity, such as a weeklong mission trip to an urban area, an Indian reservation, Appalachia, Mexico, or the national Lutheran Youth Gathering. Supplementing Sunday morning classes for children, youth, and adults are mid-week Bible studies and prayer groups and age-specific activities. Pastor Sims accepted a call to Grace, Winchester in 2001, and the congregation called the Rev. David Nelson as co-pastor. Pastors Vought and Nelson worked hard to model a team approach to ministry and encouraged lay ministries to function as teams. From 2001 to 2008, the budget of the congregation doubled and average worship attendance increased from 348 to 520. During the past twenty-five years, the congregation has gradually moved to three Sunday worship services and two mid-week services. Worship, preaching, and music have been a hallmark of Muhlenberg liturgies.

New members are welcomed every ninety days and the membership of the congregation is now over 1,400. Responding to a definite need for expansion of the church facilities, the congregation voted in 2001 to enter into a capital campaign to build an activities center, completed in 2003 and fondly known as "The MAC." The facility was offered to the Boys & Girls Club for an after-school program. In 2004, Muhlenberg instituted Second Home, a latchkey program for children at a nearby elementary school, which continues today. The congregation also committed to an expansion of full-time staff. Between 2006 and 2009, Muhlenberg called a full-time director of Christian Formation, a director and an associate director of liturgical arts, a parish nurse, and a lay youth and campus minister. These positions resulted in new avenues of ministry. In 2008, Pastor Vought resigned to accept a call to Community Lutheran in Sterling. The Rev. Robert F. Humphrey joined Pastor David Nelson as co-pastor in 2010, and continues, following Pastor Nelson's acceptance of a call to a North Carolina parish in 2012. In September 2012, Muhlenberg extended a ten-month call to seminary graduate Brett Davis, who was ordained at Muhlenberg that year. The congregation embraced a new vision for future ministry and mission: "We strive to be a wellspring of God's grace in Jesus Christ! Open + Authentic + Relational + Serving."

Pastors
Rev. John Derrick, 1976–1991
Rev. K. Roy Nilsen, 1991–1996
Rev. Joe Vought, 1997–2008
Rev. Martha Miller Sims, associate, 1998–2001
Rev. David Nelson, 2001–2012
Rev. Robert F. Humphrey, 2010–
Rev. Brett Davis, 2012–

Trinity, Keezletown

In 1987, as the ELCA was being formed, Trinity, Keezletown was celebrating its 200th anniversary of organization. Improvements were made to the church building—painting, kitchen upgrades, and ceiling fan installations in the sanctuary. After a long history of being part of a multiple-church parish, Trinity became a single-point church in 1995. Also in that year, new chancel furniture was dedicated. In 2000, a memorial garden was blessed in memory of Pastor Bill Hoffmeyer, who served the congregation from 1996 to 1998. In 2007, we celebrated 150 years of worship in the present church building, and in 2012, we observed the 225th anniversary of organization. Youth delegates attended national Youth Gatherings in 2003, 2006, 2009, and 2012 and also have attended synod youth events—Winter Celebration, Lost and Found, and Seventh Day. Trinity is strong in its outreach ministries—World Hunger, Mission Partners, Child Fund, Blue Ridge Area Food Bank, weekday religious education, Mercy House, People Helping People, and the Free Clinic—as well as helping local needy families at Christmas, a neighboring food pantry and an elementary school backpack program.

Pastors
Rev. Richard N. Umberger, 1985–1991
Rev. Sharon A. Israel, 1992–1994
R. W. "Bill" Hoffmeyer, licensed lay minister, 1996–1997
Rev. R. W. "Bill" Hoffmeyer, 1997–1998
Rev. Karen S. Church, 1999–2012

Bethany, Lexington

Bethany was organized with New Mt. Olive, Fairfield as the Rockbridge Parish until they separated in 2007. The congregation celebrated its 150th anniversary in 2002. The fellowship hall was renovated, air conditioning and kitchen paneling were installed, and woodwork on the bell tower was replaced.

Pastors
Rev. Wade Coffey, 1985–1990
Rev. Janyce Jorgensen, 1990–1992
Rev. Heather Bumstead, 1993–1997
Rev. Alfred Fogleman, 2000–

Good Shepherd, Lexington

Good Shepherd, Lexington came into being in the year 1958 under the auspices of the Board of American Missions of the former United Lutheran Church in America and services began in 1959, starting at Lee Chapel and DuPont Hall on the Washington and Lee University campus. A church school met in W&L Student Union. A church building was completed in 1963 and Boxwoods, a house behind the church, was renovated for Sunday School quarters. That building is still in use for a pastor's office, general office area, and Sunday School. Good Shepherd is a small but vigorous, vibrant, and welcoming congregation. It continues to reach out to students from Washington and Lee University and cadets from Virginia Military Institute, honoring the congregation's roots in campus ministry. Good Shepherd serves through the riches of Lutheran worship, through education in the meaning of life in Christ, and by sharing the love of God with neighbors and one another.

Pastors
Rev. Wayne R. Shelor, 1986–1990
Rev. Tracie L. Bartholomew, 1991–1993
Rev. Brian K. Peterson, 1994–1998
Rev. Arthur J. Henne, 1999–2001
Rev. Mark S. Schroeder, 2001–2010
Rev. Lyndon D. Sayers, 2011–

Redeemer, McKinley

Twenty-four years ago, Redeemer called Pastor JoAnn Bunn—unusual, because at that time there were not as many women clergy as today. More unusual is that the vote was unanimous. Even more unusual is that she is still our pastor! Over these years we have continued to have yearly chicken barbeques serving over 800 people in the community and beyond, making it possible financially to support things in our church and in our community. A handicapped ramp, bathroom, kitchen, Sunday School room, several sets of paraments and banners, and Lutheran Study Bibles are among the new additions in the last twenty-five years. But those things may not be as important as the ministries being carried out by our members. Our small congregation of dedicated and talented members continues to serve Christ by working in the community for their neighbors. Cutting wood, mowing, sitting with those in need, and shopping for those who cannot are everyday ministries of Redeemer's people. Over the years we have sponsored youth going to camp, provided Bible studies and Vacation Bible Schools, and provided presents and food for hundreds of children and adults at Christmas through the Christmas Alive program at Riverheads Elementary School. Among our new ministries is the collection of a "noisy offering" every Sunday during worship by the children which is given to a chosen charity. This ministry began when we helped other congregations of the synod sponsor Peace Lutheran in Slidell, Louisiana, after Hurricane Katrina. Our Social Ministry committee is a new ministry with money set up specifically for people in our community who have needs with which we can help. Though we are small and remote, our members are active and ministering in our area.

Pastors
Rev. JoAnn Bunn, 1988–

Mt. Tabor, Middlebrook

In the past twenty-five years, Mt. Tabor has gone through lots of changes. In 1995, Pastor Harold Fuller retired after serving for twenty years. Pastor Art Henne was Mt. Tabor's interim. Pastor Terry Edwards, Mt. Tabor's next pastor, served from 1996 to 1998. While Pastor Kenneth Price was interim from 1998 to 2000, this congregation began cooperation with other congregations in the community to have Lenten services each Wednesday night during Lent and Holy Week. From 2000 to 2004, Pastor Stan Wickett served as pastor of Mt. Tabor. While Pastor Wickett was serving, a Roanoke College marker was dedicated on Mt. Tabor Road just outside the church. Dr. Norman Fintel, president of Roanoke College, came to the ceremony. Presently, Pastor JoAnn Bunn has been serving at Mt. Tabor for the past seven years. The organ console has been replaced and the organ interior has been upgraded to a modern electronic organ. The Property Committee is overseeing massive renovations to the social hall, offices, all Sunday School rooms, and bathrooms, making them totally handicapped-accessible. Though Mt. Tabor has been through many changes over the years, it is growing and thriving through all of them. Thanks be to God for His blessings.

Pastors
Rev. Harold Fuller, 1975–1995
Rev. Terry Edwards, 1996–1998
Rev. Kenneth Price, interim, 1998–2000
Rev. Stan Wickett, 2000–2004
Rev. JoAnn Bunn, 2005–

Salem, Mt. Sidney

Since the formation of the ELCA, much growth and change has taken place at Salem. Pastor Barney Troutman entered the ministry in 1953 at Salem, served a second call here in 1987, and retired three years later. In 1991, Pastor David Skole began a five-year tenure and Pastor Wayne Shelor came to Salem in 1997, serving for three years. Pastor Kenneth Price began as interim pastor in 2000, enthusiastically leading Salem through our bicentennial year in 2002 with a large celebration that included a parade of parishioners representing all the ways folks traveled to worship over the past 200 years. Christopher Carr was ordained by Bishop James F. Mauney in the first Service of Ordination held at Salem in 2003. Salem's physical campus has grown. A picnic shelter and an exterior handicapped ramp and gazebo were constructed. A playground was built by members. Indoors, an office remodeling project created office spaces for the pastor and church secretary and handicapped-accessible restrooms. The largest physical change was the addition of a $1.5-million fellowship hall/activity center, dedicated in June 2011 and named The Imagine Center. This brick structure, designed to match the existing church building, is handicapped-accessible; is double our previous square footage; provides space for congregational, community, and regional church gatherings; and seats over 250 people. Salem has had many outreach projects. A prison ministry began in the early 1980s and volunteers began collecting food and serving more than eighty clients/families monthly at the Verona Community Food Pantry. Service projects have been undertaken with Thrivent support and/or participation. Between 2007 and 2010, we participated with multiple local Thrivent for Lutherans chapters in building Thrivent Builds/Habitat for Humanity homes in Staunton and Waynesboro. The Stephen Ministry began in 2010 to serve those grieving or in need of a listening ear. Four members were trained as Stephen leaders and eight have completed fifty hours of training and been commissioned as Stephen ministers, providing over 600 hours of Christian caregiving. Members of the Youth Group work to attend all ELCA Youth Gatherings and they meet monthly for Bible study, lead worship for Youth Sunday, and serve as acolytes, choir members, and assisting ministers. Young children (pre-K–5) collect a monthly "noisy offering" to buy dishes for The Imagine Center and to purchase mosquito nets for children in Africa. We give thanks for the blessings God has given us and the ways in which we are allowed to be a blessing and to minister in Christ's name.

Pastors

Rev. C. Bernard Troutman, 1987–1990

Rev. David Skole, 1991–1996

Rev. Wayne Shelor, 1997–2000

Rev. Kenneth Price, interim, 2000–2003

Rev. Christopher Carr, 2003–

St. Paul, Mount Solon

In 1989, we had a Sesquicentennial Celebration service with Pastor Lance Braun leading the worship and Bishop Richard Bansemer delivering the sermon. In 1990, the exterior and roof of the church were painted. The front of the church was remodeled by church members in 1992 and carpet was installed. In 1994, the 155th anniversary service was led by Pastor Lance Braun and former Pastor Ray Hatcher. Money was raised for a special Flood Relief Fund in 1996; $7,248 was used to help people in the community. In 1997, toys and books were sent to children in North Dakota who lost everything in a flood. In 1998, a picnic was held to celebrate the 160th anniversary. In 2000, the altar was moved out to be freestanding and church members built a cabinet at the wall to hold the cross and flowers. A brass cross was donated by St. Peter's Lutheran in Churchville to replace a wooden one. In 2007, St. Paul was one of the congregations in the North River Ministerial Association that built a house near our church for a family with a handicapped member. We donated money and food for Thrivent/Habitat for Humanity houses in Augusta County in 2008–2010. In 2010 and 2011, a new front porch with a better wheelchair ramp was added and a new sign was installed. The bathroom was made more handicapped-accessible. The inside of the church was painted. A Potluck for Hunger raised $230 for World Hunger. In 2005–2012, with the help of Thrivent's Caring in Communities, generous food baskets have been delivered to needy families or shut-ins at Christmas. In 2008–2012, we were part of Samaritan's Purse: Operation Christmas Child.

Pastors

Rev. Lance Braun, 1988–1994

Rev. David Skole, vice pastor and supply, 1995

Rev. L. Warren Strickler, 1995–2007

Rev. Ted Schultz, vice pastor, 2008

Don Stonesifer, synodically authorized worship leader, 2009–2010

Hank Tomlinson, synodically authorized worship leader, 2009–2012

Rev. Kim Triplett, vice pastor, 2009–2013

St. Jacob's-Spaders, Mt. Crawford

As the ELCA was in its infancy, St. Jacob's decided it was time to combine its two names. The official name of the church at that time was "St. Jacob's-Bethany"; however, the community had long been known as "Spader's Church," after Jacob Spader, our founder. In fact, the county named the street on which we sit "Spaders Church Road." So on March 8, 1989, we adopted

"St. Jacob's-Spaders Lutheran Church" as our name. During the last twenty-five years, St. Jacob's-Spaders Lutheran Church has grown in outreach both locally and worldwide. The church has supported a number of causes in the Harrisonburg-Rockingham community, including the Grottoes Food Pantry, Generations Crossing, the Salvation Army shelter, the Minnick School, and Mercy House. St. Jacob's supports the United Lutheran Appeal, ELCA World Hunger, and the Malaria Campaign. As we sit right in a rapidly growing area of Rockingham County, we are poised to follow God into a future of transformation so that we may do God's work.

Pastors
Rev. Richard Umberger, 1985–1991
Rev. Sharon Israel, 1992–2001
Rev. Dianna Horton, 2003–2009
Rev. G. William Nabers, 2010–2013

New Mt. Olive, Rockbridge

New Mt. Olive was aligned with Bethany, Rockbridge Baths in the Rockbridge Parish until they separated in 2007. Since that time, services have been led by the Rev. Phil Carr, a Presbyterian pastor.

Pastors
Rev. Wade Coffey, 1985–1990
Rev. Janyce Jorgensen, 1990–1992
Rev. Heather Bumstead, 1993–1997
Rev. Alfred Fogleman, 2000–2007
Rev. Phil Carr, 2007–

Christ, Staunton

Many congregations reflecting on their twenty-five-year history might supply a list of pastors who have served. At Christ Lutheran it would be just as appropriate to provide a list of church musicians. Sharon Porter Shull, William Polhill, and Benjamin Heizer are a few of the recent organists and music directors whose influence continues to shape the worship and ministry of the congregation. In 2003, when Christ Lutheran celebrated its 150th anniversary, a hymn was commissioned by the congregation. "Clouds of Witnesses Surround Us" is based on Hebrews 11:8-12:3 and was written by Nancy Raabe with music by May Schwarz. The most significant moment in the last twenty-five years was the purchase and installation of a locally crafted, 24-rank tracker organ. The Taylor Boody Opus 24 organ was made in Swoope, about nine miles away from Christ Lutheran. Installed in 1994, the organ has for twenty years filled the congregation with the rich heritage of Lutheran and Christian hymnody. The new organ brought with it a chance to engage Staunton's musical community. The first of Christ Lutheran's organ concerts in 1994 featured David Boe of Oberlin College Conservatory of Music. In November 1997, Paul Manz, professor of Church Music from the Lutheran Theological School of Chicago, conducted a festival hymn sing that filled Christ's sizable sanctuary. As an extended prelude to Good Friday, Christ holds a five-week Lenten Concert Series. These concerts feature both local and international artists on most Friday evenings of Lent, with an occasional Wednesday noon offering. A similar Advent Series serves as a lead-in to Christmas Eve worship. The musical variety of the concerts has at times shaped special worships on Sunday mornings. Christ has celebrated both bluegrass and Celtic Sunday worships. Additionally, a variety of singers and instrumentalists have joined Christ's choir for our Sunday morning praise of God.

Pastors
Rev. Kenneth Price, 1981–1996
Rev. Robert Holley, 1997–2007
Rev. Cynthia Long, 2006–2008
Rev. Robert McCarty, 2008–

Faith, Staunton

Faith, Staunton, formed from Christ, Staunton, in 1959, purchased the former Christ church building, added a new façade, and remodeled the nave and sanctuary. The congregation continues to witness to the richness of the Lutheran Christian tradition although its membership is small. The inside of the nave and sanctuary represent the best of the Lutheran tradition with a 22-rank Reuter pipe organ in the loft and etched glass windows depicting themes from the Old and New Testaments and the Reformation. The congregation has been reestablishing itself within a larger ecumenical environment and continues to seek ways to witness and serve the area.

Pastors
Rev. Peter Olsen, 1987
Rev. Lance Braun, 1990–1992
Rev. Harold Fuller, 1995–2005
Rev. Kenneth Price, supply, 2005
Rev. Kim Triplett, 2008–2012

Pleasant View, Augusta County

For the last twenty-five years, Pleasant View in Augusta County has maintained the spirit of a small country church dedicated to worshiping God and doing good works for its community and the world at large. A large number of physical changes were made to our church in the last twenty-five years—air conditioning, electrical system update, picnic shelter and playground, windows replacement, a sacristy/workroom next to the church sanctuary, and a kitchen renovation "from the ground up." An eternal flame candle was placed in the church as a memorial to all deceased members. A very major project was the beautiful copper roof installed over the sanctuary in 1995. On July 17, 2004, Pleasant View celebrated its 125th anniversary. A dedication ceremony was attended by Bishop Jim Mauney, former Pastors William Batterman and Howard Ratcliffe, Interim Pastor Jackson Martin, and seminary student Jeremy Magoon. Frances Leach resigned as youth choir director in 1995 after thirty-nine years of service. Her talent and dedication are still appreciated by many members. In 1997, a food pantry, a major outreach program spearheaded by Hunter Fauber, began operation out of the Fauber home and it has continued to grow in the Augusta County Government Center. In 2010, another outreach program, established by Pastor Kenneth Price, was the Giving Tree Project (based on the children's book) to raise $10,000 for outreach programs.

Pastors
Rev. Howard Ratcliffe, 1984–2000
Rev. Lyla Harold, 2001–2005
Rev. Margaret Ashby, 2006–2009
Rev. Kenneth Price, interim, 2009–

Bethlehem, Waynesboro

Bethlehem Lutheran Church, Waynesboro started in 1854 as a daughter congregation of Trinity Church in Crimora. In 1926, the congregation united with Melanchthon Chapel to form a joint parish lasting until 1969. The church bought the parcel of land adjoining its existing property in 1997 to prevent commercial development on the corner next to the church building. In 2004, Lucy Coyner made an extraordinarily generous donation to the congregation that allowed it to renovate and expand the parish building—adding classrooms and a new roof—and pay the remaining $85,000 on the mortgage for the corner lot. For three years the congregation again joined in a ministry partnership, this time with Zion, Waynesboro and St. James, Fishersville. Bethlehem has since returned to being an independent parish.

Pastors
Rev. Susan L. Tyykila, 1983–1989
Rev. Randall N. Lohr, 1990–2009
Rev. Karen R. Taylor, 2010–

Grace, Waynesboro

In 1993, Grace congregation initiated a yearlong celebration of our one-hundredth anniversary. Activities included honoring our "mother" church, Bethlehem Lutheran in Ladd; inviting previous pastors back to preach; honoring those children of the congregation who have entered ordained ministry, including Bishop Emeritus V. A. Moyer and Pastor Roger Kluttz; dinners; creation of a centennial banner and plate; and the development of a Grace cookbook. In the 1990s, plans were developed for much-needed renovations, and they began in 2000. Showers were added so that groups could be hosted for youth events and for disaster relief. A new chapel was dedicated in 2010, and a columbarium with a sculptural surround designed by Joan Ranzini, artist and member of Grace, was dedicated on Reformation Sunday 2010 by Bishop Jim Mauney. The congregation made a commitment to its ministry of hospitality by opening our facilities for Virginia Synod and community events and organizations. Numerous synod committee meetings and events are held at Grace, including serving as the main site for ACTS. We have housed programs for Lutheran Family Services and Lutheran Disaster Relief. The Valley

Music Academy and the Waynesboro YMCA use our facilities, and we are active participants in the Waynesboro LARCUM, helping to host the statewide LARCUM Conference in 2011. Early in the 1990s, the congregation began to live out its ministry by sponsoring groups on mission trips to assist with rebuilding homes damaged in disasters, including four youth mission trips to Michigan and Vermont, two to Southwest Virginia, and seven adult mission trips: four to New Orleans after Hurricane Katrina, one to Southwest Virginia, one to Nashville, and one to Swans Quarter, North Carolina. This ministry has expanded to building and repairing homes in our local community through Habitat for Humanity and ReBuild Augusta. In September 2008, we celebrated fifty years in our present church building. The Rev. Bob Hock, who was the pastor during construction, returned for the celebration. We have been blessed to sponsor six members to attend seminary and subsequently become ordained in pastoral ministry: Janice Marie Ely Lowden in 1988, Linda Mitchell Motley in 1990, Karen Shumate Van Stee in 2000, Patricia Smith Nabers in 2003, Kathryn Ruth Gosswein in 2006, and Tonya Lynn Eza in 2012.

Pastors
Rev. Glenn L. London, 1985–1989
Rev. Robert F. Humphrey, 1990–2010
Rev. Eric Childers, interim, 2010–2011
Rev. William Stewart, interim, 2011–2012
Rev. Paul Pingel, 2012–

Zion, Waynesboro

Zion, Waynesboro, dating back to 1823, operated in a joint parish with St. James for many years until the congregations voted to separate in 1970. In 1994, Zion celebrated the one-hundredth anniversary of the laying of the cornerstone of the sanctuary. In 2006, Zion accepted St. James' offer to explore the possibility of a partnership between the two congregations, and in 2008, thanks to the guidance and direction of the Rev. Chip Gunsten, the Augusta County Lutheran Partnership was created. For two years that partnership included three congregations: Zion, St. James, and Bethlehem, Waynesboro. Since 2010, the partnership has been between Zion and St. James.

Pastors
Rev. Bob Humphrey, 1988
Rev. Rich Jorgensen, 1990–1992
Rev. Jim Pence, 1993–

Melanchthon Chapel, Weyers Cave

One family provided most of the support for Melanchthon Chapel and its cemetery.

Pastor
Rev. Peter Olsen, 1987–2013

TIDEWATER CONFERENCE
Grace, Chesapeake

Grace, Chesapeake has been blessed with wonderful, spirit-filled pastors. Our roster over the last twenty-five years is comprised of five pastors: the Revs. Harold "Hal" Hizer, William "Bill" Bolden, David Stacy, Rick Gates, and Joel Neubauer. Pastors Hal and Rick now watch over us from their eternal home. Like many congregations, our numbers have ebbed and flowed, but we soldier on! Our food pantry has grown from a small closet of food to an organization that feeds between 120 to 150 people per week. It has received several charitable grants, and continues to feed those most in need in our community. In January 2013, Grace Lutheran Day School celebrated forty years of Christian education. The church celebrated its fiftieth anniversary in 2013. We are truly blessed at Grace. We have a solid roof over our heads, a small and loving congregation, and the desire to serve God in all we do.

Pastors

Rev. Harold Hizer, 1974–1992

Rev. William Bolden, 1993–2000

Rev. David Stacey, 2001–2005

Rev. Rick Gates, 2006–2011

Rev. Joel Neubauer, 2012–2014

Grace, Franklin

Grace, Franklin traces its beginnings back to the mid-1960s, when a small group of Lutherans began worshiping at St. John, a congregation at Emporia in the Slovak District of the Synod of Evangelical Lutheran Churches (SELC) affiliated with the Lutheran Church-Missouri Synod. They worshiped in Emmanuel Episcopal Church in Franklin for over twenty years. In 1979, they transferred to the Association for Evangelical Lutheran Churches (AELC) and later joined the Virginia Synod when the AELC joined in the merger to form the ELCA in 1988. The congregation began looking for its own worship center and they purchased the closed Inland Restaurant in nearby Courtland and held their first service there in 1998. Much renovation was needed to adapt the former restaurant to a church. When Hurricane Floyd devastated the Franklin/Southampton County area in 1999, Grace provided housing for a Mennonite Disaster Response Team while it was rebuilding for seven months. The team made major improvements to Grace's kitchen and other parts of the building. Members of Grace provided appliances for some flood victims. The church sanctuary was dedicated in 2003. The original sanctuary has since been transformed into fellowship and Sunday School rooms. Members provided much of the hard work, prayer, talent, skills, and elbow grease for a modern facility. Grace joined Thrivent Financial for Lutherans and the Faith, Apostles, and Rejoice Lutheran congregations to paint the Children's Center in Franklin. The congregation has helped the local food pantries and provided food baskets for those in need and care packages for college students and military personnel overseas.

Pastors
Rev. Alan Schulz, 1986
Rev. M. Gary Lecroy, 1991–1995
Rev. Harold J. Harter, 1996–2005
Rev. Dennis Buchholz, 2007–

First, Norfolk

Worship, learning, youth, and service have been important areas of ministry for our congregation during the first twenty-five years of the ELCA. We give thanks for vibrant traditional worship where Holy Communion is celebrated at all Sunday worship services. Learning opportunities are numerous and address a wide spectrum of issues to assist persons in their faith formation. Our youth participate with joy in local, synodical, regional, and churchwide events. Our worship, learning, and youth ministries have moved us to expand our ministries locally by establishing a weekly Wednesday lunch ministry for persons who are hungry and by joining other people of faith to form Norfolk Emergency Shelter Team (NEST), which provides overnight shelter during winter months for persons who are homeless. We also participate in the ministries of the International Seamen's House, Ghent Area Ministries, the Dwelling Place, Lutheran Family Services of Virginia, and Lutheran Theological Southern Seminary. Our global mission efforts expanded as well with support for and mission trips to the Faraja Primary School for children with physical disabilities in Tanzania, Africa. Two major building programs were completed which reconfigured and enhanced the existing facility, from the front doors to the rear parking lot entrance and from the first-floor offices to the third-floor kitchen. The 1992–1993 renovations included changing the auditorium-style hall into a community room that is used by numerous "step" programs each week and the NEST program in the winter. The 2007 renovations greatly expanded the welcome center area and staff offices, established a suite of offices for our rostered leaders, updated our kitchen, and added Sunday School classrooms, a handicapped-accessible elevator, and access to our balcony area in the nave. An indoor columbarium was also constructed in 2003 and dedicated on All Saints Sunday. Judith Ann Cobb served as an associate in ministry (AIM) from 1988 to 1997 and Jane F. Nicholson was an AIM from 2003 to 2010.

Pastors
Rev. James G. Cobb, senior pastor, 1988–1999
Rev. Judith Ann Cobb, associate, 1997–2000
Rev. Jeremy R. Gamelin, associate, 2001–2005
Rev. William B. Trexler, Jr., senior pastor, 2001–2009
Rev. Nathan T. Gragg, associate, 2006–2010
Rev. James P. Blalock, interim senior pastor, 2009–2010
Rev. Richard J. Goeres, senior pastor, 2010–
Rev. Lauren T. Carlson, associate, 2011–
Rev. Paul J. Carlson, associate, 2011–

St. John, Norfolk

St. John retired the mortgage on its building in 1987 and celebrated the tenth anniversary of its school in 1988. A pipe organ was purchased. A silver flagon and cruet were purchased for communion in 1996, and the congregation marked its forty-fifth anniversary in 1998. The school began a Step Up program for children aged two and a half through kindergarten, offering activities on an educational theme. A chairpersons committee was formed to better utilize church committees. A tape ministry began for the homebound. In 2003, following a constitutional change, Jim Owen became the first lay president of the congregation. That title was formerly held by the pastor. The fiftieth anniversary theme was "Recommitted to His Call: Serving, Welcoming and Loving all God's Children." The youth group took its first mission trip to work with the homeless, youth, and people in need in the St. Petersburg, Florida area in 2004. A freestanding altar was dedicated, a communion home care ministry was established with guidance from Pastor Sid Nelson, and a prayer shawl ministry was started. In 2010, Barbara Krumm, former director of the church school, entered Gettysburg Seminary on a track to ordained ministry. In 2011, an annual German Christmas service was held. St. John inherited the choral music library of Park Place Baptist Church, Norfolk. A columbarium site was selected, adjacent to the pastor's study.

<u>Pastors</u>

Rev. Peter Stiller, 1986–1991

Rev. Mark Schroeder, 1993–2001

Rev. Clayton Bailey, 2002–2005

Rev. Keith Olivier, 2006–

St. Timothy, Norfolk

Founded in 1955, St. Timothy Evangelical Lutheran Church relocated to our first permanent and current site at 1051 Kempsville Road, Norfolk, in 1956. Following steady growth in mission and ministry, the congregation voted to expand the building in 1989. Bishop Richard Bansemer was present for a groundbreaking ceremony on February 25, 1990. The expansion, which included a new entrance, worship space, and classrooms, was completed in less than a year, and culminated with Bishop Bansemer returning to dedicate the building on November 18, 1990. Through the generosity of anonymous donors and the faith and determination of other members, the $450,000 mortgage was retired in just ten years in 2000. In June 2007, Pastor Sidney K. Nelson retired. In 2008, Pastor David Penman accepted a call to serve. With the help of some very special financial assistance led by Pastor Penman, and including grants from the ELCA and the synod, we contracted with Pastor Lucille "CeCee" Mills to be co-pastor from July 2011 through December 2013. Desiring to increase our faith through education and prayer, we offer several new ministries to our members through small group study. These groups include a quarterly Men's Prayer Breakfast that meets on Sunday morning prior to worship, a Searchers Bible Study that meets weekly on Wednesday mornings, and a Splash Bible Study that meets twice a month on Tuesday evenings. We instituted Holy Communion every Sunday, and changed from using wafers to bread in 2008. To add more variety to our worship, in 2011 we designated the first Sunday as Processional Sunday, and every fifth Sunday as Youth Sunday. Then in 2012, we designated the last Sunday of the month as a Praise Service, and we also held our first series of outdoor worship services. Thrivent for Lutherans issued a grant of $5,000 in support of all three of our hunger ministries, including our annual sheltering ministry. In addition, Thrivent offered another match of 50¢ on the dollar, up to $5,000, on all donations made to these ministries through March 31, 2013. We at St. Timothy share a rich history and are richly blessed with a caring and committed congregation.

Pastors
Rev. Sid Nelson, 1977–2007
Chaplain Steve Beyer, interim, 2007
Rev. John Himes, interim, 2007–2008
Rev. David Penman, 2008–
Rev. Lucille Mills, 2011–2013

First, Portsmouth

The Portsmouth landscape has substantially changed in the last few decades. It can be called "urban renewal," but it is better described as "urban removal." As the surrounding suburban communities grew First Lutheran sponsored two strategically located mission churches. The new outlying areas grew with young families, vastly changing the location requirements for schools, professional offices, and places of employment. Of course, First Lutheran had to deal with an aging and reduced congregation and with a surrounding area of empty stores, vacant houses, and an archaic metro infrastructure. For organizational survival, this required a total rethinking of church goals by our succeeding officers and pastors. We now have an active membership in the Old Town Business Association, which keeps us apprised of governmental changes "in direction" and allows us an important voice in decisions. The city government has supplied its answers by revitalizing the downtown area and encouraging the growth of new business. Also, we have the ability to actively participate in downtown festivals and other events that give First Lutheran needed exposure. We introduced a parking lot for service attendees. Bible studies and formal services are structured to appeal to local varied groups (young singles, retired couples, visiting military personnel, racial mixes). We work with the city and local businesses to help us encourage people back for a Sunday sojourn for church and dinner at one of many new restaurants in downtown Portsmouth. We do our utmost to make sure that the "near-in" population knows that we are here to help with their religious needs and "spread the Word."

Pastors
Rev. H.J. Hund, 1971–1990
Rev. David K. Stouter, 1991–1993
Rev. Larry Ugarte, 2001–

Holy Communion, Portsmouth

A pavilion was constructed in 2005, the fiftieth anniversary was celebrated in 2008, and Precious Angels Preschool began in 2011.

Pastors
Rev. Otis Zirkle, 1965–1990
Rev. Dennis Buchholz, 1993–2004
Rev. Stephen McGinnis, 2004–2013
Rev. Aaron Fuller, 2013–

St. Andrew, Portsmouth

The first worship service for St. Andrew was held on November 10, 1963, in a local elementary school with an attendance of seventy-one. Our first sanctuary was dedicated in 1967 and, after much growth, a new sanctuary was built in 1978, and an educational wing in 1987. In 1989, we received a memorial gift of a new Zimmer pipe organ. Seven pastors and one intern have served our church over the years: William J. Ridenhour was our mission pastor and Marilyn Ascarza served as our intern from 1989 to 1990. We have had two vice pastors, Joel Neubauer and Cathy Mims, and several interim pastors. St. Andrew is very active in the community with Meals on Wheels, local clothes closets and food pantries, nursing home visits, weekly Bible study, and an Alzheimer's support group. In November 2013, we celebrated fifty years of sharing God's love in our community.

Pastors
Rev. Weldon R. Sheets, 1973–1981
Rev. Stephen L. Moose, 1981–1993
Rev. William H. Batterman, 1993–1998
Rev. Karen S. Van Stee, 2000–2005
Rev. Cathy A. Fanslau, 2006–2011
Rev. Aaron Fuller, 2013–

Faith, Suffolk

Worshipers first met at John Yeates Middle School beginning in April 1990. Our organizing pastor was Richard Browder, who with his wife, Jo, visited much of northern Suffolk, extending the community an invitation to be part of Faith Lutheran Church. We moved to Sturtevant Funeral Home, immediately next to the current church, in 1995. Our land was purchased and construction began in early 1997. Our dedication day was October 26, 1997. We placed a time capsule in the corner of the narthex, to be opened in 2047. After Pastor Browder left, we were served by Interim Pastor Richard F. Batman for one and a half years. Pastor Scott Benson, with his wife, Babs, and daughters Kelly and Emily, arrived in August 2000. We began a contemporary liturgical service in 2001. Youth, women's, and men's groups were founded that year as well. We started our Wednesday evening service, also contemporary in nature, in December 2010. Our membership as of December 2011 was 218 baptized members with an average attendance of 168.

<u>Pastors</u>

Rev. Richard Browder, 1990–1997

Rev. Richard Batman, interim, 1997–2000

Rev. Scott Benson, 2000–

Emmanuel, Virginia Beach

In 1987, the Ballentine Wing was completed and the congregation held the first service in the new edifice on June 7. In the early 1990s, Emmanuel Preschool was reestablished for two-, three-, and four-year-olds. After several years, the program was expanded to include eighteen-month-olds. The program now includes before and after-school care and offers a summer program. In 1997, the house next to the church became available for purchase, and the church was given first right of refusal. Through personal loans from members, we purchased the house now known as "ET," or Emmanuel Too. From 2000 to 2003, Emmanuel committed to provide for three interns as a vital part of their training. Emmanuel worked closely with the Lutheran Council of Tidewater, who partnered with Lutheran Family Services and obtained Hurricane Katrina grant money from Disaster Aid. As a result, we were able to sponsor two Hurricane Katrina New Orleans families from 2005 to 2007. Other projects we are involved in are Partners in Hope and the Human Warmth Fund. In 2010, the ordination and installation of the Rev. Aaron P. DeBenedetto was held on October 31.

<u>Pastors</u>

Rev. Andrew W. Ballentine, 1983–1991

Rev. Terry D. Clark, 1993–2008

Rev. Heidi S. Moore, 2003–2010

Rev. Jean Bozeman, senior vice pastor, 2008–2010

Rev. Aaron P. DeBenedetto, 2010–

Good Shepherd, Virginia Beach

In 1987, when the ELCA was formed, Good Shepherd, Virginia Beach had already existed for thirty-two years. Pastor Bruce Modahl had been our pastor for six years. In 1987, the congregation voted on a three-year fund drive in the amount of $100,000 to fund the installation of a Zimmer pipe organ. It was dedicated in May 1989 and, after extensive repairs, rededicated in 2001. In 1988, Pastor Modahl accepted a call to Christ Our Redeemer in Temple Terrace, Florida. Pastor Russell Siler followed. Pastor Gary Lyerly became our fifth pastor. He resigned to become part of the chaplaincy program in Spartanburg, South Carolina. The Rev. C. Marcus Engdahl then faithfully served our congregation for nine and a half years. Our church went through many capital improvements, including a new roof, outside lighting, tuck pointing, handicapped ramps, and a new HVAC system. A fund drive, "Growing with Good Shepherd," continued for three years and realized over $100,000, which exceeded our goal. A columbarium was built, with enhancements made to the courtyard to create a beautiful setting. One addition in our courtyard was the gift of a bronze statue by Gabriel Glasheen in memory of his wife. The statue of Jesus holding a lamb followed by a pig was given when Glasheen heard about the destruction of our original wooden cross by vandals. His statue, "The Good Shepherd," found a home with us. A new steel cross was also added and both were dedicated on June 1, 2003. In 2007, Pastors Scott and Cathy Mims accepted our call and our youth and community outreach has grown dramatically during their leadership. This youth involvement has helped our church grow as young families seek out a congregation where their children can grow in faith. Our youth program has also been enhanced by the dedication of our organist, Steve Sunderland, who has strengthened our youth choir, which also includes hand bells used by both the youth and adult choirs. The need for food assistance was growing in our community and our food pantry was created to help with the needs of those less fortunate. We currently provide food to families twice a week. This endeavor is strongly supported by our congregation in their generous offerings of time, food, and monetary contributions. We have helped over 690 families each year. Good Shepherd is looking forward to the years ahead as we are Christ's hands and voice in the world!

Pastors

Rev. Bruce Modahl, 1981–1988
Rev. Russell Siler, 1989–1992
Rev. Gary Lyerly, 1994–1995
Rev. Marcus Engdahl, 1996–2006
Rev. Scott Mims, 2007–
Rev. Cathy Mims, 2007–

Our Saviour, Virginia Beach

Our Saviour, Virginia Beach was founded in 1955 as a mission development in the Bayside area of Virginia Beach with seventy-five charter members, starting under the United Lutheran Church in America and later as a congregation of the Lutheran Church in America and finally as part of the ELCA. Under the pastoral leadership of the Rev. Kenneth Carbaugh, the founding pastor, the first sanctuary was built in 1960. In its fifty-nine years, Our Saviour has been served by only two called pastors, Pastors Carbaugh and Harry Griffith. Between their service, Our Saviour had two interim pastors, Chaplain Timothy Eichler and Pastor Larry Shoberg. All four pastors served on active duty as Navy chaplains. Pastor Carbaugh served the congregation for fifty-three years. Under his leadership, a second sanctuary was built in 1978. The old sanctuary, used as the congregation's social hall, was named Carbaugh Hall in 2011 to honor his ministry and the service to the congregation of his late wife, Elizabeth Carbaugh. Other highlights include the establishment in 1989 of two endowment funds from the estates of two beloved members, Helen Brower and Mildred Bugge. In the 1990s, Our Saviour had twenty-six members enrolled in colleges and universities. The congregation built and dedicated a covered pavilion in 2007 to host outdoor community gatherings and picnics.

Pastors

Rev. Kenneth R. Carbaugh, 1956–2009

Chaplain Timothy Eichler, interim, 2009

Rev. Larry Shoberg, interim, 2009–2011

Rev. Harry Griffith, 2011–

St. Michael, Virginia Beach

Beginning in 1984, a Joint Planning Council of congregations among Lutherans in America determined that a new congregation should be developed and a three-acre site was purchased at the Southgate subdivision in the S. General Booth Boulevard area of Virginia Beach. Pastor Ray Hatcher began development, services were held in Courthouse Elementary School, and St. Michael was organized with 156 charter members in 1986. A building fund campaign started in 1988 and the first building with an education wing was dedicated by Bishop Richard Bansemer in June 1989. Pastor Hatcher was followed by Pastor Peter Stiller, who served until 2000. Vice Pastor Cliff Olsen led worship three Sundays a month until Pastor John Himes served from 2001 until he resigned for medical reasons in 2007. Michael Burke was called as minister of music and the church secretary, Beth Araujo, became the first preschool director. Sharon Long became the minister of administration and coordinator of lay ministry. From 2001 to 2003, St. Michael grew rapidly, ranking as one of the fastest-growing Lutheran congregations in the country. A capital campaign raised $400,000 in three years to build a new sanctuary and expand the education wing. Part of the cost was financed by the Mission Investment Fund. The construction was completed in 2004. Pastor Chris Bowen was installed as associate pastor in 2004 and Pastor Dave Johnson had interim service in 2007–2008, followed by Pastor Rob Cosmas as senior pastor in 2008–2009. An outdoor ministry facility was enclosed for youth ministry. In 2008, Aaron Fuller was accepted at Luther Seminary, St. Paul, Minnesota, becoming the first ministerial candidate from St. Michael. Juliet Hutchins was accepted at Gettysburg Seminary in 2008, but she was installed as director of faith development later that year. Holly Sunderland was installed as minister of liturgical and choral music. Kerry Wadzita was accepted at Gettysburg Seminary in 2010. She began discernment for ministry while serving in Project Connect at a Tampa, Florida area congregation. St. Michael continues to expand its ministry with nearly 200 people regularly attending Sunday services. With God's help, the ministry at St. Michael will continue to spread the good news of Christ through the many programs that are offered to His glory and the faith community that is so evident in this special place.

<u>Pastors</u>
Rev. Ray Hatcher, 1986–1991
Rev. Peter Still, 1991–2000
Rev. Cliff Olsen, vice pastor, 2000
Rev. John Himes, 2001–2007
Rev. Chris Bowen, associate, 2004–2009
Rev. David Johnson, 2008–2009
Rev. Rob Cosmas, 2008–2009
Rev. Chris Bowen, 2009–2013

EPILOGUE
AN HISTORICAL GATHERING OF LUTHERANS IN VIRGINIA

Here in this place the new light is shining, now is the darkness vanished away;
See in this space our fears and our dreaming brought here to you in the light of this day.
Gather us in, the lost and forsaken, gather us in, the blind and the lame;
Call to us now, and we shall awaken, we shall arise at the sound of our name.

We are the young, our lives are a myst'ry, we are the old who yearn for your face;
We have been sung throughout all of hist'ry, called to be light to the whole human race.
Gather us in, the rich and the haughty, gather us in, the proud and the strong;
Give us a heart, so meek and so lowly, give us the courage to enter the song.

Here we will take the wine and the water, here we will take the bread of new birth,
Here you shall call your sons and your daughters, call us anew to be salt for the earth.
Give us to drink the wine of compassion, give us to eat the bread this is you;
Nourish us well, and teach us to fashion lives that are holy and hearts that are true.

Not in the dark of buildings confining, not in some heaven, light years away;
Here in this place the new light is shining, now is the kingdom and now is the day.
Gather us in and hold us forever, gather us in and make us your own;
Gather us in, all peoples together, fire of love in our flesh and our bone.

GATHER US IN
Text: Marty Haugen b. 1950
Music: Marty Haugen[1]

---

1. Text Copyright (www.GIAMusic.com). All rights reserved. Used by permission.

The voices of over 700 Virginia Lutherans sang out in unison this opening hymn of the "Service of Worship for the Burial of the Dead in Certain Hope of the Resurrection of Paul Gerhard Gunsten" held at 1:00 p.m. on Saturday, December 15, 2012. Gathered in the familiar baroque sanctuary of St. Andrew's Roman Catholic Church, Roanoke, the hearts of all present were in need of "new light shining" and the "darkness vanished away."

Chip, as he was lovingly known, died unexpectedly Tuesday evening, December 11, at Duke University Hospital, Durham, North Carolina, while participating in a protocol trial of chemotherapy to treat the advance of a cancer known as Chronic Lymphocytic Leukemia (CLL). The cause of death was a cardiac arrest within twelve hours of receiving a medication to prepare his body for the first chemotherapy treatment. Kris, his wife, called Bishop Mauney shortly after 11:00 p.m. to inform him of Chip's death. Mauney and Chaplain Paul Henrickson, Roanoke College, traveled to Durham to be by her side and help arrange for Chip to come home to Virginia.

The Rev. Paul "Chip" Gunsten, July 16, 1954–December 11, 2012

Chip's death was a great shock to the synod. Many had come to love him and embrace his stature of faith and devotion to the gospel and the Church of Jesus Christ. In his twelve years as assistant to the bishop, he had endeared himself to his Virginia Synod family—fellow staff, his ordained colleagues, lay leaders, and members of congregations in every part of the synod. He had also become well known and highly respected among other leaders in the ELCA, the Islands District of the Evangelical Lutheran Church in Papua New Guinea, other synods in Region 9, and among ecumenical partners of the synod who came to know him as he traveled the circuits of service to the churches in Virginia.

Bishop James F. Mauney presided and preached at the funeral service, assisted by Bishop Emeritus Richard F. Bansemer. Other assisting ministers were Pastors David Derrick and Kelly Derrick, St. Philip Lutheran Church, Roanoke, and the Rev. Dr. David K. Delaney, synodical director for Youth and Young Adult Ministries. Judge Charles Poston, vice president of the synod; Sue Dugas, synod office manager; and Pastor Andy Ballentine, St. Stephen, Williamsburg served as lectors.

Pam Gunsten, Chip's sister, shared family reflections and explained the true origins of his nickname, given to him by his maternal grandmother who called him a "chip off the old block." Even at six feet, seven inches tall, the name stuck throughout his life. Chaplain

Paul Henrickson, dean of the Chapel, Roanoke College, told stories of their friendship and adventures in serving on the staff with Chip at Caroline Furnace and the Koinonia Lutheran camp and retreat centers.

Mauney proclaimed in his sermon a message of hope and new life, offering comfort to those gathered and giving thanks for the witness of Chip's life and ministry. Mauney captured the depth of sorrow felt across the synod and expressed his own grief with a play on Gunsten's nickname.

I so want to have a big chip on my shoulder today because I don't understand the things that happen in this world and I don't know all the workings of God. I need a holy companion, a lasting friend and a church to constantly walk with me. There is such sadness because Chip was so loving, such a witness and example, so hope-filled down to his very last day.

But we are not hopeless, and we are convinced, and we gather to swap stories and to remember our brother, father, husband, beloved pastor and friend who lives in the life of Jesus Christ.

Holy Communion was shared at several stations throughout the sanctuary. Hymns were sung with a mixture of joy and tears as voices combined to proclaim hope and comfort in the words of "Children of the Heavenly Father," "The Strife Is O'er," "How Great Thou Art," "I Am the Bread of Life," and "O Christ, Our Hope, Our Heart's Desire." The strong voices of more than one hundred youth were heard above all in singing "Preparing Ye the Way of the Lord."

The service booklet included a message from Kris:

I would like to express my deep sorrow to all of those here today—Chip's colleagues in the VA synod, all who he knew through synod events, meetings, and anywhere else I can't think of. He loved his job because it meant that he could work with all of you, get to know you—sharing congregational struggles and joys because it meant sharing God's love for all of you. Please keep his love for mission and ministry going! Thank you so much for your prayers for me and my family! My prayers, too, to all of his friends and our family. We will miss "dear" so much but he will always be with us and for that I am thankful.

Blessing and Peace to all of us who struggle with this loss. May the hope of Advent and promise of the resurrection see us through. Love to all—Kris

In keeping with the wishes of the family and to honor Chip and his years of ministry, the Synod Council authorized the establishment of the Paul Gerhard Gunsten Fund for Mission to receive gifts in memory of and thanksgiving for his witness and dedication to the mission of Christ's Church and to advance the mission of the Virginia Synod of the Evangelical Lutheran Church in America.

† † †

Sixteen days before the end of 2012, the twenty-fifth anniversary year of the synod, faithful voices united in worship just as they had twenty-five years earlier at the Constituting Convention of a new Virginia Synod. In both settings of worship there was an awareness of endings and beginnings; sad loss, yet joyful hope in the promise of a new life to come for God's people and the Church in which they are called, gathered, enlightened, and sanctified by the Holy Spirit.

In both settings of worship separated by twenty-five years, a sure and certain confidence was proclaimed in Word, celebrated in Holy Communion, and united in voices of old hymns and new songs. In both settings of worship a new unity was experienced as the Holy Spirit gathered in a good and faithful people to remember their heritage, a gifted brother in Christ, and pray for the coming of a new day in God's Kingdom when all things will be made new. In both settings of worship they embraced their journey together as the Virginia Synod—a new expression of the Church in which God in Jesus Christ would continue in the years ahead to give new life in, under, around, and through this evangelical people in Virginia.

APPENDICES

Appendix I: Virginia Synod/Evangelical Lutheran Church in America Statistics

Year	Baptized Members	Confirmed Members	Average Sunday Attendance
1987	42,987	33,495	14,156
1988	42,678	33,027	14,226
1989	43,660	33,326	14,619
1990	44,041	33,554	15,132
1991	43,927	33,428	15,441
1992	44,431	33,690	15,507
1993	44,377	33,513	15,510
1994	43,887	33,288	15,666
1995	43,537	33,144	15,837
1996	43,623	33,029	15,951
1997	43,821	33,215	16,439
1998	43,930	33,555	16,459
1999	43,699	33,349	16,526
2000	43,726	33,573	16,803
2001	44,074	33,615	17,100
2002	44,035	33,533	16,809
2003	44,078	33,709	16,747
2004	44,055	33,801	16,719
2005	43,516	33,578	16,436
2006	42,966	33,248	16,486
2007	42,042	32,437	16,077
2008	41,886	32,391	15,775
2009	40,954	32,348	15,546
2010	37,326	29,707	13,820
2011	36,384	29,083	13,203
2012	36,089	28,782	12,884

Appendix II: Virginia Synod Ordinations[1]

1988
Janice Marie Lowden, Grace, Waynesboro, Sept. 8
Brent Mason Thomas, Trinity, Newport News, June 17
Harold F. Burnette, College, Salem, Nov. 13
Kenneth P. Lane, College, Salem, Nov. 13
Murray Ann Ziegenfuss, College, Salem, Nov. 13

1989
Carl Edward Norman-Trost, Emmanuel, Virginia Beach, Feb. 25
Pat McLaughlin, Williamsburg United Methodist Church, May 26
Boyce D. Whitener, Jr., St. Mark's, Roanoke, Sept. 8
Tracie L. Bartholomew, St. Mark's, Roanoke, Sept. 8
Karen S. Church, St. Mark's, Roanoke, Sept. 8
Janyce Jorgensen, Bethany, Rockbridge Parish, Dec. 17

1990
John D. Ericson, Holy Trinity, Martinsville, Feb. 11
Anthony W. Brewton, St. Andrew's Catholic Church, Roanoke, May 19
David B. McCoy, St. Andrew's Catholic Church, Roanoke, May 19
Darla J. Kincaid, St. Andrew's Catholic Church, Roanoke, May 19
Linda S. Mitchell, St. Andrew's Catholic Church, Roanoke, May 19
Randall N. Lohr, St. Stephen, Williamsburg, July 29

1991
David K. Stouter, First Lutheran, Portsmouth, Feb. 28
Cynthia Lea Long, Reformation, Newport News, June 25
Lynn Ann Bechdolt, St. Mark, Charlottesville, Dec. 14

1992
Charlotte Strecker-Baseler, Grace, Rural Retreat, Sept. 16
John Strecker-Baseler, Grace, Rural Retreat, Sept. 16

1993
Heather Lynn Bumstead, College, Salem, Dec. 5

1994
Robin L. Henrickson, St. Andrew's Catholic Church, Roanoke, May 14
Mary Clay Peters, St. John, Roanoke, June 26
Martha Marie Miller, Grace, Rural Retreat, June 26

---

1. Women and men who were ordained by Bishop Richard Bansemer and Bishop James Mauney and the place and date of their ordination from 1988 to 2012.

1995
Linda Louise Anderson, First English, Richmond, March 19
Terrie L. Sternberg, Trinity, Pulaski, Oct. 1
Matthew W. Henning, Trinity, Pulaski, Oct. 1
Sherry Poole Teves, Reformation, New Market, Dec. 5

1996
David Rhodes Wooly, St. Andrew's Catholic Church, Roanoke, June 1
Terry Lee Edwards, Grace, Waynesboro, Sept. 8
Frederick Allen Hodges, Grace, Waynesboro, Sept. 8
James R. Larsen, Grace, Waynesboro, Sept. 8
Amy Melissa Oehlschlaeger, Christ, Roanoke, Oct. 27

1997
Jeffrey Scott Plummer, St. Andrew's Catholic Church, Roanoke, May 31
David Christopher Derrick, Christ, Fredericksburg, July 20
Judith Ann Cobb, First, Norfolk, Sept. 13
Gary Curtis Chenoweth, Reformation, New Market, Sept. 14
Paul Eric Walters, Reformation, New Market, Sept. 14
Ralph William Hoffmeyer, Jr., Reformation, New Market, Sept. 14

1998
William David Brooks, Mt. Nebo, Rochelle, July 12
Cecelia Haxton, Wheatland, Buchanan, Sept. 26

1999
Rosemary Wheeler Backer, Bethlehem, Lynchburg, Feb. 7
Ruth Lynne Rinker, St. Andrew's Catholic Church, Roanoke, June 5
James Lewin Armentrout, Muhlenberg, Harrisonburg, Sept. 26
Scott James Maxwell, Muhlenberg, Harrisonburg, Sept. 26

2000
Karen Van Stee, Grace, Waynesboro, March 11
Meredith Dare Patrick Williams, Immanuel, Bluefield, Aug. 27
John Himes, St. Andrew's Catholic Church, Roanoke, June 9
Lyla Harold, St. Andrew's Catholic Church, Roanoke, June 9

2001
Robert A. Vogl, Messiah, Virginia Beach, July 21

2002
Richard A. Krasneck, St. Andrew's Catholic Church, Roanoke, June 8
Shelby DePriest, St. Andrew's Catholic Church, Roanoke, June 8
Timothy Orell, St. Andrew's Catholic Church, Roanoke, June 8
Paul W. St. Clair, Reformation, New Market, Dec. 14

Pastor Robert Vogl was ordained and installed at Messiah Lutheran, Virginia Beach, on July 21, 2001. His daughter Sarah rushes up to greet him at the conclusion of the service.

2003
Heidi Schakel Moore, Our Saviour, Norge, July 27
Patricia Smith Nabers, Grace, Waynesboro, Aug. 20
Christopher David Carr, Salem, Mt. Sidney, Aug. 31

2004
Philip Bouknight, Leesville, South Carolina, June 13
David Penman, St. Peter, Stafford, Sept. 11

2005
Laura Sinche-Vitucci, Christ, Fredericksburg, Feb. 28
Harvey Atkinson, St. Andrew's Catholic Church, Roanoke, June 4

2006
Judy Tavela, St. Andrew's Catholic Church, Roanoke, June 17
Margaret Ashby, St. Andrew's Catholic Church, Roanoke, June 17
Patricia Covington, Muhlenberg, Harrisonburg, July 22
Kathryn Gosswein, Grace, Waynesboro, Dec. 10
Mary Louise Brown, Good Shepherd, Front Royal, Dec. 16

2007
Kelly Bayer Derrick, St. Andrew's Catholic Church, Roanoke, June 9
Candis O'Meara, Faith, Suffolk, Dec. 2
Louis A. Florio, Jr., Messiah, Mechanicsville, Nov. 26

2008
Nathan Robinson, Gloria Dei, Hampton, Aug. 9
Sarah Trone Garriott, Martin Luther, Bergton, Aug. 23

2009
Kristin Hunsinger, St. Andrew's Catholic Church, Roanoke, June 20
Ryan Viands, St. Andrew's Catholic Church, Roanoke, June 20
Andrew Bansemer, St. Andrew's Catholic Church, Roanoke, June 20
Kathryn Schroeder, St. Stephen, Williamsburg, Aug. 30

2010
Patrice Thisted Arthur, St. Peter, Toms Brook, Jan. 3
David Collin Drebes, Prince of Peace, Basye, Oct. 10
Aaron Paul DeBenedetto, Emmanuel, Virginia Beach, Oct. 31

2011
Paul Christian, St. Andrew's Catholic Church, Roanoke, June 4

2012
Cathryn Proctor Costa, St. Luke, Culpeper, Jan. 14
Jonathan M. Boynton, St. Andrew's Catholic Church, Roanoke, June 9
Deanna S. Boynton, St. Andrew's Catholic Church, Roanoke, June 9
Brett Meredith Davis, Muhlenberg, Harrisonburg, Oct. 12
Phylis Diamond, Christ, Roanoke, Nov. 10

Appendix III: United Lutheran Appeal, First Year Report of Response By Conference[1]

Conference	Total Congregations Participating /Congregations in Conference	Amount
Central Valley	20/28	$10,117.56
Germanna	11/12	$6,351.00
Highlands	21/24	$7,235.00
New River	11/13	$4,457.00
Northern Valley	7/9	$3,189.13
Page	4/8	$1,555.00
Peninsula	7/8	$6,314.32
Richmond	8/10	$9,961.69
Southern	13/18	$13,704.00
Southern Valley	13/20	$6,118.00
Tidewater	10/15	$2,512.90
Anonymous		$510.00
Totals	124/165	$72,655.60

1. Minutes, 8th Annual Synod Assembly, Virginia Synod/ELCA, 1995, p. 62.

Appendix IV: United Lutheran Appeal, Response By Year

Year	Amount
1995	$72,655
1996	$58,071
1997	$80,181
1998	$92,894
1999	$138,627
2000	$102,417
2001	$104,921
2002	$104,910
2003	$82,977
2004	$104,720
2005	$111,637
2006	$118,554
2007	$120,975
2008	$117,480
2009	$82,647
2010	$77,745
2011	$67,870
2012	$74,271
Total Giving in 18 Years	$1,713,552

Appendix V: Power in the Spirit Programs and Leaders

1986, July 24-26
"Worship and Witness"
Dr. Paul Manz (Lutheran School of Theology at Chicago), Organist & Hymn Festival
Dr. Thomas Ridenhour (Lutheran Theological Seminary at Gettysburg), Bible Study
Rev. Jerry Schmalenberger (Evangelical Outreach, Lutheran Church in America; Pastor at St. John, Des Moines, IA), Preacher
Rev. Deborah Steed (Pastor, Prince of Peace, Loveland, OH), Chaplain
Gordon Beaver (Organist, St. Mark, Charlotte, NC), Choir/Choral Aspects of Worship
Rev. James Connelly (Division for Parish Services, Lutheran Church in America), Plenary Sessions

1987, July 30-August 1
"Equipping for Ministry," 115 attendance
Dr. Robert Benne (Professor of Religion, Roanoke College, Salem), Keynote Speaker
Rev. Karen Bockelman (Campus Pastor, Luther College, IA), Preacher
Dr. Donald Busarow (Associate Professor of Church Music, Wittenburg), Keyboard/Choral Direction
Dr. Richard Jeske (Professor of New Testament and Greek, Lutheran Theological Seminary at Philadelphia, PA), Bible Study
Rev. John Largen (Director of Church Relations, Lutheran Theological Southern Seminary, Columbia, SC), Chaplain

Elizabeth Smythe, Coordinator of Power in the Spirit, 2006–

1988
No Event

1989, July 20-22
"Equipping for Ministry—Our Journey Together," 145 attendance
Dr. Walter Bouman (Professor of Systematic Theology, Trinity Lutheran Seminary, Columbus, OH), Keynoter and Bible Study
Rev. Mark Radecke (Pastor, Christ Lutheran, Roanoke), Chaplain
Wayne Wold (Director of Music Ministry, First Lutheran, Ellicott City, MD), Musician
Dr. Robert Benne (Professor of Religion, Roanoke College, Salem), Banquet Speaker

1990, July 19-21
"Visioning for the '90s," 152 attendance
Dr. H. George Anderson (President, Luther College, Decorah, IA), Keynoter/Banquet Speaker
Dr. Robert L. Hock (Pastor, St. John Lutheran, Winter Park, FL), Bible Study
Rev. Susan Tyykila (Chair, Evangelism Committee, Virginia Synod), Chaplain
John Horman (Director of Music, Warner Memorial Presbyterian, MD), Musician

1991, July 18-20
"All Things Bright and Beautiful," 173 attendance
Dr. John E. Schramm (Assistant to the Bishop, Minneapolis Synod/ELCA), Keynoter
Rev. Richard F. Bansemer (Bishop, Virginia Synod/ELCA), Bible Study
Rev. Frank G. Honeycutt (Pastor, St. John Lutheran, Abingdon), Chaplain
Mark Glaeser (Minister of Music, Christ Lutheran, Charlotte, NC), Musician

1992, July 9-11
"For Everything There Is a Season," 250 attendance
Dr. James A. Nestingen (Associate Professor of Church History, Luther Northwestern Seminary, St. Paul, MN), Keynoter
Dr. Paul Manz (Christ Seminary-Seminex Professor of Church Music, Lutheran School of Theology at Chicago), Musician
Daryl S. Everett (Professor of Pastoral Care and Counseling, Lutheran Theological Southern Seminary), Bible Study
Rev. Marilyn Ascarza (Pastor, Christ Church, Charlotte, NC), Chaplain

1993, July 15-17
"I Love to Tell the Story" 243 attendance
Rev. Ronald J. Lavin (Pastor, Our Saviour Lutheran, Tucson, AZ), Keynoter
Rev. Robin D. Mattison (Professor of New Testament, Lutheran Theological Seminary, Philadelphia, PA), Bible Study
Rev. Frank Stoldt (Director of Music and Worship, Augsburg Fortress, ELCA), Musician
Rev. William T. Stewart II (Pastor, Peace Lutheran, Charlottesville), Worship Planner
Festival of the Arts: Play, *Mass Appeal*, Rev. Eric Moehring and Members of Christ Lutheran, Richmond

1994, July 21-23
"The Walk to Emmaus," 237 attendance
Robert Hobby (Director of Music, Trinity English, Fort Wayne, IN), Musician
Rev. Sarah S. Henrich (Professor of New Testament, Luther Northwestern Theological Seminary, St. Paul, MN), Bible Study
Rev. Dr. Patrick R. Keifert (Professor of Systematic Theology, Luther Northwestern Theological Seminary, St. Paul, MN), Keynoter
Rev. Mark William Menees (Bishop, North Carolina Synod/ELCA), Preacher
Rev. Paul Millholland (Pastor, St. Paul Lutheran, Hampton), Worship Coordinator

1995, July 13-15
"A New Song for a New Day," 282 attendance
Rev. Walter P. Kallestad (Pastor, Community Church of Joy, AZ), Keynoter
Dr. Walter Michel (Professor of Old Testament, Lutheran School of Theology at Chicago), Bible Study
Rev. Carole Burns (Pastor, Austin Messiah Lutheran, Chicago), Chaplain
Musician and Special Event: "Festival Song Fest," John Ylvisaker, Composer

1996, July 11-13
"Choose This Day," 359 attendance
Rev. Dr. Walter Wangerin, Jr. (Valparaiso University, Valparaiso, IN), Keynoter
Rev. Dr. James Forbes (Minister, Riverside Church, NY), Bible Study
Edith Hockspeier (Associate Minister of Music, Mt. Tabor Lutheran, West Columbia, SC), Musician
Rev. Sharon Israel (Pastor, St. James-Spader, McGaheysville), Worship Coordinator
Special Event: "Voices of Faith"

1997, July 10-12
"Foretaste of the Feast," 276 attendance
Dr. Marva J. Dawn (Theologian, Author, Washington State), Keynoter
Dr. Walter Taylor, Jr. (Professor of New Testament, Trinity Lutheran Seminary, Columbus, Ohio), Bible Study
Mr. David Cherwien (Director of Music, Church of the Good Shepherd, Minneapolis, MN), Musician
Rev. Murray Ziegenfuss (Pastor, Mt. Zion Lutheran, Fairview), Worship Coordinator
Special Event: "Their Fine Group," Robin and Linda Williams, Folk Musicians (Middlebrook)

1998, July 9-11
"Our Hope for Years to Come," 367 attendance
Bishop H. George Anderson (Presiding Bishop, ELCA, Chicago, IL), Keynoter
Rev. Barbara R. Rossing (Professor of New Testament, Lutheran School of Theology at Chicago), Bible Study
Scott Weidler (Associate Director of Worship and Music, ELCA, Chicago), Musician
Special Event: Sing Along with Scott Weidler and local singers, "Men of Praise"

1999, July 15-17
"Lift Every Voice," 284 attendance
Bishop Callon W. Holloway, Jr. (Bishop, Southern Ohio Synod/ELCA), Keynoter
Rev. Dr. David K. Delaney (Associate Pastor, St. John Lutheran, Roanoke), Bible Study
May Schwarz (Director of Church Music, Trinity Lutheran Seminary, Columbus, OH), Musician
Rev. Bill Boldin, Janice Bunting, Pat Morgan (Virginia Synod Worship Committee), Worship
Special Event: "Hands of Peace" Puppet Ministry, Entertainers

2000, July 13-15
"M2K: Ambassadors for Christ," 279 attendance
Rev. Claire S. Burkat (Director of Mission and Resource Development, Southeastern Pennsylvania Synod/ELCA), Keynoter
Rev. Dr. James F. Mauney (Bishop, Virginia Synod/ELCA), Bible Study
Brian Larson (Cantor, All Saints Lutheran, Port Orange, FL), Musician
Rev. Rhodes Woolly (Pastor, Bethel Lutheran, Winchester), Worship Coordinator
Special Event: Entertainer Ed Stivender, Storyteller

2001, July 12-14
"Fanning the Flame," 217 attendance
Rev. Richard Webb (Pastor, Lutheran Church of Hope, West Des Moines, IA), Keynoter
Dr. Paul Hinlicky (Professor of Religion, Roanoke College, Salem), Bible Study
Dr. Gerald R. McDermott (Associate Professor of Religion, Roanoke College, Salem), Bible Study
David Atkins (Music Director, Christ the King, Richmond), Musician and Worship Coordinator
Special Event: Rev. Webb and Mr. Atkins

2002, July 11-13
"Filling the Cup: Prayer and Spirituality," 261 attendance
Dr. Dorothy Bass (Director of the Valparaiso Project, Valparaiso, IN), Keynoter
Rev. Daniel Erlander (Teaching Pastor, Trinity Lutheran Church, Freeland, WA), Bible Study
Rev. James Capers (Assistant to the Bishop, Southeastern Synod/ELCA), Musician
Rev. John Herman and Rev. Rosemary Backer (Pastors, Bethlehem Lutheran, Lynchburg), Worship Coordinators
Special Event: "Their Fine Group," Robin and Linda Williams, Folk Musicians (Middlebrook)

2003, July 10-12
"Spilling the Cup: Faith Active in Love," 245 attendance
Dr. Bill Fintel, M.D. (Oncologist; Member, Christ Lutheran, Roanoke), Keynoter
Rev. Marty Stevens (Visiting Assistant Professor of Old Testament, Union Theological Seminary, Richmond), Bible Study
Rev. Paul Weber (Associate Professor of Church Music, Lenoir Rhyne College, Hickory, NC), Musician
Florence Jowers (Assistant Professor of Music, Church Organist, Lenoir Rhyne, Hickory, NC), Musician
Special Event: "When in Our Music God is Glorified," Jowers & Weber

2004, July 15-17
"Stamped By Christ ... Sent With a Message," 280 attendance
Bishop Mark Hansen (Presiding Bishop, ELCA), Keynoter
Rev. James Mauney (Bishop, Virginia Synod/ELCA), Bible Study
Musicians and Entertainers: Jay Beech Trio (Trinity Lutheran, Moorhead, MN)

Presiding Bishop Mark Hanson, 2004 presenter at Power in the Spirit.

2005, July 7-9
"Christ, the Kaleidoscope of Light Around the World," 199 attendance
Rev. Rani Abdulmasih (Pastor, Abundant Life Arabic Lutheran, Dearborn, MI), Keynoter
Rev. Rafael Malpica Padilla (Executive Director of the Division for Global Mission, ELCA), Bible Study
Musicians and Entertainers: Jubilee (Portland, OR)

2006, July 6-8
"Spiritual Disciplines: Habits of the Heart," 251 attendance
Rev. Susan Briehl (Associate with the Valparaiso Project, Valparaiso, IN), Keynoter
Dr. David Rhoads (Professor of New Testament, Lutheran School of Theology at Chicago), Bible Study
Aaron Garber (Director of Music at College Lutheran, Salem), Musician
Special Event: The Rev. Richard Bansemer (Librettist) and Aaron Garber (Composer), a Presentation on the Oratorios "Job" and "Mary, the Mother of Jesus"; Tara and Philip Bouknight, Soloists

2007, July 5-7
"Nurturing Faith in Home, Church, and School," 257 attendance
Rev. James A. Nestingen (Professor Emeritus of Church History, Luther Seminary, St. Paul, MN), Keynoter
Rev. Susan W. McCarver (Associate Professor of Christian Education, Lutheran Theological Southern Seminary), Bible Study
Mark Mummert (Seminary Musician, Lutheran Theological Seminary at Philadelphia, PA), Musician
Special Event: Doug Berky, Mask/Movement Artist (First United Methodist, Anderson, IN)

2008, July 10-12
"God Gives! We Care! We Share!" 180 attendance
Charles "Chick" Lane (Assistant to the Bishop, Northwestern Minnesota Synod/ELCA), Keynoter
Rev. Andrea DeGroot Nesdahl (Bishop Emeritus, South Dakota Synod/ELCA), Bible Study
Special Event: Exit Nine (Virginia Synod) Worship Musicians/Entertainers

2009, July 9-11
"Power Through Scripture: Fueling Our Faith," 195 attendance
Dr. Mark Allan Powell (Professor of New Testament, Trinity Lutheran Seminary, Columbus, OH), Keynoter and Bible Study
J. Bert Carlson (Composer and Performer), Musician
Special Event: Rev. Leslie Hunter (Youth Director and Assistant Minister, Holy Family Lutheran, Chicago)

2010, July 8-10
"Shaped By the Master's Hands," 226 attendance
Rev. Susan Briehl (Valparaiso Project on the Education and Formation of People of Faith, Valparaiso, IN; Distinguished Professor of the Art of Ministry, Wartburg Seminary, Dubuque, IA), Keynoter

Dr. Diane Jacobson (Director of Book of Faith, ELCA; Assistant Professor, Luther Seminary, St. Paul, MN), Bible Study
Marty Haugen (Composer-in-Residence at Mayflower Community, Minneapolis, MN), Musician
Entertainers: Night Crossing (Marion)

2011, July 7-9
"We Love to Tell the Story," 218 attendance
Dr. Walter Wangerin (Jochum Chair, Valparaiso University, Valparaiso, IN), Keynoter
Rev. John Largen (Pastor, Seminary Community, Lutheran Theological Southern Seminary, Columbia, SC), Bible Study
Kevin Barger (Director of Music, Epiphany Lutheran, Richmond), Musician
Entertainer: Isaac Freeman (Royal Oak Presbyterian, Marion)

2012, July 12-14
"Welcoming the Stranger," 176 attendance
Rev. Ruban Duran (Director for New Evangelizing Congregations, ELCA), Keynoter
Rev. Margaret Payne (Bishop, New England Synod/ELCA), Bible Study
Special Event: Power Praise (Music Leaders, Mt. Rogers Parish, VA), Musicians, and Ed Kilbourne (Rock Hill, SC), Storyteller

Appendix VI: Ambassadors Community for Theological Study (ACTS) Courses

A total of 502 (325 women, 177 men) members from eighty-one different congregations of the synod participated in at least one course of ACTS between 2001 and 2013. In addition to the "Core Courses," twenty "Elective Courses" were offered in Christian Education, Stewardship, Worship, and Evangelism from 2004 through 2008 with 251 students attending. Four spiritual retreats were offered with seventy-eight in attendance. Three study trips were offered for those interested: Paul's Second and Third Missionary (November 2008), German Reformation Tour and Oberammergau Passion Play (August 2010), and Lenten Tides in the Holy Land (April 2012). There were a total of thirty-one course leaders, sixty small group leaders, and seven leaders of the spiritual retreats.

The Rev. Rubén F. Durán, program director, New Congregations for ELCA Evangelical Outreach and Congregational Mission, lecturer for ACTS.

Course Subject	Leaders	Students	New Students	Time
Lutheran Confessions	Timothy Wengert	57		Fall 2002
Old Testament	Lamontte Luker	54	9	Winter 2003
New Testament	Brian Peterson	41	2	Spring 2003
Christian Nurture	Robert Benne	46	10	Fall 2003
Lutheran Confessions	Timothy Wengert	77	63	Fall 2004
Old Testament	Dave Delaney	34	6	Spring 2005
New Testament	Brian Peterson	45	17	Fall 2005
Christian Nurture	Robert Benne	34	2	Spring 2006
Old Testament	Dave Delaney	59	36	Fall 2006
Lutheran Confessions	Timothy Wengert	70	26	Spring 2007
New Testament	Brian Peterson	40	10	Fall 2007
		34	6	Grace, Waynesboro (first live simulcast)[1]
Christian Life	Robert Benne	23	2	Spring 2008
		18		Grace, Waynesboro
		5		Gloria Dei, Hampton
Old Testament	David Delaney	14	2	Fall 2008
Spirituality and Leadership	John Largen	75	25	Spring 2009
		59		Grace, Waynesboro
		16		St. John, Norfolk
Lutheran Confessions	Michael Root	49	19	Fall 2009
		45		Grace, Waynesboro
		4		Gloria Dei, Hampton
Biblical Models of Leadership	James Thomas	91	37	Spring 2010
		45		Grace, Waynesboro
		46		St. John, Norfolk
New Testament	Brian Peterson	72		Fall 2010
		38		Grace, Waynesboro
		7		St. John, Norfolk
		27		Ebenezer, Marion
Christian's Call	Rubén Durán and Mary Sue Drier	87	39	Spring 2011
		62		Grace, Waynesboro
		25		St. John, Norfolk
Old Testament	Lamontte Luker	63	13	Fall 2011
Spirituality and Leadership	John Largen	43	3	Spring 2012
Lutheran Confessions	Paul Hinlicky	74	38	Fall 2012
Biblical Models of Leadership	James Thomas	67	23	Spring 2013
New Testament	Brian Peterson	75	23	Fall 2013

---

1. Beginning in the fall of 2007, Gloria Dei, Hampton hosted the first live simulcast. Other locations added are noted with attendance numbers that contain some new students.

Appendix VII: The Ministerium Covenant, Virginia Synod/ELCA

As the Ministerium of the Virginia Synod/ELCA, we are rooted in the gospel, affirm and cherish our call to Word and Sacrament and Service, and honor one another. As a community of rostered leaders, we covenant with one other to

1. Care for and support one another
2. View our ministry context as part of the wider church
3. Care for family and self in healthy ways
4. Engage in professional development (i.e. continuing education, mentoring, and consultation)
5. Meet regularly with other rostered leaders for prayer, support, study, and fellowship
6. Live and serve in accordance with the Vision and Expectations
7. Renew this covenant annually

Values:
- Christ-centered
- Grounded in Scripture and Confessions—open to the Holy Spirit
- Discovering and valuing our giftedness and places of ministry
- Passionate Proclaimers
- Sent into the world for witness and service
- Agents of reconciliation, revelation, and transformation

Appendix VIII: Virginia Synod Assembly Themes

1988	We, the Family of God
1989	Proclaim Him Lord of All[1]
1990	God's Baptized People in the World
1991	A Legacy of Strengthened Vision—The College and the Church
1992	We Are Not Ashamed
1993	Light, Bread, Salt—That Christ May Be Seen
1994	Live and Give—That Christ May Be Seen
1995	Educating the Faith—That Christ May Be Seen
1996	Educating for Faith—That Christ May Be Seen
1997	True Confessions, A Study of Martin Luther's Small Catechism
1998	Planting New Churches, Congregational Mission, Global Outreach, Trust Fund, Senior Adults, Youth and Young Adults—That Christ May Be Seen
1999	Our Church in a Hungry World—That Christ May Be Seen
2000	Created as the People of God
2001	Ambassadors for Christ—Disciples Under Construction, Pardon Our Dust
2002	Ambassadors for Christ—Go in Peace, Serve the Lord
2003	Ambassadors for Christ—Stewards of the Kingdom
2004	Ambassadors for Christ—Sent On Purpose, With a Purpose
2005	Ambassadors for Christ—Friends of Jesus
2006	Ambassadors for Christ—God's Appeal Through Us as Global Partners
2007	Ambassadors for Christ—Baptized Disciples

---

1. The 1989 Synod Assembly met at the College of William and Mary, Williamsburg. All of the other assemblies were held at Roanoke College.

2008   Ambassadors for Christ—Blessed to Be a Blessing
2009   Ambassadors for Christ—God's Work, Our Hands
2010   Ambassadors for Christ—Reaching Out, Sharing the Good News
2011   Ambassadors for Christ—Sharing the Story, Living the Faith
2012   Ambassadors for Christ—Running the 5Ks (Knows)

Appendix IX: Ordained Ministers in Special Situations

1987–2012

Rev. Floyd Addison, President, Virginia Lutheran Homes
Rev. Patrick Appleget, Chaplain, U.S. Army
Rev. Richard Bansemer, Bishop, Virginia Synod
Rev. William Boldin, Hospital Chaplain
Rev. Jean Bozeman, Assistant to the Bishop, Virginia Synod
Rev. Cecil Bradfield, Professor, James Madison University
Rev. Lance Braun, Campus Pastor, Richmond
Rev. Daphne Burton, Campus Pastor, Fredericksburg
Rev. Randall Chapman, Chaplain, U.S. Navy
Rev. Robert Chell, Campus Pastor, Harrisonburg
Rev. Terry Clark, Regional Specialist, Evangelism/Witness, Division of Congregational Life, ELCA
Rev. Mark Cooper, Director, Clinical Pastoral Education, Medical College of Virginia
Rev. David Couchman, Chaplain, U.S. Army
Rev. Kenneth Crumpton, Jr., Associate Director, Department of Church Extension, LCA
Rev. Gary Danielsen, Executive Director, Lutheran Council of Tidewater
Rev. David Delaney, Director, Synod Youth and Young Adult Ministry
Rev. Lewis Doggett, Jr., Associate Chaplain, Mary Washington Hospital, Fredericksburg
Rev. Charles Easley, Chaplain, Brandon Oaks, Roanoke
Rev. Robert Fellows, President, Virginia Synod Lutheran Homes
Rev. Stephen Gragg, Chaplain, U.S. Navy
Rev. Kathleen Haines, Lutheran-Presbyterian Campus Pastor, Harrisonburg
Rev. Robert Hale, Chaplain, U.S. Navy
Rev. George Handley, Secretary, Virginia Synod
Rev. Richard Harris, Institutional Chaplain, Roanoke Valley
Rev. Willetta Heising, Chaplain/Consultant to Williamsburg Task Force
Rev. Paul Henrickson, Chaplain, Roanoke College
Rev. Paul Hinlicky, Professor, Roanoke College
Rev. Byron Holderby, Chaplain, U.S. Navy
Rev. Walter Huffman, Associate Professor, Trinity Seminary, Columbus, Ohio

The Rev. Darryl Morton, assistant to the bishop for federal chaplaincies, ELCA, reads the retirement certificate and commendations received by Captain Stephen Gragg, chaplain, U.S. Navy, on June 7, 2008.

Rev. Carl Jensen, Executive Director, Peninsula Counseling Center
Rev. Daniel Jungkuntz, Executive Director, Peninsula Counseling Center
Rev. John Keister, Director, Signal Knob Retreat Center
Rev. William King, Campus Pastor, Blacksburg
Rev. Jack Dean Kingsbury, Professor, Union Seminary, Richmond
Rev. Carl Koch, Chaplain, U.S. Navy
Rev. John Koehnlein, Graduate Study
Rev. Larry Lafon, Chaplain, U.S. Navy
Rev. John Largen, Director of Church Relations, Southern Seminary
Rev. Arthur Lewis, Executive Director, Lutheran Council of Tidewater
Rev. Luther Lindberg, Professor, Southern Seminary
Rev. Michael Lippard, Graduate Study
Rev. Lamontte Luker, Professor, Southern Seminary
Rev. Robert Marshall, Professor, Southern Seminary
Rev. Jackson Martin, Regional Director, Division for Mission in North America
Rev. Janet Marvar, Campus Pastor, Harrisonburg
Rev. James Mauney, Assistant to the Bishop, Virginia Synod
Rev. Luther Mauney, Jr., Chaplain, Medical College of Virginia, Richmond
Rev. M.L. Minnick, Jr., Director of Church Extension, Division for Mission in North America, LCA
Rev. Virgil A. Moyer, Bishop, Virginia Synod
Rev. Terence Mullins, Editor, Division for Parish Services, LCA
Rev. James Nichols, Chaplain, U.S. Navy
Rev. Kenneth Nilsen, Executive Director, Caroline Furnace Lutheran Camp
Rev. Jack Nussen, Chaplain/Counselor, Portsmouth Psychiatric Center
Rev. Clifford A. Olsen, Chaplain, Seamen's Friend Society, Norfolk
Rev. James W. Pence, Campus Pastor, Charlottesville
Rev. Brian Peterson, Professor, Southern Seminary
Rev. Thomas Prinz, Assistant Director, Department of Ecumenical Relations, Division for Mission in North America
Rev. Jeffrey Plummer, Chaplain, U.S. Navy
Rev. A.E. Purdham, Chaplain, U.S. Navy
Rev. Gordon Putnam, Chaplain, University of Virginia Cancer Center
Rev. Janet Ramsey, Chaplain, Virginia Synod Lutheran Home, Roanoke
Rev. James Ritchie, Jr., Chaplain, Veterans Administration
Rev. James Roepke, Chaplain, Chaplain Service of Virginia
Rev. William Rosenow, Regional Representative, Bethel Series
Rev. Robert Scharlemann, Professor, University of Virginia, Charlottesville
Rev. Paul Schulz, Chaplain/Administrator, Good Samaritan Society, Franklin, West Virginia
Rev. Carol Schweitzer, Professor, Union Seminary, Richmond
Rev. Wayne Shelor, Executive Director, Caroline Furnace Lutheran Camp
Rev. George Sims, Regional Gift Planner, Synod Office of Planned Giving
Rev. Richard Sipe, Jr., Chaplain, U.S. Navy
Rev. Trygve Skarsten, Professor, Trinity Seminary, Columbus, Ohio
Rev. Charles Spraker, Special Ministry, Staunton
Rev. Carl Swanson, Chaplain, U.S. Air Force
Rev. David Tholstrup, Missionary to Peru, Division for Mission in North America
Rev. Carl Trost, Chaplain, U.S. Navy

Rev. Philip Tundel, Chaplain, U.S. Navy
Rev. Harold Uhl, Bishop's Liaison for Mobility
Rev. Timothy Waltonen, Chaplain, Campus Christian Community, Fredericksburg
Rev. Bob Ward, Chaplain, Brandon Oaks
Rev. Carroll Wessinger, Appalachian Counselor, Division for Mission in North America
Rev. Dwayne Westermann, Assistant to the Bishop, Virginia Synod
Rev. Robert Wilken, Professor, University of Virginia, Charlottesville
Rev. Wayne Williams, Director of Outdoor Ministries, Virginia Synod

Appendix X: Associates in Ministry (AIM)

Patricia Arthur, St. Peter, Toms Brook
Lindsay Barr, Bethel, Winchester
Sue Clark, Synod Church Worker
Judith Cobb, Church Educator, Norfolk
Frances Halcrow, Director of Christian Education, On Leave
Daniel Hannemann, Grace, Winchester
Dr. Robert Hawkins, Professor, Southern Seminary
Patricia Jabre, St. Luke, Richmond
Louise Jacobson, Church Musician, St. Luke, Richmond
Jeanne Lindemann, Church Musician, Newport News
Shirley Lucore, Church Administrator, Richmond, On Leave
Jane Nicholson, First Lutheran, Norfolk
Katherine Reier, Church Musician, Christ, Roanoke
Steven Shaner, Church Musician, On Leave
Sharon Shull, Christ, Staunton
Judith Smith, Stafford, On Leave from Call
Louise Sparrer, Deaconess, Midlothian
Lavelva Stevens, Church Musician, St. Mark, Charlottesville and Holy Trinity, Wytheville
Christine Van O'Linda, Diaconal Minister, Epiphany, Richmond
Sonya Williams-Giersch, St. Paul, Strasburg

Appendix XI: Number of Congregations

1987...159	2000...163
1988...160	2001...163
1989...161	2002...161
1990...161	2003...164
1991...163	2004...165
1992...162	2005...165
1993...164	2006...165
1994...164	2007...166
1995...163	2008...164
1996...163	2009...162
1997...162	2010...159
1998...162	2011...155
1999...162	2012...155

Appendix XII: New Congregations Received

Apostles, Gloucester, March 21, 1988
Resurrection, Fredericksburg, Nov. 17, 1989
Faith, Suffolk, Sept. 10, 1991
All Saints, Chesterfield, Nov. 14, 1993
Lakeside, Littleton, North Carolina, Nov. 10, 1996
Peace, Clarksville, established as authorized worshiping community, March 2000
Grace and Glory, Palmyra, established as authorized worshiping community, Jan. 2001
Rejoice, Chesapeake, approved Oct. 21, 2001
Massaponax, approved for mission development, Oct. 2001
St. Thomas, Bealeton, 2005
Bedford, approved as mission under development, 2008
Living Water, Kilmarnock, approved as mission under development, 2008

Appendix XIII: Congregations Closing or Leaving

Realignment of Fairview Parish, Maurertown transferred to West Virginia-Western Maryland Synod, 1991
Sale of property of St. Matthew, Richmond to The Church of Our Lord Jesus Christ, March 7, 1996
Emmanuel, Roanoke closed, Oct. 27, 1996
Dissolution of Giles Parish, Pembroke merged into Redeemer, Pearisburg, June 29, 1997
Dissolution of All Saints, Chesterfield, June 2001
Dissolution of All Saints, Covington, Jan. 2002
Approval of St. Paul, Roanoke to leave ELCA, 2007
Approval of The Life, Richmond to dissolve, 2007
Three congregations voted to leave ELCA: Apostles, Chesapeake; St. John, Roanoke; and Morning Star, St. James, 2010
Three congregations voted to leave ELCA: Lebanon Church, Lebanon; Reformation, Culpeper; and United, Crockett, 2011
Five congregations voted to dissolve: Grace, Spottsylvania; Messiah, Virginia Beach; Furnace Hill, Smyth County; Corinth, Wythe County; and Rejoice, Chesapeake, 2011

Appendix XIV: Necrology

Deaths of Pastors and AIMs, 1988–2012

Rev. Allan H. Fenner, Feb. 18, 1989
Rev. J. Luther Mauney, Jan. 29, 1990
Rev. Malcolm L. Minnick, June 18, 1991
Rev. Henry M. Schumann, Oct. 15, 1991
Rev. Adrian K. Yount, June 28, 1992
Rev. Paul L. Himmelman, March 6, 1993
Rev. Martin L. Shaner, April 28, 1993
Rev. Franklin P. Cauble, July 6, 1993
Rev. Steven M. Anderson, Nov. 5, 1993
Rev. Albert J. Shumate, Nov. 10, 1993
Rev. Curtis H. Brandt, June 27, 1994
Rev. Auburn F. Bowers, Sr., Nov. 16, 1994
Rev. Willis S. Buchanan, Jan. 23, 1995
Rev. Elmer H. Ganskopp, May 9, 1995
Rev. Luther C. Florstedt, June 30, 1995
Rev. Harold J. Hizer, Sept. 14, 1995
Rev. Arthur L. Smeland, April 20, 1996
Rev. Carl W. Beyer, July 14, 1996
Rev. Otis W. Zirkle, Oct. 2, 1996
Gary E. Kelly, lay minister, Jan. 1, 1997
Rev. Joseph Huntley, March 14, 1997
Rev. James K. Cadwallader, March 19, 1997
Rev. Susan M. Hove, Aug. 16, 1997
Rev. Evans R. Keim, Jr., Oct. 9, 1997
Rev. Charles G. Tusing, Jan. 14, 1998
Rev. Elmer E. Bosserman, Feb. 28, 1998
Rev. Thomas K. Spande, April 16, 1998
Rev. R. William Hoffmeyer, Jr., June 16, 1998
Louise M. Iverson Jacobson, AIM, Sept. 4, 1998
Rev. John J. Kylie, Dec. 6, 1999
Rev. William E. Eisenberg, Jan. 13, 2000
Rev. Paul A. Scholz, March 22, 2000
Sara Crumley Lindemann, AIM, Dec. 3, 2000
Rev. Robert R. Sala, Jan. 15, 2001
Rev. John C. Bellingham, May 13, 2001
Rev. Roger S. Kluttz, Aug. 8, 2001
Rev. Frederick M. Ritter, Jr., Feb. 3, 2002
Rev. Hensil Arehart, June 13, 2003
Rev. Henry J. Hund, Jan. 3, 2004
Rev. John J. Cooper, April 16, 2004
Rev. Harris L. Willis, Aug. 29, 2004
Rev. Louis A. Smith, Nov. 30, 2004
Rev. James Hughes, Jan. 17, 2005
Rev. Gordon Hite, May 31, 2005
Rev. Lawrence O. Sanger, Dec. 6, 2005
Rev. George K. Bowers, May 23, 2006
Rev. Walter Vierling, July 14, 2006
Rev. Charles L. Lesemann, Feb. 27, 2009
Rev. William E. Kinser, March 29, 2009
Rev. Donald R. Pichaske, April 18, 2009
Rev. L. Douglas Stowe, July 31, 2009
Rev. Lucille A. Dorband, Oct. 27, 2009
Rev. George L. Ziegenfuss, Nov. 10, 2009
Rev. John F. Byerly, Jr., April 27, 2010
Rev. Patti T. Arthur, Sept. 10, 2010
Rev. Kenneth Crumpton, Sept. 24, 2010
Rev. Richard Gates, Dec. 18, 2011
Rev. Gordon K. Zirkle, June 5, 2012
Rev. Ruth L. Rinker, Aug. 25, 2012
Rev. Stephen J. McGinnis, Nov. 2, 2012
Rev. Paul "Chip" Gunsten, Dec. 11, 2012
Rev. Jesse S. Hangen, Dec. 26, 2012

Appendix XV: Ambassadors Community for Theological Study (ACTS) Certificates Awarded[1]

Name	Date Received	Home Congregation
Karren Light	October 24, 2004	Bethel, Winchester
Charlene Seibert	December 5, 2004	St. Peter, Stafford
Elizabeth Smythe	December 5, 2004	Ebenezer, Marion
Pamela Walters Estes	March 6, 2005	Epiphany, Richmond
Nancy Schmitz	June 26, 2005	Peace, Charlottesville
Bob Blair	July 10, 2005	Holy Trinity, Lynchburg
Gene Gomez	July 31, 2005	Apostles, Gloucester
Janet Gomez	July 31, 2005	Apostles, Gloucester
Delores Harris	July 31, 2005	Our Saviour, Richmond
Ron Lawson	September 11, 2005	Christ, Wise
Michael Samerdyke	September 11, 2005	Christ, Wise
Candyce Sylling	September 25, 2005	St. Peter's, Stafford
Ellen Miller	October 20, 2005	St. John, Abington
Patty Franz	October 30, 2005	Christ, Richmond
Paula Stensvaag	November 20, 2005	St. Paul, Hampton
Jim Stensvaag	November 20, 2005	St. Paul, Hampton
Bill Roberts	February 10, 2007	Peace, Charlottesville
Tom Barron	February 11, 2007	St. Paul, Strasburg
Joe Fleming	November 11, 2007	Mt. Zion, Woodstock
Debbie Mintiens	January 20, 2008	Salem, Mt. Sidney
Cynthia Anders	March 29, 2009	Mt. Rogers Parish, Faith, Whitetop[2]
Pamela Badin	March 29, 2009	Mt. Rogers Parish, Faith, Whitetop
Sharon Compton	March 29, 2009	Mt. Rogers Parish, Faith, Whitetop
May Hill	March 29, 2009	Mt. Rogers Parish, Faith, Whitetop
Barbara Jones-Butcher	March 29, 2009	Mt. Rogers Parish, Faith, Whitetop

Commissioning of Dr. Jim and Paula Stensvaag as ELCA missionaries to Slovakia on July 11, 2010, by the Rev. Jean Bozeman and their pastor, the Rev. Chris Farrow, St. Paul, Hampton.

---

1. Updated January 16, 2015.
2. Mt. Rogers Parish represents a group of congregations sharing one pastor with lay ministers certified through the ACTS program to serve all congregations. The church designation indicates where the person has congregational membership.

Dave Raecke	May 16, 2009	Our Saviour, Warrenton
Dean Freeburn	October 18, 2009	Our Redeemer, Petersburg
Linda Roberts	March 14, 2010	St. Mark, Charlottesville
Barbara Krumm	April 18, 2010	St. John, Norfolk
Richard Hartman	April 25, 2010	Our Saviour, Norge
Joyce Moore	April 25, 2010	Our Saviour, Norge
Angela Dunn	June 5, 2010[3]	Mt. Rogers Parish, St. James, Chilhowie
Ellen Greene	June 5, 2010	St. Andrew, Portsmouth
Gail Penman	June 5, 2010	St. Timothy, Norfolk
Terri Larsen	June 5, 2010	Apostles, Gloucester
Don Stonesifer	June 5, 2010	St. Peter, Churchville
Sherrill Miller	June 5, 2010	St. Paul, Edinburg
Betty Jasmund	June 5, 2010	St. Peter, Stafford
Sara Kegley	June 5, 2010	Mt. Rogers Parish, St. James, Chilhowie
Diana Shane	June 5, 2010	Resurrection, Fredericksburg
Hank Tomlinson	June 5, 2010	St. Peters, Churchville
Thelma Shirley	June 13, 2010	Muhlenberg, Harrisonburg
Glen Dewire	June 20, 2010	Our Saviour, Richmond
Margaret Fleet	June 27, 2010	First, Norfolk
Sandy Croushore	July 4, 2010	St. Stephen, Williamsburg
Heidi Flatin	July 4, 2010	St. Stephen, Williamsburg
Bob Mullen	October 3, 2010	Emmanuel, Virginia Beach
Mark Merz	November 14, 2010	Mt. Rogers Parish, St. James, Chilhowie
Kristine Leafgreen	November 14, 2010	Mt. Rogers Parish, St. James, Chilhowie
Deb Meyers	June 4, 2011	Peace, Charlottesville
Peggy Malzi Bizjak	June 4, 2011	Peace, Charlottesville
Jewel Thomas	June 12, 2011	Apostles, Gloucester
Anne Collins	January 22, 2012	Our Saviour, Norge
Ann Charlton	April 15, 2012	St. Mark, Charlottesville
Helen Ida Moyer	April 15, 2012	St. Mark, Charlottesville
Carolyn Rader	April 15, 2012	St. Mark, Charlottesville
Karen Schmidt	April 15, 2012	St. Mark, Charlottesville
Mac McAlister	May 13, 2012	Messiah, Mechanicsville
Barbara Gaskill	May 13, 2012	Messiah, Mechanicsville

Mt. Rogers lay assistants on February 21, 2007. Front row (left to right): Kristine Steel Hughes, Pam Badin, Cindy Anders, May Hill, and Barbara Jones-Butcher. Second row (left to right): Bishop James Mauney, Sharon Compton, Angela Dunn, and Pastor Joe Shumate. Third row (left to right): Sarah Kegley and Mark Merz. This unique group of lay assistants was appointed by Bishop Mauney to preach and lead worship, under pastoral supervision, with ACTS certification as their training.

---

3. Certificates were normally awarded in one's home congregation but on June 5, 2010, the certificates were awarded at Synod Assembly.

Kristine Florio	May 13, 2012	Messiah, Mechanicsville
Sue G. Wymer	June 23, 2013	St. Stephen, Strasburg
Imogene Ryman	June 23, 2013	St. Stephen, Strasburg
Peggy Baseler	June 23, 2013	Emmanuel, Woodstock
Linda Meyer	November 3, 2013	Grace, Waynesboro
Stephenie Gregg	November 10, 2013	St. Mark, Yorktown
Jean Shafferman	November 10, 2013	St. Mark, Yorktown
Lola Heffner	December 1, 2013	Muhlenberg, Harrisonburg
Kathy Thompson	December 1, 2013	Muhlenberg, Harrisonburg
Dottie Self	December 15, 2013	Trinity, Newport News
Eugene McClurkin	May 4, 2014	St. Mark, Charlottesville
Russell Martin	July 13, 2014	St. Peter's, Stafford

Karren Light, Bethel, Winchester, was the first student to receive ACTS certification on October 24, 2004.

Appendix XVI: Synod Council Members and Officers

1988
Officers
Bishop Richard F. Bansemer
Leroy R. Hamlett, Jr., vice president
Clifton W. Anderson, secretary
Kathryn K. Buchanan, treasurer

Members
Robert Benne
Rev. Marshall F. Mauney
Kendra Brown
Rev. Susan L. Springer
Richard K. Gerlitz
Anne W. Ashby
George A. Kegley
Rev. James H. Bangle
Sue S. Lane
Frances Hammond
Rev. Willetta B. Heising
Rev. Mark W. Radecke
Betty Kipps

1989
Officers
Bishop Richard F. Bansemer
Leroy R. Hamlett, Jr., vice president
Clifton W. Anderson, secretary
Kathryn K. Buchanan, treasurer

Members
Rev. Willetta B. Heising
Frances Hammond
Betty Kipps
Rev. Mark W. Radecke
Rev. Marshall F. Mauney
Katherine Ashby
Rev. Susan L. Springer
Robert Benne
Anne W. Ashby
Humes J. Franklin, Jr.
Rev. James H. Bangle
George A. Kegley
Sue S. Lane

1990
Officers
Bishop Richard F. Bansemer
Leroy R. Hamlett, Jr., vice president
Clifton W. Anderson, secretary
Kathryn K. Buchanan, treasurer

Members
Anne W. Ashby
Humes J. Franklin, Jr.
Rev. James H. Bangle
George A. Kegley
Frances Hammond
Sue S. Lane
Rev. Mark W. Radecke
Rev. Conrad J. Christianson
Katherine Ashby
Rev. Frank C. Honeycutt
Robert Benne
Betty Kipps
Rev. Susan L. Springer

1991
Officers
Bishop Richard F. Bansemer
Leroy R. Hamlett, Jr., vice president
Clifton W. Anderson, secretary
Kathryn K. Buchanan, treasurer

Members
Katherine Ashby
Rev. Frank C. Honeycutt
Robert Benne
Betty Kipps
W. Ernest Boldin
Rev. Susan L. Springer
George A. Kegley
Anne W. Ashby
Sue S. Lane
Callister Dailey
Rev. Conrad J. Christianson, Jr.
Rev. W. Richard Fritz
Rev. Gary Schroeder

1992
Officers
Bishop Richard F. Bansemer
Leroy R. Hamlett, Jr., vice president
Clifton W. Anderson, secretary
Kathryn K. Buchanan, treasurer

Members
Rev. Conrad J. Christianson
Rachael Dietz
Rev. Frank C. Honeycutt
Rev. W. Richard Fritz, Jr.
Betty Kipps
Rev. Gary R. Schroeder
Rev. Susan L. Springer
W. Ernest Boldin
Anne W. Ashby
Martha Edwards
Callister Dailey
Joe Leafe
Mark Reed

1993
Officers
Bishop Richard F. Bansemer
Leroy R. Hamlett, Jr., vice president
Clifton W. Anderson, secretary
Kathryn K. Buchanan, treasurer

Members
Anne W. Ashby
Martha Edwards
Callister Dailey
Joe Leafe
Rachael Dietz
Mark Reed
Rev. W. Richard Fritz, Jr.
Rev. Steven M. Anderson
Rev. Gary R. Schroeder
Rev. Terry D. Clark
W. Ernest Boldin
Martha Miller
Rev. Linda S. Mitchell

1994
Officers
Bishop Richard F. Bansemer
Leroy R. Hamlett, Jr., vice president
Clifton W. Anderson, secretary
Kathryn Buchanan, treasurer

Members
W. Ernest Boldin
Rev. Murray Ann Ziegenfuss
Martha Edwards
Ruthie Covington
Joe Leafe

Callister Dailey
Mark Reed
Rev. Gary R. Schroeder
Rev. Richard M. Carbaugh
Rev. Robert R. Ward
Rev. Terry D. Clark
Brian Taminger
Martha Miller

1995
Officers
Bishop Richard F. Bansemer
Kathryn K. Buchanan, vice president
Mark N. Reed, secretary
Martha A. Edwards, acting treasurer

Members
Rev. Richard M. Carbaugh
Rev. Gary R. Schroeder
Rev. Terry D. Clark
Rev. Robert R. Ward
Martha Miller
Brian Taminger
Rev. Murray Ann Ziegenfuss
Diane Baun
Ruthie Covington
Martha Edwards
Callister Dailey
Josiah Tlou
James Wilson

1996
Officers
Bishop Richard Bansemer
Kathryn K. Buchanan, vice president
Mark N. Reed, secretary
Martha A. Edwards, treasurer

Members
Ruthie Covington
Bill Smith
Callister Dailey
Mary P. Hartman
Rev. Gary R. Schroeder
Rev. W. Arthur Lewis
Rev. Robert R. Ward
Rev. Terry D. Clark
Brian Taminger

Jackie Bourque
Diane Baun
Rev. Murray Ziegenfuss
James F. Wilson

1997
Officers
Bishop Richard F. Bansemer
Kathryn K. Buchanan, vice president
Mark N. Reed, secretary
Martha A. Edwards, treasurer

Members
Diane Baun
Rev. Murray Ann Ziegenfuss
James F. Wilson
Rev. Robert R. Ward
Bill Smith
Judy Ann Fray
Mary P. Hartman
Rev. Larry A. Shoberg
Rev. W. Arthur Lewis
James Sheets
Rev. Terry D. Clark
Aaron Freid
Jackie Bourque

1998
Officers
Bishop Richard F. Bansemer
Kathryn K. Buchanan, vice president
Mark N. Reed, secretary
Martha A. Edwards, treasurer

Members
Rev. Judith Cobb
Rev. Larry A. Shoberg
Rev. Terry D. Clark
James Sheets
Jackie Bourque
Aaron Freid
Rev. Murray Ann Ziegenfuss
Janice Bunting
Rev. Robert R. Ward
James Wilson
Judy Ann Fray
Bill Smith
Judyth Timm

1999
Officers
Bishop James F. Mauney
Kathryn K. Buchanan
Mark N. Reed, secretary
Martha A. Edwards, treasurer

Members
Rev. Robert R. Ward
Bill Smith
Judy Ann Fray
Judyth Timm
Rev. Larry A. Shoberg
Rev. Judith Cobb
James Sheets
Betty Jean Fawcett
Janice Bunting
Rev. Sharon Israel
James F. Wilson
Rev. George Sims

2000
Officers
Bishop James F. Mauney
Kathryn K. Buchanan, vice president
Mark N. Reed, secretary
Martha A. Edwards, treasurer

Members
Janice Bunting
Rev. Sharon Israel
James Wilson
Rev. George Sims
Bill Smith
Judy Ann Fray
Judyth Timm
James Sheets
Rev. J. Christopher Price
Rev. Linda Mitchell
Betty Jean Fawcett
Rev. James Utt

2001
Officers
Bishop James F. Mauney
Kathryn K. Buchanan, vice president
Mark N. Reed, secretary
Martha Edwards, treasurer

Members
Rev. J. Christopher Price
Rev. Linda Mitchell
Betty Jean Fawcett
Rev. James Utt
Rev. George L. Sims
W. Martin Paulson
Rev. Robert F. Humphrey
Janice Bunting
Judy Ann Fray
Connie Koiner

2002
Officers
Bishop James F. Mauney
Kathryn K. Buchanan, vice president
Mark N. Reed, secretary
Martha Edwards, treasurer

Members
Judy Ann Fray
Connie Koiner
Rev. Linda Mitchell
Brian Taminger
Rev. James Utt
Betty Jean Fawcett
James Sheets
Rev. William Nabers
W. Martin Paulson
Rev. Christopher Price
Janice Bunting
Rev. Karen Van Stee

2003
Officers
Bishop James F. Mauney
Mark N. Reed, vice president
Patricia Morgan, secretary
Martha A. Edwards, treasurer

Members
Janice Bunting
Rev. Christopher Price
Connie Koiner
Rev. Karen Van Stee
W. Martin Paulson
Rev. James Kniseley
Brian Taminger

Lynda L. McConnell
Betty Jean Fawcett
Judge Charles Poston
Rev. G. William Nabers
Rev. James Utt

2004
Officers
Bishop James F. Mauney
Mark N. Reed, vice president
Patricia Morgan, secretary
Adolph Moller, treasurer

Members
Betty Jean Fawcett
Judge Charles Poston
Rev. G. William Nabers
Rev. James Utt
Rev. J. Christopher Price
Janet Gomez
Rev. Karen Van Stee
W. Martin Paulson
Rev. James C. Kniseley
Elizabeth Smythe
Lynda L. McConnell
James Stensvaag

2005
Officers
Bishop James F. Mauney
Mark N. Reed, vice president
Patricia Morgan, secretary
Adolph Moller, treasurer

Members
Patty Franz
Elizabeth Smythe
Rev. James C. Kniseley
James Stensvaag
Judge Charles Poston
Patrice T. Arthur
Rev. James Utt
Rev. Paul Henrickson
Janet Gomez
Rev. William Nabers
W. Martin Paulson
Rev. Karen Van Stee

2006
Officers
Bishop James F. Mauney
Mark N. Reed, vice president
Patricia Morgan, secretary
Adolph Moller, treasurer

Members
Janet Gomez
Rev. William Nabers
W. Martin Paulson
Rev. Karen Van Stee
Elizabeth Smythe
Patty Franz
James Stensvaag
Rev. James Kniseley
Patrice T. Arthur
Judge Charles Poston
Rev. R. Paul Henrickson
Rev. Meredith Williams

2007
Officers
Bishop James F. Mauney
Judge Charles Poston, vice president
Janet Gomez, secretary
Adolph Moller, treasurer

Members
Patrice T. Arthur
Rev. James Kniseley
Rev. R. Paul Henrickson
Rev. Meredith Williams
Rev. G. William Nabers
Charles Downs, Jr.
Rev. Karen Van Stee
Jane Nicholson, AIM
Ryan Sullivan
Elizabeth Smythe
Patty Franz
James Stensvaag

2008
Officers
Bishop James F. Mauney
Judge Charles Poston, vice president
Janet Gomez, secretary
George "Skip" Zubrod, treasurer

Members
Patty Franz
Elizabeth Smythe
Rev. James C. Kniseley
James Stensvaag
Rev. Meredith Williams
Patrice T. Arthur, AIM
Lucas Hakkenberg
Rev. David Derrick
Charles Downs, Jr.
Rev. Paul Henrickson
Jane Nicholson, AIM
Rev. Patricia Nabers

2009
Officers
Bishop James F. Mauney
Judge Charles Poston, vice president
Janet Gomez, secretary
George "Skip" Zubrod, treasurer

Members
Patty Franz
Elizabeth Smythe
Rev. James C. Kniseley
James Stensvaag
Rev. Meredith Williams
Patrice Arthur, AIM
Lucas Hakkenberg
Rev. David Derrick
Charles Downs, Jr.
Rev. Paul Henrickson
Jane Nicholson, AIM
Rev. Patricia Nabers

2010
Officers
Bishop James F. Mauney
Judge Charles Poston, vice president
Janet Gomez, secretary
George "Skip" Zubrod, treasurer

Members
Charles Downs, Jr.
Rev. David Derrick
Jane Nicholson, AIM
Rev. Paul Henrickson
Elizabeth Smythe
Rev. Patricia Nabers

James Stensvaag
Patty Franz
Lucas Hakkenberg
Rev. Meredith Williams
Patrice Arthur, AIM
Rev. John Wertz, Jr.

2011
Officers
Bishop James F. Mauney
Judge Charles Poston, vice president
Janet Gomez, secretary
George "Skip" Zubrod, treasurer

Members
Dana Cornett
Rev. Meredith Williams
Rev. David Derrick
Rev. John Wertz, Jr.
Rev. R. Paul Henrickson
Rose Stevens Booker
Rev. Patricia Nabers
Jackie Bourque
Patty Franz
Charles Downs, Jr.
John Stover II
Linus Ellis, AIM

2012
Officers
Bishop James F. Mauney
Judge Charles Poston, vice president
Janet Gomez, secretary
George "Skip" Zubrod, treasurer

Members
Patty Franz
Charles Downs, Jr.
John Stover II
Linus Ellis, AIM
Rev. Meredith Williams
Dana Cornett
Rev. John Wertz, Jr.
Rev. David Derrick
Rose Stevens Booker
Rev. Cathy Mims
Jackie Bourque
Rev. Patricia Nabers

Synod Council Officers

Leroy Hamlett
Vice President, 1988–1995

Clifton Anderson
Secretary, 1988–1995

Kathryn Buchanan
Treasurer, 1988–1995
Vice President, 1995–2003

Mark Reed
Secretary, 1995–2003
Vice President, 2003–2007

Martha Edwards
Treasurer, 1995–2004

Patricia Morgan
Secretary, 2003–2007

Adolph Moller
Treasurer, 2004–2008

Judge Charles Poston
Vice President, 2007–

Janet Gomez
Secretary, 2007–

George "Skip" Zubrod
Treasurer, 2008–

Appendix XVII: Ordained/Rostered Leaders Statistics

	1988	2012
Total Ordained/Rostered Leaders	200	262
Total Retired	34 (17%)	97 (37%)
Men, Retired	34	92
Women, Retired	0	5
Total Active	166	165
Men, Active	157 (95%)	114 (69%)
Women, Active	9 (5%)	51 (31%)

Appendix XVIII: Distribution of Congregations By Size

	1988 Total	%	2012 Total	%
Very Small (1-175)	73	45.34	86	55.84
Small (176-350)	44	27.32	35	22.75
Moderately Small (350-500)	19	11.8	11	7.14
Medium (501-700)	11	6.83	9	5.84
Moderately Large (700-950)	13	8.07	5	3.25
Large (951-1,500)			6	3.9
Very Large (1,500+)				

Appendix XIX: Worship Attendance Statistics

	1988	2012
Total Weekly Attendance	14,226	12,884
Average Weekly Worship Attendance	90	84
Baptized Members Attending	33.33%	35.70%

Appendix XX: Baptized Members By Congregation Size

	1988 Total	%	2012 Total	%
Very Small (1-175)	6,189	14.5	6,698	18.56
Small (176-350)	11,586	27.14	8,776	24.32
Moderately Small (350-500)	7,917	18.55	4,916	13.63
Medium (501-700)	8,753	15.82	5,268	14.6
Moderately Large (700-950)	10,231	23.9	3,819	10.5
Large (951-1,500)			6,610	18.32
Very Large (1,500+)				

Appendix XXI: Baptisms By Year

	Children	Adults (16 and older)
1988	691	101
1989	738	105
1990	754	105
1991	752	146
1992	679	87
1993	695	110
1994	739	109
1995	731	117
1996	694	99
1997	684	102
1998	687	93
1999	692	110
2000	611	101
2001	633	130
2002	547	84
2003	526	103
2004	527	100
2005	518	108
2006	549	89
2007	512	75
2008	463	68
2009	431	68
2010	438	62
2011	396	45
2012	439	72
Totals	15,126	2,389

Total   17,515

Appendix XXII: Membership Analysis[1]

1988
Congregations Reporting Ethnic Group Members and Percentage of Congregations

White	154	95.65%
Native American	7	4.34%
Black	27	16.77%
Asian/Pacific Islander	35	21.73%
Hispanic/Spanish	17	10.55%
Other	8	4.96%

Total Ethnic Baptized Membership and Percentage of Total Membership

White	41,152	96.42%
White Hispanic	35	0.08%
Native American	19	0.04%
Native American Hispanic		0.00%
Black	148	0.34%
Black Hispanic	7	0.01%
Asian/Pacific Islander	134	0.31%
Asian/Pacific Islander Hispanic	1	0.00%
Other	20	0.04%
Other Hispanic	2	0.00%

2012
Congregations Reporting Ethnic Active Participants and Percentage of Congregations

African American/Black	45	29.22%
African National/African Caribbean	8	5.19%
American Indian/Alaska Native	6	3.90%
Arab/Middle Eastern	10	6.49%
Asian/Pacific Islander	38	24.68%
Latino/Hispanic	38	24.68%
Multi-racial	41	26.62%
White/Caucasian	152	95.74%
Other	4	2.60%

Total Ethnic Active Participants and Percentage of Total Active Participants

African American/Black	378	1.32%
African National/African Caribbean	25	0.09%
American Indian/Alaska Native	10	0.03%
Arab/Middle Eastern	72	0.25%
Asian/Pacific Islander	175	0.61%
Latino/Hispanic	249	0.87
Multi-racial	306	1.06%
White/Caucasian	27,520	95.74%
Other	9	0.03%

---

1. Office of the Secretary, Evangelical Lutheran Church in America, Form A, Summary of Congregational Statistics, as reported by those congregations submitting parochial reports for the years 1988 (153) and 2012 (95).

INDEX

Subject Index

20/20 Vision Goals, 121
2009 Churchwide Assembly of the ELCA, 167

A

A Call into Covenant, 193
Ambassadors Community for Theological Study (ACTS), 142, 143, 294
Ambassadors Community for Theological Study (ACTS) Certificates Awarded, 302
Ambassadors Community for Theological Study (ACTS) Courses, 294
Ambassadors for Christ, 120, 121, 122, 123, 124, 127, 132, 143, 144, 146, 147, 149, 154, 171, 173, 291, 296, 297
American Lutheran Church (ALC), 18, 21, 34, 187, 200, 210, 248, 260, 261
Apostles, Gloucester, 53, 145, 148, 155, 239, 300, 302, 303
Ascension, Danville, 15, 22, 26, 253, 320
Associates in Ministry, 67, 90, 91, 102, 105, 160, 300
Association for Evangelical Lutheran Churches (AELC), 271

B

Ballots for Bishop, 18, 41, 45, 46, 47, 48, 49, 95, 107, 108, 110, 111, 112, 113
Baptism, Eucharist, and Ministry, 191
Baptisms By Year, 312
Baptized Members By Congregation Size, 312
Bedford Mission, Bedford, 183, 251, 252, 254
Beth Eden, Luray, 236, 237
Bethany, Columbia Furnace, 199
Bethany, Lexington, 263
Bethel, Edinburg, 199
Bethel, Winchester, 234, 299, 302, 304
Bethlehem, Luray, 237
Bethlehem, Lynchburg, 23, 253, 286
Bethlehem, Waynesboro, 269, 270
Bishop Bansemer Retirement, 108, 113
Bishop's Representatives, 62, 63
Brandon Oaks, 179, 259, 298, 299
Bridgebuilders, 8, 137, 139, 140, 161, 162

C

Called to Common Mission, 191, 195
Called to Integrity—Called to Be a Safe Place, 105
Campus Ministry, 9, 28, 37, 92, 98, 124, 127, 129, 174, 187, 188, 189, 190, 194, 195, 211, 225, 232, 249, 261, 263
Candidacy Committee, 95, 116, 151
Care of Spouses—Luncheons and Retreats, 89
Care of the Call/Care of the Soul, 91, 92, 102
Caroline Furnace Lutheran Camp and Retreat Center, 76, 132, 178
Celebration Art, 87, 117, 149
Central Valley Conference, 133, 198, 203, 206
Central, Burke's Garden, 218, 219, 220
Chaplain Service of the Churches of Virginia, 29, 30, 76, 177
Chief Ecumenical Officer, 192
Christ the King, Richmond, 23, 31, 34, 41, 182, 248, 292
Christ, Fredericksburg, 23, 27, 97, 213, 286, 287
Christ, Radford, 22, 63, 117, 232
Christ, Richmond, 57, 155, 247, 303
Christ, Roanoke, 256, 286, 287, 300
Christ, Staunton, 267, 268, 300
Christ, Wise, 244, 303
Clergy Misconduct, 104, 106, 114
College, Salem, 28, 259, 289
Commission for a New Lutheran Church (CNLC), 21, 23, 36, 39
Communications Task Group, 33, 96
Companion Synod, 79, 79, 80, 82, 83, 119, 151, 152, 153, 154, 155, 156, 181, 228, 254

Concordat of Agreement, 195
Congregations Closing or Leaving, 300
Congregations Contributed and Received, 34
Conscience-bound Belief, 168, 169
Constitutional and Legal Task Group, 26, 39
Constituting Convention Task Group, 24, 25
Council of Deans, 38, 63, 72, 74, 75, 101

D

Day of the Ministerium, 124, 156, 157
Deans, 12, 37, 38, 59, 62, 63, 72, 74, 75, 101, 109, 113, 117, 119, 123, 124, 135, 164
Diaconal Minister for Healthy Leadership and Wellness, 161
Director of Youth and Young Adult Ministries, 127, 129, 130
Disaffiliate Congregations, 171
Disaster Response, 134, 184, 195, 271
Distribution of Congregations By Size, 311

E

Eastern District of the American Lutheran Church, 34, 210
Ebenezer, Marion, 53, 63, 87, 97, 221, 296, 303
Ecumenical Relationships, 174, 190, 198
Ecumenical Representative, 192, 196, 197
Emanuel, Woodstock, 86, 201, 208
Emmanuel, Virginia Beach, 149, 276, 285, 287, 304
Emphases in Our Life Together, 173
Epiphany, Richmond, 64, 138, 148, 153, 157, 249, 299, 302
Evangelical Lutheran Church in Papua New Guinea (ELC-PNG), 79, 81, 84, 119, 151, 281

F

Faith Formation, 67, 114, 123, 130, 146, 147, 150, 151, 235, 238, 244, 272
Faith, Fort Valley, 200
Faith, Staunton, 268
Faith, Suffolk, 276, 287, 300
Faith, Whitetop, 221, 223, 302
Finance Task Group, 28
Finances Contributed and Received, 35
First Call, 57, 124, 128, 142, 156, 159, 162, 242
First English, Richmond, 23, 24, 50, 249, 286
First, Norfolk, 63, 97, 148, 157, 272, 286, 303
First, Portsmouth, 53, 274
From Transition to Formation, 35

G

Gathering of the Ministerium, 150, 157, 158, 159, 160
Germanna Conference, 209
Glade Creek, Blue Ridge, 23, 63, 85, 86, 252
Gladesboro, Carroll County, 230
Global Missions Committee (GMC), 78, 79, 80, 81, 82, 83, 116, 151, 152, 153, 154, 155
Gloria Dei, Hampton, 151, 240, 287, 295
Good Shepherd, Front Royal, 232, 233, 287
Good Shepherd, Galax, 230
Good Shepherd, Lexington, 64, 263
Good Shepherd, Orange, 215
Good Shepherd, Virginia Beach, 145, 148, 277
Grace and Glory, Palmyra, 129, 212, 300
Grace, Chesapeake, 34, 63, 271
Grace, Franklin, 271
Grace, Luray, 236, 237
Grace, Waynesboro, 23, 29, 41, 50, 64, 138, 143, 144, 147, 148, 155, 165, 269, 285, 286, 287, 295, 304
Grace, Winchester, 11, 14, 15, 16, 22, 23, 29, 64, 115, 133, 138, 235, 261, 299, 320
Gravel Springs, Star Tannery, 233

314 † Journey Together

H

Headquarters Site and Staffing Task Group, 31
Healthy Congregations, 119, 137, 138, 139, 140, 141, 142, 146, 147, 159, 161, 162, 163
Healthy Starts, 141
Hebron, Madison, 64, 140, 215
Highland Conference, 60, 218
Historical Sketches of Congregations by Conference, 14, 198
Holy Advent, Lebanon, and St. Luke, Walker Mountain, 222
Holy Communion, Portsmouth, 275
Holy Trinity, Lynchburg, 155, 251, 254, 302
Holy Trinity, Martinsville, 255, 285
Holy Trinity, Wytheville, 63, 87, 117, 224, 299
Human Sexuality—Gift and Trust, 167
Hungry Mother Retreat Center, 30

I

Immanuel, Bluefield, West Virginia, 219, 220
Inclusiveness and Minorities Ministries Committee, 93
Installation of Bishop Bansemer, 60, 61
Installation of Bishop Mauney, 117
Institutions, Agencies, and Social Ministry Organizations Task Group, 27, 29
Islands District of the Evangelical Lutheran Church in Papua New Guinea (ELC-PNG), 79, 81, 84, 151, 281

J

Joint Declaration of Justification, 195, 231

L

Lakeside, Littleton, North Carolina, 245, 300
LARCUM Covenant, 193
Lifelong, Monogamous, Same-gender Relationships, 168, 169, 170
Living Water, Kilmarnock, 86, 242, 300
Lost and Found, 55, 125, 126, 128, 130, 131, 262
Luther League, 66, 125
Luther Memorial, Blacksburg, 115, 225
Lutheran Campus Ministry, 187, 189, 190, 211, 225
Lutheran Church in America (LCA), 18, 20, 125, 186, 187, 259
Lutheran Council of Tidewater, 30, 75, 132, 145, 180, 276, 297
Lutheran Family Services of Virginia (LFS/VA), 30, 61, 66, 67, 71, 72, 75, 89, 100, 101, 124, 132, 138, 140, 177, 178, 184, 235, 246, 272
Lutheran Partners in Mission (LPM), 135, 136, 137
Lutheran Theological Southern Seminary, 28, 51, 59, 63, 72, 74, 76, 88, 118, 132, 133, 151, 157, 158, 175, 272, 289, 290, 293, 294, 320
Lutheran World Federation, 182, 193, 195
Lutheran Youth Organization (LYO), 116, 119, 125, 126, 127, 128, 129, 153
Lutheran, Anglican, and Roman Catholic (LARC), 59, 193, 211
Lutheran, Anglican, Roman Catholic, and United Methodist (LARCUM), 192, 193, 194, 196, 270
Lutheran-Episcopal Day, 196

M

Martin Luther, Bergton, 34, 198, 287
Massanetta Summer Assembly, 58, 65, 86, 125
Melanchthon Chapel, Weyers Cave, 270
Members Contributed and Received, 35
Membership Analysis, 313
Messiah, Mechanicsville, 246, 287, 303, 304
Metropolitan Washington, DC Synod, 22, 34, 35, 36, 56, 64, 136, 188, 193
Ministerium Covenant, 296
Ministerium Team, 158, 159, 160, 162
Ministry Program Agencies, 30
Mission Office for Planned Giving, 124, 131, 132, 133, 134, 135, 136, 235
Morning Star, Luray, 237
Mt. Calvary, Mt. Jackson, 201
Mt. Nebo, Rochelle, 216, 286
Mt. Tabor, Middlebrook, 264
Mt. Zion, New Market, 200, 203, 205
Mt. Zion, Woodstock, 209, 302
Muhlenberg, Harrisonburg, 23, 28, 31, 64, 129, 261, 286, 287, 303, 304, 305

N

National Lutheran Communities and Services, 134, 176, 235
National Lutheran Home, 30, 73, 74, 75, 76, 132, 176, 204
Necrology, 301
New Congregations Received, 300
New Leaders Orientation, 122, 124, 142, 150, 157, 163
New Mt. Olive, Rockbridge, 267
New Mt. Zion, Blacksburg, 225
New River Conference, 225
Nominating Task Group, 24, 33
Nominations for Constituting Convention, 41
Northern Valley Conference, 232, 233, 320
Number of Virginia Synod Congregations, 299

O

Office of the Bishop-East, 14, 87, 101, 114, 150
Officers of the Synod, 14, 44, 116, 132
Ordained Ministers in Special Situations, 297
Ordained/Rostered Leaders Statistics, 311
Our Redeemer, Petersburg, 247, 303
Our Saviour, Christiansburg, 227
Our Saviour, Norge, 244, 287, 303
Our Saviour, Richmond, 129, 148, 155, 184, 250, 302, 303
Our Saviour, Virginia Beach, 278
Our Saviour, Warrenton, 144, 145, 217, 303
Outdoor Ministry, 30, 37, 40, 181, 228, 229

P

Page Conference, 236
Pastoral Leadership Consulting Groups, 141
Patmos, Woodstock, 209
Peace, Charlottesville, 22, 44, 64, 184, 210, 302, 303
Pectoral Cross, 117, 118
Peninsula Conference, 239
Pleasant View, Augusta County, 268
Porter-Hess Fund, 81, 139
Power in the Spirit, 53, 80, 82, 84, 85, 86, 87, 88, 93, 101, 114, 145, 147, 149, 150, 155, 174, 289, 292
Power in the Spirit Programs and Leaders, 289
Prince of Peace, Orkney Springs/Basye, 204

R

Rader, Timberville, 206
Redeemer, Bristol, 219
Redeemer, McKinley, 264
Redeemer, Pearisburg, 231, 300
Reformation, New Market, 64, 133, 201, 204, 286
Reformation, Newport News, 149, 150, 242, 285
Region 8 or Region 9, 39
Region 9 Center for Mission, 59, 97, 184, 187
Report and Recommendation on Ministry Policies, 167
Responses to the Issues of Human Sexuality, 163
Resurrection, Fredericksburg, 53, 214, 300, 303
Richmond Conference, 245
Roanoke College, 11, 15, 18, 25, 28, 31, 32, 36, 50, 54, 56, 63, 70, 71, 72, 73, 74, 75, 76, 79, 82, 83, 84, 85, 86, 87, 90, 97, 102, 110, 122, 132, 136, 149, 153, 155, 157, 166, 173, 174, 182, 185, 188, 231, 245, 264, 281, 282, 289, 292, 296, 297
Roots & Wings, 146, 148, 149, 150, 151

S

Salem, Mt. Sidney, 129, 265, 287, 302
Seventh Day, 126, 214, 236, 262
Shepherd of the Valley, Dayton, 79, 153, 260
Shiloh, Blacksburg, 226
Social Ministry Organizations, 27, 29, 30, 36, 62, 67, 71, 73, 77, 78, 134
Solomon, Mt. Jackson, 201
Southern Conference, 251
Southern Valley Conference, 260
Special Financial Appeals, 71, 72, 74, 93
St. Andrew, Portsmouth, 275, 303
St. Jacob's-Spaders, Mt. Crawford, 266
St. Jacob's/Zion, Edinburg, 199
St. James, Chilhowie, 87, 220, 223
St. James, Fishersville, 261, 269
St. James, Hudson Crossroads, Mt. Jackson, 202
St. John, Abingdon, 129, 218
St. John, Norfolk, 273, 295, 303
St. John, Singers Glen, 183
St. John, Timberville, 207
St. John's, Winchester, 236
St. Luke, Culpeper, 212, 287
St. Luke, Richmond, 64, 149, 166, 250, 299
St. Luke, Stanley, 64, 238, 239
St. Luke, Woodstock, 209
St. Mark, Charlottesville, 23, 26, 44, 50, 85, 129, 211, 225, 285, 299, 303, 304
St. Mark, Forestville, Quicksburg, 200
St. Mark, Luray, 64, 97, 149, 237
St. Mark, Willis, Floyd-Willis, 154, 229

St. Mark, Yorktown, 128, 245, 304
St. Mark's, Roanoke, 257, 285
St. Martin, New Market, Quicksburg, 200, 205
St. Mary's Pine, Mt. Jackson, 202
St. Matthew, Konnarock, 221, 223
St. Matthew, Red Oak, and Sharon, Bland, 218
St. Matthew, Toms Brook, 203, 208
St. Michael, Blacksburg, 63, 148, 154, 155, 226
St. Michael, Virginia Beach, 145, 279
St. Paul and Grace, Rural Retreat, 222
St. Paul, Hampton, 53, 101, 302
St. Paul, Jerome, 201
St. Paul, Mount Solon, 266
St. Paul, Shenandoah, 155, 238, 239
St. Paul, Strasburg, 90, 149, 166, 205, 299, 302
St. Paul, Timberville, 206, 207
St. Peter, Churchville, 145, 260, 303
St Peter, Shenandoah, 22, 238, 239
St. Peter, Toms Brook, 206, 207, 287, 299
St. Peter's, Stafford, 148, 216, 302, 304
St. Philip, Roanoke, 149, 159, 255, 257
St. Stephen, Strasburg, 206, 208, 304
St. Stephen, Williamsburg, 50, 166, 244, 281, 285, 287, 303

St. Thomas, Bealeton, 209, 300
St. Timothy, Norfolk, 63, 273, 303
St. Timothy, Vinton, 259
Statistical Realities, 33, 35
Strategy 2000, 96, 97, 98, 99, 100, 101, 102, 103, 108, 110, 113, 114, 122, 124, 127, 131, 132, 166
Synod Council Members and Officers, 304, 310
Synod Functions and Activities Task Group, 32, 37
Synod Trust Fund for Mission, 67, 69, 70, 132
Synodical Minister for Christian Formation, 150

T

That Christ May Be Seen, 96, 99, 100, 102, 103, 109, 110, 113, 114, 166, 296
The Need for Church to Be a Safe Place, 103
Tidewater Conference, 79, 114, 130, 271
Transition Team, 13, 15, 19, 21, 22, 23, 24, 25, 26, 27, 28, 29, 30, 31, 32, 33, 34, 35, 36, 37, 38, 39, 40, 41, 45, 46, 54, 96
Transition Team Members, 22, 23
Trinity Ecumenical Parish, Moneta, 90, 194, 255
Trinity Lutheran Seminary, 74, 75, 289, 291, 293
Trinity, Keezletown, 262

Trinity, Newport News, 23, 31, 64, 79, 138, 149, 154, 166, 243, 285, 304
Trinity, Pulaski, 80, 86, 231, 286
Trinity, Roanoke, 258
Trinity, Stephens City, 234
Trust Fund for Mission, 67, 68, 69, 70, 102, 121, 131, 132

U

United Lutheran Appeal, 71, 76, 77, 78, 135, 136, 137, 216, 241, 267, 288
United Lutheran Appeal, First Year Report of Response By Conference, 288
United Lutheran Appeal, Response By Year, 288
United Lutheran Church in America (ULCA), 11, 15, 66, 125, 244, 263, 278

V

Virginia Council of Churches, 30, 59, 192, 195
Virginia Ecumenical Groups, 30
Virginia Lutheran Homes (VLH), 73, 75, 132, 136, 179, 297
Virginia Lutheran Men in Mission (VLMM), 182, 183, 184
Virginia Synod Assembly Themes, 296
Virginia Synod Homes, 71
Virginia Synod Ordinations, 285
Virginia Synod Statistics, 284

Virginia Synodical Women's Organization (VSWO), 81, 155, 156, 181, 182

W

Walker Mountain Parish, Wythe County, 86, 222, 225
Welcoming Traditional Lutherans Resolution, 172
West Virginia-Western Maryland Synod, 22, 34, 35
Wheatland, Buchanan, 252, 286
Winter Celebration, 55, 115, 125, 126, 128, 262
World Hunger Appeal, 61, 70, 204
Worship Attendance Statistics, 311

Y

Youth Ministry, 24, 33, 40, 65, 66, 92, 93, 125, 126, 127, 128, 130, 131, 194, 196, 204, 205, 207, 232, 242, 279
Youth Ministry Task Group, 33
Youth-to-Youth Project, 119, 153, 154

Z

Zion, Cripple Creek, 220
Zion, Floyd, Floyd-Willis, 149, 154, 155, 228
Zion, Waynesboro, 148, 269, 270

Name Index

A

Addison, Floyd, 74, 75, 135, 180, 254, 297
Agner, Chris, 192
Ahern, Renee, 74, 75
Albright, Kenneth, 213
Almen, Lowell G., 110, 112
Anderson, Clif, 14, 22, 23, 42, 44, 74, 75, 112, 304, 305, 310
Anderson, David W., 148
Anderson, H. George, 117, 118, 165, 289, 291
Anderson, Linda, 236, 237, 286
Anderson, Tim, 257
Armentrout, James L., 224, 225, 255, 257, 286
Arthur, Patrice, 207, 208, 246, 287, 299, 301, 308, 309
Ashby, Anne, 45, 73, 74, 304, 305
Ashby, Margaret, 269, 287
Atkinson, Barbara, 182
Atkinson, Harvey, 86, 124, 222, 223, 225, 287
Austin, A.G. "Chip", 243

B

Backer, Rosemary, 253, 254, 286, 292
Bailey, Clayton, 273
Ballance, William "Bill", 201, 202
Ballard, Richard, 53
Ballard, Ruby, 53
Ballentine, Andrew W., 212, 244, 276, 281
Bang, Charles, 151, 221, 241
Bangle, James H., 42, 45, 47, 63, 111, 218, 221, 304, 305
Bansemer, Andrew, 117, 184, 221, 287
Bansemer, David C., 60
Bansemer, Richard F., 7, 13, 14, 18, 23, 31, 32, 46, 47, 48, 49, 51, 57, 60, 61, 67, 74, 103, 107, 109, 110, 112, 118, 183, 193, 200, 207, 222, 224, 226, 230, 232, 236, 258, 266, 273, 279, 281, 285, 290, 293, 297, 304, 305, 306
Bansemer, Ronald W., 60
Bartholomew, Tracie L., 64, 257, 263, 285
Barton, Raymond, 193

Baseler, James, 44, 64, 158, 203, 206, 215
Batka, Lubo, 222
Batman, Richard, 276
Batterman, William, 46, 247, 268, 275
Beasley, Helen, 230
Beaver, Gordon, 85, 289
Beaver, Grady, 231
Bechdolt, Lynn, 111, 112, 199, 233, 236, 255, 285
Becker, Marcia, 189
Behlendorf, Jack, 241, 244
Behr, David, 15
Bengston, John W., 64, 184, 251
Benne, Robert "Bob", 43, 45, 85, 87, 88, 174, 289, 295, 304, 305
Benson, Babs, 276
Benson, David, 190
Benson, Scott, 158, 201, 202, 276
Beyer, Steve, 53, 274
Blackwelder, Till, 83
Blalock, James P., 272
Bland, Richard M., 46, 200, 205, 218
Blansett, Ray, 87
Bohannon, Stephen, 213, 248
Bohm, Robert K., 206

Boldin, William "Bill", 63, 110, 111, 119, 239, 291, 297
Bollinger, Larry, 222
Boschen, Henry "Hank", 86, 111, 116, 253, 254
Bosserman, Elmer, 46, 212, 301
Bosserman, Thomas L., 23, 31, 32, 46, 47, 48, 64, 111, 138, 166, 243, 249
Bost, Raymond, 186
Bouknight, Anna Rose, 90
Bouknight, Philip, 148, 155, 229, 256, 287, 293
Bouknight, Tara, 90, 293
Bourque, Jackie, 185, 306, 309
Bowman, Kenneth, 64, 236, 237
Boynton, Deanna, 203, 206, 208, 217, 287
Boynton, Jonathan, 203, 206, 208, 235, 287
Bozeman, Jean, 8, 14, 65, 66, 67, 73, 85, 87, 88, 89, 90, 93, 94, 100, 101, 102, 105, 106, 107, 110, 114, 116, 119, 123, 124, 142, 143, 144, 145, 146, 147, 148, 150, 184, 224, 247, 276, 297, 302, 320
Braaten, Conrad A., 232

Bradshaw, Larry, 176
Brady, James, 247
Brandt, Curtis H., 243, 301
Branham, Mack C., 176
Braswell, James, 201
Braun, Lance, 64, 189, 190, 208, 217, 233, 236, 266, 268, 297
Briehl, Gregory John, 46, 210, 211, 260
Briehl, Pamela, 90
Broker, Rod, 256
Brooks, David, 215, 216, 286
Browder, Richard, 276
Brown, Genie, 56
Brown, Janette, 56
Brown, Janice, 182
Brown, Keith, 7, 14, 23, 24, 28, 42, 44, 55, 56, 58, 62, 73, 93, 94, 114, 116, 119, 127, 129, 186
Brown, Mary Louise, 209, 233, 287
Brown, Sabra, 56
Bruns, Roger, 248
Buchanan, Kathryn, 11, 14, 56, 69, 74, 75, 87, 88, 97, 102, 116, 117, 157, 185, 304, 305, 306, 307, 310
Buchholz, Dennis, 272, 275
Bugg, Garrett, 240, 241
Bullock, Cynthia Happel, 250
Bumstead, Heather, 263, 267, 285
Bunn, JoAnn K., 64, 231, 239, 264, 265
Bunting, Crystal, 83
Burke, Michael, 279
Burke, Wayne, 148
Burnette, Harold, 83, 201, 224, 285
Burnish, Jim, 184
Burr, William, 202
Burton, Daphne, 297
Busch, Robert, 260
Byerly, John F., Jr., 8, 49, 64, 65, 119, 250, 301

C

Caldwell, Clarence, 18
Campbell, Brian, 219, 225
Carbaugh, Richard, 27, 46, 97, 111
Carlson, Duane H., 22
Carlson, Lauren T., 272
Carlson, Paul J., 272
Carlstadt, Rhoda, 82
Carmichael, Standrod, 230
Carpenter, Mac, 222
Carr, Christopher, 265, 266
Casteele, Judy, 182
Chaffee, Brian, 222
Chapman, Peg, 117
Chappell, Melissa, 218, 220
Chell, Bob, 189
Chelton, Ronald K., 43, 210, 211
Chenoweth, Gary C., 219
Childers, Eric, 270
Chilstrom, Herbert W., 58, 60, 67
Christian, Paul T., 247
Christianson, Conrad, 47, 234
Chudd, Donald, 244
Clark, Sue, 62, 85, 185, 299
Clark, Terry D., 18, 276, 297, 305, 306
Clough, Grace, 129
Cobb, James G., 63, 272
Cobb, Judith Ann, 272, 286, 299, 306, 307
Cobb, Marion, 208
Coffey, Wade, 263, 267
Connelly, James, 85, 289
Conradt-Eberlin, Paul, 214
Cooper, John, 221
Cooper, Mark, 160, 297
Copenhaver, W. Eugene, 220
Costa, Kate, 212
Costie, Jim, 184
Covington, Patricia, 238, 239, 287
Cox, Carol, 23, 32
Crout, Tim, 184
Crump, Amy, 203
Crumpton, Kenneth, 26, 46, 251, 297, 301

D

Dailey, Callister, 18, 43, 60, 305, 306
Daley, James "Jim", 203, 206, 236, 239
Danielson, Gary, 180
David-Young, Heidi, 234
Davis, Brett, 262
Davis, James B., 200, 205
Day, Caldwell Newton, 18
DeBenedetto, Aaron P., 276
Delaney, David, 111, 245, 291, 295, 297
Depew, Emily, 129
DePriest, Shelby, 200, 286
Derrick, David, 159, 160, 213, 258, 281, 286, 309
Derrick, John, 261, 262
Derrick, John L., 64
Derrick, Kelly, 246, 258, 281, 287
DeVilbiss, Vickie, 87, 149
Dew, Steve, 221
Dewire, Glen, 148, 303
Diamond, Phyllis, 238, 239
Diehl, Matthew, 201, 254
Donahoe, Fred, 29, 217
Dooley, Larry, 257
Dorband, Lucille, 46, 202
Downs, Amanda, 129
Dugard, Maurice, 178
Dugas, Sue, 14, 116, 281
Dukes, Debbie, 203
Duncan, Richard, 216, 217
Durán, Rubén, 157, 294, 295

E

Easley, Charles, 179, 257, 297
Edwards, John, 29
Edwards, Martha, 14, 69, 116, 305, 306, 307, 310
Edwards, Terry, 158, 198, 219, 220, 222, 264, 265, 286
Ehlers, Edwin L., 22
Eichelberger, R. Nicholas "Nick", 64, 119, 237, 238
Eichler, Timothy, 278
Eichner, Fred, 246
Einarsen, Thord, 244
Eisemann, Richard, 246
Eisenberg, William Edward, 5, 11, 14, 235, 301
Ellis, Linus, 249, 250, 309
Engdahl, C. Marcus, 111, 277
England, Mark, 249
Erdos, Gary M., 245
Erickson, John, 217
Erickson-Pearson, Jan, 106

F

Fanslau, Cathy A., 275
Farrow, Christine, 241
Feldman, George R., 200, 205, 207, 208, 220
Fendley, Ruth, 117
Ficken, Carl, 186
Fields, John Blair, 66
Fintel, Norman, 174, 175, 264
Fitzsimmons, Mark, 235
Fix, Kay, 22
Florio, Lou, 213, 246
Fluckinger, Fred, 43, 184
Fogleman, Alfred, 212, 263, 267
Foré, James, 212, 217, 222
Forgacova, Magda, 222, 223
Franklin, Humes J., Jr., 29, 104
Fray, Judy Ann, 78, 81, 182, 306, 307
Freeborn, Edmund T., III, 241
Fritch, David, 208
Fritts, Geneva, 83
Fritz, Richard, 48, 253, 305
Frizzell, Thomas, 111
Froehlich, Mary, 15
Frye, Debbie, 217
Fuller, Aaron, 275, 279
Fuller, Harold, 264, 265, 268
Fuller, Kayla, 14
Funkhouser, Frank, 178

G

Gamelin, Jeremy R., 272
Ganskopp, Elmer H., 19, 301
Garriott, Sarah T., 198, 287
Garst, Stephanie, 87
Gates, Rick, 271
Gerlitz, Betty, 78
Gerlitz, Richard K., 45
Giessler, Diane, 81, 153, 154, 155, 228
Giessler, Richard, 228, 229
Gillespie, Dennis, 231
Goeres, Richard J., 166, 205, 206, 272
Gomez, Gene, 53, 302
Gomez, Janet, 14, 53, 86, 145, 148, 302, 308, 309, 310
Gosswein, Katie, 199
Gragg, Nathan T., 272
Graham, Mark A., 46, 63, 111, 112, 119
Gray, Austin, 200, 205

Greene, Ellen, 148, 150, 303
Griffin, Cheryl, 160, 243, 244
Griffith, Harry, 278
Gring, David, 174, 175
Gross, Donald, 193
Gum, Donna, 143, 144
Gunderlach, David, 243
Gunsten, Anna, 114
Gunsten, Kris, 114, 154, 281, 282
Gunsten, Pam, 281
Gunsten, Paul Gerhard "Chip", 5, 8, 14, 107, 108, 111, 114, 115, 116, 119, 124, 151, 153, 154, 160, 161, 162, 173, 184, 185, 224, 227, 233, 235, 242, 257, 258, 270, 281, 282, 301
Gunsten, Sarah, 114
Guy, Frederick P. "Fred", 63, 243, 255

H

Hahle, Dennis, 245, 246
Haines, Kathleen, 189, 297
Hall, Billie, 116
Hall, William, 47, 110
Hamlett, Leroy, 11, 14, 28, 69, 72, 85, 94, 104, 110, 185, 304, 305, 310
Hamman, Jonathan, 148, 222, 253
Handley, George E., 14, 15, 23, 26, 28, 46, 47, 48, 49, 50, 61, 84, 85, 297
Hangen, Judi, 178
Hannan, Shauna, 158
Hanson, Barbara, 222
Hanson, Robert, 29
Harold, Lyla, 213, 269, 286
Harris, Phil, 113
Harter, Harold J., 78, 243, 272
Hatcher, Ray, 209, 210, 266, 279
Haugen, Doug, 184
Haugen, Marty, 280, 294
Hawn, John, 257
Haxton, Cecie, 253
Heckathorn, Michael, 209
Heintzelman, Warren C., Jr., 233, 236
Heising, Willetta B., 18, 22, 32, 42, 45, 46, 297, 304
Heneberger, James, 200
Henne, Arthur J., 64, 119, 263, 264
Henrickson, Paul, 110, 111, 115, 174, 188, 281, 282, 297, 308, 309
Henrickson, Robin, 226, 256, 285
Herman, John, 46, 111, 210, 211, 253, 254, 292
Herring, Ronald L. "Ron", 67, 74, 75, 132, 138, 139, 178
Hill, Paul, 148
Himes, John, 274, 279, 286
Hinlicky, Ellen, 8, 14, 136, 137
Hinlicky, Paul, 226, 256, 257, 292, 295, 297
Hinlicky, Wynemah, 259
Hite, Patrick, 148

Hizer, Harold, 271
Hodges, Anjanette, 182
Hodges, Fred, 227
Holgersen, Arnold H., 261
Holley, Robert "Bob", 46, 111, 211, 268
Homesley, Scott, 218
Honeycutt, Frank, 78, 111, 218, 234
Horn, David, 179
Horton, Dianna, 204, 207, 208, 222, 267
Hougen, John, 189
Hove, Susan, 198, 199
Howard, Karin, 252
Howell, C.W., 219
Huber, Philip C., 22
Huddle, Crockett, 200
Huddle, Paul, 222
Hudy, Stacy, 126
Huffman, Christy V., 160, 249
Hughes, Robert T., 47, 226, 255
Humbert, Larrie, 215, 216
Humphrey, Robert F., 47, 107, 110, 144, 262, 270, 307
Hund, H.J., 274
Hunsinger, Kristin, 248, 287
Huntley, Harvey, Jr., 186

I

Irasua, Mary, 156
Israel, Sharon, 64, 267, 291, 307

J

Jackson, Diana, 231
Jacobsen, Karl, 248
Jacobsen, Kristin, 248
Jacobsen, Kevin, 82
Jansen, E. Harold, 18, 47, 61
Jeffcoat, Dorothy "Dot", 184, 185, 186, 187
Jennings, Angela, 212
Joe, Jimmy, 154
Johnson-Holt, Lavonne, 219, 225
Jones, Robert H. "Bob", 44, 45, 78, 119, 233
Jones, Wayne, 129
Jorgensen, Janyce, 263, 267, 285
Jung, John, 69
Jungkuntz, Daniel, 138, 298

K

Kammerer, Charlene, 193
Keefer, Owen, 144
Kegley, George, 10, 45, 73, 178, 320
Keister, Dee, 90
Keister, John D. "Pat", 47, 191, 192, 298
Kelley, Shelly, 69
Kelly, Gary, 220
Kerr, Jerry, 15, 235
Keyl, Rudolph, Jr., 235
Kidabing, Rose, 155
Kigasung, Wesley, 153, 154
Kincaid, Darla, 110

Kindt, Lois, 78
Kindt, Warren, 69, 74
King, William "Bill", 43, 189, 190, 225, 298
Kinser, William E. "Bill", 44, 46, 47, 68, 113, 250, 251, 256, 301
Kipps, Betty, 23, 31, 32, 42, 45, 105, 304, 305
Kipps, Joyce, 182
Kipps, Paul, 28
Klein, Lisa, 225
Kleindt, Adolph, 51
Kluttz, Roger, 218, 224, 225, 269
Kniseley, Carol, 214
Kniseley, Jim, 307, 308, 309
Koehnlein, John M., 44, 64, 204, 298
Koiner, Connie, 68, 307
Krasneck, Rick, 202
Kristo, Arne, 180
Krumm, Barbara, 219, 273, 303
Kuhn, Alvin, 64, 117, 119, 241

L

Lambie, James A., 28
Lamson-Andrew, Liv, 222
Lance, Susan, 201
Lane, Kenneth P., Jr., 258, 285
Lane, Sue, 43, 66, 78, 79
Larsen, Daniel L., 74
Larsen, James R., 145, 215, 240, 286
Larson, Shirley, 226
Lasher, Cynthia Long, 252
Lasher, John, 184
Lazareth, William H., 192
Leafe, Joe, 97, 305
Lecroy, M. Gary, 272
Lewis, W. Arthur, 180, 298, 306
Lillie, John, 217
Lineberger, Robert B., 219
Lippard, Michael A., 47, 63, 198, 298
Liskey, Henry, 238
Litchford, Thomas, 180
Lohr, Randy, 248, 269, 285
London, Glenn L., 44, 45, 47, 64, 219, 224, 270
Lutz, Benton, 244
Lyerly, Gary, 277

M

MacKey, Larry L., 219
Mahanes, Susie, 78, 153
Maier, Robert J., 19, 63, 85, 86, 221, 242, 251, 321
Mammoser, Tom, 215, 216
Mangus, Cary, 86
Marble, Jeffrey, 199, 237, 253
Marcoux, Frederick, 251
Marshall, Robert J., 18, 25, 41, 46, 47, 48, 298
Martin, Danielle, 155
Martin, Kenneth, 212
Martin, Philip, 249
Martinson, Roland D., 149
Marvar, Janet, 189, 200, 298

Mauney, James F., 7, 8, 10, 12, 14, 55, 57, 73, 107, 110, 111, 112, 113, 196, 201, 202, 203, 208, 212, 213, 220, 223, 224, 233, 236, 247, 248, 265, 281, 285, 291, 292, 298, 303, 307, 308, 309
Mauney, J. Luther, Jr., 22, 44, 50, 117, 139, 196, 298, 301
Mauney, Lynda, 113
Mauney, Marshall F., 19, 43, 45, 46, 47, 68, 117, 304
Maxey, Michael C., 11, 15, 82, 160, 166, 174, 175
Maxwell, Scott, 234, 249
May, Bill, 83
May, Jeff, 203
Mayer, Charles, 240
Mayer, Jacob L., 46, 47, 63, 227
Mayer, Karen, 154, 155
Mayer, Starr, 160, 166
McAllister, Jane, 78
McArver, Susan, 88
McCandlish, John W., 19, 63, 117, 119, 232, 252, 253, 257
McCarty, Robert, 268
McClanahan, William, 177
McGinnis, Stephen, 275, 301
McLaughlin, Pat, 260, 285
Mendes, Sergio, 73
Meromar, Roselyn, 151
Merz, Anna, 87
Messick, Walter, 223
Miko, Kathleen, 160, 179, 207
Milburn, Roger, 15
Milholland, Paul, 185, 241
Miller, Kate, 26, 41, 44, 45, 49, 73
Miller, Linda, 15
Miller, Marcus J., 176
Miller, Mark F., 11, 15
Miller, Martha, 285, 305, 306
Mills, CeCee, 53, 273
Milton, Phyllis, 14, 150
Mims, Cathy, 148, 275, 277, 309
Mims, Scott, 145, 277
Minnick, Anne, 182
Mintiens, Debbie, 86, 145, 302
Mitchell, Ann, 154, 155
Mitchell, Linda, 227, 256, 270, 285, 305, 307
Modahl, Bruce, 277
Moehring, Eric, 196, 218, 247, 290
Moller, Adolph, 14, 308, 310
Moore, Sylvia, 78
Moose, Stephen, 47, 246, 275
Morgan, Harold E., III, 230
Morgan, Pat, 14, 291, 307, 308, 310
Morrill, John C., 26, 47
Motec, Hynna, 154
Moyer, V.A. "Virgil", Jr., 11, 14, 15, 18, 21, 26, 50, 59, 60, 67, 206, 269
Muyambe, Miriam, 156
Myers, Jennie, 252
Myers, Jonathan, 225, 252

N

Nabers, Patricia, 215, 216, 222, 270, 287, 309
Nabers, William "Bill", 111, 204, 206, 267, 307, 308
Neal, Richard, 22, 178
Nelson, David, 184, 261, 262
Nelson, Sidney K., 63, 273, 274
Nestleroth, David, 178
Neubauer, Joel, 245, 271, 275
Nicholson, Jane, 148, 272, 299, 308, 309
Nickols, James P., 150, 243, 244
Nilsen, K. Roy, 23, 29, 61, 183, 261, 262
Nilsen, Kenneth A., 76, 179, 183, 199, 298
Nilsen, Timothy R., 209
Nimal, Dorothy, 166, 238, 251

O

O'Hara, Sabine, 174, 175
O'Meara, Candis, 220, 221, 223, 287
Oehlschlaeger, Amy, 222, 223, 260
Olivier, Keith, 273
Olson, Richard, 111, 250
Orrell, Timothy D., 209
Orso, Paul, 111
Osmondson, Lenae, 14, 116
Osterhout, Bruce, 256

P

Padilla, Rafael Malpica, 293
Paradise, Scott, 201
Parvin, Viktoria, 210, 211
Peery, Rufus Benton, 11
Pence, Jim, 189, 270, 298
Penman, David, 210, 273, 274, 287
Peterson, Brian, 295, 298
Peterson, Herb, 183, 184
Peterson, Kent, 218
Peterson, Mary, 190, 250
Phillips, Paul, 192
Pingel, Paul, 83, 151, 153, 222, 228, 270
Plummer, Jay, 209, 210
Poole, Robert, 108
Poston, Charles, 11, 14, 281, 308, 309, 310
Price, J. Christopher "Chris", 43, 45, 46, 74, 107, 110, 111, 112, 138, 185, 243, 248, 249, 307, 308
Price, Kenneth, 215, 216, 224, 260, 264, 265, 266, 268, 269
Prinz, Thomas, 47, 111, 201, 298
Purdham, Aldon, 239, 245, 246

R

Radecke, Mark, 45, 73, 256, 289, 304, 305
Ramsey, Janet, 180, 260, 298
Ratcliffe, Howard, 268, 269